# Advanced Research and Trends in Human-Computer Interaction

# Volume II

# Advanced Research and Trends in Human-Computer Interaction
# Volume II

Edited by **Stanley Harmon**

LANRYE
INTERNATIONAL

New Jersey

Published by Clanrye International,
55 Van Reypen Street,
Jersey City, NJ 07306, USA
www.clanryeinternational.com

**Advanced Research and Trends in Human-Computer Interaction: Volume II**
Edited by Stanley Harmon

International Standard Book Number: 978-1-63240-025-3 (Hardback)

# Contents

# Preface

Human-computer interaction is a field that involves the study, planning, design and use of the process of interaction between people or users and computers. The term 'human-computer interaction' was established around the 1980s. The term can be simplified through the fact that unlike other tools with only limited and one dimensional uses, a computer has many uses and these functions take place in an open-ended dialog between the user and the computer. It is an interdisciplinary field of study with foundations in computer science, behavioural science, media studies, design, and several other arenas. It studies how computers and people interact with each other and to what extent computers are developed for such successful interactions. There are many ways for a user to interact with computers, and the interface used for this interaction between humans and the computers is crucial. Desktop applications, internet browsers, handheld computers, and computer are examples of human-computer interfaces that we use daily. There are constant and rapid developments in this field and they all have ramification on our day to day lives. Thus there is always a demand for graduates who can work towards better and more efficient interfaces.

This book is an attempt to compile and collate all available research on human-computer interaction under one aegis. I am grateful to those who put their hard work, effort and expertise into these research projects as well as those who were supportive in this endeavour.

**Editor**

# A Comparison of Field-Based and Lab-Based Experiments to Evaluate User Experience of Personalised Mobile Devices

**Xu Sun[1] and Andrew May[2]**

[1] *Science and Engineering, University of Nottingham Ningbo, 199 Taikang East Road, Ningbo 315100, China*
[2] *Loughborough Design School, Loughborough University, Ashby Road, Loughborough, Leicestershire LE11 3TU, UK*

Correspondence should be addressed to Xu Sun; xu.sun@nottingham.edu.cn

Academic Editor: Caroline G. L. Cao

There is a growing debate in the literature regarding the tradeoffs between lab and field evaluation of mobile devices. This paper presents a comparison of field-based and lab-based experiments to evaluate user experience of personalised mobile devices at large sports events. A lab experiment is recommended when the testing focus is on the user interface and application-oriented usability related issues. However, the results suggest that a field experiment is more suitable for investigating a wider range of factors affecting the overall acceptability of the designed mobile service. Such factors include the system function and effects of actual usage contexts aspects. Where open and relaxed communication is important (e.g., where participant groups are naturally reticent to communicate), this is more readily promoted by the use of a field study.

## 1. Introduction

Usability analysis of systems involving stationary computers has grown to be an established discipline within human-computer interaction. Established concepts, methodologies, and approaches in HCI are being challenged by the increasing focus on mobile applications. Real-world ethnographic studies have received relatively little attention within the HCI literature, and little specific effort has been spent on delivering solid design methodologies for mobile applications [1]. Researchers and practitioners have been encouraged to investigate further the criteria, methods, and data collection techniques for usability evaluation of mobile applications [2]. Lab-based experiments and field-based experiments are the methods most discussed in relation to evaluating a mobile application [2–4].

There has been considerable debate over whether interactions with mobile systems should be investigated in the field or in the more traditional laboratory environment. There seems to be an implicit assumption that the usability of a mobile application can only be properly evaluated in the field, for example, Kjeldskov and Stage [5]. Some argue that it is important that mobile applications are tested in realistic settings, since testing in a conventional usability lab is unlikely to find all problems that would occur in real mobile usage (e.g., [2, 6, 7]). For example, Christensen et al. [6] presented a study of how ethnographic fieldwork can be used to study children's mobility patterns via mobile phones. Authors consider that field studies make it possible to carry out analysis that can broaden and deepen understanding of peoples' everyday life. However, some authors have highlighted how ethnographic field experiments are time consuming, complicate data collection, reduce experimental control, or are unacceptably intrusive [1, 3, 5].

Laboratory experiments are generally not burdened with the problems that arise in field experiments as the conditions for the experiment can be controlled, and it is possible to employ facilities for collection of high-quality data [5, 8]. However, Esbjörnsson et al. [9] and many other authors have argued that traditional laboratory experiments do not adequately simulate the context where mobile devices are used and also lack the desired ecological validity. This may lead to less valid data, where there is a potential disconnect between stated preferences, intentions, and actual experiences [4].

There are alternatives to field studies when assessing the impact of mobile devices. Adding contextual richness to laboratory settings through scenarios and context simulation can contribute to the realism of the experiment while maintaining the benefits of a controlled setting [3, 5, 10]. The extent to which simulated scenarios represent a real-life situation is a critical determinant of the validity of the usability experiment [11]. In addition, for mobile devices, two basic contextual factors which need to be considered are mobility and divided attention. To replicate real-world mobility within a lab setting, test participants have been asked to use a treadmill or walk on a specifically defined track in a lab setting (e.g., [12]). To replicate divided attention, a range of measures have been used in the past. For example, to assess the impact of information provision on drivers, a range of simulators have been used, from low-fidelity personal computer-based simulations [13] to high-fidelity simulators with large projection screens involving real dashboards [14]. These simulators recreate divided attention, as well as enabling task performance measurement.

This paper reports a combination of a field and lab-based evaluation in order to assess the impact of personalisation on the user experience at sports events. This mixed approach enabled a comparison of evaluation methodology, and comments on their relative effectiveness for mobile users.

## 2. Background

*2.1. Mobile Personalisation.* Personalization techniques can be classified into three different categories [15]: rule-based filtering systems, content-filtering systems, and collaborative filtering systems. Some recent techniques used in collaborative filtering are based on data mining in order to infer personalisation rules or build personalisation models from large data sets.

The main aspects of personalization which are relevant within this paper are *what* is personalized and *how* this is achieved. This paper focuses on content personalization [16], that is, the tailoring of information within a particular node within the human-device navigation space. This form of personalization is based on the key assumption that the optimal content for an individual is dependent on contextual factors relating to the individual, the situation they are in, and the activities they are undertaking—these factors can be used as triggers for the adaptation of content for the individual [17] in order to enhance their user experience.

The personalization framework in this research contains four modules, which (1) cooperate to perform the functions of classification of information, (2) collect relevant contextual factors, and (3) personalize content accordingly (Figure 1).

The overall context of this research (which enabled the field versus laboratory comparison described here) was the investigation of the benefits of personalisation of mobile-based content. However, the research project also investigated the benefits/drawbacks of either the user or the system performing personalisation of content. Some research favours user-initiated personalisation and its focus on the natural intelligence of the user, while others found that system-initiated approaches were more effective for dynamic contexts [18].

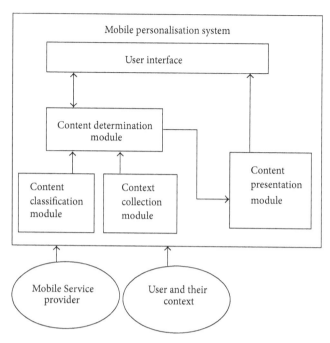

FIGURE 1: Modules forming a mobile personalization application.

*2.2. User Experience.* "User experience" is a broader concept than usability. As user experience affects the success of a product, studies of user experience should therefore be considered as an important part of the product development process [19]. The importance of user experience stems from mobile devices being personal objects used by individuals with particular social and cultural norms, within an external context defined by their environment.

There is much interest in user experience from design, business, philosophy, anthropology, cognitive science, social science, and other disciplines. Among these, there have been some initial efforts to create theories of user experience. Rasmussen [20] argues that as society becomes more dynamic and integrated with technology, there is a need for a greater multidisciplinary approach in tackling human factors problems. Arhippainen and Tähti [21], in evaluating mobile application prototypes, describe five categories of influences on the user experience, evoked through interaction with an application. These are user factors, social factors, cultural factors, context of use, and product (i.e., application) related factors. They also list specific attributes for each category, such as the age, emotional state of the user, habits and norms as cultural factors, the pressure of success and failure as social factors, time and place as context of use factors, and usability and size as product factors. Similarly, Hassenzahl and Tractinsky [22] define user experience as "a consequence of a user's internal state (predispositions, expectations, needs, motivation, mood, etc.), the characteristics of the designed system (e.g., complexity, purpose, usability, functionality, etc.) and the context (or the environment) within which the interaction occurs (e.g., organizational/social setting, meaningfulness of the activity, voluntariness of use, etc.)."

Despite the emerging importance of user experience, there are several barriers to using this concept as a key design objective, and, hence, how they may be employed within either a field or lab-based evaluation process. There is not yet a common definition of user experience because it is associated with a broad range of both "fuzzy" and dynamic concepts, for example, emotion, affect, experience, hedonic, and aesthetics [24]. There is also currently a lack of consensus regarding the constructs that comprise user experience, and how they may be measured [25].

This research follows the approach taken by Arhippainen and Tähti [21] and Hassenzahl and Tractinsky [22] in considering user experience to comprise multiple components, namely: user, social, usage context, cultural, and product. Consequently, multicomponent user experience was measured using 15 agree-disagree scales, addressing the five components. This approach therefore considers *user experience* to be a formative construct that is measured in terms of its components [26].

## 3. Field-Based Evaluation of Content Personalisation

*3.1. Aims.* The first empirical study was a field experiment, the aims of which were to evaluate the impact of using a mobile device, and personalising that device, for a spectator within a real sports environment. Field studies typically sacrifice some experimental control in order to maximise the ecological validity of the experiment.

*3.2. Method*

*3.2.1. Setup.* The study took place in a sports stadium during a competition involving local football clubs. This competition comprised fast-moving sporting action and a large gathering of spectators, most of whom were unfamiliar with each other. The user experience was therefore typical of that encountered during a large sports event. Information was broadcast to spectators over a public address system and shown on a large display screen in one corner of the stadium.

*3.2.2. Experimental Scenarios.* The successful use of scenarios takes into account the diversity of contexts encountered by spectators; these were derived from previous studies [27, 28]. Four scenarios were developed including (1) checking the schedule of forthcoming matches and finding one of particular interest; (2) obtaining information on a particular player of interest; (3) reviewing the progress of the current match (dynamic information access); (4) joining a "community" and participating in community-based activities in the stadium.

*3.2.3. Prototypes.* Prior to the experiments described in this paper, a total of seven field studies were undertaken with spectators at large sports events [27, 28]. These studies found that a large number of contextual factors influenced the design of service/information provision to a spectator, but that three had the greatest potential impact on the user experience. These were the *sporting preferences* of the spectator, their *physical location* in the stadium, and the *event progress*.

Following the previous studies, one paper prototype and two mobile prototypes (a personalised prototype and a nonpersonalised prototype) were developed that provided content to support the experimental scenarios above.

Both mobile prototypes were identical in terms of their functionality and visual design. The personalised prototype had the option to manually configure the presentation of information according to the key contextual factors using the content filtering personalisation technique (description of the technical development is out of scope of this paper). With this prototype, users were asked to set their preferences relating to the sports types and athletes taking part from an extended tree menu structure (Figure 2). As a result, tailored event-based information (e.g., information on athletes) and event schedules were presented to the spectator (Figure 3). In contrast, the nonpersonalised mobile prototype did not require the user to set the personalisation attributes and as a result presented information and services applicable for a more general audience (Figure 4).

The personalised prototype also enabled users to assign themselves to virtual communities with common interests within the stadium using collaborative filtering technique, based on their stated interests. This was via online chat and media sharing within groups defined by their personal preferences. The nonpersonalised mobile prototype enabled the same chat and media sharing, but within a larger group not differentiated according to personal interests.

In addition, a paper leaflet was prepared that was based on the information that a spectator would traditionally get during a real event from posters and programs. It provided information on match schedules and players' profiles.

*3.2.4. Participants.* Eighteen participants were recruited by an external agency. Their ages ranged from 18 to 45 years, mean 28.5, with an equal gender split. A range of occupations were represented, including sales, journalist, engineer, teacher, secretary, and accountant; eight participants were university students. A recruitment criterion was that all participants should have undertaken personalisation of their ringtone, screen background, or shortcut keys at least once a week. In addition, all participants had watched a large sports event in an open stadium within the last six months.

*3.2.5. User Experience Measurement.* The key dependent variable was the user experience that resulted from using the prototypes. User experience was measured in terms of the multidimensional components described in Section 2. User experience was therefore rated by participants in a multicomponent assessment that was theoretically grounded and empirically derived (see the appendix).

*3.2.6. Procedure.* A pilot study was used to check the timings, refine the data collection methods, and resolve any ambiguities with the instructions and data collection tools. This was carried out in a stadium.

At the beginning of the study, participants were given instruction on how to use the mobile prototype. Participants then undertook the scenario-based tasks, using either the

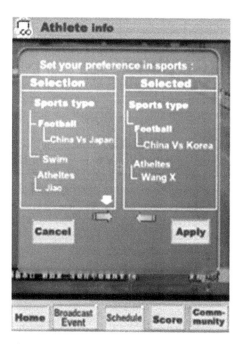

FIGURE 2: Setting personalisation preferences.

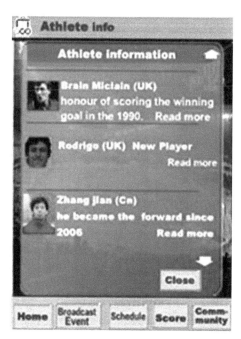

FIGURE 4: Obtaining *general* information on all athletes.

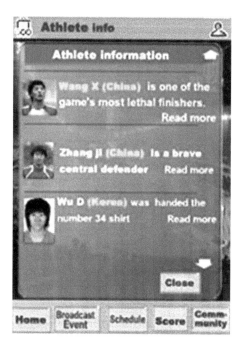

FIGURE 3: Obtaining *personalised* information on particular athletes.

paper-based programme or one of the mobile prototypes. They then completed the 15-item questionnaire that differentiated the five components of user experience.

Finally, they were interviewed in a semistructured format to discuss the experiment design in the field study. The study lasted around 60 minutes for each user.

*3.2.7. Data Collection.* A multiplicity of data collection methods was used within the study to enable a limited triangulation of subjective rating, verbal report, and observational

data. A video camera was used to record their interactions with the mobile prototypes. Users were encouraged (but not required) to "think aloud" during the trial. A user assessment in relation to overall user experience was captured using six-point agree/disagree rating scales. Direct observation was also used, and informal interaction with the researcher was encouraged during the trial. A posttrial structured interview was video recorded.

*3.2.8. Analysis of Data.* For quantitative data, Friedman nonparametric tests for three related samples were calculated for the main within-subjects factors. Multiple paired comparisons were undertaken using the technique described in Siegel and Castellan [23, page 180], to take into account the increased likelihood of a type I error with multiple comparisons. The qualitative data (interview transcripts and concurrent verbal reports) and observational data were analyzed using an affinity diagram technique [29] to collate and categorise this data.

*3.3. Field Study Results.* The field experiments generated large amounts of rich and grounded data in relatively short time. For all tasks, the personalised mobile device consistently generated the highest user experience rating (see Table 1). The nonpersonalised device was consistently worse but still an improvement over the control condition (paper-based programme). The control condition (paper-based programme) was consistently rated poor—a limitation also noted by Nilsson et al. [30] in their field observations of sports events.

To make sure that the user interface itself (rather than the personalization approach) was not majorly influencing the experiment outcome, the user-initiated interface was evaluated by calculating the percentage of tasks completed by participants and analysing user comments. The experiment

TABLE 1: The overall user experience assessment for each task.

| Task | Friedman (3 related samples) | Multiple paired comparisons [23, page 180], ($\alpha = .05$) |
|------|------------------------------|--------------------------------------------------------------|
| Checking match schedules | $\chi^2(2) = 31.3$ $P < .001$ | $N = 18, \left\|R_{\text{Personalized}} - R_{\text{Nonpersonalized}}\right\| = 21.5, >Z = 14.36^*$ <br> $N = 18, \left\|R_{\text{Personalized}} - R_{\text{paper}}\right\| = 29.5, >Z = 14.36^*$ <br> $N = 18, \left\|R_{\text{Nonpersonalized}} - R_{\text{paper}}\right\| = 8, <Z = 14.36$ |
| Obtaining player information | $\chi^2(2) = 34$ $P < .001$ | $N = 18, \left\|R_{\text{Personalized}} - R_{\text{Nonpersonalized}}\right\| = 17, >Z = 14.36^*$ <br> $N = 18, \left\|R_{\text{Personalized}} - R_{\text{paper}}\right\| = 34, >Z = 14.36^*$ <br> $N = 18, \left\|R_{\text{Nonpersonalized}} - R_{\text{paper}}\right\| = 17, >Z = 14.36^*$ |
| Reviewing match progress | $\chi^2(2) = 30.6$ $P < .001$ | $N = 18, \left\|R_{\text{Personalized}} - R_{\text{Nonpersonalized}}\right\| = 16.5, >Z = 14.36^*$ <br> $N = 18, \left\|R_{\text{Personalized}} - R_{\text{paper}}\right\| = 33, >Z = 14.36^*$ <br> $N = 18, \left\|R_{\text{Nonpersonalized}} - R_{\text{paper}}\right\| = 16.5, >Z = 14.36^*$ |
| Building a community | $\chi^2(2) = 32.1$ $P < .001$ | $N = 18, \left\|R_{\text{Personalized}} - R_{\text{Nonpersonalized}}\right\| = 17, >Z = 14.36^*$ <br> $N = 18, \left\|R_{\text{Personalized}} - R_{\text{paper}}\right\| = 34, >Z = 14.36^*$ <br> $N = 18, \left\|R_{\text{Nonpersonalized}} - R_{\text{paper}}\right\| = 17, >Z = 14.36^*$ |

$^*$Indicates a significant difference.

recorded approximately 18 hours of video capturing the 18 subjects' interaction steps while completing each task. In summary, 95.5% of the tasks were completed successfully. For the 4.5% of unfinished tasks, 35 usability problems with the personalized mobile prototype were reported.

Participants in the field experiment stressed problems of mobile "use" rather than simply application "usability," and typically those problems were expressed in the language of the situation. For example, users were concerned about spending too much time personalizing the application during the event (detracting from the event itself) and the font on the interface being too small to read in an open stadium under bright sunlight. The field study also identified issues of validity and precision of the data presented by the application. For example, users were concerned about the reliability of information provided by the prototypes after they found that some player information presented on the mobile device did not match with the real events.

To the participants, the field experiment environment felt fairly informal, and the users talked freely about the use of the application and their feelings. Users expressed how the field experiment allowed them to feel relaxed and able to communicate with the researcher as they undertook the evaluation scenarios. Rather than focusing on interface issues, users generally expressed broader views and were able to give a wide range of evaluation-related information during the experiment, such as expressing contextually related requirements. A particular example of the kind of data generated during the field study was the need for the mobile content (and its delivery) to be highly integrated into the temporal flow of the sporting action.

Using a field experiment approach, it may be possible to obtain a higher level of "realism." However, this evaluation method is not easy to undertake. Experiments in the field are influenced by external factors, such as the weather, and moreover, it is more difficult to actually collect data from participants. Users were impacted by events happening in the field, such as noise and other disturbances. For example, some participants actually forgot that they were taking part in a research study—until prompted, they focused their attention on the competition happening in the stadium and were substantially distracted from the field experiment. Flexibility and pragmatism are needed to still collect useful data, while not detracting unduly from the experience generated within the field setting.

## 4. Lab-Based Evaluation of Personalisation Approach

*4.1. Aims.* Whereas the previous section has described a field-based study, this section describes a very similar lab study, this time centred around a multievent athletics meeting. The specific objectives of this study were to use a more controlled experimental setup to compare the user experience for a spectator at a large sports event under three conditions: (1) using paper-based (not mobile) content; (2) using a mobile prototype where personalisation parameters were set by the user; (3) using a similar prototype where parameters were set automatically. Similar procedures and data collection methods enable a comparison of findings with the field-based study described in Section 3.

*4.2. Method*

*4.2.1. Setup.* This evaluation took place in a usability laboratory in the UK. The usability lab was set up to resemble a part of the sports stadium. To mimic the divided attention that would result from a spectator watching a sporting event, sports footage, including auditory output, was projected onto the front wall of the laboratory. A crowd scene was replicated on each of the two side walls. In contrast to typical mobile applications such as tourist guides [31], a spectator is usually seated and relatively static at a sporting event. Therefore, mobility per se did not need to be incorporated into the experimental environment. A video camera was used to record users' interaction with the prototypes (Figure 5).

FIGURE 5: User study in a usability lab.

*4.2.2. Experimental Scenarios.* Five scenarios were developed, based on the same key spectator activities as used in the previous field-based experiment. Four of the experimental tasks were the same as those employed in the field experiment. This lab-based study also employed a fifth task which required the participant to select a suitable viewing angle for a mobile broadcast on the device. This enabled the participants to follow the sporting action from wherever they were in the stadium.

*4.2.3. Prototypes.* Two personalised mobile prototypes were developed using content filtering and collaborative filtering personalisation technique. They shared the same look and feel as those used in the field study described in Section 3.

One prototype enabled *user-initiated* personalisation of content, using an extended menu structure as before (see Figure 2). As a result, this prototype presented event information such as athlete details and event schedules based on the users' settings.

In contrast, the prototype with *system-initiated* personalisation did not require that participants set personalisation parameters. Personalised content was then presented automatically to the participant using the content and collaborative filtering personalisation technique.

As for the field experiment, a control condition was included that was representative of a nondigital event programme that a spectator would typically have. This was a paper leaflet that provided information on competition times and athlete information.

*4.2.4. Participants.* A different cohort of eighteen participants took part in the study, again split equally male-female, aged between 18 and 38, and with various occupations. As in the previous field-based study, all participants had regular experience of personalising mobile devices and had attended a large sports event within the last six months.

*4.2.5. Procedure and Analysis of Data.* A pilot study was used to maximise the realism of the simulation and ensure that the data collection methods that were used during the field trial were effective within a laboratory setting. Two key changes were made: rearrangement of speakers to broadcast audience noise; the side projection of a video of the audience was replaced with large-scale posters. This enhanced the perceived social atmosphere within the laboratory without unnecessarily distracting the participant from the main projected view (the sporting action).

The procedure followed that used for the field experiment described in Section 3. Each task was completed in turn, with the three personalisation conditions counterbalanced across participants within each task. The design of the lab experiment was also discussed with participants at the end of the study. The study lasted approximately one hour for each participant.

As for field study, the data comprised quantitative rating scale data, concurrent verbal reports and posttrial interview data, and observational data. This was analysed as described previously.

*4.3. Lab Study Results.* Across all tasks, there were clear advantages to having personalised content delivered over a mobile device. The control condition (representing that present at current stadium environments) was significantly worse in all scenarios (see Table 2). Table 2 also indicates that in terms of the impact on user experience, neither user nor system-initiated personalisation emerged as a *single* best approach across the range of tasks studied.

The experiment recorded approximately 18 hours of video during the lab study. In summary, 92% of the tasks were completed successfully. For the 8% of unfinished tasks, 42 usability problems with the personalized mobile prototype were reported. In general, participants considered the user interface of both personalized mobile prototypes easy to use.

The laboratory study was relatively easy to undertake and collect data from. During the lab study, participants quickly revealed considerable information about how a spectator uses the prototypes. The lab environment also offered more control over the conditions for the experiment. In comparison to the field study, participants were more focused on the experiment being undertaken, and were not influenced by external factors, such as weather, noise, or others disturbances from the sporting environment.

There were some drawbacks to the lab experiment, including only a limited representation of the real world, and greater uncertainty over the degree of generalization of results outside laboratory settings. This laboratory study tried to "bring" the large sporting event into the experiment by carefully setting up the lab to resemble a stadium, designing scenarios based on previous studies of context within large sports events, and involving users who were familiar with the usage context. It also addressed the issue of users' divided attention by requiring subjects to watch a sport event video which was projected on the front wall of the lab room while performing the scenario-based tasks with the mobile prototypes. As a result, participants were able to identify some context related problems (e.g., the font was too small to read in an open stadium) during the lab experiment. In addition, participants expressed their concerns with using the personalized prototypes from contextual and social perspectives, including concerns over spending too much time personalizing the device during the event, and therefore actually missing some of the sporting action.

TABLE 2: The overall user experience assessment for each task.

| Task | Friedman (3 related samples) | Multiple paired comparisons [23, page 180] ($\alpha = .05$) |
|---|---|---|
| Follow sporting action | $N = 18$, $\chi^2(2) = 27.5$, $P < .001$ | $N = 18$, $\left\|R_{\text{system-initiated}} - R_{\text{use-initiated}}\right\| = 15, >Z = 14.36^*$ <br> $N = 18$, $\left\|R_{\text{system-initiated}} - R_{\text{paper}}\right\| = 49, >Z = 14.36^*$ <br> $N = 18$, $\left\|R_{\text{user-initiated}} - R_{\text{paper}}\right\| = 34, >Z = 14.36^*$ |
| Obtaining athlete information | $N = 18$, $\chi^2(2) = 29.4$, $P < .001$ | $N = 18$, $\left\|R_{\text{system-initiated}} - R_{\text{use-initiated}}\right\| = 2, <Z = 14.36$ <br> $N = 18$, $\left\|R_{\text{system-initiated}} - R_{\text{paper}}\right\| = 16, >Z = 14.36^*$ <br> $N = 18$, $\left\|R_{\text{user-initiated}} - R_{\text{paper}}\right\| = 18, >Z = 14.36^*$ |
| Reviewing athletics event results | $N = 18$, $\chi^2(2) = 35.5$, $P < .001$ | $N = 18$, $\left\|R_{\text{system-initiated}} - R_{\text{use-initiated}}\right\| = 17.5, >Z = 14.36^*$ <br> $N = 18$, $\left\|R_{\text{system-initiated}} - R_{\text{paper}}\right\| = 35, >Z = 14.36^*$ <br> $N = 18$, $\left\|R_{\text{user-initiated}} - R_{\text{paper}}\right\| = 17.5, >Z = 14.36^*$ |
| Building a community | $N = 18$, $\chi^2(2) = 29.6$, $P < .001$ | $N = 18$, $\left\|R_{\text{system-initiated}} - R_{\text{use-initiated}}\right\| = 6, <Z = 14.36$ <br> $N = 18$, $\left\|R_{\text{system-initiated}} - R_{\text{paper}}\right\| = 24, >Z = 14.36^*$ <br> $N = 18$, $\left\|R_{\text{user-initiated}} - R_{\text{paper}}\right\| = 30, >Z = 14.36^*$ |
| Checking event schedules | $N = 18$, $\chi^2(2) = 34.5$, $P < .001$ | $N = 18$, $\left\|R_{\text{system-initiated}} - R_{\text{use-initiated}}\right\| = 16.5, >Z = 14.36^*$ <br> $N = 18$, $\left\|R_{\text{system-initiated}} - R_{\text{paper}}\right\| = 34.5, >Z = 14.36^*$ <br> $N = 18$, $\left\|R_{\text{user-initiated}} - R_{\text{paper}}\right\| = 18, >Z = 14.36^*$ |

$^*$Indicates a significant result.

The lab experiment did not allow users to feel relaxed during the experimental procedure. Participants acted more politely during the study, and they pointed out that they were uncomfortable about expressing negative feelings about the applications. In one example, when interviewing a participant about aspects of his user experience, he generally stated that it was fine. However, when presented with the Emotion Cards (a group of cartoon faces that were used to help promote discussion of affective aspects of interaction), he tended to pick up one emotion card and talked a lot about concerns over the time and effort required to manually personalize the application, without feeling that he was being overly critical.

## 5. Discussion and Conclusion

In recent years, there has been much debate on whether mobile applications should be evaluated in the field or in a traditional lab environment, issues including users' behaviour [11]; identification of usability problems [3]; the experiment settings [5, 8, 32]; the communication with participants [33]. This research enabled a comparison between field and laboratory experiments, based on similar users, mobile applications, and task-based scenarios. In particular, a similar user-initiated prototype was used in each, even though the field experiment took place at a football competition, and the lab experiment recreated an athletics meeting.

The number of usability problems identified during both the field and lab experiments was similar (over all participants, when using the user-initiated prototype, there were 35 usability problems identified in the field setting, and 42 found in the lab setting). These findings are consistent with those of Kjeldskov et al. [3]. They specifically compared lab and field-based usability results and found that the difference in effectiveness of these two approaches was nonsignificant

in identifying most usability problems. Also, some context related problems, such as the font being too small to read in an open stadium, were identified in both experiment settings. However, some key differences in the effectiveness of the field and laboratory approaches were found; the lab experiment identified problems related to the detail of the interface design, for example, the colours and icons on the interface; the field experiment identified issues of validity and precision of the data presented by the application when using the application in a stadium. The field experiment also stressed the problems of mobile "use" rather than simply application usability, and typically these problems were expressed in the language of the situation [11].

An analysis of positive versus negative behaviours [11] was undertaken. This data included verbal reports and rating scale data according to the user experience definitions. Accepting the limitations of a direct comparison, participants reacted more negatively in the laboratory setting when completing similar tasks (using the similar user-initiated personalisation approach). In the field, individuals were influenced by the atmosphere surrounding the sports event, and this resulted in an enhanced user experience. In addition, they focused more attention on the actual usage of personalisation on the mobile device, instead of issues to do with the interface. The lab setting was less engaging than the field setting; participants were more likely to be critical, and in general they took longer to perform certain tasks by focusing (and commenting) on interface issues such as fonts and colours used.

The field experiment was more difficult to conduct than the lab experiment, a point noted by many authors, including Kjeldskov et al. [3] and Baillie [8]. Confounding factors were present, for example, variations in the weather and noise from other spectators. In addition, although it was desirable that participants engaged in the sporting action, spectators' foci of attention could not be controlled and was difficult to predict.

Some participants were "distracted" from the experimental tasks, and this did not occur during the laboratory setting. The greater control possible with a laboratory study (as discussed by a range of authors, including [2, 5, 8]) was clearly demonstrated during these studies.

Where there is an interest in qualitative data, good communication between the researcher and participants is vital. The field experiment provided a more open and relaxed atmosphere for discourse. Users more freely discussed their use of the mobile applications, their underlying beliefs, and attitudes that arose during the study. The field experiment helped the communication tensions with the participants as they felt they were not being directly examined. As well as generally promoting the generation of qualitative data, the field experiments encouraged the expression of broader, as well as more contextually relevant views. An example is the identification of contextually dependent requirements, which occurred much less frequently during the lab-based studies.

Some suggestions for user impact assessment with mobile devices can be made based on the findings of this study. A lab experiment is recommended when the focus is on the user interface and device-oriented usability issues. In such cases, a well-designed lab study should provide the validity required, while being easier, quicker, and cheaper to conduct. However, the results suggest that a field experiment is better suited for investigating a wider range of factors affecting the overall acceptability of mobile services, including system functions and impact of usage contexts. Where open and relaxed communication is important (e.g., where participant groups are naturally reticent to communicate), this is more readily promoted by the use of a field study.

The natural tension between a deductive and inductive research design was also apparent. This research in general was essentially deductive, since it set out to explain causal relationships between variables, operationalized concepts, controlled variables, and used structured and repeatable methods to collect data. However, the field study in particular also comprised an inductive element, as there was a desire to understand the research context and the meanings attached to events in order to help design the lab study. Van Elzakker et al. [2] underline how it is often desirable to combine approaches within the same study. The undertaking of a field experiment followed by a lab experiment was an attempt at multiplicity of methods from an essentially deductive viewpoint. This recognised that the natural research process is often that of moving from a process of *understanding* to one of *testing*, whilst attempting to avoid the unsatisfactory middle ground of user evaluations that are divorced from any underlying research objectives.

## Appendix

### Likert Items Used to Assess User Experience

In all cases, participant responses were based on a six-point scale ranging from 1 (strongly disagree) to 6 (strongly agree).

*User Aspect*:

(1) I feel happy using [A/B/C] during the event.

(2) My expectations regarding my spectator experience in the stadium are met using [A/B/C].

(3) My needs as a spectator are taken into account using [A/B/C].

*Social Aspect*:

(4) Using [A/B/C] helps me feel I am communicating, and sharing information with others in the stadium.

(5) The [A/B/C] helps me create enjoyable experiences within the stadium.

(6) The [A/B/C] helps me share my experiences with others within the stadium.

*Usage Context Aspect*:

(7) The [A/B/C] provides me with help in the stadium while watching the sporting action.

(8) The [A/B/C] provides me with information about other spectators in the stadium.

(9) The [A/B/C] helps provide me with a good physical and social environment in the stadium.

*Culture Aspect*:

(10) The [A/B/C] helps me feel part of a group.

(11) The [A/B/C] helps me promote my group image.

(12) The [A/B/C] helps me interact with my group.

*Product Aspect*:

(13) The [A/B/C] is useful at the event.

(14) The [A/B/C] is easy to learn how to use.

(15) The [A/B/C] is easy to use.

## Acknowledgments

This work has been carried out as part of the Philips Research Programme on Lifestyle. The authors would like to thank all the participants who were generous with their time during this study.

## References

[1] D. Raptis, N. Tselios, and N. Avouris, "Context-based design of mobile applications for museums: a survey of existing practices," in *Proceedings of the 7th International Conference on Human Computer Interaction with Mobile Devices & Services*, 2005.

[2] C. P. J. M. Van Elzakker, I. Delikostidis, and P. J. M. Van Oosterom, "Field-based usability evaluation methodology for mobile geo-applications," *Cartographic Journal*, vol. 45, no. 2, pp. 139–149, 2008.

[3] J. Kjeldskov, M. B. Skov, B. S. Als, and R. T. Høegh, "Is it worth the hassle? Exploring the added value of evaluating the usability of context-aware mobile systems in the Field," in *Proceedings of the 6th International Mobile Conference (HCI '04)*, Springer, 2004.

[4] X. Sun, D. Golightly, J. Cranwelly, B. Bedwell, and S. Sharples, "Participant experiences of mobile device-based diary studies," *International Journal of Mobile Human Computer Interaction*. In press.

[5] J. Kjeldskov and J. Stage, "New techniques for usability evaluation of mobile systems," *International Journal of Human Computer Studies*, vol. 60, no. 5-6, pp. 599–620, 2004.

[6] P. Christensen, M. Romero, M. Thomas, A. S. Nielsen, and H. Harder, "Children, mobility, and space: using GPS and mobile phone technologies in ethnographic research," *Journal of Mixed Methods Research*, vol. 5, no. 3, pp. 227–246, 2011.

[7] E. G. Coleman, "Ethnographic approaches to digital media," *Annual Review of Anthropology*, vol. 39, pp. 487–505, 2010.

[8] L. Baillie, "Future Telecommunication: exploring actual use," in *Proceedings of the International Conference on Human-Computer Interaction*, IOS press, 2003.

[9] M. Esbjörnsson, B. Brown, O. Juhlin, D. Normark, M. Östergren, and E. Laurier, "Watching the cars go round and round: designing for active spectating," in *Proceedings of the Conference on Human Factors in Computing Systems (CHI '06)*, pp. 1221–1224, New York, NY, USA, April 2006.

[10] X. Sun, "User requirements of personalized mobile applications at large sporting events," in *Proceedings of the IADIS Multi Conference on Computer Science and Information Systems(MCCSIS '10)*, Freiburg, Germany, 2010.

[11] H. B. L. Duh, G. C. B. Tan, and V. H. H. Chen, "Usability evaluation for mobile device: a comparison of laboratory and field tests," in *Proceedings of the 8th International Conference on Human-Computer Interaction with Mobile Devices and Services (MobileHCI '06)*, pp. 181–186, September 2006.

[12] A. Pirhonen, S. Brewster, and C. Holguin, "Gestural and audio metaphors as a means of control for mobile devices," in *Proceedings of the Conference on Human Factors in Computing Systems (CHI '02)*, pp. 291–298, New York, NY, USA, April 2002.

[13] R. Graham and C. Carter, "Comparison of speech input and manual control of in-car devices while on-the-move," in *Proceedings of the 2nd Workshop on Human Computer Interaction with Mobile Devices (HCI '1999)*, Edinburgh, UK, 1999.

[14] J. Lai, K. Cheng, P. Green, and O. Tsimhoni, "On the road and on the web? Comprehension of synthetic and human speech while driving," in *Proceedings of the Conference on Human Factors in Computing Systems (CHI '01)*, pp. 206–212, New York, NY, USA, April 2001.

[15] B. Mobasher, "Data mining for personalization," in *The Adaptive Web: Methods and Strategies of Web Personalization*, P. Brusilovsky, A. Kobsa, and W. Nejdl, Eds., pp. 1–46, Springer, Berlin, Germany, 2007.

[16] D. Wu, I. Im, M. Tremaine, K. Instone, and M. Turoff, "A framework for classifying personalization schemes used on e-commerce websites," in *Proceedings of the 36th Hawaii International Conference on Systems Sciences (HICSS '03)*, p. 222b, Maui, Hawaii, USA, 2003.

[17] L. Norros, E. Kaasinen, J. Plomp, and P. Rama, *Human-Technology Interaction Research and Design. VTT Roadmap*, VTT Research Notes 2220, Espoo, Finland, 2003.

[18] E. Frias-Martinez, S. Y. Chen, and X. Liu, "Evaluation of a personalized digital library based on cognitive styles: adaptivity versus adaptability," *International Journal of Information Management*, vol. 29, no. 1, pp. 48–56, 2009.

[19] J. Dewey, *Art as Experience*, Perigee, New York, NY, USA, 1980.

[20] J. Rasmussen, "Human factors in a dynamic information society: where are we heading?" *Ergonomics*, vol. 43, no. 7, pp. 869–879, 2000.

[21] L. Arhippainen and M. Tähti, "Empirical Evaluation of User Experience in Two Adaptive Mobile Application Prototypes," in *Proceedings of the 2nd International Conference on Mobile and Ubiquitous Multimedia*, Luleå, Sweden, 2003.

[22] M. Hassenzahl and N. Tractinsky, "User experience—a research agenda," *Behaviour and Information Technology*, vol. 25, no. 2, pp. 91–97, 2006.

[23] S. Siegel and N. J. Castellan, *Nonparametric Statistics For the Behavioral Sciences*, McGraw-Hill, New York, NY, USA, 1988.

[24] E. Law, V. Roto, A. P. O. S. Vermeeren, J. Kort, and M. Hassenzahl, "Towards a shared definition of user experience," in *Proceedings of the 28th Annual Conference on Human Factors in Computing Systems (CHI '08)*, pp. 2395–2398, Florence, Italy, April 2008.

[25] E. L. C. Law and P. van Schaik, "Modelling user experience—an agenda for research and practice," *Interacting with Computers*, vol. 22, no. 5, pp. 313–322, 2010.

[26] C. H. Lin, P. J. Sher, and H. Y. Shih, "Past progress and future directions in conceptualizing customer perceived value," *International Journal of Service Industry Management*, vol. 16, no. 4, pp. 318–336, 2005.

[27] X. Sun and A. May, "Mobile personalisation at large sports events—user experience and mobile device personalisation," in *Human-Computer Interaction 2007*, vol. 11, Springer, Berlin, Germany, 2007.

[28] X. Sun and A. May, "The role of spatial contextual factors in mobile personalization at large sports events," *Personal and Ubiquitous Computing*, vol. 13, no. 4, pp. 293–302, 2009.

[29] J. Hackos and J. Redish, *User and Task Analysis For Interface Design*, John Wiley & Sons, New York, NY, USA, 1998.

[30] A. Nilsson, U. Nuldén, and D. Olsson, "Spectator information support: exploring the context of distributed events," in *Proceedings of the International ACM SIGGROUP Conference on Supporting Group Work*, 2004.

[31] B. Oertel, K. Steinmuller, and M. Kuom, "Mobile multimedia services for tourism," in *Information and Communication Technologies in Tourism 2002*, K. W. Wober, A. J. Frew, and M. Hitz, Eds., pp. 265–274, Springer, New York, NY, USA, 2002.

[32] D. D. Salvucci, "Predicting the effects of in-car interfaces on driver behavior using a cognitive architecture," in *Proceedings of the Conference on Human Factors in Computing Systems (CHI '01)*, pp. 120–127, New York, NY, USA, April 2001.

[33] A. Kaikkonen, A. Kekäläinen, M. Cankar, T. Kallio, and A. Kankainen, "Usability testing of mobile applications: a comparison between laboratory and field testing," *Journal of Usability Studies*, vol. 1, pp. 4–16, 2005.

# 2

# Assessment of Learners' Motivation during Interactions with Serious Games: A Study of Some Motivational Strategies in Food-Force

## Lotfi Derbali and Claude Frasson

*Département d'Informatique et de Recherche Opérationnelle, Université de Montréal,*
*C.P. 6128, Succursale Centre-Ville, Montréal, QC, Canada H3C 3J7*

Correspondence should be addressed to Lotfi Derbali, derbalil@iro.umontreal.ca

Academic Editor: Francesco Bellotti

This study investigated motivational strategies and the assessment of learners' motivation during serious gameplay. Identifying and intelligently assessing the effects that these strategies may have on learners are particularly relevant for educational computer-based systems. We proposed, therefore, the use of physiological sensors, namely, heart rate, skin conductance, and electroencephalogram (EEG), as well as a theoretical model of motivation (Keller's ARCS model) to evaluate six motivational strategies selected from a serious game called Food-Force. Results from nonparametric tests and logistic regressions supported the hypothesis that physiological patterns and their evolution are suitable tools to directly and reliably assess the effects of selected strategies on learners' motivation. They showed that specific EEG "attention ratio" was a significant predictor of learners' motivation and could relevantly evaluate motivational strategies, especially those associated with the *Attention* and *Confidence* categories of the ARCS model of motivation. Serious games and intelligent systems can greatly benefit from using these results to enhance and adapt their interventions.

## 1. Introduction

It is widely acknowledged that learners' psychological and cognitive states have an important role in intelligent systems and serious games (SGs). For instance, engagement and motivation or disaffection and boredom obviously affect learners' wills and skills in acquiring new knowledge [1]. SGs cannot, therefore, ignore these states and should take them into account during learning process. One important learners' state is motivation which plays a crucial role in both the learners' performance and the use of intelligent systems over time [2]. Motivation is generally defined as that which explains the *direction* and *magnitude* of behaviour, or in other words, it explains *what* goals people choose to pursue and *how* they pursue them [3]. It is considered as a natural part of any learning process. Several researches have showed that motivated learners are more likely to be more engaged, to undertake challenging activities, and to exhibit

enhanced performance and outcomes [4, 5]. Therefore, it is of particular relevance to study motivation and its role in improving learners' performance during gameplay.

Learners' interactions with Intelligent Tutoring Systems (ITSs) and especially SGs have always been considered to be intrinsically motivating. One possible explanation is the fact that ITSs generally use pictures, sounds, videos, and so forth, that are considered, crudely, as motivational factors. Intrinsic motivation is possibly gained through challenge, curiosity, control, sensory stimuli, interaction, and fantasy when using SGs [6, 7]. However, many researchers have argued that learners' negative emotions or amotivational states such as boredom or disengagement have been known to appear following a certain period of interaction with computer systems. These states can be overwhelming to learners and cause motivational problems and decrease learning benefits [2, 8, 9]. Once learners' psychological and cognitive states are identified, intelligent systems are in a much better position to act upon them. In this perspective, several studies have described intelligent systems that can provide adapted emotional or cognitive strategies for coping with, or at least reducing, the negative learners' states [8–12]. Computer systems can also use motivational strategies which are the actions (or tactics) taken in order to scaffold learners' motivation toward tasks and goals of learning process and to make learning easier, faster, more enjoyable, more self-directed, and more effective. However, it is surprising to find so little mention of the motivational strategies and relatively little is known about coping with motivational problems, which motivational strategies should be used, and to what extent they are employed. Within the researchers who have tackled this issue, some have found that SGs seemed to show a promising potential from a motivational standpoint. It has been consistently shown that SGs have inherent motivational properties and different strategies, allowing them to be used for improving educational applications [7, 13–15]. Game designers, for example, employ a range of Artificial Intelligence (AI) techniques (e.g., controlling the behaviour of the nonplayer characters, providing performance feedback) to promote long-term user engagement and motivation [16].

Moreover, evaluating systems interventions is obviously related to differences in learners' performance (successful completion of tasks) or judgement (self-report questionnaires). However, by using only performance or judgement in evaluating motivational strategies, intelligent systems risk obtaining delayed or imperfect evaluations or interrupting learning process by repeatedly using self-report questionnaires. This may offer misleading information regarding the impact of motivational strategies on learners' motivation. Therefore, it is of particular relevance to investigate new ways of evaluating motivational strategies. One promising way is the use of physiological sensors. This is notably explained by the significant results of recent studies involving physiological sensors to assess motivational learners' states as well as emotional and cognitive systems strategies [10, 17–19].

The present paper examines the implication of different physiological sensors to evaluate some motivational strategies employed in SGs and to highlight the corresponding learners' patterns. To this end, we use an existing SG called Food-Force presented by the United Nations World Food Programme (WFP) and intended to learn players about the fight against world hunger. The ultimate objective of this intervention study is to assess learners' motivation when motivational strategies haves been used by SGs. We ask the two following research questions: Can we empirically find physiological patterns to evaluate the effects of motivational strategies on learners' motivation during interactions with Food-Force? If so, Can these patterns feed AI models to predict the level of learners' motivation to the motivational strategies? Hence, two hypotheses are postulated: (1) it is possible to model learners' physiological reactions and trends towards motivational strategies in an SG environment and (2) we can discriminate between effective and ineffective motivational strategies using physiological manifestations as well as self-report questionnaires. We designed an experiment using an existing SG called Food-Force and combined both the theoretical ARCS model of motivation

and empirical physiological sensors (heart rate (HR), skin conductance (SC), and electroencephalogram (EEG)) to assess the effects of motivational strategies on learners.

The organization of this paper is as follows. In the next section, we present previous work related to our research. In the third section, we explain our empirical approach in assessing learners' motivation. In the fourth section, we describe the theoretical ARCS strategies to support motivation and the studied strategies in Food-Force. In the fifth section, we detail our experimental methodology. In the sixth section, we present the obtained results and discuss them. Finally, we give a conclusion in the last section, as well as present future work.

## 2. Related Research

Csikszentmihalyi [20] observed that people enter in a "flow" state when they are fully absorbed in activity during which they lose their sense of time and have feelings of great satisfaction. Games generally catalyze conditions of flow state by their clear goals, balance between challenges and skills, immediate feedback, progress, and control. Furthermore, Ryan and Deci [21] defined the Self-Determination Theory (SDT) and distinguished between intrinsic motivation (to understand the subject) and extrinsic motivation (for the reward of a certificate or employment). They assumed that the individual is normally inclined to be active, motivated, curious, and eager to succeed. They also recognized that some people mechanically perform their tasks, or even people passive and unmotivated. They reported that environments that facilitate the satisfaction of psychological needs can boost the internal dynamism of people to maximize their motivation and to maximize results in personal development and behavior. Ryan and colleagues [22] have studied the SDT and stated that the motivational pull of computer games is attributed to the combination of optimal challenge and informational feedback. Bartle [23], one of the pioneers of the massively multiplayer online games and known for his work on the first MUD (An MUD (originally Multiuser dungeon, with later variants Multiuser Dimension and Multiuser Domain) is a computer program, usually running over the Internet, that allows multiple users to participate in virtual-reality role-playing games.), distinguished several motivational profiles among players: the killer (competitiveness), the per-former (success), the explorer (curiosity), and socializer (cooperation). He reported that some players strive to achieve all the challenges offered by the gameplay while others seek the company of other players, or want to discover the whole virtual world.

Nevertheless, the effectiveness of any study regarding the assessment of learners' motivational states depends on two important factors: (1) the choice of proper assessment tools and (2) the accuracy of the selected tools. For example, Schunk et al. [5] used Keller's ARCS model (see next section for a description of this model) and proposed several rules to infer motivational states from two sources: the interactions of the students with the tutoring system and their motivational traits. Some researchers have analyzed log files and have established correlations between learners' actions in log files and their motivational states (e.g., [24]). Other researchers have used physiological sensors to assess learners' motivation and correlate physiological learners' responses to some dimensions of motivation such as attention and confidence (e.g., [17, 25]). They have identified that the combination of various physiological sensors may provide perfect measures of learners' states and consequently enhance systems intervention strategies. They have involved a variety of sensors to assess physiological learners' states and responses to stimuli in Computer-Based Education (CBE) environment: mouse, electromyogram (EMG), respiration (RESP), HR, SC, and more recently EEG. For instance, Conati [19] has used biometric sensors (HR, SC, EMG, and RESP) and facial expression analysis to develop a probabilistic model of detecting students' affective states within an educational game. Arroyo and colleagues [26] have used four different sensors (camera, mouse, chair, and wrist) in a multimedia adaptive tutoring system to recognize students' affective states and embed emotional support.

Others studies have shown that learners have also been known to experience a lower sense of relatedness to the educational systems [27], thus increasing their feeling of isolation and possibly leading to further motivational issues. For example, learners lack the substantial self-monitoring skills that CBE systems require and possibly start "gaming" the system [9]. In addition, CBE systems generally place fewer restrictions on learners and learners must take greater responsibility for their educational experiences. Hannafin and colleagues [28] recommended that students need more support and must be empowered to acquire the necessary skills to effectively progress in an educational environment. For example, it has been found that when collaborative learning strategy is used, a fewer errors are made than in individual learning situations, resulting in better outcomes performance, increased confidence, and decreased frustration levels of the learners [29, 30]. Dörnyei [31] has reported that motivational strategies are used not only to maintain students' motivation but also to generate and increase it. He has defined that more than one hundred motivational strategies can be used by teachers in the classroom. These strategies integrate the creation of the basic motivational conditions, the generation of initial motivation, the maintaining and the protection of motivation, and the encouragement of positive and retrospective self-evaluation. Furthermore, efforts to overcome learners' motivational problems have mainly been focused on tutor's strategies or instructional design aspects of the systems. For example, Hurley [12] developed interventional strategies to increase the learner's self-efficacy and motivation in an online learning environment. She extracted and then validated rules for interventional strategy selection from expert teachers by using an approach based on Bandura's Social Cognitive Theory and by observing the resulting learners' behaviour and progress. Goo and colleagues [32] showed that tactile feedback, sudden view point change, unique appearance and behaviour, and sound stimuli played an important factor in increasing students' attention in virtual reality experience. Arroyo and colleagues [8] evaluated the impact of a set of noninvasive interventions in an attempt to repair students' disengagement while solving geometry

problems in a tutoring system. They claimed that showing students' performance after each problem reengages students, enhances their learning, and improves their attitude towards learning as well as towards the tutoring software.

## 3. Assessment of Learners' Motivation

There are a few studies that have particularly considered the evaluation of motivational strategies. It is of particular significance for this research work that motivational strategies are identified and their impacts on learners are evaluated in a specific CBE environment, precisely serious games. In addition to ARCS self-reported questionnaires, the present study uses three physical sensors (SC, HR, and EEG) to assess motivational strategies while interacting with a serious game called Food-Force. We first need to present the tools used to measure motivation itself.

*3.1. ARCS Model of Motivation.* In the present study, the ARCS model of motivation [33] has been chosen to theoretically assess learners' motivation in SG. Keller used the existing research on psychological motivation to identify four components of motivation: *Attention, Relevance, Confidence,* and *Satisfaction.* His model has been used in training and games and has also been validated in numerous studies with all education levels and in many different cultures (e.g., [3, 34, 35]), and therefore, it is of particular interest in our study.

(i) *Attention:* to attract learners' attention at the beginning and during the process of learning. Diverse activities should be considered to maintain students' feelings of novelty thus the attention can be sustained.

(ii) *Relevance:* to inform learners of the importance of learning and to explain how to make the learning meaningful and beneficial.

(iii) *Confidence:* to allow learners to know the goal and to believe that the goal can be achieved, if enough effort (physical and/or intellectual) has been made.

(iv) *Satisfaction:* to provide feedback on performance and to allow learners to know how they are able to perform well and apply what is learned in real life situations.

The ARCS questionnaire asks students to rate ARCS-related statements in relation to the instructional materials they have just used. Examples of items related to each ARCS component are as follows.

(i) "uses questions to pose problems or paradoxes." (*Attention*);

(ii) "uses language and terminology appropriate to learners and their context." (*Relevance*);

(iii) "provides feedback on performance promptly." (*Confidence*);

(iv) "makes statements giving recognition and credit to learners as appropriate." (*Satisfaction*).

Assessment of Learners' Motivation during Interactions with Serious Games: A Study of Some Motivational Strategies in Food-Force

13

*3.2. Physiological Sensors.* Considering the motivation as a state of both cognitive and emotional arousal, we have decided to combine several noninvasive physiological sensors in order to empirically evaluate the motivational strategies in serious games context. Besides the SC and HR sensors which are typically used to study human affective states [36], we have considered relevant to use the EEG sensor in our proposed approach. Indeed, brainwave patterns have long been known to give valuable insight into the human cognitive process and mental state [37]. More precisely, our EEG analysis relies on differences between slow and fast wave ratios (i.e., "attention ratio" or Theta/low-Beta) which are correlated with responses to motivational stimuli and emotional traits [38, 39]. For instance, low-level attention is characterized by "a deviant pattern of baseline cortical activity, specifically increased slow-wave activity, primarily in the Theta band, and decreased fast-wave activity, primarily in the Beta band, often coupled" [40]. The power of the EEG "attention ratio" can be explained by Putman and colleagues [39]. According to the authors, a negative correlation exists between the attention ratio and learners' *Attention* level. A high Theta/low-Beta ratio is usually correlated with excessive Theta and consequently inattentive state. Conversely, a low Theta/low-Beta ratio is normally correlated with excessive Low-Beta brainwave activity reflecting normal state in adults.

## 4. Motivational Strategies

The key issue in this paper is related to the identification and assessment of motivational strategies in SGs that support and enhance learners' motivation. We define a motivational strategy as the use of a game element (or factor) [41] susceptible of providing motivational support for players. Motivational strategies in SG are the key to finding and harnessing players' motivation to learn and achieve their goals. For example, a virtual companion in SG can offer encouragement to players as well as offering additional aid in their current task. This is can be considered as a motivational strategy related to the *Confidence* category of the ARCS model only if it increases learners' belief in competence and consequently their effectiveness. Otherwise, it is simply an SG element and not a motivational strategy. Each of the four categories has also subcategories that are useful in identifying learners' motivational profiles and in creating motivational tactics (or strategies) that are appropriate for specific situations in SG [3].

*Attention Getting Strategies (Capture Interest, Stimulate Inquiry, and Maintain Attention).* Before any learning can take place, the learner's attention must be engaged. The challenge with the attention is to find the right balance of consistency, novelty, and understanding how people differ, what tactics to use, and how to adjust the tactics for the learners and how the tutor will be able to keep them focused and interested.

*Relevance Producing Strategies (Relate to Goals, Match Interests, and Tie to Experiences).* It is very difficult for students to be motivated to learn if they do not perceive there to be any relevance in the instruction. To stimulate the motivation to learn, it is best to build relevance by connecting instruction to the learners' backgrounds, interests, and goals.

*Confidence Building Strategies (Success Expectations, Success Opportunities, and Personal Responsibility).* When people believe that they have little or no control over what happens to them, they experience anxiety, depression, and other stress-related emotions. In contrast, when they believe that they can predictably influence their environment by exercising their efforts and abilities in pursuit of their goals, then they are more motivated to be successful.

*Satisfaction Generating Strategies (Intrinsic Satisfaction, Rewarding Outcomes, and Fair Treatment).* One of the most important elements of satisfaction is intrinsic motivation; that is, if learners believe that they achieved a desirable level of success while studying topics that were personally meaningful, then their intrinsic satisfaction will be high. Another component of satisfaction is based on social comparisons and comparisons to expected outcomes.

The present study invited participants to play the freely downloadable SG called Food-Force [42]. It is an initiative of the World Food Program (WFP) of the United Nations intended to educate players about the problem of world hunger. Food-Force is comprised of multiple arcade-type missions, each intended at raising players' awareness towards specific problems regarding worldwide food routing and aid. Food-Force also presents players' objectives in a short Instructional Video before the beginning of each mission. A virtual tutor also accompanies the player throughout each mission by offering various tips and lessons relative to the obstacles and goals at hand. All participants have never played Food-Force before. We have investigated in details six motivational strategies in Food-Force in order to answer our main research question. (Can we empirically find physiological patterns to evaluate motivational strategies during serious game play?) These strategies are related to the four categories of the ARCS model, see Figure 1.

*Problem Solving.* Keller's ARCS motivation theory tells us that the learner's motivation is also aroused by the mean of "solving a problem or resolving an open issue..." called inquiry arousal. Mission 2 (nutritious meal preparation) presents to learners a challenging problem that consists of finding the right combination of different food items (rice, beans, vegetable oil, sugar, and iodized salt) to create a nutritious and balanced diet, all at a target cost of 30 US cents per person per meal. It has been investigated in our experiment to study the Problem Solving strategy used by Food-Force.

*Alarm Trigger.* According to Brophy [43], situational interest is triggered in response to something in the situation (e.g., unexpected sound) that catches our attention and motivates us to focus on it and explore it further. Keller's ARCS motivation theory also argues that the learner's motivation

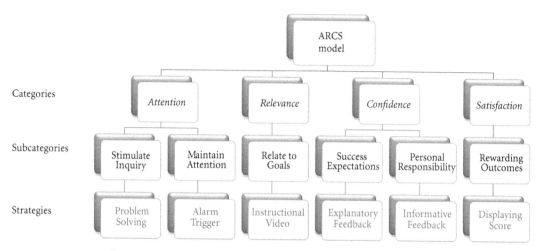

FIGURE 1: ARCS model and the corresponding motivational strategies.

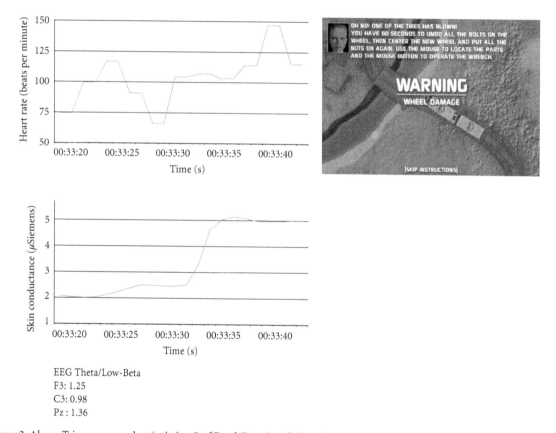

FIGURE 2: Alarm Trigger screen shot (mission 5 of Food-Force) and three physiological data (HR, SC, and EEG "attention ratio").

is possibly gained by a perceptual arousal (novel, surprising, or incongruous events). We have decided to investigate the three Alarm Triggers as a strategy supporting motivation in mission 5 (UN. food delivery) of Food-Force. An example of an alarm trigger is shown in Figure 2.

*Instructional Video.* Motivational strategies rely on some game elements that make a lesson content relevant to the learners. Keller has reported that the instructor has to

tie instruction into the learner's experience by providing examples that relate to the learner's work. In Food-Force, Instructional Video segments that draw on players' existing knowledge have been used in order to show them the real application of presented mission in the field and connect each mission to the problem of world hunger.

*Informative Feedback.* It is important to raise learner's confidence by offering suitable feedback. According to [44],

Assessment of Learners' Motivation during Interactions with Serious Games: A Study of Some Motivational Strategies in Food-Force

15

negative or positive Informative Feedback tells learners what they are doing. It works much better then Controlling Feedback which simply tells them what to do. For Informative Feedback used in Food-Force, comments like "What was a dangerous drop! Try to be more accurate and watch the wind gauge" (mission 3) or "Won't arrive immediately, but that might be ok for you" (mission 4) indicate the effects (or benefits) of actions taken by the player.

*Explanatory Feedback.* The learner is open to a brief instructional explanation that will help build the right mental model and/or correct misconceptions. Explanatory Feedback resulted in much better learning than Corrective Feedback [45], which can be automated in many authoring tools with only a few key strokes. The virtual companion of Food-Fore makes comments, such as "Rice: we need a lot of rice. It provides nutrition and energy" (mission 2), to explain user actions.

*Displaying Score.* Motivational strategies aimed at increasing learner's satisfaction usually focus on allowing students to display their work, encouraging them to be proud of themselves and celebrate success, and using rewards. Displaying Score strategy is used at the end of each mission in order to show players their current scores and their overall progress.

## 5. Experimental Methodology

*5.1. Procedure.* Thirty-three volunteers (11 females) took part in the study in return of a fixed compensation. Participants were recruited from the University of Montreal. The sample's mean age was 26.7 (SD = 4.1). Following the signature of a written informed consent form, each participant was placed in front of the computer monitor to play the game. Set on a fictitious island called Sheylan riven by drought and war, Food-Force invites participants to complete 6 virtual missions that reflect real-life obstacles faced by WFP in its emergency responses both to the tsunami and other hunger crises around the world. All participants have played only the first five missions of Food-Force. A pretest and posttest were also administered to compare learners' performance regarding the knowledge presented in the serious game. We have used 10 multiple choice questions about general problem of world hunger. Figure 3 presents a flow diagram of the experiment.

*5.2. Data Collection.* The motivational measurement instrument called Instructional Materials Motivation Survey (IMMS) was used following each mission to assess learners' motivational state. It is derived from four categories of ARCS motivation model. Due to time constraints and in order to achieve minimum disruption to learners, we used a short IMMS form which contained 16 out of the 32 items after receiving the advice and approval from Dr. John Keller. IMMS used a 5-point Likert-type scale (where 1 is strongly disagree and 5 is strongly agree). Furthermore, two cameras were also used to simultaneously record learners' facial expressions and game progress. Physiological data was also

recorded in synchrony to both camera feeds throughout the experiment. The Galvanic Skin Resistance (GSR) electrodes and the blood volume pulse (BVP) sensor were attached to the fingers of participant's nondominant hands, leaving the other hand free for the experimental task. BVP sensor is a blood volume pulse detection sensor housed in a small finger worn package, to measure heart rate (HR). GSR electrodes measure the conductance across the skin (SC). An EEG cap was also conveniently fitted on participant's head and each cerebral sensor spot slightly filled with a saline nonsticky solution. EEG refers to the recording of the brain's spontaneous electrical activity over a period of time as recorded from multiple electrodes placed on the scalp. HR, SC, and EEG recordings were managed by the Thought Technology ProComp Infiniti Encoder [46]. This encoder has 8 protected pin sensor inputs with two channels sampled at 2048 samples per second and six channels sampled at 256 samples per second. The first two channels were used to record HR and SC. The last six other channels were used to record EEG at sites Fz, F3, C3, Pz, A1, and A2 according to the international 10–20 system. A ground is located at Fpz. Electrode impedances were maintained below 5 KΩ. Participants were asked to minimize eye blinks and muscle movements during physiological recordings. Furthermore, an additional notch filter is typically used to remove artifact caused by electrical power lines (60 Hz in Canada). According to [47], "the reference electrode should be placed in a location that is not susceptible to artifact. An extra midline electrode is suitable". Thus all EEG sites were referenced online to Cz. Electrophysiological data were recorded during the whole of the experiment. A 60s-baseline was also computed before the beginning of the game.

*5.3. Data Analysis.* The offline processing of the HR, SC, and EEG data was performed using BioGraph Infiniti software. EEG data were rereferenced offline to the mean of the activity at the two mastoid leads (A1 and A2). For each site $s \in \{Fz, F3, C3, Pz\}$, the corrected $s$ is calculated using the following formula:

$$\text{corrected}_s = s - \frac{(A1 + A2)}{2}, \quad s \in \{Fz, F3, C3, Pz\}. \quad (1)$$

Four participants (2 females) were excluded from the EEG analysis because of technical problems at the time of recording. Technical Fz recording problem with some participants leads us to exclude all Fz data from our analysis. Furthermore, manual editing of the recorded signals has been carried out to remove artifact-contaminated data caused by muscle activity and eye blinks or movements. The EEG raw signal is filtered through a band pass filter from 2 to 48 Hz. A necessary normalization technique (min-max [48]) was applied to HR and SC physiological data using the baseline data. Indeed, normalizing the data keeps the physiological patterns for individual subjects and establishes a common metric for intersubject comparisons. Min-max normalization performs a linear transformation on the original data. It has the advantage of preserving exactly all

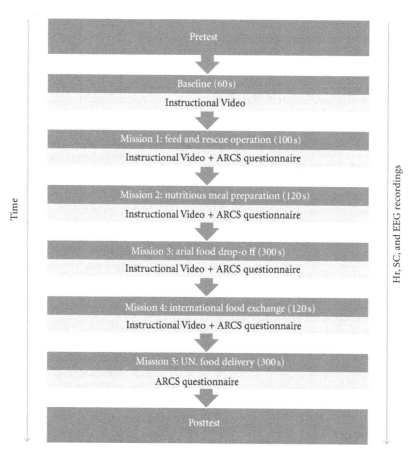

FIGURE 3: Progress diagram of the experiment.

relationships in the data. We have normalised each HR and SC data using the following modified formula [49]:

$$\text{normalised signal}(i) = \frac{\text{signal}(i) - \text{baseline}}{\text{signal}_{\max} - \text{signal}_{\min}}, \quad (2)$$

where $\text{signal}_{\max}$ and $\text{signal}_{\min}$ refer, respectively, to maximum and minimum values during interaction period and baseline refers to the average value of physiological data before the beginning of the game. These normalized physiological data reflect signal changes from baseline.

EEG data were segmented into one-second epochs and power spectral densities were calculated for each epoch using Fast Fourier Transformation. Power spectral data were averaged within Theta (4–8 Hz) and Low-Beta (12–20 Hz) bands. For each epoch of every participant the attention ratios (Theta/low-Beta) were calculated as described in Section 3.

*5.4. Percent of Time (PoT) Index.* We have defined an index representing players' physiological evolution throughout each mission of the serious game with regards to each signal signification. This index, called Percent of Time (PoT), represents the amount of time, in percent, that player's signal amplitude is lower (or higher) than a specific threshold. The PoT index is a key metric enabling us to sum up players' entire signal evolution for a mission. A simple method would

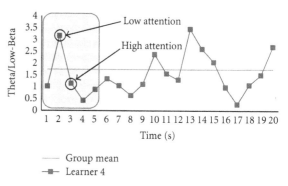

FIGURE 4: Learner's EEG "attention ratio" evolution.

be to choose the mean players' signal amplitude of each physiological sensor as the threshold. The PoT index of HR (or SC) for each player was calculated using values above the HR (or SC) threshold, whereas the PoT index for each EEG sites was calculated when player's attention ratio was below the threshold since we are looking for positive evolutions. Figure 4 illustrates an EEG attention ratio evolution during 20 seconds. The PoT for the selected 5-second window was 80% (4 values below divided by 5 values) and 70% for the entire 20 seconds (14 values below divided by 20 values).

The idea is to analyze, in a joint venture, PoT indexes of HR, SC, and EEG signals to determine, or at least estimate,

Assessment of Learners' Motivation during Interactions with Serious Games: A Study of Some Motivational Strategies in Food-Force

17

relations between the motivational strategies used in the serious game and the physiological learners' responses. To that end, various AI models have been constructed using gathered data in order to classify learners in two distinct classes: "Below" and "Above". Indeed, subjects have been separated into two groups based on their self-reported scores of the ARCS model after each mission of game: those with scores below the overall average (group "Below") and those with scores above the overall average (group "Above"). For instance, the evaluation of an Attention Getting strategy (e.g., Alarm Trigger or Problem Solving) used by Food-Force will consider the *Attention* scores to determinate the "Below" and "Above" groups of subjects and compare their physiological reactions [50]. The same procedure has been applied for all other strategies. Consequently, the members of each group are different from one strategy to another. A detailed description of all these possibilities is given in the following section.

## 6. Experimental Results

Before presenting our results, we considered it necessary to quickly explain the statistical approach used in this section. Indeed, we could not rely on the usual parametric statistical tools such as ANOVA and $t$-test because (1) our sample population is small ($N = 29$ participants), (2) no justifiable assumptions could be made with regards to the normal distribution of the data, and (3) normality tests run on our data confirmed its nonnormal distribution. Hence, nonparametric Friedman's ANOVA by ranks (counterpart of the parametric one-way ANOVA) and nonparametric Wilcoxon's signed ranks test (counterpart of paired sample $t$-test) have been used. However, $P$ value is interpreted in the same manner in both approaches and to that effect, reported significant $P$ values were all computed at the 0.05 significance level (95% confidence).

*6.1. Performance and Motivation.* In order to determine if the IMMS scale is reliable, a Cronbach's Alpha was run on IMMS data gathered after the first mission of Food-Force. The simplified IMMS yielded reliability (Cronbach's Alpha coefficient) of 0.88 for the overall motivation measure and Cronbach's Alpha for *Attention*, *Relevance*, *Confidence*, and *Satisfaction* was 0.91, 0.71, 0.79, and 0.87, respectively. These reliability coefficients are analogous to those found in [51] and showed that the motivational measurement instrument used in the present study was highly reliable.

Since we intend to study several motivational strategies in different missions within the Food-Force game, we evaluated the effects of these strategies on learners' performance as well as their motivation. We have then conducted statistical tests and we have obtained several results regarding knowledge acquisition (pre- and posttests) and learners' motivation (ARCS scores). The results of Wilcoxon signed ranks test displayed in Table 1 showed a significant difference between the participants' scores of the pre- and posttests in terms of knowledge acquisition ($Z = 4.65$, $P < 0.001$). Number of correct answers after finishing the game is significantly

TABLE 1: Results of Wilcoxon signed ranks test.

| Test | Mean | Median | SD | Z | Sig. P |
|------|------|--------|-----|-----|--------|
| Pretest | 6,07 | 6 | 1,387 | 4,657 | .000* |
| Posttest | 8,86 | 9 | .990 | | |

*Significance at the .05 level.

higher than that of correct answers before start playing. The results of Friedman's ANOVA by ranks between ARCS scores are displayed in Table 2. Significant differences for the general motivational scores as well as each category of the ARCS model were also observed between missions, except for *Relevance* (motivation overall score: $F(1,4) = 10.16$, $P < 0.05$; *Attention*: $F(1,4) = 19.51$, $P < 0.001$; *Relevance*: $F(1,4) = 7.38$, $P = 0.12$; *Confidence*: $F(1,4) = 16.8$, $P < 0.05$; *Satisfaction*: $F(1,4) = 10.85$, $P < 0.05$). Nonsignificant results of the Relevance category can be explained by the fact that the Relevance Producing strategy (Instructional Video) presented between missions was roughly the same: video segments explain the goal of each mission or its real application in order to connect each mission to the problem of world hunger. Conversely, the *Attention* category which showed the strongest difference and rank has used various game strategies throughout the missions. Indeed, Food-Force maintains learners' attention by using Alarm Trigger when they are confronted with an unexpected situation such as attacks to the convoy by local rebel forces or flat tires of trucks (mission 5). It also includes mental tasks that require concentration and attention: drop food from the air without risking human lives (mission 3) and guide a convoy of trucks safely to a feeding centre while overcoming challenges from clearing land mines to rebuilding bridges and negotiating with local rebel forces (mission 5). Finally, learners' attention is possibly gained by using Problem Solving strategy such as finding the right combination of different food items (rice, beans, vegetable oil, sugar, and iodized salt) to create a nutritious and balanced diet, all at a target cost of 30 US cents per person per meal (mission 2).

An example of an Alarm Trigger used in mission 5 is shown in Figure 2. As described in Section 4, Alarm Trigger is a motivational strategy (Attention Getting strategy) associated to *Attention* category of the ARCS model. We have then considered self-reported Attention scores to separate participants into two groups: a "Below" class (4 females and 7 males) representing participants who reported an *Attention* score below that of the overall mean and an "Above" class (5 females and 13 males) presenting the opposite (a score above the overall mean). Three alarms in mission 5 have been investigated. They are a sound trigger followed by Food-Force logistics officer's comments used to help players to overcome challenges—from clearing land mines to rebuilding bridges and negotiating with local rebel forces. To detect physiological changes for each player, we considered two 5-second windows computed before and after each alarm and calculated their means ($mean_{Before\ Alarm}$, $mean_{After\ Alarm}$). Fifteen Wilcoxon signed ranks tests (3 alarms × 5 physiological sensors) were run between Before Alarm and After Alarm data and significant results were

TABLE 2: Results of Friedman's ANOVA by ranks.

(a)

| Motivation | Mean | Median | SD | Chi-Square | Sig. $P$ |
|---|---|---|---|---|---|
| Mission 1 | 55,14 | 55 | 10,347 | | |
| Mission 2 | 54,66 | 55 | 11,321 | | |
| Mission 3 | 52,00 | 50 | 11,206 | 4,657 | .000* |
| Mission 4 | 58,93 | 62 | 10,535 | | |
| Mission 5 | 56,45 | 54 | 10,377 | | |

* Significance at the .001 level.

(b)

| Attention | Mean | Median | SD | Chi-Square | Sig. $P$ |
|---|---|---|---|---|---|
| Mission 1 | 14,334 | 15 | 3,351 | | |
| Mission 2 | 16,310 | 18 | 3,883 | | |
| Mission 3 | 16,000 | 17 | 3,595 | 19,512 | .001* |
| Mission 4 | 16,862 | 17 | 3,090 | | |
| Mission 5 | 17,620 | 19 | 3,121 | | |

* Significance at the .01 level.

(c)

| Relevance | Mean | Median | SD | Chi-Square | Sig. $P$ |
|---|---|---|---|---|---|
| Mission 1 | 12,689 | 14 | 5,745 | | |
| Mission 2 | 11,000 | 9 | 5,855 | | |
| Mission 3 | 9,482 | 7 | 5,369 | 7,379 | .117 |
| Mission 4 | 12,620 | 12 | 5,747 | | |
| Mission 5 | 10,758 | 10 | 4,852 | | |

* Significance at the .05 level.

(d)

| Confidence | Mean | Median | SD | Chi-Square | Sig. $P$ |
|---|---|---|---|---|---|
| Mission 1 | 14,689 | 16 | 4,629 | | |
| Mission 2 | 12,655 | 14 | 4,760 | | |
| Mission 3 | 11,241 | 12 | 4,725 | 16,833 | .002* |
| Mission 4 | 14,586 | 16 | 4,452 | | |
| Mission 5 | 12,344 | 14 | 4,466 | | |

* Significance at the .01 level.

(e)

| Satisfaction | Mean | Median | SD | Chi-Square | Sig. $P$ |
|---|---|---|---|---|---|
| Mission 1 | 13,413 | 14 | 2,872 | | |
| Mission 2 | 14,689 | 15 | 3,495 | | |
| Mission 3 | 15,275 | 16 | 3,463 | 10,852 | .028* |
| Mission 4 | 14,862 | 15 | 2,812 | | |
| Mission 5 | 15,724 | 15 | 2,986 | | |

* Significance at the .05 level.

obtained for all data. The 3 Alarms Triggers and learners' physiological trends are presented in Figure 5. Each dot on the graph represents the difference between the two means for each alarm (mean$_{\text{After Alarm}}$ − mean$_{\text{Before Alarm}}$). Figure 5 shows almost complete opposite trends for all physiological data between the "Below" and "Above" classes, *except* for SC. The physiological analysis pointed towards the fact that the "effect" of an Alarm Trigger seems to decrease over time. We can see on Figure 5(a) that the effect of those alarms on

SC seems to slowly fade after the second alarm, contrary to the popular belief. Indeed, one may think that intervening with color and sound tends to capture learners attention, but our findings seem to indicate that this is only partially true. There seems to be a certain "adaptation" on the part of the learner with regards to SC at the very least. Nevertheless, any permanent diagnosis regarding learners' attention level in reaction to an Alarm Trigger based only on SC at this point may be hasty or even wrong for there are numerous other

Assessment of Learners' Motivation during Interactions with Serious Games: A Study of Some Motivational Strategies in Food-Force

19

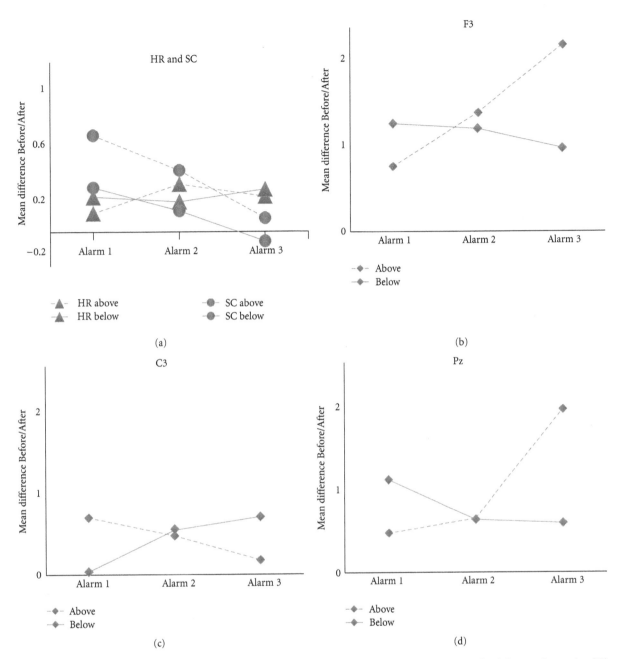

FIGURE 5: HR, SC, and EEG trends for three Alarm Triggers (mission 5 of Food-Force): each dot in all subfigures shows the difference between Mean$_{\text{After Alarm}}$ and Mean$_{\text{Before Alarm}}$ physiological data.

physiological trends to consider first. Indeed, even if no clear trends were found in HR, the cerebral data provided clarity in distinguishing between the two classes.

In fact, variations in the attention ratio are clearly evident for both classes. We found numerous occasions when two participants from different classes had the same SC and HR trends but have shown very opposite trends in EEG sites, especially C3 area. An example of this situation is illustrated in Figure 6: two participants had the same HR and SC trends but only an opposite trend in C3 helped us identify their respective attention classes. These results seem to show the relevance and importance of adding the EEG in assessing

learners' attention change, even more so when this change cannot be clearly established by the use of HR and SC alone. Thus, the EEG "attention ratio" generally increases for participants who reported a *low Attention* category score (class "Below") whereas the same ratio decreases for the learners in the class "Above".

6.2. *Logistic Regression Analysis.* Subjects have been separated into two groups according to their ARCS scores after each mission: those with scores below the overall average (group "Below") and those with scores above the overall average (group "Above"). We have run logistic regressions

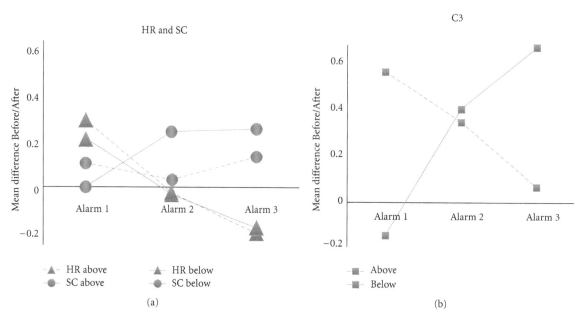

FIGURE 6: Comparison of physiological trends of 2 learners in 2 different classes: the same HR and SC trends (a) and opposite C3 mean difference Before/After trends (b).

TABLE 3: Omnibus tests of model coefficients (logistic regression).

| Strategy | Chi-Square | df | Sig. | Nagelkerke $R^2$ |
|---|---|---|---|---|
| Problem Solving | 15,893 | 5 | .007* | .574 |
| Alarm Trigger | 18,706 | 5 | .002* | .647 |
| Instructional Video | 7,563 | 5 | .182 | .312 |
| Informative Feedback | 15,468 | 5 | .009* | .563 |
| Explanatory Feedback | 12,103 | 5 | .033* | .464 |
| Displaying Score | 11,974 | 5 | .035* | .460 |

*Significance at the .05 level.

to predict learners' group ("Above" or "Below") for each studied strategy. The dependent variable in logistic regression is usually dichotomous, that is, the "Above" group coded as "1" whereas the "Below" group coded as "0". Furthermore, logistic regression makes no assumption about the distribution of the independent variables. These variables do not have to be normally distributed, linearly related or of equal variance within each group. Our prediction models used all computed PoT indexes as predictor variables (PoT-SC, PoT-HR, PoT-F3, PoT-C3, and PoT-Pz) and the Enter method for variable selection. Table 3 reports the results of adding five predictors (df = 5) to the regression model. Results indicated that adding predictors to the model has significantly increased our ability to distinguish between "Above" and "Below" groups for all studied motivational strategies, except for Instructional Video (see Table 3: Chi-Square and Sig. values with conventional significance level of 0.05). In addition, Nagelkerke's $R^2$ values of Table 3 ranged from 46% to 65% and indicated a moderately high relationship between the predictors and the dependent variable. Table 5 showed the classification tables which tell us how many of the cases where the observed values of the dependent variable were 1 or 0, respectively have been

correctly predicted. In each classification table, the columns are the two predicted values of the dependent, while the rows are the two observed values of the dependent. Prediction success overall was between 65.5% and 79.3% (see Table 5). The Wald criterion demonstrated that PoT-C3 especially made a significant contribution to prediction (see Table 4). Other variables were not significant predictors. Results of regression models clearly showed that physiological data, especially EEG "attention ratio", were relevant to evaluate motivational strategies. The most significant differences between groups were shown for *Attention Getting Strategies* though. One reason may be the limitation of the "attention ratio" (Theta/low-Beta) which seems to be inappropriate to identify EEG patterns other than those correlated with the *Attention* category. Regarding the physiological analysis, it is preferable to explore alternative EEG frequency ratios based on additional brainwaves such as Alpha (8–12 Hz) and High-Beta (20–32 Hz) in order to highlight other patterns correlated with learner's motivation. Furthermore, F3 and C3 areas showed more significant differences of PoT trends than Pz area which showed roughly similar trends between groups. This is can be explained by specific functions associated with the middle parietal (Pz) area. These functions

Assessment of Learners' Motivation during Interactions with Serious Games: A Study of Some Motivational Strategies in Food-Force

21

TABLE 4: Tables of variables in the equation (logistic regression).

| | B | SE | Wald | df | Sig. | Exp(B) |
|---|---|---|---|---|---|---|
| **Problem Solving** | | | | | | |
| PoT-HR | −.072 | 1,246 | .003 | 1 | .954 | .931 |
| PoT-SC | .733 | .958 | .586 | 1 | .444 | 2,082 |
| PoT-F3 | .271 | .681 | .159 | 1 | .691 | 1,312 |
| PoT-C3 | −3,473 | 1,580 | 4,829 | 1 | .028* | .031 |
| PoT-Pz | −.039 | 1,075 | .001 | 1 | .971 | .961 |
| Constant | 3,995 | 2,359 | 2,867 | 1 | .090 | 54,335 |
| **Alarm Trigger** | | | | | | |
| PoT-HR | −1,733 | 1,210 | 2,053 | 1 | .152 | .177 |
| PoT-SC | 1,990 | 1,459 | 1,861 | 1 | .173 | 7,314 |
| PoT-F3 | .785 | .802 | .960 | 1 | .327 | 2,193 |
| PoT-C3 | −4,462 | 1,890 | 5,576 | 1 | .018* | .012 |
| PoT-Pz | .282 | 1,263 | .050 | 1 | .823 | 1,326 |
| Constant | 4,733 | 2,430 | 3,795 | 1 | .051 | 113,643 |
| **Instructional Video** | | | | | | |
| PoT-HR | −.618 | .684 | .815 | 1 | .367 | .539 |
| PoT-SC | .879 | .729 | 1,455 | 1 | .228 | 2,408 |
| PoT-F3 | .462 | .471 | .960 | 1 | .327 | 1,587 |
| PoT-C3 | −.914 | .565 | 2,620 | 1 | .106 | .401 |
| PoT-Pz | −.378 | .790 | .229 | 1 | .633 | .685 |
| Constant | 1,150 | 1,283 | .804 | 1 | .370 | 3,160 |
| **Explanatory Feedback** | | | | | | |
| PoT-HR | −.828 | .919 | .812 | 1 | .368 | .437 |
| PoT-SC | 1,523 | 1,134 | 1,804 | 1 | .179 | 4,588 |
| PoT-F3 | −.102 | .637 | .026 | 1 | .873 | .903 |
| PoT-C3 | −1,969 | 1,180 | 2,784 | 1 | .095 | .140 |
| PoT-Pz | −.717 | 1,099 | .426 | 1 | .514 | .488 |
| Constant | 3,237 | 1,749 | 3,426 | 1 | .064 | 25,452 |
| **Informative Feedback** | | | | | | |
| PoT-HR | .950 | .789 | 1,450 | 1 | .229 | 2,585 |
| PoT-SC | 1,795 | .997 | 3,241 | 1 | .072 | 6,018 |
| PoT-F3 | −1,872 | .938 | 3,978 | 1 | .046 | .154 |
| PoT-C3 | 2,084 | .868 | 5,759 | 1 | .016* | 8,033 |
| PoT-Pz | −.316 | .605 | .272 | 1 | .602 | .729 |
| Constant | −1,848 | 1,354 | 1,864 | 1 | .172 | .158 |
| **Displaying Score** | | | | | | |
| PoT-HR | .806 | .953 | .716 | 1 | .398 | 2,239 |
| PoT-SC | .478 | 1,001 | .227 | 1 | .633 | 1,612 |
| PoT-F3 | −.068 | .526 | .017 | 1 | .897 | .934 |
| PoT-C3 | −1,149 | .534 | 4,635 | 1 | .031* | .317 |
| PoT-Pz | −1,221 | .784 | 2,424 | 1 | .119 | .295 |
| Constant | 2,074 | 1,457 | 2,027 | 1 | .155 | 7,957 |

* Significance at the .05 level.

incorporate appreciation of form, sensory combination and comprehension (pain, pressure, heat, cold, and touch) which are quite sparse or even absent in all missions. Learners tended to rely mostly on the frontal cortex (F3) because it is known to be strongly implicated in taking quick decisions under pressure. The central region of the brain (C3) seems to be the most solicited when a more "generalized" problem solving approach is used. Not only our results show that physiological data can provide an objective evaluation of motivational strategies for clearly distinguishing between learners' reactions, but also the relevance and importance of adding the EEG in our empirical study. The obtained

TABLE 5: Classification tables (logistic regression).

**Problem Solving**

| Observed | Predicted | | |
|---|---|---|---|
| | Below | Above | Percentage correct |
| Below | 7 | 4 | 63,6 |
| Above | 2 | 16 | 88,8 |
| Overall percentage | | | 79,3 |

**Alarm Trigger**

| Observed | Predicted | | |
|---|---|---|---|
| | Below | Above | Percentage correct |
| Below | 8 | 3 | 72,7 |
| Above | 4 | 14 | 77,7 |
| Overall percentage | | | 75,8 |

**Instructional Video**

| Observed | Predicted | | |
|---|---|---|---|
| | Below | Above | Percentage correct |
| Below | 10 | 6 | 62,5 |
| Above | 4 | 9 | 69,2 |
| Overall percentage | | | 65,5 |

**Explanatory Feedback**

| Observed | Predicted | | |
|---|---|---|---|
| | Below | Above | Percentage correct |
| Below | 8 | 2 | 80 |
| Above | 4 | 15 | 78,9 |
| Overall percentage | | | 79,3 |

**Informative Feedback**

| Observed | Predicted | | |
|---|---|---|---|
| | Below | Above | Percentage correct |
| Below | 7 | 3 | 70 |
| Above | 4 | 15 | 78,9 |
| Overall percentage | | | 75,8 |

**Displaying Score**

| Observed | Predicted | | |
|---|---|---|---|
| | Below | Above | Percentage correct |
| Below | 6 | 2 | 75 |
| Above | 4 | 17 | 80,9 |
| Overall percentage | | | 79,3 |

results also open the door to the possibility to evaluate other motivational strategies used in different intelligent systems.

## 7. Conclusion and Future Work

In this paper, we have assessed the effects of some motivational strategies in Food-Force on learners' motivation using the ARCS theoretical model as well as three physiological sensors: HR, SC, and EEG. We have successfully answered our first research question by identifying physiological patterns, especially EEG Theta/low-Beta ratio, to evaluate motivational strategies. We then successfully answered our second research question by using these physiological trends to build prediction models of learners' motivation. These models were able to moderately distinguish motivating strategies

from those with low impacts on learners' motivation. Our findings showed that SC and HR may reach their limits in some cases for evaluating the impacts of motivational strategies on learners. In fact, no clear trends were found in SC and HR for evaluating some studied strategies. However, C3 Theta/low-Beta ratio has showed different trends between groups for almost all studied strategies. It can give valuable evaluation of motivational strategies.

Statistical and physiological study of our data has given some insights into the assessment of learners' motivation during playing a serious game. It has shown that physiological parameters are suitable to assess the effects of motivational strategies on learners' motivation. The obtained results are very encouraging to an ITS because (1) it is possible to assess the effects of tutor's interventions on learners' motivation, (2) we can rely on this assessment as a substitute for self-reports that can disrupt a learning session, and (3) it is possible to enrich the Learner Model (which describes learners' behaviors and evaluates their knowledge) with a motivational component based on our results, thus enabling the Tutor Model (which uses the Learner Model and customizes learning environments by adapting learning strategies in order to respond intelligently to learners' needs, objectives, and interests) to properly adapt its interventions.

However, one limitation in this work is the assumption that the ARCS categories are independent from each other. Simultaneous strategies in SG can be related to different categories of the ARCS model. One possible extension of the present work would be to consider dependencies between ARCS categories. In addition, we can extend the present work to study more than two classes of motivation. Multinomial logistic regression will be used in this case in counterpart of binary logistic regression. It is also possible to add other variables that can improve the prediction quality of our models. Indeed, some personals characteristics (age, gender, player style, hours spent playing video games, etc.) can be additional predictors for players' motivation. Furthermore, brain activity can also be better analysed in the future and other EEG analysis methods, such as the event-related potential (ERP) technique, can be used to test whether different events in serious game evoke differential EEG responses. We plan, therefore, to address all these possibilities in a further complementary study.

## Conflict of Interests

The authors declare that they have no conflict of interests in the research.

## Acknowledgments

The authors would like to thank all the reviewers for their insightful and helpful comments. They acknowledge the support of the Tunisian government and the National Science and Engineering Research Council (NSERC) of Canada for this work. They also address their thanks to Pierre Chalfoun for his participation in the experiment setup and his useful comments.

# References

[1] A. Bandura, *Social Foundations of Thought and Action: A Social Cognitive Theory*, Prentice-Hall, Englewood Cliffs, NJ, USA, 1986.

[2] A. de Vicente and H. Pain, "Informing the detection of the students' motivational state: an empirical study," in *Proceedings of the 6th International Conference on Intelligent Tutoring Systems*, pp. 933–943, Springer, Biarritz, France, 2002.

[3] J. M. Keller, *Motivational Design for Learning and Performance: The ARCS Model Approach*, Springer, New York, NY, USA, 2010.

[4] T. S. Chan and T. C. Ahern, "Targeting motivation—adapting flow theory to instructional design," *Journal of Educational Computing Research*, vol. 21, no. 2, pp. 151–163, 1999.

[5] D. H. Schunk, P. R. Pintrich, and J. L. Meece, *Motivation in Education: Theory, Research and Applications*, Pearson/Merrill, Upper Saddle River, NJ, USA, 3rd edition, 2008.

[6] M. Prensky, *Digital Game-Based Learning*, McGraw Hill, New York, NY, USA, 2001.

[7] R. Garris, R. Ahlers, and J. E. Driskell, "Games, motivation, and learning: a research and practice model," *Simulation and Gaming*, vol. 33, no. 4, pp. 441–467, 2002.

[8] I. Arroyo, K. Ferguson, J. Johns et al., "Repairing disengagement with non invasive interventions," in *Proceedings of the 13th International Conference on Artificial Intelligence in Education*, pp. 195–202, IOS Press, Los Angeles, Calif, USA, 2007.

[9] R. S. J. D. Baker, A. T. Corbett, K. R. Koedinger et al., "Adapting to when students game an intelligent tutoring system," in *Intelligent Tutoring Systems*, pp. 392–401, Springer, Jhongli, Taiwan, 2006.

[10] S. Chaffar, L. Derbali, and C. Frasson, "Inducing positive emotional state in intelligent tutoring systems," in *Proceedings of the 14th Conference on Artificial Intelligence in Education*, IOS Press, 2009.

[11] G. Rebolledo-Mendez, B. du Boulay, and R. Luckin, "Motivating the learner: an empirical evaluation," in *Proceedings of the 8th Conference on Intelligent Tutoring Systems*, pp. 545–554, Springer, Berlin, Germany, 2006.

[12] T. Hurley, "Intervention strategies to increase self-efficacy and self-regulation in adaptive on-line learning," in *Adaptive Hypermedia and Adaptive Web-Based Systems*, pp. 440–444, Springer, Berlin, Germany, 2006.

[13] T. Barnes, E. Powell, A. Chaffin, and H. Lipford, "Game2Learn: improving the motivation of CS1 students," in *Proceedings of the 3rd International Conference on Game Development in Computer Science Education (GDCSE'08)*, pp. 1–5, ACM, Miami, Fla, USA, March 2008.

[14] D. S. McNamara, G. T. Jackson, and A. C. Graesser, "Intelligent tutoring and games (iTaG)," in *Proceedings of the Workshop on Intelligent Educational Games at the 14th International Conference on Artificial Intelligence in Education*, pp. 1–10, IOS Press, Brighton, UK, 2009.

[15] W. H. Huang, W. Y. Huang, and J. Tschopp, "Sustaining iterative game playing processes in DGBL: the relationship between motivational processing and outcome processing," *Computers and Education*, vol. 55, no. 2, pp. 789–797, 2010.

[16] W. L. Johnson, H. H. Vilhjálmsson, and S. Marsella, "Serious games for language learning: how much game, how much AI?" in *Proceedings of the 12th International Conference on Artificial Intelligence in Education*, pp. 306–313, IOS Press, Amsterdam, The Netherlands, 2005.

[17] L. Derbali and C. Frasson, "Prediction of players' motivational states using electrophysiological measures during serious game play," in *Proceedings of the 10th IEEE International Conference on Advanced Learning Technologies (ICALT'10)*, pp. 498–502, IEEE Computer Society, Sousse, Tunisia, July 2010.

[18] G. Rebolledo-Méndez, S. de Freitas, J. R. Rojano-Caceres, and A. R. Garcia-Gaona, "An empirical examination of the relation between attention and motivation in computer-based education: a modeling approach," in *Proceedings of the 23rd International Florida Artificial Intelligence Research Society Conference (FLAIRS-23)*, pp. 74–79, Daytona Beach, Fla, USA, May 2010.

[19] C. Conati, "Probabilistic assessment of user's emotions in educational games," *Applied Artificial Intelligence*, vol. 16, no. 7-8, pp. 555–575, 2002.

[20] M. Csikszentmihalyi, *Flow: The Psychology of Optimal Experience*, Harper Perennial, 1990.

[21] R. M. Ryan and E. L. Deci, "Self-determination theory and the facilitation of intrinsic motivation, social development, and well-being," *American Psychologist*, vol. 55, no. 1, pp. 68–78, 2000.

[22] R. M. Ryan, C. S. Rigby, and A. Przybylski, "The motivational pull of video games: a self-determination theory approach," *Motivation and Emotion*, vol. 30, no. 4, pp. 347–360, 2006.

[23] R. Bartle, "Hearts, clubs, diamonds, spades: players who suit MUDs," *The Journal of Virtual Environments*, vol. 1, 1996.

[24] M. Cocea and S. Weibelzahl, "Log file analysis for disengagement detection in e-Learning environments," *User Modelling and User-Adapted Interaction*, vol. 19, no. 4, pp. 341–385, 2009.

[25] G. Rebolledo-Méndez, S. de Freitas, J. R. Rojano-Caceres, and A. R. Garcia-Gaona, "An empirical examination of the relation between attention and motivation in computer-based education: a modeling approach," in *Proceedings of the 23rd International Florida Artificial Intelligence Research Society Conference (FLAIRS-23)*, pp. 74–79, Daytona Beach, Fla, USA, May 2010.

[26] I. Arroyo, D. G. Cooper, W. Burleson, B. P. Woolf, K. Muldner, and R. Christopherson, "Emotion sensors go to school," in *Proceedings of the 14th Conference on Artificial Intelligence in Education*, pp. 17–24, IOS Press, 2009.

[27] A. P. Rovoi and R. Lucking, "Sense of community in a higher education television-based distance education program," *Educational Technology Research and Development*, vol. 51, no. 2, pp. 5–16, 2003.

[28] M. J. Hannafin, J. R. Hill, and S. M. Land, "Student-centered learning and interactive multimedia: status, issues, and implications," *Contemporary Educational Psychology*, vol. 68, pp. 94–97, 1997.

[29] T. VanDeGrift, "Coupling pair programming and writing: learning about students' perceptions and processes," in *Proceedings of the 35th SIGCSE Technical Symposium on Computer Science Education*, pp. 2–6, ACM, Norfolk, Va, USA, March 2004.

[30] C. A. Collazos, L. A. Guerrero, J. A. Pino, and S. F. Ochoa, "Evaluating collaborative learning processes," in *Proceedings of the 8th International Workshop on Groupware: Design, Implementation and Use*, pp. 203–221, Springer, 2002.

[31] Z. Dörnyei, *Motivational Strategies in the Language Classroom*, Cambridge University Press, Cambridge, UK, 2001.

[32] J. Goo, K. Park, M. Lee et al., "Effects of guided and unguided style learning on user attention in a virtual environment," in *Technologies For e-Learning and Digital Entertainment*, pp. 1208–1222, Springer, Berlin, Germany, 2006.

[33] J. M. Keller, "Development and use of the ARCS model of instructional design," *Journal of Instructional Development*, vol. 10, no. 3, pp. 2–10, 1987.

[34] J. V. Dempsey and R. B. Johnson, "The development of an ARCS gaming scale," *Instructional Psychology*, vol. 25, pp. 215–221, 1998.

[35] G. A. Gunter, R. F. Kenny, and E. H. Vick, "A case for a formal design paradigm for serious games," *International Digital Media and Arts Association*, vol. 3, pp. 93–105, 2006.

[36] T. Lin, A. Imamiya, W. Hu, and M. Omata, "Display characteristics affect users' emotional arousal in 3D games," in *Universal Access in Ambient Intelligence Environments*, C. Stephanidis and M. Pieper, Eds., pp. 337–351, Springer, Berlin, Germany, 2007.

[37] G. F. Wilson and F. Fisher, "Cognitive task classification based upon topographic EEG data," *Biological Psychology*, vol. 40, no. 1-2, pp. 239–250, 1995.

[38] D. J. L. G. Schutter and J. van Hon, *Electrophysiological Ratio Markers for the Balance Between Reward and Punishment*, Elsevier, Amsterdam, The Netherlands, 2005.

[39] P. Putman, J. van Peer, I. Maimari, and S. van der Werff, "EEG theta/beta ratio in relation to fear-modulated response-inhibition, attentional control, and affective traits," *Biological Psychology*, vol. 83, no. 2, pp. 73–78, 2010.

[40] M. M. Lansbergen, M. Arns, M. van Dongen-Boomsma Martine, D. Spronk, and J. K. Buitelaar, "The increase in theta/beta ratio on resting-state EEG in boys with attention-deficit/hyperactivity disorder is mediated by slow alpha peak frequency," *Progress in Neuro-Psychopharmacology and Biological Psychiatry*, vol. 35, no. 1, pp. 47–52, 2011.

[41] L. Derbali, P. Chalfoun, and C. Frasson A, "Theoretical and empirical approach in assessing motivational factors: from serious games To an ITS," in *Proceedings of the Florida Artificial Intelligence Research Society Conference*, pp. 513–518, Palm Beach, Fla, USA, 2011.

[42] United Nation's Food-Force Game, World Food Programme, 2005, http://www.wfp.org/how-to-help/individuals/food-force.

[43] J. Brophy, "Other ways to support students intrinsic motivation," in *Motivating Students to Learn*, pp. 220–248, Lawrence Erlbaum Associates, Mahwah, NJ, USA, 2004.

[44] A. Hiam, "Motivating with informative feedback," in *Motivating and Rewarding Employees: New and Better Ways to Inspire Your People*, Adams Media Corporation, 1999.

[45] R. Moreno and R. E. Mayer, "Role of guidance, reflection, and interactivity in an agent-based multimedia game," *Journal of Educational Psychology*, vol. 97, no. 1, pp. 117–128, 2005.

[46] Pro-Comp Infinity Encoder, Thought Technology Ltd, http://www.thoughttechnology.com/proinf.htm.

[47] D. Gregory, "Guidelines for digital EEG," *American Journal of Electroneurodiagnostic Technology*, vol. 39, no. 4, pp. 278–288, 1999.

[48] J. Han and M. Kamber, *Data Mining: Concepts and Techniques*, The Morgan Kaufmann Series in Data Management Systems, Morgan Kaufmann, 2006.

[49] T. Lin, A. Maejima, and S. Morishima, "An empirical study of bringing audience into the movie," in *Proceedings of the 9th International Symposium on Smart Graphics*, pp. 70–81, Springer, Berlin, 2008.

[50] L. Derbali and C. Frasson, "Physiological evaluation of attention getting strategies during serious game play," in *Proceedings of the 15th International Conference on Artificial Intelligence in Education*, Springer, Auckland, New Zealand, 2011.

[51] S. H. Song and J. M. Keller, *Effectiveness of Motivationally Adaptive Computer-Assisted Instruction on the Dynamic Aspects of Motivation*, Springer, Heidelberg, Germany, 2001.

# 3

# Towards Brain-Computer Interface Control of a 6-Degree-of-Freedom Robotic Arm Using Dry EEG Electrodes

**Alexander Astaras,**[1,2] **Nikolaos Moustakas,**[1,2]
**Alkinoos Athanasiou,**[1,3] **and Aristides Gogoussis**[2]

[1] *Lab of Medical Informatics, Medical School, Aristotle University of Thessaloniki, Thessaloniki, Greece*
[2] *Department of Automation, Alexander Technological Educational Institute of Thessaloniki, Thessaloniki, Greece*
[3] *Department of Neurosurgery, Papageorgiou General Hospital, Thessaloniki, Greece*

Correspondence should be addressed to Alexander Astaras; alexander.astaras@gmail.com

Academic Editor: Panagiotis Bamidis

*Introduction.* Development of a robotic arm that can be operated using an exoskeletal position sensing harness as well as a dry electrode brain-computer interface headset. Design priorities comprise an intuitive and immersive user interface, fast and smooth movement, portability, and cost minimization. *Materials and Methods.* A robotic arm prototype capable of moving along 6 degrees of freedom has been developed, along with an exoskeletal position sensing harness which was used to control it. Commercially available dry electrode BCI headsets were evaluated. A particular headset model has been selected and is currently being integrated into the hybrid system. *Results and Discussion.* The combined arm-harness system has been successfully tested and met its design targets for speed, smooth movement, and immersive control. Initial tests verify that an operator using the system can perform pick and place tasks following a rather short learning curve. Further evaluation experiments are planned for the integrated BCI-harness hybrid setup. *Conclusions.* It is possible to design a portable robotic arm interface comparable in size, dexterity, speed, and fluidity to the human arm at relatively low cost. The combined system achieved its design goals for intuitive and immersive robotic control and is currently being further developed into a hybrid BCI system for comparative experiments.

## 1. Introduction

Brain-computer interfaces (BCIs) are interactive systems that aim at providing users with an alternative way of translating their volition into control of external devices. Their most popular applications lie within the scope of rehabilitation and motor restoration for patients with severe neurological impairment [1]. Although BCI research is currently undergoing a transitional stage of exploratory efforts [2], commercial applications of BCIs are beginning to emerge [3].

The use of brainwaves to control robotic devices has produced promising clinical results in terms of feasibility [4]. Restoration of a certain degree of motor functions [5, 6] and high accuracy control of robotic prosthetic arms using invasive BCIs has already been demonstrated [7]. Nevertheless, in order for such BCI-controlled robotic applications to achieve end-user maturity, the use of noninvasive, portable, and relatively low-cost systems is considered a required development.

Given these recent technological advances, we have focused our research efforts in noninvasive, minimally intrusive, and low-cost BCI. We have designed, partly implemented, and tested an electromechanical robotic system to investigate the capabilities and limitations in combining these technologies for biomedical applications [8]. All components used for the developed system presented in this paper have been designed, implemented, and tested by our research and development team.

Design requirements included fast robotic movement that approximates the natural movement of a human operator's arm, an intuitive and immersive interface, portability, potential for further development, scalability, and relatively

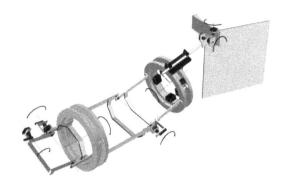

FIGURE 1: CAD diagram of the 6-DOF exoskeletal position sensing harness. The curved arrows show the axis of 7 axes of rotation (the 7th DOF is used to control the robotic gripper). The harness is worn around the human operator's arm.

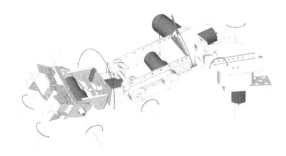

FIGURE 2: CAD diagram of the 6-DOF robotic arm and gripper. The 6 dark cylinders are DC motors, each accommodating a degree of freedom.

low cost (i.e., less than $3000). We targeted investigative comparative neurophysiological scenarios in which an operator remotely controls a 6-degree-of-freedom (DOF) robotic arm using their arm movement, their brainwaves, or both.

## 2. Materials and Methods

The hybrid system under development comprises two input devices and a robotic arm. The input devices are an exoskeletal position sensing harness (EPSH) and a commercially available dry electrode BCI headset. The robotic arm is the actuator device in our system and was also developed entirely by the authors. There is no feedback to the human operator in the proof-of-concept prototype described in this system.

The human arm, excluding the hand, possesses the ability to move along 7 DOF: pitch, yaw, and roll at the shoulder joint, pitch and roll at the elbow, pitch and yaw at the wrist. Only three DOF are needed to move the hand at a particular point in space, while the remaining 4 DOF permit humans to approach and grasp objects from different angles.

In order to simplify the design of both the EPSH and the robotic arm, we made the choice to omit wrist yaw, since it does not significantly affect the ability of the robot to manipulate objects. Still, a 7th DOF was added in order to operate the gripper.

All parts were designed using computer-aided design (CAD) software, manufactured using computer numerical control (CNC) and laser cutting machines, and assembled and tested by our team.

*2.1. The Exoskeletal Position Sensing Harness.* An EPSH was developed as a form of minimally intrusive, intuitive, and immersive interface for the robotic arm. It copies the operator's arm movement with measurable and repeatable accuracy (Figure 1). Apart from providing research data directly on immersive human computer interfaces, it will also form the basis for future comparative neurophysiological experiments in which a dry electrode BCI headset is evaluated against other forms of immersive robotic remote control.

The harness sensors and accompanying electronics provide real-time data on the position of the human operator's

joints from wrist to shoulder. Hand and finger position is not sensed; however, a finger-operated switch allows the user to operate the robotic arm's gripper in order to pick up and release items.

Copying of the human operator's movements is achieved through the EPSH which is worn around their arm. The harness measures the angles between the different parts of the arm and hand. Electronic output originating from the sensing harness is passed on to the robotic arm's control circuit, which also takes into account feedback output from the robotic arm itself. During the design phase, we, therefore, faced a classic automation closed-loop control challenge: the input is provided by the EPSH worn by the operator, the robotic arm is the recipient of the control output, and a feedback loop takes into account the actual position of the arm.

*2.2. The Robotic Arm.* The robotic arm is capable of the 6 following types of movement.

   (i) 2 DOF for the "shoulder" joint ("right–left" and "up–down").

  (ii) 1 DOF for the "elbow" joint.

 (iii) 1 DOF for the "wrist" joint.

 (iv) 2 DOF for rotation between the "shoulder–elbow" and "elbow–wrist" parts.

The robotic arm (Figure 2) is also equipped with an electromechanical gripper, which is operated by two servomotors controlled through a separate 7th communication channel.

*2.3. The Dry Electrode BCI Headset.* The selection of a commercially available BCI headset depended on the number of sensing channels, signal quality, price, and ease of use [9]. The ability of electrodes to perform dry was set as an important requirement. The inconvenience caused by the application of conductive gel to the scalp and the time-consuming preparation routine were considered decisive factors in limiting our selection to dry electrode headsets. While gel-contact electrodes provide better contact and measurement accuracy, the goals of the planned MERCURY comparative experiments are better served by a less precise, less expensive wearable headset.

Furthermore, the ideal BCI headset would need to meet the requirements of multiple data acquisition channels, low weight, and low cost. Frequency-based automatic classification of mental states by the hardware device and the ability to export the raw EEG signal were considered, the former being a strong factor for preference, the latter a decisive requirement. The maximum number of automatically detected mental states was not considered a priority, since this feature can be provided by the signal processing capabilities of our experimental setup. Still, the capacity of a commercial system to automatically detect multiple mental states was considered an indirect indication of the quality and breadth of its sensing capabilities. Thus, it was deemed a desirable—albeit less significant—advantage.

For this reason we examined two low-cost, commercially available headsets (Figure 3), the Emotiv EPOC [3] and NeuroSky MindWave [9].

Both devices export raw EEG as well as processed, automatically classified mental state data. Our choice between them depended on their sensing capabilities where the NeuroSky MindWave uses one sensor that can provide only three values: attention, meditation, and eye blinking. The Emotiv EPOC uses a series of 16 sensors, which are capable of detecting specific conscious thoughts, levels of attention, facial expressions, and head movements (the latter using the embedded gyroscope). The sampling frequency of the Emotiv EPOC is 4 times greater than the NeuroSky MindWave making it comparable to more complex and expensive virtual rehabilitation EEG devices [10].

The drawback of both devices is the occasional unreliability of signal quality, primarily associated with the use of dry electrodes. For this reason, the designers of the Emotiv headset suggest that users further improve skin conductance by the moistening of the sensors using a saline solution. While this procedure is not ideal for our purposes, it was considered the least inconvenient among commercially available low-cost solutions.

Despite this drawback, we selected the Emotiv EPOC for use in our hybrid system design, since it integrates the largest number of sensors at the highest sampling rate among all portable low-cost BCI headsets available in the market at the time this paper was submitted.

In the MERCURY hybrid setup, frequency-based EEG data classification is performed both inside the Emotiv EPOC device [11] as well as on the PC accepting raw data, depending on the mode of operation. The PC supporting the MERCURY hybrid system performs frequency-based analysis on selected channels and communicates results to the microcontroller operating the robotic arm, through a digital wired connection. The microcontroller can subsequently choose to control the arm based on incoming data from the EPOC or the exoskeletal sensing harness (Figure 4) or redirect both to a fusion algorithm that produces movement instructions (hybrid interface mode).

## 3. Results and Discussion

Development of the first two components of the hybrid system, the robotic arm and EPSH, has recently been completed. Validation and characterization tests have been performed in order to measure response times, angular velocity and acceleration, maximum payload, and power consumption (Figure 5).

*3.1. Response Time.* The average response time of M2, the motor operating within the shoulder joint of the robotic arm, was measured to be 120 ms ± 10. This was measured using an oscilloscope, measuring (10 repetitions average) the drop in current consumption by the motor as soon as the rotor started rolling. This motor is the slowest in the robot, so this measurement is used to formulate worst-case scenario comparisons. The aforementioned value was obtained using an oscilloscope to measure the initial setup time before the motor starts accelerating continuously. Anecdotal evidence from initial tests indicates that this delay is hardly noticeable by human operators.

*3.2. Angular Velocity and Acceleration.* A typical range of values for the average angular velocity of a human arm has been reported in the literature [12] to be $23°$–$50°$/sec for relaxed, $36°$–$87°$/sec for regular, and $122°$–$251°$/sec for strained quick movement. The equivalent ranges for average angular acceleration were $29°$–$41°$/sec$^2$, $72°$–$135°$/sec$^2$, and $721°$–$1151°$/sec$^2$, respectively. These average values were extracted from a series of experiments involving multiple subjects moving a horizontally rotating handle, a task which combined shoulder, elbow, and wrist movements.

We experimentally measured the average angular velocity of motors M2 (shoulder) and M4 (elbow) of our robotic arm throughout their full range of motion, $180°$ and $150°$, respectively [12]. These two motors were selected since they are known to be the slowest in the robotic arm, carry the most weight, and consume the largest share of power.

The experiments were set up so that the robotic arm be in an upwards movement (impeded by gravity) and were performed twice, with and without an additional 50 gr load. The robot input was to move as fast as possible, and multiple measurements were made in order to obtain average values. Results are summarised in Table 1.

Even though the experimental results are not directly comparable, focusing on the slowest response times of the robot—a deliberately pessimistic scenario—leads to some useful conclusions. The robotic arm

(i) is capable of combining speed and acceleration that exceed the typical range of regular human arm movements [13], even when impeded by gravity and carrying a small load,

(ii) is capable of accelerating faster than the human arm,

(iii) has an average speed reduction of less than 6% when carrying a small 50 gr load (averaged across the full range for motion for any joint),

(iv) has a qualitative attribute, not quantified yet, informally indicated by testing engineers: motion is smooth and the control is immersive and "feels natural";

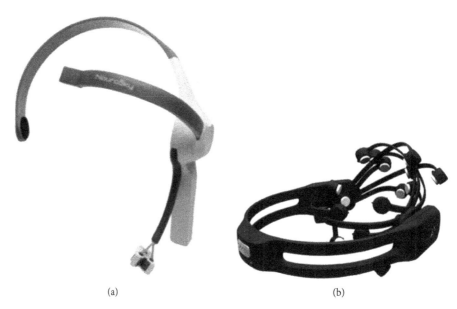

(a)　　　　　　　　　　　　　　　　　　　(b)

FIGURE 3: The two commercially available dry electrode BCI headsets considered. The NeuroSky MindWave (a) and Emotiv EPOC (b).

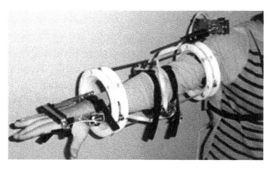

FIGURE 4: The first prototype exoskeletal position sensing harness, which is worn around the extended arm of a human operator. All parts used for the assembly were manufactured by the developers to design requirements.

TABLE 1: Experimental results of average angular velocity and acceleration measurements from the robotic arm. Motor M2 moves the shoulder joint, M4 moves the elbow. The load used was 50 gr.

| | Avg angular velocity (°/sec) | Avg angular acceleration (°/sec²) |
|---|---|---|
| M2 (free) | 108 ± 1 | — |
| M2 (load) | 102 ± 1 | 1535 ± 10 |
| M4 (free) | 134 ± 1 | — |
| M4 (load) | 128 ± 1 | — |

　(v) combined with the EPSH and the BCI headset, the entire integrated device is portable and suitable for carriage by a single person.

Complete qualitative assessment studies are planned in the immediate future, prior to the comparative experiments mentioned in following sections.

*3.3. Dimensions, Payload, and Power Consumption.* The EPSH measures 21 × 21.4 × 69 cm and weighs 3 kg. Including its wooden base, the robotic arm weighs 5.9 kg. When extended vertically, the robotic arm measures 25 × 73.9 × 30.2 cm. The moving part of the arm measures 25 × 12.5 × 46 cm. Its working space is approximately a hemisphere with a radius equal to its reach (46 cm), approximately 60% the reach of an adult human arm [14].

　The robotic arm prototype has a rated maximum payload of 300 gr. The maximum payload is 750 gr. These figures are a direct consequence of striving to maintain low development cost and can be dramatically improved in future prototypes. No tests were performed with loads greater than 750 gr in order to prevent damage to the prototype.

　The robotic arm is powered by a 24 V DC power supply. The peak current is 3.5 A ± 0.1, and the average power consumption is 25.3 W ± 0.1. All measurements were made with gravity impeding movement without additional load.

## 4. Future Work

With respect to electromechanics and electronics, the next development steps involve integrating the selected dry electrode headset with the EPSH and robotic arm into a hybrid device. A PC will be capable of recording experimental sessions in which the operator uses the headset, the harness, or both to control the robotic arm. Once experiments are concluded with the hybrid setup, there are further plans to introduce a feedback loop so that the operator gains a tactile feeling of resistance when the robotic arm touches an object or obstacle.

　With respect to software development, MATLAB-based (the MathWorks Inc., Natick, Massachusetts, USA) software code will process the output of the BCI headset, evaluate it against precise motion data captured by the harness and arm, and draw comparative conclusions. Our team is interested in comparing the BCI output to that of a conventional 10/20 EEG data acquisition system as well as to the output of the EPSH.

FIGURE 5: The first prototype robotic arm developed by our team. It is capable of moving at angular speed comparable to the natural motion of a human operator's arm. It comprises 6 DC motors (one for each DOF) and 2 servomotors for the gripper.

*4.1. Comparative Experiments.* The novelty of our experimental setup is the ability to capture all 6 degrees of freedom of the human arm's physical movement electromechanically, at low cost, with relative accuracy, and in real time. Furthermore, we plan to proceed with comparing our results to those acquired through the use of both a commercial BCI headset and a more conventional multichannel EEG-BCI paradigm, while the subject actually performs motor execution tasks. It is also among our research plans to comparatively investigate the role of virtual reality (VR) in controlling a virtual prosthetic arm versus controlling an actual robotic arm.

A series of neurophysiological experiments involve comparison of brain activation results between scenarios of motor execution (ME) versus motor imagery (MI) [15] and an unrelated control scenario. We plan to compare brain activation maps during ME tasks performed with the EPSH of the robotic arm, as well as the dry electrode headset BCI versus similar maps acquired during MI tasks performed with the BCI system.

The role of functional connectivity (FCN) of the brain in the fluid motions of the arm is also within our scope of experimentation. We wish to explore whether graph analysis of FCN during ME and MI of the arm can contribute towards the goal of making BCI systems more intuitive, easy to learn and easy to use.

A hybrid man-machine interface (MMI) and brain-computer interface (BCI) systems offer numerous investigative research advantages. Fluid and intuitive control of a prosthetic robotic arm using BCI is yet to be demonstrated, due to limitations of current BCI data acquisition and classification technologies. Those limitations could be addressed using the added benefit the MMI-control parameter for the robotic arm and artificial intelligence classifiers. The main question to be answered, as far as this hybrid system is concerned, can be identified in whether the unintuitive, hard-to-adjust-to and limited in functionality BCI systems which are currently commercially available can benefit from this approach. Are BCIs after all destined to be exclusively used for research and clinical purposes or could they evolve into a mature mainstream technology?

## 5. Conclusions

We have developed an intuitively controlled 6 DOF robotic arm and accompanying operator's sensing harness, satisfying the design requirements for an immersive, hybrid robotic control system. The first proof-of-concept prototype has been developed, evaluated, and deemed adequate for the next development step: integration with a commercial dry-electrode BCI headset. The intended research objectives for this system include BCI optimization through comparative experiments, using the motion and position sensing harness, the dry electrode BCI headset, and a combination of both. The ultimate research goals are to better understand the function of the motor cortex, improve neurofeedback training for people suffering from neurological disorders, and optimize robotic prosthetics.

## Acknowledgments

The research leading to these results has received funding from the European Union's Seventh Framework Programme (FP7/2007-2013) under grant agreement no 288532. For more details, please see http://www.usefil.eu/.

## References

[1] A. Athanasiou and P. D. Bamidis, "A review on brain computer interfaces: contemporary achievements and future goals towards movement restoration," *Aristotle University Medical Journal*, vol. 37, no. 3, pp. 35–44, 2010.

[2] B. Allison, J. D. R. Millan, A. Nijholt et al., "Future directions in Brain/Neuronal computer interaction (Future BNCI)," in *Proceedings of the BCI Meeting 2010*, Asilomar, Calif, USA, 2010.

[3] L. F. Nicolas-Alonso and J. Gomez-Gil, "Brain computer interfaces, a review," *Sensors*, vol. 12, no. 2, pp. 1211–1279, 2012.

[4] F. Galán, M. Nuttin, E. Lew et al., "A brain-actuated wheelchair: asynchronous and non-invasive Brain-computer interfaces for continuous control of robots," *Clinical Neurophysiology*, vol. 119, no. 9, pp. 2159–2169, 2008.

[5] J.-H. Lee, J. Ryu, F. A. Jolesz, Z. H. Cho, and S. S. Yoo, "Brain-machine interface via real-time fMRI: preliminary study on thought-controlled robotic arm," *Neuroscience Letters*, vol. 450, no. 1, pp. 1–6, 2009.

[6] L. R. Hochberg, M. D. Serruya, G. M. Friehs et al., "Neuronal ensemble control of prosthetic devices by a human with tetraplegia," *Nature*, vol. 442, no. 7099, pp. 164–171, 2006.

[7] T. Yanagisawa, M. Hirata, Y. Saitoh et al., "Real-time control of a prosthetic hand using human electrocorticography signals: technical note," *Journal of Neurosurgery*, vol. 114, no. 6, pp. 1715–1722, 2011.

[8] N. Moustakas, Υδράργυρος-*Six Degree of FreeDom Robotic Arm*, Aristotle University of Thessaloniki, Thessaloniki, Greece, 2011.

[9] J. I. Ekandem, T. A. Davis, I. Alvarez, M. T. James, and J. E. Gilbert, "Evaluating the ergonomics of BCI devices for research and experimentation," *Ergonomics*, vol. 55, no. 5, pp. 592–598, 2012.

[10] G. N. Ranky and S. Adamovich, "Analysis of a commercial EEG device for the control of a robot arm," in *Proceedings of the 36th Annual Northeast Bioengineering Conference (NEBEC '10)*, pp. 1–2, March 2010.

[11] M. Duvinage, T. Castermans, T. Dutoit, M. Petieau, T. Hoellinger, C. De Saedeleer et al., "A P300-based Quantitative Comparison between the Emotiv Epoc Headset and a Medical EEG Device," Biomedical Engineering/765: Telehealth/766: Assistive Technologies: ACTA Press, 2012.

[12] N. Moustakas, *Design and construction of a robotic arm capable of movement with 6 degrees of freedom and an exoskeleton sensor harness for its control [M.S. thesis]*, Alexander Technological Educational Institute of Thessaloniki, Sindos, Greece, 2011.

[13] H. Nagasaki, "Asymmetric velocity and acceleration profiles of human arm movements," *Experimental Brain Research*, vol. 74, no. 2, pp. 319–327, 1989.

[14] S. Plagenhoef, "Anatomical data for analyzing human motion," *Research Quarterly For Exercise and Sport*, vol. 54, no. 2, pp. 169–178, 1983.

[15] J. A. Stevens and M. E. P. Stoykov, "Using motor imagery in the rehabilitation of hemiparesis," *Archives of Physical Medicine and Rehabilitation*, vol. 84, no. 7, pp. 1090–1092, 2003.

# 4

# Estimation Algorithm of Machine Operational Intention by Bayes Filtering with Self-Organizing Map

**Satoshi Suzuki[1] and Fumio Harashima[2]**

[1] *School of Science and Technology for Future Life, Department of Robotics and Mechatronics, Tokyo Denki University, 2-2 Kanda-Nishiki-cho, Chiyoda-ku, Tokyo 101-8457, Japan*
[2] *Tokyo Metropolitan University, 1-1 Minami-Osawa, Hachioji-Shi, Tokyo 192-0397, Japan*

Correspondence should be addressed to Satoshi Suzuki, ssuzuki@fr.dendai.ac.jp

Academic Editor: Holger Kenn

We present an intention estimator algorithm that can deal with dynamic change of the environment in a man-machine system and will be able to be utilized for an autarkical human-assisting system. In the algorithm, state transition relation of intentions is formed using a self-organizing map (SOM) from the measured data of the operation and environmental variables with the reference intention sequence. The operational intention modes are identified by stochastic computation using a Bayesian particle filter with the trained SOM. This method enables to omit the troublesome process to specify types of information which should be used to build the estimator. Applying the proposed method to the remote operation task, the estimator's behavior was analyzed, the pros and cons of the method were investigated, and ways for the improvement were discussed. As a result, it was confirmed that the estimator can identify the intention modes at 44–94 percent concordance ratios against normal intention modes whose periods can be found by about 70 percent of members of human analysts. On the other hand, it was found that human analysts' discrimination which was used as canonical data for validation differed depending on difference of intention modes. Specifically, an investigation of intentions pattern discriminated by eight analysts showed that the estimator could not identify the same modes that human analysts could not discriminate. And, in the analysis of the multiple different intentions, it was found that the estimator could identify the same type of intention modes to human-discriminated ones as well as 62–73 percent when the first and second dominant intention modes were considered.

## 1. Introduction

Estimation of human intention is quite practical for various applications such as assistance software [1], prediction of users' requests on the internet [2], and marketing [3]. In the robotics fields, realization of the intention estimator is desired especially for power assist systems [4] and for co-operative robots [5] since users' intentions are significant for their control. A function to estimate users' internal status and their intention is embedded in social robots [6] or interactive human-friendly robots [7, 8]. Thus, such technology is becoming a requisite technology to realize advanced human-computer interaction. Interaction techniques used in their applications are, however, designed on a case-by-case basis since practical design methodology for a general artificial

system has not yet been established. Especially, function of existing intention estimators were determined at the design phase against a limited circumstance of encounter and target user group; hence, there is no design method for an intention estimator which can deal with dynamic change of user's environment and of user's individual characteristics such as skill and experience. In some cases, we user needs familiarization with the use of the estimator's function, for instance we implicitly select adequate candidates of keywords when we use some data-search system. Due to this issue, there are many gadgets requiring user efforts in the case of not only intention estimators but also of other machines although a machine has been developed to support humans basically (remember how long and hard training to get a car license was in order to drive a vehicle that was

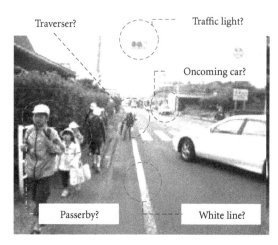

FIGURE 1: Example of difficult situation to specify environmental factor to estimate intentions: on the crossroad.

developed to make human mobility convenient). Against this background, new need of mechatronics supporting operational skill of user, that is a human adaptive mechatronics (HAM), was pointed out [9, 10]. Even to realize HAM, a function of an intention-estimation is desired to enhance the human-computer interaction. Specifications of the intention-estimation for HAM are the following.

(S1) Adaptivity to natural circumstance which is always varying.

(S2) Real time processing to cope with events in real world.

(S3) Ease of designing not depending on ability of application developers.

Below, reasons of these specifications will be explained with discussion on research background and existing methods.

### 1.1. Existing Methods and the Issues

*1.1.1. Difficulty to Specify Adequate Environmental Status.* Estimation of intentions at general human-machine system is more difficult than above-mentioned successful examples since it is difficult to identify the information types which are utilized for the user's decision making. Further, it is hard for a machine to measure all types of environmental information that was perceived by a human. And, the machine recognition of events' causality is also hard since many factors and events affect each other. We can understand these difficulties easily when considering a driving situation at a crossroad, as shown in Figure 1. Since a driver has to perceive and recognize many factors—traffic light, oncoming cars, traversers, passersby, and their white line on the road—his/her attention to them should be always changing. Therefore, it is difficult for a machine to detect what the driver is paying attention to. For all these reasons, adequate selection of these environmental elements/status for an intention estimator requires trial and errors and an experience by the developers. If this troublesome work, that

is, selection of environmental variables, is automatically performed, the above-mentioned specifications (S1) and (S3) will be achieved.

*1.1.2. Real time Processing.* Estimation of timings of events/factors is significant for an operation assistance. Similarly, the intention-estimation has to be executed in real time. However, a sensitive human model that can estimate operator's action/intention under time-varying circumstance is not established yet. Generally, a discrete event modeling is proper to describe human cognitive behavior/action, and several effective methods such as GOMS [11] and Therblig [12] were developed. It is, however, unexpectedly difficult to embed time factors into a frame of these discrete models. As attempts to solve this issue, many researchers proposed a wide variety of hybrid systems. As an example, the stochastic switched ARX model was presented [13]. The model consists of continuous-time linear subsystems and the switching probabilities of the subsystems, are trained using an EM algorithm. The other is a hybrid system consisting of a finite state automaton and multiple liner dynamical systems [14]. Although effectiveness of these methods was demonstrated, the applicable conditions are limited, that is, the number of the discrete modes were relatively small. Because the number of network links increases drastically as the nodes increase, and then computation also increases. The countermeasure is to decrease the links by considering the context of events since the context of action plays a significant role in the decision of users' intentions. For this reason, event-driven models based on graph theories, such as hidden Markov model [15] and fuzzy automata [16], are used frequently. Building of these graph networks needs, however, experiences; hence, this issue comes down to the issue of the developer side as pointed out in (S3).

Moreover, as a research on behavior analysis of humans, activity recognition (AR) is known [17]. AR aims to recognize the actions from a series of observations like a lifelog. AR was performed by classifying measured data of human behavior, and the change/pattern of the data is analyzed mainly. On the other hand, intentions of action are so-called internal status of the human, and the intention does not always appear to the outside as behavior. Hence, methods for AR cannot be applied to the intention-estimation problem for human-support machines.

*1.1.3. Usability without Dependency on Developer's Skill.* Performance of algorithm depends on ability of the system developer. This fact is not unique to a design of an intention estimator; however, there are several awkward processes even to the skilled developer. For instance, if the aforementioned graph theory approaches are adopted, the system designer has to make the network structures by sufficiently considering relations of transition states and of events causality, that is, the developer has to know sufficiently the task contents. When we use "traditional metrics, an application developer would get conflicting information from the frame and the event level analysis [18]," in short, an experience is demanded to resolve it.

In summary, a design of intention-estimation using AR, Therblig, or graph theories entails human judgement and experience of developers; hence, these are not feasible for an automatic supporting system that has to execute computation without interposition of human developers online.

*1.1.4. Merit and Demerit of Related Mathematical Tools.* Since the estimation of intentions basically can be traced to a classification problem depending on environment and events, development of various clustering methods such as a support-vector machine and a k-nearest neighbor method makes it possible to realize applications of the intention-estimation. To resolve issues mentioned in Section 1.1.1, if many sensors were used to measure the environmental status, effectiveness of the above-mentioned liner classifiers are reduced due to the increase of the number of variables [19] and the intention estimator by these techniques would not work well. On the other hand, since other intention estimators based on graph theories assume Gaussian distribution for their probability computation, these methods cannot deal with transition of human intention changing under non-Gaussian probability. To resolve such issues, Bayesian approaches are well leveraged in recent years [19]. Bayesian techniques are utilized in wide areas, especially for the information technology field [20]. Since the Bayes approach is faithful to measured data, it is expected that intentions estimation is possible regardless of designers' ability and preoccupation. Although Bayesian method is a powerful tool, huge amount of computation is a similar problem if the number of elements increases.

*1.2. Countermeasure and the Approach.* From the discussion above, an intention-estimation algorithm that satisfies specifications (S1) and (S3) requires the following functions: a component analysis function which enables to extract dominant factors from multivariable information and a clustering function which can identify information relating to intentions. Therefore, the present authors focused on SOM that can perform the compression and identification of information. SOM is a type of artificial neural network to discriminate multidimensional data [21], and it models the cerebral cortex in the human brain. SOM is adequate for data processing of large dimensional data since the SOM technique can compress multidimensional information into lower (two-) dimensional map by keeping original topological information. Similar types of nodes gather close to each other on the map, and different types are assigned there apart from each other. The Bayesian probability embedded in the SOM is expected to be utilized to predict transition of status. Utilizing such property of SOM, the present authors presented automatic method to identify machine operation [22]. By expanding the method, a basic idea of *SOM-Bayes intention estimator* was also proposed [23, 24]. The merit given by SOM is labor saving for the developer; it is not necessary to specify the type of information utilized in the operator because selection of the informations is performed automatically through the SOM computation. This merits are helpful as solutions for specifications (S1) and (S3).

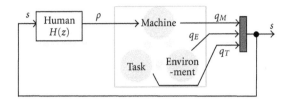

FIGURE 2: System architecture of human-machine system.

*1.3. Purpose.* In this paper, the details of algorithm of the SOM-Bayes intention estimator presented in [23, 24] are explained, and characteristics, design method, issues, and benefits are discussed comprehensively. Moreover, additional analyses of individual differences in human discrimination about intention modes and of multiple different intention are reported.

An organization of this paper is as follows: Section 2 explains an idea of the SOM-Bayes intention estimator and the algorithm. In Section 3, a particle filtering algorithm to realize the intention estimator is presented. In Section 4, a remote operation experiment system to apply the estimator and preparations to use it are explained. Section 5 shows analyses of the applied example and discusses the results. An improvement of the estimator and the related analysis are mentioned there. Section 6 presents several analyses concerning the estimator's behavior. Lastly Section 7 contains a conclusion and discussion.

## 2. Algorithm of SOM-Bayes Intention Estimator

As a preparation to design the intention estimator, a human-machine system structure is considered, and an internal status of the human model is assumed as intentions. Then, the design issues are formulated as an observer design problem that estimates the internal status. Elements in the human-machine system are a human (operator), a machine (to be manipulated), an environment, and the work task, as shown in Figure 2. This scheme is interpreted as the following: *human* operates *machine*, motion of the *machine* affects to *environment*, status of *task* is changed by the *environment*, and the change affects the status of *machine* again [25]. Describing these three types of statuses as the machine status ($M$-status, $q_M$), the environment status ($E$-status, $q_E$), and the task substance ($T$-status, $q_T$), a human during machine operation can be defined as an information-processing system, $\rho = H(z) \cdot s$, where $s := [q_M^T, q_E^T, q_T^T]^T$ is an information to be recognized by a human, $\rho$ is an output of operation commands to the machine, and $z$ is intentions of the human. Since it is impossible to describe the function $H$ by using algebraic equations, $H$ is required to be expressed using some mathematical model that can give numerical solution. Therefore, $H$ is approximated by a mapping relation corresponding to transition property of $H$ as an alternative way. Under this framework, the present authors devised a computation of belief bel($z$) of intentions $z$ from measurable data $s$ and $\rho$ using Bayesian estimation method in order to obtain numerical solution

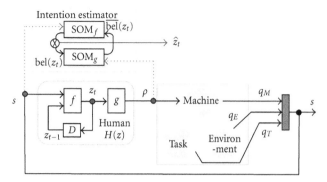

FIGURE 3: Block diagram involving a human model and the intention estimator in human-machine system.

from the function $H$. This is a computation method to infer probability of reasons using information of measured events. Probability of events is predicted based on the prior distribution, and the prediction is modified using the postmeasurement probability. Repeating this process, an internal status of the dynamical system, that is, intentions in this case, is estimated. Applying the Bayesian estimation approach to the computation of $H$, the computation of $H(z) \cdot s \to \rho$ is formulated as follows:

$$z_t = f(z_{t-1}, s_t), \tag{1}$$

$$\rho_t = g(z_t), \tag{2}$$

where the subscript $t \in \mathcal{N}$ is a time counter, the function $f$ is a state transition function describing change of the intention $z$, and the function $g$ corresponds to selection of operational commands based on the intention $z$. Based on a concept of "spotlight of selective attention" in global workspace theory (GWT) [26], so-called *spotlight models*, mathematical expression $z$ is defined as a vector $z \in [0,1]^{n_z}$ of which element corresponds to one intention strength of one operation action ($n_z$ is a size of vector $z$). According to the *spotlight models*, several types of consciousness exist simultaneously inside human brain, and one of them floats from unconsciousness level as a conscious awareness. Since there are several operational modes in case of a general machine operation, the vector-form expression of intentions can fit a concept of *spotlight models*.

The probabilistic distribution bel($z$) is estimated using a technique of the Bayes filtering with (1) and (2). Although other intentions not involving the machine operation exist inside the human brain simultaneously, only intentions determining the operation are considered since the information which relates to the operation is solely treated; hence, such internal status is called simply as "intention."

Basic algorithm for estimation of bel($z$) using Bayes filtering is explained below.

*Algorithm 1* (Bayes filter). Consider the following:

$$\overline{\text{bel}}(z_t) = \int p(z_t \mid s_t, z_{t-1}) \cdot \text{bel}(z_{t-1}) dz_{t-1}, \tag{3}$$

$$\text{bel}(z_t) = \eta \cdot p(\rho_t \mid z_t) \cdot \overline{\text{bel}}(z_t). \tag{4}$$

This algorithm is defined with iterative equations that are computed from time (index) $t = 1$ to the final time $T$. $p(z_t \mid s_t, z_{t-1})$ corresponds to a probabilistic distribution of a transition of intention from $z_{t-1}$ to $z_t$ given input $s_t$. $p(\rho_t \mid z_t)$ is the conditional probabilistic distribution of judgment that outputs $\rho_t$ if the intention $z_t$ happens to be true. Equation (3) is a *prediction* to obtain a belief $\overline{\text{bel}}(z_t)$ at the time of $t$. Equation (4) is called *measurement update* and adjusts the prediction $\overline{\text{bel}}(z_t)$ by considering the probability $p(\rho_t \mid z_t)$. Via this update, a new belief bel($z_t$) at time $t$ is obtained. $\eta$ is a so-called Bayes normalization constant. In the proposed approach, mapping relations shown below are acquired by utilizing a mapping relation of the SOM:

$$z_t \longleftarrow \text{SOM}_f(z_{t-1}, s_t), \tag{5}$$

$$\rho_t \longleftarrow \text{SOM}_g(z_t), \tag{6}$$

where arrows in the above equations represent a mapping relation that gives variables written in the left side using $\text{SOM}_*$ by using variables written inside parentheses. The mapping relation of $\text{SOM}_f$ and $\text{SOM}_g$ are acquired offline at the training phase, and these are used as static mapping functions at the computation in (5) and (6). In short, $\text{SOM}_f$ for the state transition function $f$ is trained using the input vector sequence including the training time series data of $\{s'\}$ and $\{z'\}$, and then the SOM reference vectors $^f\xi_i$ ($i = 1, \ldots, L_f$) are obtained, where $L_f$ is the number of all nodes in $\text{SOM}_f$. Similarly, training the $\text{SOM}_g$ for the measurement function $g$ by using sequences $\{\rho'\}$, and $\{z'\}$, the other SOM reference vectors $^g\xi_i$ ($i = 1, \ldots, L_g$) are obtained, where $L_g$ is the number of all nodes in $\text{SOM}_g$. Here, $\{s'\}$ and $\{\rho'\}$ are made from the experimental logging data, and $\{z'\}$ is prepared by an analyst watching the record video of the expert's operation. Details of preparation of $\{s'\}$, $\{\rho'\}$, and $\{z'\}$ will be explained in Section 4.3.

Figure 3 shows a block diagram describing an operator model and the intention estimator. As shown at the upper left area in the figure, prediction $\overline{\text{bel}}(z)$ is computed through $\text{SOM}_f$ using input $s$, the prediction is updated through $\text{SOM}_g$ by referring $\rho$, and bel($z$) was obtained. Finally estimated intention $\hat{z}$ is derived from bel($z$). Details of the computation concerning (5) and (6) will be described at Algorithm 2 in Section 3.

## 3. Implementation by Particle Filter Algorithm

Bayesian computation described by (3) and (4) is implemented using the particle filtering technique. Since particle filtering expresses any shape of probabilistic distribution using multiple particles, it is widely used as a general probabilistic computation tools which can deal with non Gaussian distribution, for instance in robotics field [27]. Particle filtering is also for solution of issues discussed in Section 1.1.4. First of all, conceptual diagram of the SOM-Bayes filtering using particle filtering technique is illustrated in Figure 4. The illustration explains that this algorithm begins at the left block of the figure ((I) Prediction phase) by substituting input vectors, and that the process is succeeded

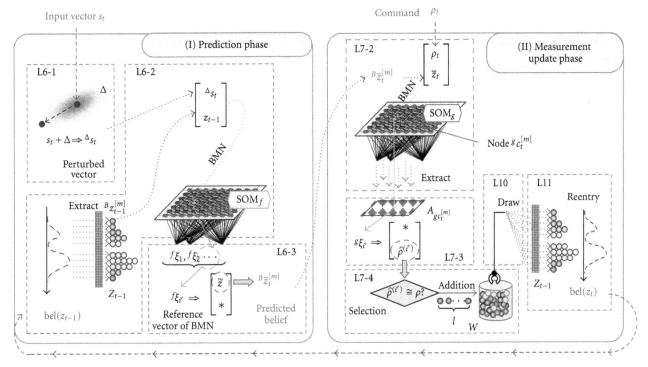

FIGURE 4: Algorithm of the SOM-Bayes estimator by particle filtering.

as "L6-1 → L6-2 → ⋯" and predicted belief is computed. In the right block of "(II) Measurement update phase", $\text{bel}(z_t)$ is computed from the predicted belief, and $\text{bel}(z_t)$ is returned to the phase I at the next sampling time The details of the processing is explained below by referring the illustration shown in Figure 4. Labels like L6-1 in the figure indicate the corresponding line in latter Algorithm 2; for instance, L6-1 means a substep 1 of the sixth line of the pseudocode.

Assuming the number of particles is $M$, the $m$ $(= 1, \ldots, M)$th particle of the belief $\text{bel}(z_t)$ at time $t$ is described as $^{B}z_t^{[m]}$. As a preparation to generate their particles, standard derivations $\sigma_i$ $(i = 1, \ldots, n_s)$ of the sequence data $\{s\} \in R^{n_s \times T}$ in each element are computed, where $n_s$ is the size of vector $s$. SOMs (which are the reference vectors $^{f}\xi$, $^{g}\xi$) defined by (5) and (6) are prepared at the SOM training step before execution of Algorithm 2.

Computation steps of the SOM particle filtering algorithm are shown by the following pseudocode. The algorithm consists of two phases: phase I for predictive computation and phase II for measurement updating. Below, notation $Z_t$ is used to express a set of particles as $Z_t := \{^{B}z_t^{[1]}, ^{B}z_t^{[2]}, \ldots, ^{B}z_t^{[M]}\}$.

Algorithm 2 (SOM particle filter).

(1)  initialize $Z_1$, prepare $\{s\}$ and $\{\rho\}$

(2)  for $t = 2$ to $T$ do

(3)  $Z_t = \varnothing$

phase I

(4)  for $m = 1$ to $M$ do

(5)  extract $^{B}z_{t-1}^{[m]}$ from $Z_{t-1}$

(6)  generate $^{B}\bar{z}_t^{[m]} \sim p(z_t \mid s_t, ^{B}z_{t-1}^{[m]})$ by $\text{SOM}_f$

(7)  $w_t^{[m]} := p(\rho_t \mid ^{B}\bar{z}_t^{[m]})$ using $\text{SOM}_g$

(8)  endfor $m$

phase II

(9)  for $i = 1$ to $M$ do

(10)  draw $m'$ with probability $\propto w_t^{[m]}$

(11)  add $^{B}\bar{z}_t^{[m']}$ to $Z_t$

(12)  endfor $i$

(13) endfor $t$.

First of the phase I is preparation of a temporal input vector which is perturbed from actual input data $s_t$ by random value. Second, a best-matching-node (BMN) that is closest to a combination of the temporal input $^{\Delta}s_t$ and old particle $^{B}z_{t-1}^{[m]}$ is searched from $\text{SOM}_f$. And the predicted particle $^{B}\bar{z}_t^{[m]}$ at time $t$ is extracted from component of the reference vector of the found BMN (this computation corresponds to line 6). This perturbation technique is popular as ordinary particle filtering approach. Measurement probability $w_t^{[m]}$ corresponding to these predicted particles is computed using $\text{SOM}_g$ for next resampling process on after-mentioned phase II (line 7). At the phase II, a particle number $m'$ is chosen in proportion to the measurement probability $w_t^{[m]}$ of each particle (line 10), and the predicted $^{B}\bar{z}_t^{[m']}$ which is indicated by the chosen number $m'$ is picked up into a new set $Z_t$ as next time particles (line 11). Then, new $M$ particles are resampled according to the measurement probability $w_t^{[m]}$. Repeating phase I and phase II till the final time $T$, $\{\mathrm{bel}(z_t)\}$, that is, a time series $\{Z_t\}$ of the belief of the intention $z$, are obtained. Sixth line of the pseudocode in Algorithm 1 corresponds to prediction defined by (3). Seventh line is a probability computation of second term in RHS of (4), that is, $p(\rho_t \mid z_t)$. Tenth and eleventh lines correspond to a probabilistic selection of same second term in RHS of (4), and the repeated computation formed by ninth and twelfth lines plays a role of Bayes normalization described at the first term in (4). The details of main parts in Algorithm 2 are explained below.

Note that pseudocode written in Algorithm 2 does not always correspond to the following computation step by step since the aim of description of Algorithm 2 is to explain semantic principle of the Bayes filtering.

*Line 6: Prediction.*

*L6-1: Preparation of Perturbation Input.* A random sample point, $^\Delta s_t$, that obeys a standard deviation $\sigma_i$ around $s_t$ is computed for all $M$ particles. Specifically, using a random value $\Delta$, the sample point is computed as

$$^\Delta s_t^{[m]} = s_t + \Delta, \quad m = 1, \ldots, M$$
$$\Delta := \mathrm{rand}([-1, 1], \sigma), \tag{7}$$

where $\mathrm{rand}([-1, 1], \sigma)$ is a function that yields pseudorandom value in the range of $[-1, 1]$ under standard deviation $\sigma$ and it is computed by a method presented in [28].

*L6-2: Search of Most Likelihood Node.* Using an old particle $^B z_{t-1}^{[m]}$, a perturbed input vector $^\Delta s_t^{[m]}$, and reference vectors $^f\xi$ of the $\mathrm{SOM}_f$, the BMN of a particle $m$ (i.e., $^f c_t^{[m]} \in \{1, \ldots, L_f\}$) is searched as

$$^f c_t^{[m]} := \arg\min_i \left\{ \left\| \begin{bmatrix} ^\Delta s_t^{[m]} \\ ^B z_{t-1}^{[m]} \end{bmatrix} - {^f\xi_i} \right\| \right\}. \tag{8}$$

*L6-3: Extraction of Prediction State.* A candidate of an intention involved in the particle that corresponds to prediction $\overline{\mathrm{bel}}(z_t)$ is extracted from a reference vector of the BMN predicted at the previous L6-2 step:

$$^B\overline{z}_t^{[m]} \Longleftarrow {^f\xi_i}(n_s + 1 : n_s + n_z), \quad i = {^f c_t^{[m]}}, \tag{9}$$

where an operation described by parentheses in the above RHS indicates an extraction of elements of the vector components.

*Line 7: Computation of Measurement Probability.* A BMN that is closest to combination of the measured command $\rho$ and the predicted belief $^B\overline{z}_t^{[m]}$ is searched newly on the $\mathrm{SOM}_g$. Then, reference vectors belonging to certain area around the new BMN are investigated. The number of nodes whose reference vectors correspond to the measured command $\rho_t$ appears to be proportional to the postmeasurement probability; hence, the measurement probability is computed

from the number of such nodes. For the resampling process at after-mentioned phase II, an information of such nodes is registered into a roulette array $W$. Numbering of particles is recorded in the array, and the number of the numbering is determined in proportion to the amount of the corresponding nodes. The following are the details.

*L7-1: Initialization.* Reset the roulette array as $W = \varnothing$.

*L7-2: Search of Most Likely Node.* Using the reference vectors $^g\xi$ of $\mathrm{SOM}_g$, a node $^g c_t^{[m]}$ that is most close to the measured $\rho_t$ and predicted status $^B\overline{z}_t^{[m]}$ is found by

$$^g c_t^{[m]} := \arg\min_i \left\{ \left\| \begin{bmatrix} \rho_t \\ ^B\overline{z}_t^{[m]} \end{bmatrix} - {^g\xi_i} \right\| \right\}. \tag{10}$$

*L7-3: Investigation of Area Around the Most Likely Node.* Computing a coordinate value $(u_c, v_c)$ of the node $^g c_t^{[m]}$ on the $\mathrm{SOM}_g$ plane map, reference vectors $^g\xi_{i'}$ of nodes that locate inside a square-like area $A_{^g c_t^{[m]}}$ are investigated, where the length of side and the center of $A_{^g c_t^{[m]}}$ are $(2L_r + 1)$ and $(u_c, v_c)$, respectively. Extracting from the vector $\xi_{i'}$ an element that corresponds to operation command, its element is described as $\hat{\rho}^{(i')}$, that is,

$$\hat{\rho}^{(i')} \Longleftarrow {^g\xi_{i'}}\left(1 : n_\rho\right), \quad \forall i' \in A_{^g c_t^{[m]}}. \tag{11}$$

Here, $L_r$ is a parameter and $n_\rho$ is a size of vector $\rho$.

*L7-4: Registration to the Roulette Array.* The number of $\hat{\rho}^{(i')}$ ($\in \mathcal{R}, \sum i' \leq (2L_r + 1)^2$) which can be rounded to an integer of $\rho_t$ ($\in I$) is counted, and the number is described as $l$. Next, "the particle number, $m$" is registered into the array $W$ $l$ times additionally,

$$W \Longleftarrow W + \{m\}^l. \tag{12}$$

*Line 10: Draw.* Since the numbering of particle that holds higher measurement probability has been registered in $W$ more times, such particles are resampled again with high ratio in a random drawing. Hence, generating a random integer $r$ within a range of $\{1, \ldots, n_W\}$, a number $m'$ that was registered on the $r$th element of the array $W$ is drawn, where $n_W$ is a length of $W$,

$$m' = W(r), \quad r = \mathrm{rand}(\{1, \ldots, n_W\}). \tag{13}$$

*Line 11: Reentry.* $m'$th particle is re-registered as one of new particles for next step as

$$^B z_t^{[m]} \Longleftarrow {^B\overline{z}_t^{[m']}}. \tag{14}$$

Algorithm 2 yields $M$ particles, that is, $\{^B z_t^{[1]}, \ldots, {^B z_t^{[M]}}\}$, every iteration time. Since the belief is expressed by a distribution of those $M$ particles, an estimated intention, say $\hat{z}$, is represented by averaging these $M$ particles as

$$\hat{z}_t = \frac{1}{M} \sum_{m=1}^{M} {^B z_t^{[m]}}. \tag{15}$$

(a)

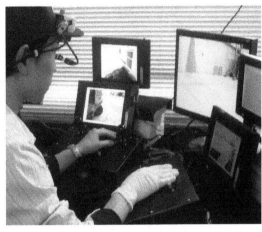
(b)

FIGURE 5: (a) Radio-controlled construction equipment on the work area and (b) the operation console.

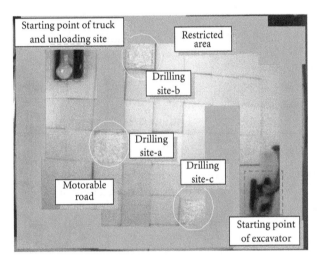

FIGURE 6: Overview of the work area.

## 4. Application to the Remote Operation Task

*4.1. Experimental Setup.* An experimental system with radio-controlled model construction equipments [29] was utilized to verify an effectiveness of the proposed intention-estimation algorithm. The purpose of the operation is a basic soil excavation work, as shown in Figure 5(a). Wireless cameras on an excavator and a truck captured video images, and displayed them on monitors for the operator, as shown in Figure 5(b). Both excavator and truck had crawler transporter systems. A bucket arm that consisted of a three-link mechanism is mounted on the superstructure of an excavator, and the mechanism are manipulated using a console system which is similar to the JIS- (Japanese Industrial Standards-) type cross-lever system. Figure 6 shows a top view of the work area. The field size is 3.3 m × 2.4 m and

consists of a motorable road, restricted areas, three drilling sites, and one unloading site. Different sample pieces are put at three drilling sites. The excavator and truck were put at their starting points at the beginning of trial.

One operator manipulated both the excavator and the truck on his/her judgement and was required to perform and optimise task scheduling. The requirements are as follows.

(i) Digging different sample pieces from three drilling sites.

(ii) Digging operation at each site is permitted only once.

(iii) Only one type of sample was permitted to be loaded into the truck at a time.

(iv) Shorten the total trial time.

(v) Collect as many samples as possible.

Standard task procedure is as follows: move to the drilling site, collect sample pieces with the excavator, load the pieces on the truck bed, and carry them to the unload site by the truck. The task procedure, however, can be chosen freely since the operator has many choices in sequence to visit three sites and in layout of positioning for digging and loading. Hence, the operator pays efforts to master the machine operation and to optimise whole task scheduling by trial and error considering the above-mentioned requirements.

To measure the positions of the excavator and truck for the intention estimator, the two equipments were observed by a camera attached to the ceiling through an infrared filter. The excavator and truck carried three and two infrared LED markers, respectively, and their positions and directions were computed using the detected positions of the LEDs. An angle of the excavator's boom and a rotation of the superstructure were measured by potentiometers. The measured signals were transmitted by wireless and recorded. Data acquisition was performed by the LabVIEW measurement system that consisted of the image acquisition, timing I/O (for digital

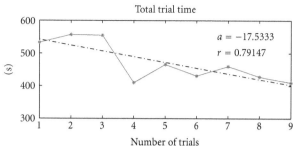

FIGURE 7: Improvement of the total trial time.

TABLE 1: Classified operational intention modes, variables, and labels.

| Variable | Label | Meanings |
|---|---|---|
| $^{(1)}z \ldots {}^{(3)}z$ | T/A-* | Truck's approach to the drilling site* |
| $^{(4)}z \ldots {}^{(6)}z$ | E/A-* | Excavator's approach to the drilling site* |
| $^{(7)}z \ldots {}^{(9)}z$ | T/P-* | Truck's positioning around the drilling site* |
| $^{(10)}z \ldots {}^{(12)}z$ | E/P-* | Excavator's positioning around the drilling site* |
| $^{(13)}z$ | E/D | Excavator's digging |
| $^{(14)}z$ | E/L | Excavator's loading of the payload |
| $^{(15)}z$ | T/TU | Transport of the payload by track and unloading |

(*a, b, c: identifier of the drilling site).

input data), and multifunction (for analog signal) modules. After capturing the video image from the ceiling camera, the images of LED markers were extracted through the video processing, and their coordinate values were obtained by centroid computation. Operations of switches on the console were also recorded via the multifunction and the I/O modules in the Labview system. The sampling frequencies of the video images and analog signals were 30 fps and 1 kHz, respectively.

*4.2. Experimental Result.* Written consent and ethical approval of one participant aged 21 yrs were obtained before experiment. As a training, three trials a day were conducted to the participant for three days; hence, total nine trials were repeated to improve the participant's operational performance. Figure 7 shows the improvement of total trial time. The gradient coefficient and correlation factor of the regression line for the total time are −17.5 and 0.79, respectively. Since the correlation factor is sufficiently large and the tendency of monotonic decrease was confirmed, it can be thought that the participant improved the skill best at the last ninth trial. Therefore, operation data and recorded movie at the ninth trial were used for the later analysis and construction of the SOM Bayes estimator.

*4.3. Preparation for the SOM-Bayes Intention Estimator.* The first preparation is to convert experimental logging data into time series sequences of $s'$ and $\rho'$. Crawler velocities for the excavator and the truck were controlled by two sliders with hands. The velocity commands were converted into the crawler operation mode $\kappa_c$ by checking the velocities of both sides of crawlers [29].

$$
\kappa_c = \begin{cases} 0: & \text{stop} \\ 1: & \text{forward} \\ 2: & \text{left-forward-turn} \\ 3: & \text{left pinwheel} \\ 4: & \text{right-backward-turn} \\ 5: & \text{backward} \\ 6: & \text{left-backward-turn} \\ 7: & \text{right pinwheel} \\ 8: & \text{right-forward-turn.} \end{cases} \tag{16}
$$

The commands for the bucket and the superstructure consist of three modes: the superstructure rotation $^e\kappa_r$, the arm $^e\kappa_a$, and the bucket $^e\kappa_b$. The operation modes were determined as follows:

$$
^e\kappa_r := \{0: \text{stop}, 1: \text{left rotation}, 2: \text{right rotation}\},
$$
$$
^e\kappa_a := \{0: \text{stop}, 1: \text{arm bend}, 2: \text{arm stretch}\}, \tag{17}
$$
$$
^e\kappa_b := \{0: \text{stop}, 1: \text{boom up}, 2: \text{boom down}\}.
$$

Difference of these operation groups appeared empirically to be utilized for inference of the operational intentions; hence, an operation command $\rho$ is defined by a vector as follows:

$$
\rho := \begin{bmatrix} ^t\kappa_c & ^e\kappa_c & ^e\kappa_h \end{bmatrix}^T \in I^3. \tag{18}
$$

Vectors of the machine and environmental status (i.e., $q_M$ and $q_E$) were chosen by considering position, posture, and geographical relation of the drilling sites and the equipments. The task status $q_T$ was defined as $q_T := \{0:$ no payload, 1: payload on bucket, 2: payload on truck bed$\}$ using the payload status. Refer to [30] for details about selection of these status. Time series sequence $\{s\}$ were obtained by combining $q_M$, $q_E$, and $q_T$, and the size of vector $s$ became as $n_s = 28$.

The second preparation is to obtain the normative intention sequence $z'$ discriminated by human analysts. Types of the remote operation for construction equipments and the definitions of elements $(^{(1)}z, \ldots, {}^{(15)}z)$ in intention vectors $z$ are summarized in Table 1. The operation modes are classified into three groups: approaching $(^{(1)}z, \ldots, {}^{(6)}z)$, positioning $(^{(7)}z, \ldots, {}^{(12)}z)$, and special operations (digging, loading, and transporting; $^{(13)}z, \ldots, {}^{(15)}z$). Sequence of reference intentions $\{z'\}$ was made through video analysis by a participant analyst who did not know the remote-operation experiment at all in order to get rid of any preconceived ideas.

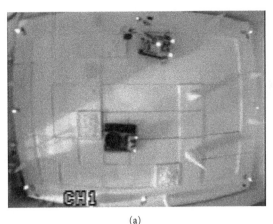

(a)                                         (b)

FIGURE 8: Sample footage for discrimination analysis: (a) view of the work area, (b) view of console desk.

Procedure to obtain the human analyst's intention $z'$ is as follows.

(1) The purpose of task, motion of equipments, geographical relationship of the work area, and the console layout are explained to the participant (below, analyst).

(2) The analyst understands the intention modes summarized in Table 1.

(3) The analyst discerns the operator's intention mode by watching the video. At that time, the analyst checks scene per frame using video editing software.

(4) Type of mode and the frame index of the found intention are recorded.

(5) After the analyst has finished decoding, the found frame indices are converted into time scale. Then, the sequence $\{z'\}$ is made by putting "1" to the corresponding element $z'_i$ at the found timing.

Footage of the work area and operator from ceiling cameras were recorded into one screen image using a multi-viewer device (Figure 8 shows a part of the images), and the analyst discriminated the operator's intention by checking the motion of equipments and body action of the operator. Discrimination data by multiple analysts that will be mentioned later in Section 6.4 was obtained similarly.

The third preparation is a training of SOM to obtain the reference vectors. The training was performed using SOM_PAK [31]. Input vectors for $SOM_f$ and $SOM_g$ are $\{[z'^T, s'^T]^T\}$ and $\{[z'^T, \rho'^T]^T\}$, respectively. Each component of the input vectors for the training was normalized into the $[-1, 1]$ range by using the maximum and minimum values of the time sequence of the input vectors. Since it is preferable for the horizontal and vertical sizes of the rectangular map of SOM to be chosen in proportion to the ratio of two square roots of the first and second maximum eigenvalues of the covariance matrix of input vector sequence [32], the sizes of the SOM lattice $(u_{\dim}, v_{\dim})$ were decided as $(50, 25)$ and $(80, 20)$ for $SOM_f$ and $SOM_g$, respectively. Hence, the number of nodes $L_f$ and $L_g$ are 1250 and 1600, respectively. A bubble-type neighborhood kernel function was chosen for updating the reference vectors at the training. On the learning process, a fine-tuned computation was performed after the rough-tuned one was computed. The learning rate and learning length were specified as 0.05, 2000 and 0.02, 1.5 million, respectively, so as to meet such requirement that the learning length is more than 500-times the number of nodes [21].

The last fourth preparation is for the particle filtering algorithm. Initial state of particles for the Bayes filtering were specified as ${}^B z_t^{[m]}|_{t=1} := [0\ 0\ 0\ 1\ 0\ \cdots\ 0\ ]^T$ for all $m\ (= 1, \ldots, M)$ since it was obvious that an initial operation in the experiment was E/A-a (i.e., ${}^{(4)}z = 1$). The number of particles was decided as $M = 1000$. $L_r$ for the area $A_{s c_t^{[m]}}$ was specified as 11.

## 5. Results of Estimation

*5.1. Preliminary Verification.* For later discussion, the intention discerned by a human analyst is described by $\tilde{z}$, and the estimated intention computed by the SOM-Bayes estimator is described as $\hat{z}$. The result of estimation is shown in Figure 9. Lines show the transitions of intention modes from T/A-a (${}^{(1)}z$) to T/TU (${}^{(15)}z$). The same intention modes of $\tilde{z}$ and $\hat{z}$ are plotted by the blue and red lines at the same vertical position, respectively. Figure 9 indicates that $\hat{z}$ overlaps with $\tilde{z}$ well concerning T/A-b (${}^{(2)}z$) - E/A-c (${}^{(6)}z$) as labeled with *Good*. There are, however, several insufficient results: *Weak*-estimation (E/D, E/L), *Delayed*-detection (T/P-c, E/P-c), *Much long* duration (T/TU, T/P-b), and estimation; *Failure* (T/A-a, T/P-a, E/P-a, a part of E/D and E/L; Similar labels are written in the figure). For quantitative assessment of $\tilde{z}$ and $\hat{z}$, the following concordance ratios were computed,

$$ {}^{(k)}R_{\text{tim}} := \frac{\sum^{\text{all} t'}\ {}^{(k)}\tilde{z}}{\sum^{\text{all} t}\ {}^{(k)}\tilde{z}} \quad t' = \left\{ t \mid {}^{(k)}\hat{z}_t > 0.3 \right\}, \quad (19) $$

$$ {}^{(k)}R_{\text{str}} := \frac{\sum^{\text{all} t'}\ {}^{(k)}\hat{z}}{\sum^{\text{all} t'}\ {}^{(k)}\tilde{z}} \quad t' = \left\{ t \mid {}^{(k)}\tilde{z}_t = 1 \right\}, \quad (20) $$

where $k = 1, \ldots, 15$, and the constant 0.3 used in above equation is a threshold parameter (this value was decided

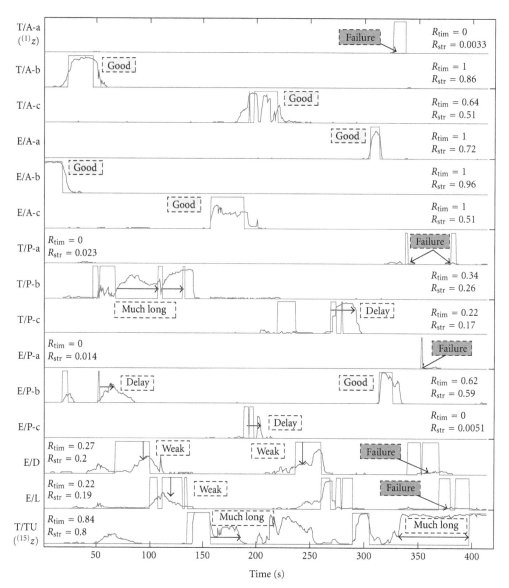

FIGURE 9: Transitions of intentions: red lines were identified by the SOM-Bayes estimator using vector $\rho$. Blue lines were discerned by human analyst.

subjectively. However, there is no problem since these ratios are used for relative comparison among $^{(1)}z \cdots ^{(15)}z$). $R_{tim}$ is a ratio of time that the analyst's $\tilde{z}$ matches to the time period of $\hat{z}$ which is identified by the estimator. $R_{str}$ shows how strongly the estimator can identify the intention level while analyst found same type of intention. In the latter discussion, these ratios are called "time-concordance ratio" and "strength-concordance ratio," respectively. Values of these ratios are also written in each graph as shown in Figure 9. Average of $R_{tim}$ and $R_{str}$ for five *Good* modes (T/A-b - E/A-c) are 0.93 (range: 0.64–1) and 0.71 (range: 0.51–0.96), respectively; hence, high concordance was confirmed since these values are close to 1. On the other hand, other insufficient eight modes except T/TU (*Much long* duration) and E/P-b (a part of this mode is *Good*) show the small values as 0.13 (range: 0–0.34) and 0.11 (range: 0–0.26) concerning $R_{tim}$ and $R_{str}$, respectively.

To clear the reason of the insufficient estimation, the trained SOM was investigated. Investigating elements corresponding to intention vectors in the reference vector ($\xi$) attached to each node on the SOM plane map, the type of intention mode included in each reference vector is discriminated. Then clusters in the SOM map are visualized as a colored map according to the discriminated modes on nodes. Figures 10 and 11 show the colored maps of $SOM_f$ and $SOM_g$, respectively. Labels described in Table 1 are written in each cluster according to the discriminated modes. For multiple clusters indicating the same mode, subindex was written as "E/L-1, E/L-2", and the dotted lines were drawn between the same clusters on the map. Figure 10 for the $SOM_f$ map shows that obvious clusters are found; however, there is cluttered area in the left side on the $SOM_g$ map as shown in Figure 11. This fact indicates that the classification in $SOM_g$ was not performed

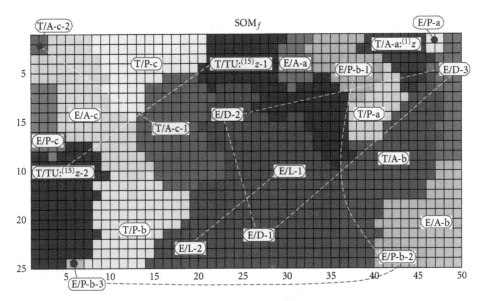

FIGURE 10: Clusters on the SOM$_f$ map.

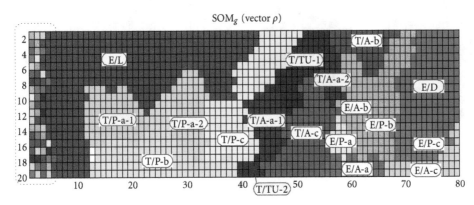

FIGURE 11: Clusters on the SOM$_g$ map (case of vector $\rho$).

sufficiently. Due to the inadequate clustering, change of probabilistic distribution using SOM$_g$ was discontinuous, and it is inferred that computation of approximation for the belief did not work well.

*5.2. Improvement of the SOM Mapping.* One technique to obtain adequate SOM clustering is to prepare adequate input data having sufficient but nonredundant information. From this viewpoint, investigating the input data that was used for the SOM training, it was found that the operator did not manipulate different types of commands defined by (18) simultaneously; hence, $\rho$ was redefined as a scalar value by

$$\rho := 1 + {}^t\kappa_c + ({}^e\kappa_c \wedge 1)({}^e\kappa_c + 8) + ({}^e\kappa_h \wedge 1)({}^e\kappa_h + 16). \quad (21)$$

Figure 12 shows new SOM$_g$ map obtained using the scalar $\rho$ newly defined by (21). Unlike a former SOM generated by vector $\rho$, clear clusters without cluttered area are confirmed all over the map. To confirm this improvement, changes of time-concordance ratio $R_{\text{tim}}$ of the result obtained using new SOM$_g$ and of the former result by old SOM$_g$ are compared, and the result was visualized as shown in Figure 13. The $x$,

$y$, and $z$ axes are the number of trials (the total is nine), intention modes (the total is fifteen), and the values of concordance ratios, respectively. Comparing the right 3D bar chart with the left one, most bars drawn in the right chart are higher than the others drawn in the left. Similar tendency of improvement was confirmed in case of the strength-concordance ratios $R_{\text{str}}$ as shown in Figure 14. These graphs prove that accuracy of the intention-estimation was improved by reduction of dimension of the input data for the SOM learning.

## 6. Analyses of the Estimator's Behavior

The SOM-Bayes intention estimator using the improved SOM mapping are investigated by comparing with the human-discerned intentions $\tilde{z}$. Figure 15 shows the transitions of $\tilde{z}$ and improved $\hat{z}$ in the same manner as Figure 9. When compared with the former result in case of the vector-$\rho$ (that are shown by red lines in Figure 9), the estimator using the scalar-$\rho$ (red lines in Figure 15) improved in eight

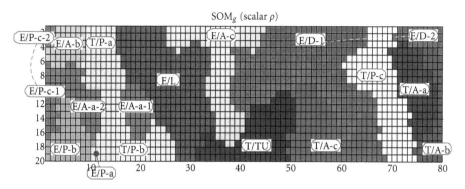

FIGURE 12: Clusters on the new $SOM_g$ map (case of scalar $\rho$).

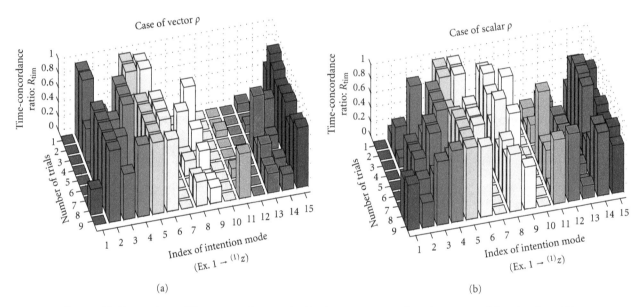

(a)

(b)

FIGURE 13: Comparison of time-concordance ratios $R_{tim}$ in two cases: results using vector $\rho$ (a) and scalar $\rho$ (b).

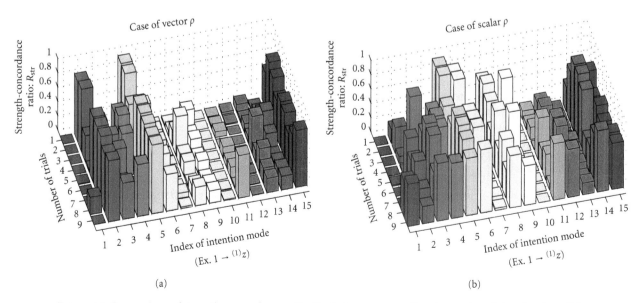

(a)

(b)

FIGURE 14: Comparison of strength-concordance ratios $R_{str}$ in two cases: results using vector $\rho$ (a) and scalar $\rho$ (b).

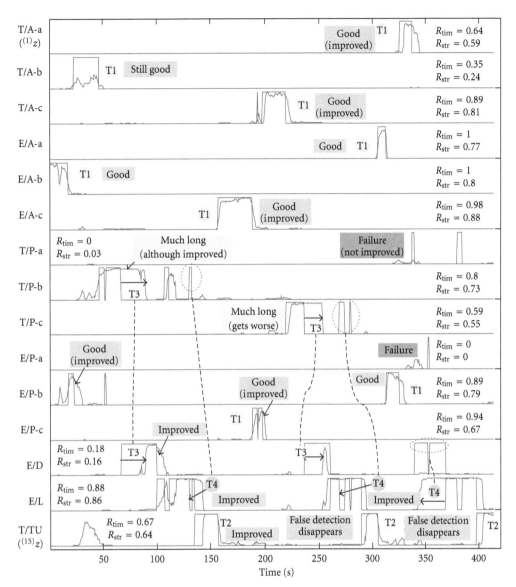

FIGURE 15: Transitions of intentions: red lines were identified by the SOM-Bayes estimator using scalar $\rho$. Blue lines were discerned by human analyst.

modes such as T/A-a, T/A-c, E/A-c, E/P-b, E/P-c, E/D, E/L, and T/TU. Detailed analysis is mentioned below.

*6.1. Tendency Analysis.* When the overlap, timing, strength, and types of the intention are qualitatively investigated by comparing $\hat{z}$ against $\tilde{z}$ in Figure 15, the following tendencies were found.

(T1) Concerning *approaching*, the operational intentions in both cases of the truck (T/A-*) and of the excavator (E/A-*) were identified adequately. And *excavator positioning* (E/P-a,b) was also identified well.

(T2) Concerning *truck's transport and unloading* (T/TU), the identification of this mode was improved; however, the starting timings of the identified intentions were delayed.

(T3) The periods identified as truck's positioning (T/P-b, T/P-c) were larger than that of the corresponding human intentions.

(T4) Although detection of the *excavator loading* (E/L) was improved, the periods were longer than human intentions.

The numberings of tendencies, (T1)–(T4), are written in Figure 15 to show relation between above-mentioned tendencies and waveforms. The reason of success mentioned in the tendency (T1) appears to come from large change in variables of the machine's status. The reason of the delay indicated by the tendency (T2) is that the analyst regarded the end of the E/L action (that occurred before the T/T action) as a start of T/T.

The tendency (T3) for *T/P* was found by investigating which status changed at the same timing of E/D in $\hat{z}$ (their

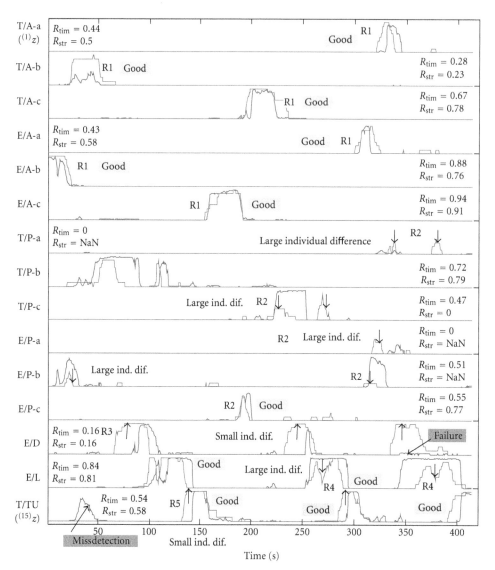

FIGURE 16: Transitions of intentions: red lines were identified by the SOM-Bayes estimator using scalar $\rho$. Blue lines were averages of results discerned by eight human analysts.

timings were about 85 [s], 255 [s]). And checking the raw logging data we found that the timing detected by the estimator was synchronized with change of the bucket's vertical manipulation while analyst's $\tilde{z}$ began to change at the time the bucket were moved in a front-back direction before the vertical manipulation. Since the analyst can check the operator's body movement (as shown in Figure 8), it appeared that the intentions were discerned by unconsciously predicting the operator's hand reaching action based on the monitoring image. In other words, the analyst appears to guess other person's action earlier than actual action by considering the sequence of events and its causality. This might be the difference between the human discrimination and the estimator's identification.

Concerning the tendency (T4), the estimator's identification might be interpreted as follows: the truck's positioning at the phase of "loading of payload" was included in the E/L operation. Such interpretation of "T/P is a part of E/L"

can be acceptable for us. If we look at this from another point of view, this fact highlights human ambiguousness of criterion to classify intentions. This question will be analyzed in Section 6.3.

6.2. Qualitative Analysis of the SOM Clusters. To confirm findings about the SOM training, relation between characteristics of clusters and the accuracies of identified intention was investigated by checking Figure 10. In terms of the relative position among clusters, the cluster corresponding to continuous operations such as "E/D → E/L" were formed close to each other. This does not contradict an intuitive feeling that intentions in continuous sequential operations resemble each other. To several modes of the excavator such as E/D, E/L, and E/P, multiple clusters were formed. This phenomenon appears to come from the difference of the working place since the number of multiple clusters are the same as the number of sites. (The transitions of their

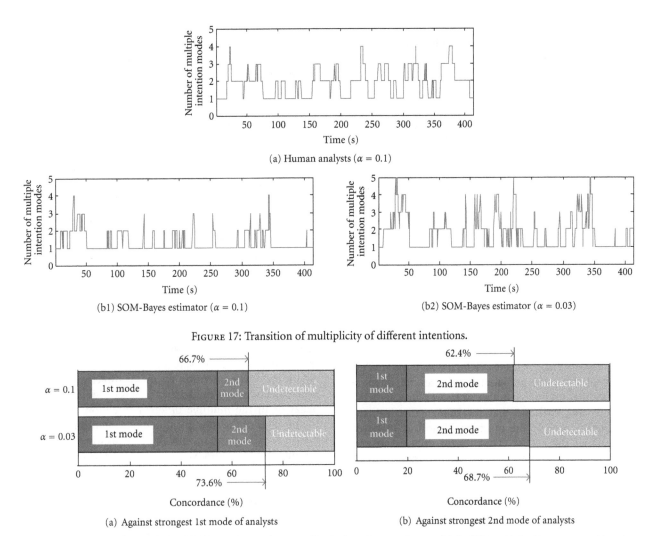

FIGURE 17: Transition of multiplicity of different intentions.

(a) Against strongest 1st mode of analysts

(b) Against strongest 2nd mode of analysts

FIGURE 18: Concordance of identified intentions to human-discriminated ones when multiple different intentions are considered.

intention modes shown in Figure 15 change widely three times).

About size of clusters, the ED and EL for excavator occupy wide area in the SOM plane map. One could interpret this to mean that many nodes are assigned to conditions of most complex and significant operation in this digging task. In contrast, intention modes having small region in the map were not identified sufficiently. For instance, the cluster size of the identification failed E/P-a—the area is located around the coordinates of $(46, 2)$ in Figure 10— is as small as four nodes which is equal to 0.3 percent of total area of the whole map. Since small cluster means small likelihood of the probability computation in the presented algorithm, it appears that this intention mode could not be identified sufficiently because of the small probability due to the small size of the corresponding cluster. Conversely, it would appear that the size of the total map should be adjusted so as to assign a sufficient number of modes to small occupied clusters.

*6.3. Analysis of Individual Differences in Human Discrimination.* In the previous section, performance of the intention

estimator was investigated by comparing with another intention, $\tilde{z}$, that was discriminated by human analyst. The $\tilde{z}$ is, however, not absolutely unique since it was discriminated subjectively. As mentioned in Section 6.1, there is a possibility that discrimination of the operator's intention differs in individuals. Therefore, other new eight participants were commissioned to discriminate intentions of the remote operation task, and individual differences among them were investigated. Intention modes discriminated by the eight participants are averaged, and the bog-standard intension is denoted by $\bar{z}$ below. Figure 16 shows renewal graph of which old blue lines of $\tilde{z}$ in Figure 15 were replaced by $\bar{z}$. The more close $\bar{z}$ is to 1, the less differences discriminations by the analysts. Investigation of the tendencies in the characteristics of humans' $\bar{z}$ yields the following results.

(R1) Concerning *approach* (T/A-a$\cdots$E/A-c): maximum of components in $\bar{z}$ are close to 1. Since their waveforms of $\bar{z}$ look like triangle, individual differences in the timing of the starting and ending are confirmed. On the other hand, the estimation $\hat{z}$ works well since $\hat{z}$ matches $\bar{z}$ relatively well.

(R2) Concerning *positioning* (T/P-a··· E/P-c): large individual differences in human discrimination are confirmed since each component in $\bar{z}$ is small. Half of the corresponding components in $\hat{z}$ were detected in the same timing of the $\bar{z}$ case.

(R3) Concerning *digging* (E/D): differences between individuals are small since the corresponding components in $\bar{z}$ are close to 1 and form a rectangular shape. Identified intention $\hat{z}$ is, however, insufficient because waveforms of $\hat{z}$ does not match $\bar{z}$.

(R4) Concerning *loading* (E/L): large individual differences are confirmed since waveforms of the components in $\bar{z}$ split into triangle shapes. The corresponding components in $\hat{z}$ cover the others in $\bar{z}$ over long periods.

(R5) Concerning *transport* (T/TU): the individual difference of the analysts is small since this component in $\bar{z}$ is large and the shape of waveform is rectangular. Although the timing of $\hat{z}$ is delayed against that of $\bar{z}$, the estimator works well.

From the result (R2) against (R1), it was found that even human analysts could not discriminate several intentions and the estimator could not also work well in such a case. The result (R3) indicates that the human discrimination differs from a way of the machine identification beyond the individual differences. This reason appears to come from human discrimination approach which utilizes also observation of operators' body motion. Or maybe human analysts utilizes task context for the discrimination by predicting the operator's intention. Therefore, a task scenario involving various judgement conditions might be required to enhance the presented intention estimator. It appears that same reason causes issues mentioned at the (R4) and (R5).

In order to evaluate the above-mentioned results quantitatively, the following indices are computed and were summarized in Table 2: the maximum of the intention level average found by eight participants, $\max(\bar{z})$, and the modified concordance ratios that are computed by (22) and (23) using new intentions identified by the improved estimator

$$^{(k)}R_{\text{tim}2} := \frac{\sum^{\text{all}\, t'\, (k)}\bar{z}}{\sum^{\text{all}\, t\, (k)}\bar{z}} \quad t' = \left\{ t \mid {}^{(k)}\hat{z}_t > 0.3 \right\}, \quad (22)$$

$$^{(k)}R_{\text{str}2} := \frac{\sum^{\text{all}\, t'\, (k)}\hat{z}}{\sum^{\text{all}\, t'\, (k)}\bar{z}} \quad t' = \left\{ t \mid {}^{(k)}\bar{z}_t > 0.7 \right\}. \quad (23)$$

$R_{\text{tim}2}$ defined by (22) is essentially the same as the former ratio defined by (19). $R_{\text{str}2}$ defined by (23) shows the degree of the strength-concordance of the estimator's result $\hat{z}$ against the intention periods which were agreed by 70 percent members of eight analysts. $\max(\bar{z})$ for ${}^{(4)}z, {}^{(7)}z-{}^{(12)}z$ described in Table 2 are as small as 0.5–0.88 while others are 1; hence, the individual differences to classify their modes were large. $R_{\text{str}2}$ of some modes could not be computed, that was $R_{\text{str}2}$ = NaN (not a number), because the $\bar{z}$-value of the mode could not

be determined due to large individual differences in the eight analysts. In other words, concerning such intention modes, it was impossible to compare the human discrimination with the machine estimation. Checking the other intention modes that have small individual differences (i.e., for ${}^{(i)}z$ satisfying $\max\left({}^{(i)}\bar{z}\right) = 1$), ${}^{(2)}z$ (T/A-b) indicates small concordance ratio as $R_{\text{tim}2} = 0.28$ and $R_{\text{str}2} = 0.23$. The upper second waveform in Figure 16 for this mode shows that the timing of $\hat{z}$'s activation coincided with $\bar{z}$ but the value of $\hat{z}$ was small. Other concordance ratio for ${}^{(13)}z$ of E/D indicates also small value as $R_{\text{tim}2} = 0.16$ and $R_{\text{str}2} = 0.16$, and this reason comes from the timing-shift given by the analysts' predictive discrimination. Except these particular cases, however, the other concordance ratios for ${}^{(1)}z, {}^{(3)}z, {}^{(5)}z, {}^{(6)}z, {}^{(14)}z$, and ${}^{(15)}z$, which were discriminable for the most human analysts, are large as $R_{\text{tim}2} = 0.44$–0.94 and $R_{\text{str}2} = 0.50$–0.91; hence, it can be said that estimation accuracies of each intention mode are comparatively good.

*6.4. Multiplicity of Different Intentions.* In former analysis relating to Figures 15 and 16, time transitions of most dominant intention-mode were mainly treated. The proposed algorithm of the intention estimator directly computes the ratio of all intention modes; hence, it is possible to investigate behavior of the multiple different intention. Transition of the number of the multiple difference intention is shown in Figure 17. The graph was obtained by drawing the change of the number of modes whose intention level becomes larger than a threshold $\alpha$. The graph (a) is for comparison, and shows the pseudomultiplicity of modes ($\bar{z}$) discriminated by eight analysts in case of $\alpha = 0.1$. Although this graph does not show strictly multiplicity of one person's intentions and expresses an individual difference of eight person, it can be thought that the maximum of the multiplicity of standard person are four. Graphs (b1) and (b2) are obtained similarly using identified modes $\hat{z}$ by the estimator, and are cases for $\alpha = 0.1$ and $\alpha = 0.03$, respectively. From these graphs, the estimator identified four or five candidates as intention modes when the threshold is set as $\alpha = 0.1$ or $\alpha = 0.03$, respectively. That is, both machine estimator and human analyst show similar possibility of multiple intentions.

Based on the results, concordance ratio between the machine estimator and human analysts were investigated by considering the multiplicity. Concordance percentage of first and second intention modes by the estimator against the human-discriminated intentions are shown in the graphs (a) and (b) in Figure 18, respectively. The upper and lower bar charts on each graph show the percentages of the concordance for $\alpha = 0.1$ and $\alpha = 0.03$, respectively. In any case shown in the figure, ratio of more than third mode is zero, that is, the estimator identified the same type of modes to human-discriminated ones by only the first or second dominant intention modes. It can be said that the proposed algorithm works comparatively well as the human does if the first and second candidates of the identified modes are considered because the sum of concordance ratio of the estimator's identification against human-discrimination indicates 62–73 percent.

TABLE 2: Maximum of intention level $(\max(\bar{z}))$ and concordance ratios $(R_{\text{tim2}}, R_{\text{str2}})$.

| Label | $^{(1)}z$ | $^{(2)}z$ | $^{(3)}z$ | $^{(4)}z$ | $^{(5)}z$ | $^{(6)}z$ | $^{(7)}z$ | $^{(8)}z$ | $^{(9)}z$ | $^{(10)}z$ | $^{(11)}z$ | $^{(12)}z$ | $^{(13)}z$ | $^{(14)}z$ | $^{(15)}z$ |
|---|---|---|---|---|---|---|---|---|---|---|---|---|---|---|---|
| | T/A-a | T/A-b | T/A-c | E/A-a | E/A-b | E/A-c | T/P-a | T/P-b | T/P-c | E/P-a | E/P-b | E/P-c | E/D | E/L | T/TU |
| $\max(\bar{z})$ | 1 | 1 | 1 | 0.88 | 1 | 1 | 0.5 | 0.88 | 0.88 | 0.5 | 0.5 | 0.75 | 1 | 1 | 1 |
| $R_{\text{tim2}}$ | 0.44 | 0.28 | 0.67 | 0.43 | 0.88 | 0.94 | 0 | 0.72 | 0.47 | 0 | 0.51 | 0.55 | 0.16 | 0.84 | 0.54 |
| $R_{\text{str2}}$ | 0.50 | 0.23 | 0.78 | 0.58 | 0.76 | 0.91 | NaN | 0.79 | 0 | NaN | NaN | 0.77 | 0.16 | 0.81 | 0.58 |

TABLE 3: List of constants.

| Symbols | Designation | Values in verification |
|---|---|---|
| $\alpha$ | Threshold to discern intention modes | 0.1 or 0.03 |
| $^f\xi_i$ | Reference vectors of the $\text{SOM}_f (i = 1,\ldots,L_f)$ | (Determined by the learning) |
| $^g\xi_i$ | Reference vectors of the $\text{SOM}_g (i = 1,\ldots,L_g)$ | (Determined by the learning) |
| $\sigma_i$ | Standard deviation of $i$th column sequence in $\{s\}$ | (Depend on data) |
| $n_s$ | Size of vector $s$ | 28 |
| $n_z$ | Number of intention types | 15 |
| $(u_{\dim}, v_{\dim})$ | Sizes of the SOM lattice | |
| $L_f$ | Number of all nodes of $\text{SOM}_f$ | 1250 (50 × 25) |
| $L_g$ | Number of all nodes of $\text{SOM}_g$ | 1600 (80 × 20) |
| $2L_r + 1$ | Number of nodes of one side of a square-like area $A_{gc_t^{[m]}}$ | 11 |
| $M$ | Number of all particles | 1000 |
| $T$ | Total time of task (integer) | (Depend on trial) |

# 7. Conclusion and Discussion

A method to estimate the operational intention in a human manipulation of a machine was introduced in the present paper. This method utilizes a clustering technique by SOM to compute a state transition probability of intentions. This method enables to omit troublesome process to specify types of information which should be used to build the estimator. By embedding the state transition property expressed by the SOM mapping into a particle filtering algorithm, the operator's intention is identified through a Bayes estimation. Applying the proposed method to the remote operation task, the estimator's behavior was analyzed, the pros and cons of the method were investigated, and ways for the improvement were discussed. Moreover, through investigation of normative data of intentions discriminated by human analysts, issues in the verification were also treated.

Concerning the design of the SOM-Bayes intention estimator algorithm, the following findings were obtained.

(F1) Reducing the redundancy in the input vector for the SOM training is effective to improve the estimator.

(F2) It was confirmed that an estimation accuracy of the intention mode is good (not good) when the corresponding cluster on the SOM plane map is large (small). Therefore, the size of the total map should be adjusted so as to assign a sufficient number of modes to small occupied clusters.

By the countermeasure mentioned in (F1), the accuracy was increased in eight intentional modes among a total of 15 modes, and the effectiveness of this findings was confirmed. Although experimental proof concerning (F2) was not performed in this paper, the proposed algorithm is a so-called frequentism method consisting of Bayes estimation; hence, the present authors predict that the approach of (F2) will be effective. As another approach for the improvement, modification of the input data can be considered in order to enhance a fixation of the related network in the SOM structure for the significant but rare events at the stage of the SOM training. A finding about individual difference in human discrimination is as follows:

(F3) there are differences in discrimination of intentions among individuals. Difficult circumstances to human analysts were also difficult to the present estimation algorithm.

For normal intention modes whose periods can be found by 70 percent members of all analysts, the concordance ratios between the identified intention by the proposed algorithm and the human-discriminated ones were as high as 0.44–0.94 if exceptional modes were removed in case of this remote operation task. Additionally, when the multiplicity of the different intentions is considered, the estimator could identify the same type of intention modes to human-discriminated ones by using the first and second dominant intention modes as high as 62–73%. The estimation accuracy is sufficiently high considering that this method does not utilize predictive estimation from the user's motion. Therefore, it can be concluded that the proposed algorithm works comparatively well.

Considering the findings based on the experiment, one method to improve the estimation is a combination with a prediction function using measurement of the operator's hand/body motion. Use of some task scenario appears to be another effective method. The former approach is, however, needs additionally the measurement device and the image-processing; hence, a tradeoff between complexity of the system and enhancement of the intention-estimation is required. The present authors would like to study such

TABLE 4: List of variables.

| Symbols | Designation | Types/range/definition |
| --- | --- | --- |
| $\eta$ | Bayes normalization parameter | Real number |
| $\kappa_c$ | Operation mode for crawlers | $\{0, 1, \ldots, 8\}$ |
| $^e\kappa_a$ | Operation mode for the arm of the excavator | $\{0, 1, \ldots, 2\}$ |
| $^e\kappa_b$ | Operation mode for the bucket of the excavator | $\{0, 1, \ldots, 2\}$ |
| $^e\kappa_r$ | Operation mode for the superstructure rotation of the excavator | $\{0, 1, \ldots, 2\}$ |
| $\rho$ | Commands to the machine from an operator | Scalar integer |
| $\hat{\rho}^{(i')}$ | Value corresponding to an operational command which is registered in $i'$th reference vector of $^g\xi$ | Real number |
| $\Delta$ | Random value having standard deviation $\sigma_i$ | Real number |
| $\mathrm{bel}(z)$ | Belief of the intention $z$ (probabilistic distribution of $z$) | Vector with real numbers |
| $\overline{\mathrm{bel}}(z_t)$ | Prediction at time $t$ (a predicted belief) | Vector with real numbers |
| $^f c_t^{[m]}$ | Node index of $m$th particle's BMN on SOM$_f$ | $\{1, \ldots, L_f\}$ |
| $^g c_t^{[m]}$ | Node index of SOM$_g$ whose reference vector is most close to a combination of the measured command and the predicted status | $\{1, \ldots, L_g\}$ |
| $i$ | Index for a particle | Integer |
| $l$ | Number of nodes whose $\hat{\rho}$ is close to $\rho_t$ | Integer |
| $m'$ | Number registered in the $r$th element of the array $W$ (a particle number) | Integer |
| $n_W$ | Length of the roulette array $W$ (this is variable on each time counter) | Integer |
| $q_M$ | Machine status ($M$-status) | Vector with real numbers |
| $q_E$ | Environmental status ($E$-status) | Vector with real numbers |
| $q_T$ | Task status ($T$-status) | Vector with real numbers |
| $r$ | Random number | $\{1, \ldots, n_W\}$ |
| $s$ | Information recognized by a human operator | Vector with real numbers |
| $^\Delta s_t$ | Random sample point around $s_t$ | Vector with real numbers |
| $t$ | Time counter | Integer |
| $(u_c, v_c)$ | Coordinate value corresponding to the node $^g c_t^{[m]}$ on the SOM$_g$ plane map | Integers |
| $w_t^{[m]}$ | Measurement probability corresponding to $m$th predicted particle at time $t$ | Real number |
| $z$ | Operational intention of a human | Vector in $[0, 1]^{n_z}$ |
| $\bar{z}$ | Average of operator's intention level discerned by eight human analysts | Vector in $[0, 1]^{n_z}$ |
| $\hat{z}$ | Intentions identified by the SOM-Bayes estimator (Average of the identified intentions given by $M$ particles) | by (15) |
| $\tilde{z}$ | Intention discerned by a human analyst | Vector in $[0, 1]^{n_z}$ |
| $^{(i)}z$ | $i$th element of vectors $z$ ($i$th intention mode) | Real number |
| $^B z_t^{[m]}$ | $m$th particle of the set $Z_t$ ($m = 1, \ldots, M$) | Vector with real numbers |
| $^B \bar{z}_t^{[m]}$ | Prediction at time $t$ by $m$th particle | by (10) |
| $^{(k)}R_{\mathrm{tim}}$ | Concordance ratio with respect to time on $k$th intention mode (time-concordance ratio) | $[0, 1]$ |
| $^{(k)}R_{\mathrm{str}}$ | Concordance ratio with respect to strength on $k$th intention mode (strength-concordance ratio) | $[0, 1]$ |
| $^{(k)}R_{\mathrm{tim2}}$ | Time-concordance ratio against average intention of eight analysts' discrimination on $k$th intention mode | $[0, 1]$ |
| $^{(k)}R_{\mathrm{str2}}$ | Strength-concordance ratio against average intention of eight analysts' discrimination on $k$th intention mode. | $[0, 1]$ |
| $A_{^g c_t^{[m]}}$ | Square-like area on the SOM$_g$ plane map around the node of $^g c_t^{[m]}$ | — |

TABLE 4: Continued.

| Symbols | Designation | Types/range/definition |
|---------|-------------|------------------------|
| $W$ | Roulette array | Size is variable |
| $Z_t$ | Set of particles at time $t$ | Set of vector |

TABLE 5: List of functions.

| Symbol | Meanings | Definitions |
|--------|----------|-------------|
| $H()$ | Conceptual human controller model. The input and output are assumed as $s$ and $\rho$, respectively | in Figure 2 |
| $f()$ | State transition function describing change of the intention | (1) |
| $g()$ | Output function of operational command | (2) |
| $p(z_t \mid s_t, z_{t-1})$ | Conditional probabilistic distribution of a transition of intention from $z_{t-1}$ to $z_t$ | |
| $p(\rho_t \mid z_t)$ | Conditional probabilistic distribution of judgment that outputs $\rho_t$ if the intentions $z_t$ happens to be true | |
| $SOM_f$ | SOM map for the function $f$ (SOM mapping function which is trained using an input vector consisting of $z$ and $s$) | (5) |
| $SOM_g$ | SOM map for the function $g$ (SOM mapping function which is trained using an input vector consisting of $z$ and $\rho$) | (6) |

a combination approach by developing the proposed SOM-Bayes intention estimator in future work since we have been studying the hand-reaching action [29].

## Appendix

Constants, variables, and functions used in this paper are summarized in the following lists. $\{x\}$ describes a time series sequence data of the vector signal $x$. Or it is used to express a set consisting of elements denoted in the braces. See Tables 3, 4, and 5.

## Acknowledgments

The present study were supported by a Grant-in-Aid for Scientific Research (A) of the Japanese Ministry of Education, Culture, Sports, Science, and Technology. The experiment was supported by many participants who embraced the authors' requests kindly. The present author appreciates their cooperation.

## References

[1] E. Horvitz, J. Breese, D. Heckerman, D. Hovel, and K. Rommelse, "The Lumière project: bayesian user modeling for inferring the goals and needs of software users," in *Proceedings of the 14th Conference on Uncertainty in Artificial Intelligence*, pp. 256–265, Madison, Wis, USA, 1998.

[2] I. Zukerman, D. W. Albrecht, and A. E. Nicholson, "Predicting users' requests on the WWW," in *Proceedings of the 7th International Conference on User Modeling*, pp. 275–284, Banff, Canada, 1999.

[3] J. Gutman, "A means-end chain model based on consumer categorization process," *Journal of Marketing*, vol. 46, pp. 60–72, 1982.

[4] K. Kasaoka and Y. Sankai, "Predictive control estimating operator's intention for stepping-up motion by exo-sckeleton type power assist system HAL," in *Proceedings of the IEEE/RSJ International Conference on Intelligent Robots and Systems, (IROS '01)*, pp. 1578–1583, Maui, Hawaii, USA, November 2001.

[5] K. Sakita, K. Ogawara, S. Murakami, K. Kawamura, and K. Ikeuchi, "Flexible cooperation between human and robot by interpreting human intention from gaze information," in *Proceedings of the IEEE/RSJ International Conference on Intelligent Robots and Systems, (IROS '04)*, pp. 846–851, Sendai, Japan, October 2004.

[6] C. Breazeal, *Designing Sociable Robots*, MIT Press, 2002.

[7] T. Shibata, "An overview of human interactive robots for psychological enrichment," *Proceedings of the IEEE*, vol. 92, no. 11, pp. 1749–1758, 2004.

[8] K.-S. Park and D.-S. Kwon, "A cognitive modeling for mental model of an intelligent robot," *International Journal of Assistive Robotics and Mechatronics*, vol. 7, no. 3, pp. 16–24, 2006.

[9] K. Furuta, "Control of pendulum: from super mechano-system to human adaptive mechatronics," in *Proceedings of the 42nd IEEE Conference on Decision and Control*, pp. 1498–1507, Maui, Hawaii, USA, December 2003.

[10] F. Harashima and S. Suzuki, "Intelligent mechatronics and robotics," in *Proceedings of the IEEE International Conference on Emerging Technologies and Factory Automation, (ETFA '08)*, Hamburg, Germany, 2008.

[11] W. D. Gray, B. E. John, and M. E. Atwood, "Project Ernestine: validating a GOMS analysis for predicting and explaining real-world task performance," *Human-Computer Interaction*, vol. 8, no. 3, pp. 237–309, 1993.

[12] B. Price, "Frank and Lillian Gilbreth and the motion study controversy, 1907–1930," in *A Mental Revolution: Scientific Management since Taylor*, D. Nelson, Ed., The Ohio State University Press, 1990.

[13] T. Suzuki, S. Sekizawa, S. Inagaki et al., "Modeling and recognition of human driving behavior based on stochastic switched ARX model," in *Proceedings of the 44th IEEE Conference on Decision and Control, and the European Control Conference, (CDC-ECC '05)*, pp. 5095–5100, Seville, Spain, December 2005.

[14] H. Kawashima and T. Matsuyama, "Multiphase learning for an interval-based hybrid dynamical system," *IEICE Transactions*

*on Fundamentals of Electronics, Communications and Computer Sciences*, vol. E88-A, no. 11, pp. 3022–3034, 2005.

[15] T. Inamura, I. Toshima, H. Tanie, and Y. Nakamura, "Embodied symbol emergence based on mimesis theory," *International Journal of Robotics Research*, vol. 23, no. 4-5, pp. 363–377, 2004.

[16] Y. Inagaki, H. Sugie, H. Aisu, and T. Unemi, "A study of a method for intention inference from human's behavior," in *Proceedings of the IEEE International Workshop on Robot and Human Communication (Ro-Man '93)*, pp. 142–145, 1993.

[17] T. Choudhury, G. Borriello, and D. Haehnel, "The mobile sensing platform: an embedded system for activity recognition," in *Proceedings of the IEEE Pervasive Magazine—Special Issue on Activity-Based Computing*, pp. 32–41, 2008.

[18] J. A. Ward, P. Lukowicz, and H. W. Gellersen, "Performance metrics for activity recognition," *ACM Transactions on Intelligent Systems and Technology*, vol. 2, no. 1, article 6, 23 pages, 2011.

[19] C. M. Bishop, *Pattern Recognition and Machine Learning*, Springer, 2006.

[20] S. Chizuwa and M. Kameyama, "Bayesian-network-based intention estimation for a user support system of an information appliance," in *Proceedings of the 5th International Conference on Information Technology and Applications (ICITA '08)*, pp. 71–76, Queensland, Australia, 2008.

[21] T. Kohonen, "The self-organizing map," *Proceedings of the IEEE*, vol. 78, no. 9, pp. 1464–1480, 1990.

[22] S. Suzuki and F. Harashima, "Segmentation and analysis of console operation using self-organizing map with cluster growing method," in *Proceedings of the IEEE/RSJ International Conference on Intelligent Robots and Systems, (IROS '09)*, pp. 4875–4880, St. Louis, Mo, USA, October 2009.

[23] S. Suzuki and F. Harashima, "Bayesian intention estimator using self-organizing map and its experimental verification," in *Proceedings of the 19th IEEE International Symposium on Robot and Human Interactive Communication (Ro-Man '10)*, pp. 290–295, Viareggio, Italy, 2010.

[24] S. Suzuki and F. Harashima, "Estimation of operational intentions utilizing self-organizing map with bayes filtering," in *Proceedings of the IEEE/RSJ International Conference on Intelligent Robots and Systems (IROS '10)*, pp. 2249–2255, Taipei, Taiwan, 2010.

[25] S. Suzuki and F. Harashima, "Skill analysis focused on the hand discrete movement for machine manipulation," in *Proceedings of the 13th IEEE Int. Conf. of Emerging Technologies and Factory Automation (ETFA '08)*, pp. 156–163, Hamburg, Germany, 2008.

[26] B. J. Baars, *A Cognitive Theory of Consciousness*, Cambridge University Press, New York, NY, USA, 1988.

[27] S. Thrun, W. Burgard, and D. Fox, *Probabilistic Robotics*, MIT Press, Cambridge, Mass, USA, 2005.

[28] G. Winkler, *Image Analysis, Random Fields, and Dynamic Monte Carlo Methods*, Springer, Berlin, Germany, 1995.

[29] S. Suzuki and F. Harashima, "Skill evaluation from observation of discrete hand movements during console operation," *Journal of Robotics*, vol. 2010, Article ID 967379, 13 pages, 2010.

[30] S. Suzuki, "Characteristics analysis of a task switching during console operation based on the self-organizing map," *International Journal of Advanced Mechatronic Systems*, vol. 2, no. 5-6, pp. 306–317, 2010.

[31] Helsinki University of Technology, Neural Networks Research Centre Web-site, http://www.cis.hut.fi/research/som-research/nnrc-programs.shtml.

[32] T. Kohonen, *Self-Organizing Maps*, Springer, Berlin, Germany, 1995.

# 5

# Tactile Modulation of Emotional Speech Samples

**Katri Salminen,[1] Veikko Surakka,[1] Jani Lylykangas,[1] Jussi Rantala,[1] Teemu Ahmaniemi,[2] Roope Raisamo,[1] Dari Trendafilov,[2] and Johan Kildal[2]**

[1] *Tampere Unit for Computer Human Interaction, School of Information Sciences,*
*University of Tampere, Kanslerinrinne 1, 33014 Helsinki, Finland*
[2] *Nokia Research Center, Itämerenkatu 11-13, 00180 Helsinki, Finland*

Correspondence should be addressed to Katri Salminen, katri.salminen@uta.fi

Academic Editor: Antonio Krüger

Traditionally only speech communicates emotions via mobile phone. However, in daily communication the sense of touch mediates emotional information during conversation. The present aim was to study if tactile stimulation affects emotional ratings of speech when measured with scales of pleasantness, arousal, approachability, and dominance. In the Experiment 1 participants rated speech-only and speech-tactile stimuli. The tactile signal mimicked the amplitude changes of the speech. In the Experiment 2 the aim was to study whether the way the tactile signal was produced affected the ratings. The tactile signal either mimicked the amplitude changes of the speech sample in question, or the amplitude changes of another speech sample. Also, concurrent static vibration was included. The results showed that the speech-tactile stimuli were rated as more arousing and dominant than the speech-only stimuli. The speech-only stimuli were rated as more approachable than the speech-tactile stimuli, but only in the Experiment 1. Variations in tactile stimulation also affected the ratings. When the tactile stimulation was static vibration the speech-tactile stimuli were rated as more arousing than when the concurrent tactile stimulation was mimicking speech samples. The results suggest that tactile stimulation offers new ways of modulating and enriching the interpretation of speech.

## 1. Introduction

In daily communication we acquire emotion-related information via several senses. Recently the investigation of the utilization of the sense of touch in technology contexts (e.g. cars, tablets, mobile phones, etc.) has been very active. Current mobile phones use routinely direct tactile manipulation for operation. Increasingly phones also utilize tactile feedback. Tactile feedback in mobile phones can be used and is aimed at mediating basically same type of information that is mediated in human-human communication. As mobile phones are still used also for conversations a natural question to come in mind is how speech and tactile information might function together.

Human touch system is designed so that via it we can get cognitive, social, and emotional information. From early studies by Harlow [1–3] we learned that tactile information is closely related to the human emotional system. People use the sense of touch when they aim, for instance, to communicate affection or to get someone's attention in a

socially acceptable manner [4]. It has also been shown that people are capable of sending and receiving emotion-related information (e.g., expressions of anger or love) through touch (e.g., [5]). In addition, studies have shown that the mediation of emotional information via tactile technology works well. Recently Smith and MacLean [6] and Bailenson et al. [7] studied how well participants could identify haptically presented emotions. In their studies one participant (i.e. the sender) used a force-feedback device to create haptic messages which would communicate certain emotions from a list (e.g., anger, sadness, and happiness). The other participant's (i.e., the receiver's) task was to try to identify intended emotion-related contents from tactile stimulations the sender had generated. The results suggested that haptic stimulation generated and interpreted this way can communicate emotion-related information at a better chance level.

Also speech can mediate emotion-related information both in human-human and human-technology contexts. For example, there is evidence that synthetically (i.e., speech synthesizers) generated speech samples with positive and negative content are in general rated as pleasant and unpleasant, respectively [8, 9]. Thus, both speech and tactile stimulations have the potential to evoke emotional experiences in humans. Although currently available vibrotactile technologies in mobile phones enable utilizing tactile modality in conjunction with speech, the potential to enrich speech communication with simultaneous tactile stimulation is largely unmapped area in human-technology interaction (HTI).

In one study by Chang et al. [10] the participants used a device prototype capable of converting hand pressure into vibration to complement speech while, for example, talking with another participant. Their results showed that the participants used tactile stimulation for emphasizing spoken messages and to indicate turn-taking behavior. In general the authors argued that their results showed that the participants can use tactile channel to transfer meaningful information simultaneously with speech. However, the potential to modulate the emotion-related responses to speech with the sense of touch in mobile contexts has not been studied.

Several studies have shown that processing of auditory and tactile information is known to have crossmodal effects on each other. Information from tactile and auditory modalities is integrated in an early phase of information processing chain and evokes responses partly in the same areas of the brain [11–14]. Further, studies have shown that auditory stimuli can affect the perception of tactile stimuli and vice versa. For example, in a study by Bresciani et al. [15] tactile taps and auditory beeps were presented to the participants who were instructed to report how many tactile taps they perceived. The results showed that the number of auditory beeps systematically modulated the perception of tactile taps regardless of the actual number of the taps. In another study by Ro et al. [16] the task of the participant was to verbally report whether or not they felt a tactile stimulus which was either accompanied by a sound or not. Their results showed that the auditory stimuli increased the detection rate especially when the tactile and auditory stimuli had the same frequency. Thus, by providing simultaneous auditory and tactile signals one can improve the cognitive performance of humans.

In addition, previous studies suggest that the form of the tactile and auditory signals has an effect to the processing of the multimodal stimulus. Especially synchronizing the signals coming from our environment affects the perception of the stimuli. A view referred as assumption of unity suggests that the brain treats information coming from different modalities as coming from the same source or object only if they share similar amodal properties. Most important of these properties is temporal coincidence [17]. Further, previous studies suggest that synchronizing tactile and auditory stimuli can affect human cognitive processing. For example, in a study by Gillmeister and Eimer [18] the task was to indicate whether a single trial contained an auditory signal near the perceivable threshold. A tactile stimulus was always delivered in the trial, and the auditory signal was presented randomly in half of the trials. The results showed that synchronous tactile stimuli improved the detection of near-threshold auditory stimuli. Similarly, in another study [19] synchronizing the auditory and tactile signal improved the detection rate of the stimuli. In another experiment by Gillmeister and Eimer [18] the participants were asked to judge the intensity (i.e., loudness) of auditory tones. The results clearly showed that intensity judgments were considerably higher in the presence of synchronous tactile stimulation than in asynchronous or no tactile stimulation trials.

Interestingly, there is also evidence suggesting that tactile information can improve the understanding of spoken syllables especially when synchronized with the speech [20]. The participants' task was to perform a forced-choice syllable decision task in which the syllables were either accompanied by additional noise or not. The syllables were presented in three modality conditions: auditory only, congruent mouthing, or incongruent mouthing manually felt from speaker's face. The results showed that congruent mouthing improved the amount of correct responses when compared with auditory only condition and incongruent mouthing but only when the syllables were accompanied by noise. In addition, there were more correct responses in auditory only condition than in incongruent mouthing condition. Based on these results the authors argue that manual tactile information relevant to speech gestures can improve auditory speech perception.

Taken together, it seems that there is only a little information on how speech and tactile stimulation are related to each other. Given that synchronized tactile and auditory or speech signals can affect human cognitive processes we selected a starting point where we first produced tactile signals that accurately mimicked the amplitude changes of the speech signal to study the effects of concurrent tactile stimulation on the emotion-related ratings of speech in a general level. Next, we proceeded in studying whether synchronizing the amplitude changes of speech and tactile signal is the optimal way to produce the concurrent tactile stimulation to evoke emotion-related experiences in the user. For this purpose the amplitude changes of the tactile signal were either mimicking the amplitude changes of the speech sample in question (i.e., congruent stimulation) or amplitude changes of another speech sample used in the study (i.e., incongruent stimulation).

To measure emotional responses the dimensional theory of emotions was used as the frame of reference for rating the effects of stimuli. According to Bradley and Lang [21–23] and Schlosberg [24] there are three basic bipolar dimensions that cover well the dimensional emotion space while rating different types of stimuli. The dimensions are valence, arousal, and dominance. Using these dimensions affective ratings can be collected with a special set of rating scales where the valence dimension varies from unpleasant to pleasant, the arousal dimension varies from relaxed to arousing, and the dominance dimension varies from feeling of being controlled by the stimulus to the feeling of being in control of the stimulus [21–23]. Although the dimensional theory of emotions suggests that the dimensions are related to a motivational tendency to approach or withdraw from emotion evoking stimulus, this tendency has not been measured frequently. Recently in some studies this fourth dimension has been taken into consideration by asking also ratings of the approach-withdrawal tendency with a bipolar rating scale varying from avoidable to approachable [25–27]. In earlier studies these four dimensions were used to evaluate how participant reacts to haptic only stimulation [28, 29]. The results have shown that varied haptic stimulus parameters (e.g., amplitude and continuity) evoke different ratings in previously mentioned four scales so that, for example, stimuli with high amplitudes are rated as more arousing and dominant than stimuli with low amplitudes.

To summarize, the present aim was to study if the emotion-related ratings of speech are affected by tactile stimulation. A handheld prototype device with four vibrating actuators produced the tactile stimulation. The participants' task was to rate the stimuli with the scales of pleasantness, arousal, approachability, and dominance. In Experiment 1 the participant's task was to rate speech only and speech tactile stimuli. The amplitude of the speech signal was mimicked as accurately as possible with tactile actuators. In Experiment 2 the speech samples were presented to the participants with both congruent and incongruent tactile stimulation. Congruent stimuli consisted of speech samples that were paired with tactile stimulation derived from that particular speech sample. Incongruent stimuli consisted of speech samples that were paired with tactile stimulations created on the basis of another speech samples.

*Experiment 1.* The aim of Experiment 1 was to study how simultaneously presented tactile stimulation affects to the subjective ratings of short speech samples. For this purpose, speech samples were presented to the participant with and without tactile stimulation. The participants rated all the stimuli, speech only and speech tactile, one at a time using the rating scales for pleasantness, arousal, dominance, and approachability.

## 2. Methods

*2.1. Participants.* Twelve voluntary male participants took part in the study (mean age 27, range 21–41 years). All the participants were students at the University of Tampere and recruited via e-mail. They did not receive any compensation for their participation. Nine of the participants were right handed, and three were left handed by their own report. Seven of the participants told that they hold a mobile phone in their right hand, and five told holding it in their left hand while typing a text message. All had normal or corrected to normal vision, and normal hearing and sense of touch by their own report. All the participants were fully informed for the purpose of the study prior to the experiment. They were also informed that they were able to abort the experiment at any point without a specific reason. A consent form was signed by all the participants.

*2.2. Apparatus.* A haptic device prototype was used in the experiment (Figure 1). The prototype was chosen for two reasons. First, its actuator solutions were more capable of producing similar variations in vibrotactile amplitude and

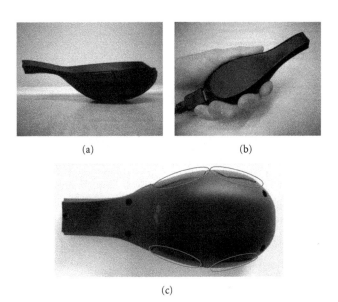

FIGURE 1: (a) Side view of the prototype device, (b) a person holding it, and (c) the bottom-up view with circles showing the placement of the actuators.

frequency than the rotating mass vibrators commonly used in standard mobile phones. Second, the shape of the prototype was designed so that the actuators would stimulate the whole palm area when the device was vibrating. The device was equipped with four Minebea Linear Vibration Motor actuators (LVM8, Matsushita Electric Industrial Co., Japan). Two actuators were located on the right side and two on the left side of the device. Actuation of these motors was based on a small electromagnetic weight which moves down when driving signal is applied and backs up using a spring when no signal is present. The resulting rapid movement in opposite directions creates the vibration. The LVM8 actuators were mounted inside separate buttons in the device in order to isolate the vibration from the body of the device. Thus, the actuation was localized to four specific areas on the device. Usable driving frequencies of 120–180 Hz and a resonant frequency of 155 Hz were measured from the LVM8 actuators after mounting. The LVM8 actuators can be driven using audiosignal which makes it easy to modify input using audiosynthesis software. A controller box was connecting the prototype device to a laptop computer with HDMI and USB connections. The controller box was designed to reduce the amount of cables between the prototype device and the computer. For more technical details, see [30].

The stimuli were controlled with an external Gigaport HD USB sound card. Pure Data Audio synthesizer software (PD, version 0.41.4) was used to create the tactile stimuli and to control the stimulus presentation. An Acer Netbook laptop computer recorded the ratings which were given with a standard computer mouse (Figure 2).

*2.3. Stimuli.* Two stimulus modalities were used in the experiment: speech only and speech tactile (see Table 1). The speech-only stimuli were selected from speech synthesizer named Loquendo text-to-speech. Speech acts refer to a

TABLE 1: The speech samples used in the experiment.

| Stimulus in English and Finnish | Emotional content | Duration (sec) | Graphical presentation of amplitude variations |
| --- | --- | --- | --- |
| "how beautiful" "oi miten kaunis" | Positive | 1.78 | |
| "nice to hear" "hauska kuulla" | Positive | 1.47 | |
| "how ugly" "miten ruma" | Negative | 1.48 | |
| "sad to hear" "ikävä kuulla" | Negative | 1.5 | |

FIGURE 2: Picture of the experimental setup.

collection of prerecorded emotional speech samples spoken by an actor. We chose four short speech samples. The samples were spoken by a native Finnish male voice. Two of the samples had a positive content, and two had a negative content. Also the tones of the speech samples were different so that the speech samples with positive content had a clear positive tone and the samples with negative content had a negative tone. The stimuli with positive content, and the stimuli with negative content were selected so that they represented bipolarity of the valence dimension. For this purpose we selected the positive and negative samples in a way that they could be seen as opposites of their semantic meaning (see Table 1).

Half of the stimuli were presented with a concurrent tactile vibration. The amplitude of the tactile stimulation followed the original amplitude of the speech. So, it was extracted from the speech sample and presented simultaneously with the speech. A 160 Hz sine wave with varying amplitude was used in each of the tactile stimulations. A fixed frequency value was used due to the LVM8 actuator's narrow range of perceivable frequencies. The frequency of 160 Hz was chosen based on piloting which showed that the

resonant frequency of 155 Hz resulted in a distracting audible noise. With 160 Hz there was noticeably less leakage of noise although the vibration felt equally strong. The amplitude level of the tactile feedback was set by using an envelope follower that took the speech signal as an input and returned its root mean square (RMS) value as an output.

The amplitude level for the tactile stimulation was set 22 times in a second based on 1000 sequential audio samples. We found the rate of 22 Hz to be sufficient for getting a perceivable tactile estimate of intensity changes in the speech stimuli. Using this feedback synthesis the amplitude of the tactile stimulation followed the original amplitude of the speech stimulus in real time. Finally, the tactile feedback signal was driven to the four LVM8 actuators. A total of 8 different stimuli (4 speech only and 4 speech tactile) was used in the study. The stimuli were presented in random order.

*2.4. Procedure.* When the participant arrived in the laboratory, the equipment and the environment were introduced to him. He was told that the purpose of the experiment was to study subjective experiences evoked by short speech samples with four rating scales. The participant was also told that some of the speech samples had only speech, but in some samples the prototype vibrated during the speech.

A soft foam cushion was under the arm of the hand holding the prototype to prevent muscle fatigue. Participants were instructed to hold the prototype on the same hand they reported holding a mobile phone while typing a text message (see Figure 1). A computer mouse was used to give ratings, and it was operated with the other hand. The participant was told that when the prototype device would be finalized, they would be able to hear the speech from the prototype. However, currently this was not yet the case, and the participants wore a Peltor HTB 79A hearing protector headset from which they could hear the speech component of the stimuli. It also blocked the noise from the prototype while producing the tactile stimulation. The participant was instructed to keep the gaze on the laptop display during the experiment. In the center of the display the participant could see instructions related to the stimulus presentation and for giving ratings.

The experiment was divided in four experimental blocks. In each block the participants' task was to rate the 8 stimuli using one of the emotion-related rating scales (i.e., pleasantness, arousal, approachability, or dominance). The ratings were given by selecting a number on the display with the mouse from nine checkboxes labeled from −4 to +4. On each of the scales 0 represented neutral experience (e.g., neither unpleasant nor pleasant). The order of the blocks was Latin square counterbalanced.

Before each experimental block there was a practice session to familiarize the participant with the stimuli and the rating scales to be used in the following experimental block. In a practice session, four different stimuli (two speech only and two speech tactile) were evaluated with one rating scale. The stimuli in the practice sessions were different than the stimuli in the experimental sessions. The practice session proceeded as follows. In the beginning of each trial the participant clicked an on-screen stimulus initiation button, and after a 2000 ms interval a stimulus was presented. During the stimulus presentation the participants were instructed to listen to the stimulus carefully and not to clench the prototype. The stimulus offset was followed by a 2000 ms interval after which a rating scale appeared on the screen and the participant was able to respond. After giving the rating, a new trial was initiated 2000 ms after the participant had clicked the stimulus initiation button again. This procedure was repeated until the participant had rated all the four practice stimuli with one rating scale. After the practice session the participant continued to rate the eight experimental stimuli with the same scale. Thus in each block there were 4 practice trials and 8 experimental trials. After the participant had rated all the stimuli with one scale, he proceeded to rate the stimuli with the next scale in the similar manner. This was repeated until all the stimuli were rated with all the four scales. Thus, the total number of the experimental trials was 32. Conducting the experiment took approximately 40 minutes.

*2.5. Data Analysis.* A Wilcoxon signed-ranks test was used for pairwise comparisons. First pairwise comparisons were conducted to study the effects of the emotional content of the speech (i.e., positive versus negative) to the ratings. Then pairwise comparisons were used to study the effects of the concurrent tactile stimulation (i.e., speech only versus speech tactile).

# 3. Results

*3.1. Pleasantness.* Means and standard error of the means (SEMs) for the ratings of the stimulus pleasantness are presented in Figure 3. For the effects of the emotional content of the speech the results showed that the speech only stimuli with positive content were rated as significantly more pleasant than the stimuli with negative content $T = 3.01$, $P < 0.01$, Cohen's $d = 2.70$. Also, the speech tactile stimuli

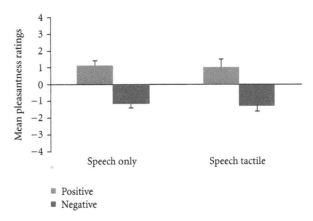

FIGURE 3: Means and SEMs for the ratings of the pleasantness of the stimuli by the emotional content of the speech sample and the stimulus presentation modality.

with positive content were rated as significantly more pleasant than the speech tactile stimuli with negative content $T = 2.99$, $P < 0.01$, Cohen's $d = 1.80$. For the effects of the concurrent tactile stimulation the results did not show any statistically significant differences.

*3.2. Arousal.* Means and SEMs for the ratings of the stimulus arousal are presented in Figure 4. For the effects of the emotional content of the speech the results showed that the speech only stimuli with negative content were rated as significantly more arousing than the speech only stimuli with positive content $T = 2.27$, $P < 0.05$, Cohen's $d = 1.01$. The speech tactile stimuli were not rated differently from each other in respect to the emotional content of the speech.

For the effects of the concurrent tactile stimulation the results showed that the speech tactile stimuli with positive content were rated as significantly more arousing than the speech only stimuli with positive content $T = 3.07$, $P < 0.01$, Cohen's $d = 1.88$. Also, the speech tactile stimuli with negative content were rated as significantly more arousing than the speech only stimuli with negative content $T = 2.82$, $P < 0.01$, Cohen's $d = 1.39$.

*3.3. Approachability.* Means and SEMs for the ratings of the stimulus approachability are presented in Figure 5. For the effects of the emotional content of the speech the results showed that the speech only stimuli with positive content were rated as significantly more approachable than the speech only stimuli with negative content $T = 3.07$, $P < 0.01$, Cohen's $d = 1.64$. Also, the speech tactile stimuli with positive content were rated as significantly more approachable than the speech tactile stimuli with negative content $T = 2.51$, $P < 0.05$, Cohen's $d = 1.16$.

For the effects of the concurrent tactile stimulation the results showed that the speech only stimuli with positive content were rated as significantly more approachable than the speech tactile stimuli with positive content $T = 2.26$, $P < 0.05$, Cohen's $d = 0.61$. The difference between the speech only stimuli with negative content and the speech tactile stimuli with negative content was not statistically significant.

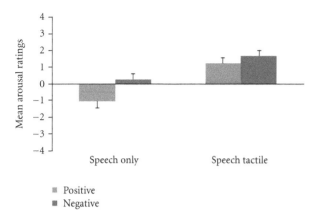

FIGURE 4: Means and SEMs for the ratings of the stimulus arousal.

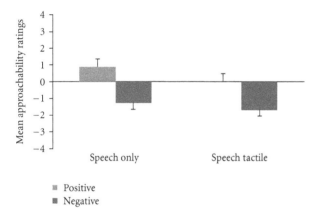

FIGURE 5: Means and SEMs for the ratings of the stimulus approachability.

### 3.4. Dominance.

*3.4. Dominance.* Means and SEMs for the ratings of the stimulus dominance are presented in Figure 6. For the effects of the emotional content of the speech the results showed no statistically significant differences in the ratings. For the effects of the concurrent tactile stimulation the results showed that the speech tactile stimuli with negative content were rated as significantly more dominant than the speech only stimuli with negative content $T = 2.21$, $P < 0.05$, Cohen's $d = 0.86$. The difference between the speech tactile stimuli with positive content and the speech only stimuli with positive content was not statistically significant.

## 4. Summary

For the effects of the emotional content of the speech the results showed that both speech only and speech tactile stimuli with positive content were rated as more pleasant and approachable than the stimuli with negative content. In addition, the speech only stimuli with negative content were rated as more arousing than the speech only stimuli with positive content. The emotional content of the speech had no statistically significant effects for the ratings of the dominance. For the effects of the concurrent tactile stimulation the results showed that the speech tactile stimuli were in general rated as significantly more arousing and more

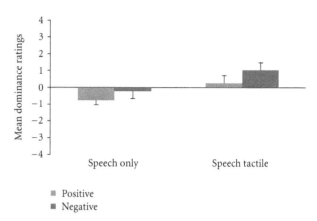

FIGURE 6: Means and SEMs for the ratings of the stimulus dominance.

TABLE 2: Emotional content of the speech sample, and the congruency of the concurrent tactile stimulation.

| Speech | Tactile congruent | Tactile incongruent | |
|---|---|---|---|
| "nice to hear" | "nice to hear" | "sad to hear" | "I see" |
| "I see" | "I see" | "nice to hear" | "sad to hear" |
| "sad to hear" | "sad to hear" | "nice to hear" | "I see" |

dominant than the speech only stimuli. The speech tactile stimuli were also rated as less approachable than the speech only stimuli. For the ratings of the pleasantness there were no significant differences between the speech tactile and speech only stimuli.

*Experiment 2.* The purpose of Experiment 2 was to study whether extracting the amplitude changes of the tactile signal from the concurrent speech sample is the optimal way to modulate the emotion-related responses related to speech. For this purpose, we varied the congruency of the tactile stimulation. By this we refer to whether the speech sample was presented simultaneously with the tactile stimulation extracted from that specific speech sample in question, or with a tactile stimulation extracted from one of the other speech samples (Table 2). In addition, we decided to use slightly longer speech samples and include neutral speech samples in Experiment 2.

## 5. Methods

*5.1. Participants.* Sixteen voluntary participants (eight female) took part in the study (mean age 23, range 19–30 years). All the participants were students at the University of Tampere. They were recruited from computer science courses and received a course credit from their participation. Fifteen of the participants were right handed, and one was left handed by their own report. Eight of the participants told that they hold a mobile phone in their right hand and seven told holding it in their left hand while typing a text message. All had normal or corrected to normal vision, and normal hearing and sense of touch by their own report. All the participants were fully informed for the purpose of

TABLE 3: The stimulus parameters varied in the experiment.

| Stimulus in English and Finnish | Emotional content | Duration (sec) | Graphical presentation of amplitude variations |
|---|---|---|---|
| "nice to hear" "hauska kuulla" | Positive | 1.5 | |
| "I see" "vai niin" | Neutral | 1.5 | |
| "sad to hear" "ikävä kuulla" | Negative | 1.5 | |

the study prior to the experiment. They were also informed that they were able to abort the experiment at any point without a specific reason. A consent form was signed by all the participants.

*5.2. Apparatus and Procedure.* The device prototype, the experimental setup, and the procedure were similar to Experiment 1.

*5.3. Stimuli.* Two stimulus modalities were used in the experiment: speech only and speech tactile (see Table 3). First parts (i.e., beginnings) of each sentence were varied in their emotion-related content while the final part was always the same. The beginning had either positive, negative, or neutral content. All the beginnings of the speech samples were 1500 ms long. The positive and negative beginnings were selected from the samples used in Experiment 1 that is, "nice to hear" and "sad to hear." There was no clear neutral counterpart for these speech samples, and therefore we created one with the Loquendo synthesizer. By this we also aimed to create neutral speech stimulation without emotional prosody evident in the prerecorded samples spoken by an actor. So, the neutral speech sample "I see" in Finnish was chosen because it had no emotion-related content. Even though the neutral beginning was created with the synthesizer, the identity of the speaker was clearly the same as in the prerecorded samples. Thus, the neutral speech sample did sound quite natural, not robotic.

As the motivation was to use longer sentences instead of short phrases, a controlled confirmation and ending was needed. The ending of all speech samples was always "everything seems to go as usual." The ending was 3000 ms long. This type of ending was chosen because it was presumed to be rather neutral in its emotional content, and it semantically continued smoothly the three possible beginnings of the sentences.

The tactile stimulation was presented only during the beginning part of the sentence (i.e., the first 1500 ms). The tactile stimulation for positive and negative speech samples (i.e., "nice to hear" and "sad to hear") was produced similarly as in Experiment 1. The tactile stimulation for the neutral speech sample was a vibration with a static frequency and

amplitude. The amplitude of the static tactile vibration created for the neutral speech sample was the mean of the amplitudes of the tactile stimuli extracted from both positive and negative speech samples. The frequency for all the tactile stimuli was 160 Hz.

Because in the current study we wanted to know whether the congruency of the tactile stimulation had an effect on the ratings, a tactile stimulation presented simultaneously with a speech sample was either the tactile stimulation extracted from the current speech sample, or tactile stimulation extracted from one of the two other speech samples. So, for example, the positive speech sample was repeated with tactile stimulation derived from positive speech sample (congruent), with tactile stimulation derived from negative speech sample (incongruent), and with static vibration (incongruent). Thus, a total of 12 stimuli (3 speech only, 3 speech tactile with congruent tactile stimulations, and 6 speech tactile with incongruent tactile stimulations) were used in the study.

*5.4. Data Analysis.* Three Friedman tests were conducted in order to test whether varying the congruency of the tactile stimulation affected the ratings of a speech sample. Then, four Friedman tests were conducted in order to test whether varying the emotional content of the speech sample affected the ratings differently between the four concurrent tactile stimulation categories used (i.e., speech only, tactile derived from positive speech sample, static vibration, and tactile derived from negative speech sample). If the Friedman test revealed statistically significant differences between the ratings of the stimuli, a Wilcoxon signed-ranks test was used for pairwise comparisons.

## 6. Results

*6.1. Pleasantness.* Means and standard error of the means (SEMs) for the ratings of the stimulus pleasantness are presented in Figure 7. Varying the congruency of the tactile stimulation affected the ratings when the emotional content of the speech sample was positive $\chi = 11.2$, $P < 0.05$. In this case the speech only stimuli were rated as more pleasant than the congruent speech tactile stimuli $T = 2.62$, $P < 0.01$, Cohen's $d = 0.78$. Other pairwise comparisons were

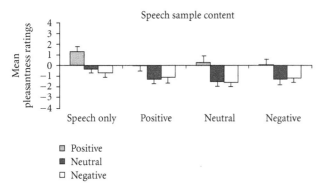

FIGURE 7: Means and SEMs for the ratings of the pleasantness by the speech sample content and the tactile stimulation.

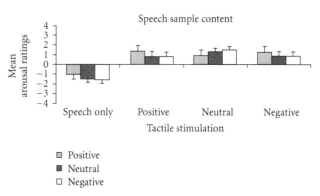

FIGURE 8: Means and SEMs for the ratings of the stimulus arousal.

not statistically significant. Varying the congruency of the tactile stimulation had no statistically significant effects on the ratings of neutral or negative speech samples.

Varying the emotional content of the speech affected the ratings of speech only stimuli $\chi = 15.0$, $P < 0.001$. It also affected the ratings of the speech tactile stimuli when the concurrent tactile stimulation was a static vibration $\chi = 6.45$, $P < 0.05$. However, when the concurrent tactile stimulation was derived from positive or negative speech samples varying the emotional content of the speech sample had no statistically significant effect on the ratings of the speech tactile stimuli. The results of the pairwise comparisons can be seen in Table 4.

*6.2. Arousal.* Means and SEMs for the ratings of the stimulus arousal are presented in Figure 8. Varying the congruency of the tactile stimulation affected the ratings when the emotional content of the speech sample was positive $\chi = 18.8$, $P < 0.001$, when the emotional content of the speech sample was neutral $\chi = 26.3$, $P < 0.001$, and when the emotional content of the speech sample was negative $\chi = 26.1$, $P < 0.001$. The results of the pairwise comparisons can be seen in Table 5. Varying the emotional content of the speech had no statistically significant effects to the ratings of the stimuli.

*6.3. Approachability.* Means and SEMs for the ratings of the stimulus approachability are presented in Figure 9. Varying the congruency of the tactile stimulation had no statistically significant effect on the ratings of the approachability. However, varying the emotional content of the speech affected the ratings of the speech only stimuli $\chi = 21.7$, $P < 0.001$. It also affected the ratings of the speech tactile stimuli when the concurrent tactile stimulation was derived from positive speech sample $\chi = 15.2$, $P < 0.001$, when the concurrent tactile stimulation was static vibration $\chi = 13.6$, $P < 0.001$, and when the concurrent tactile stimulation was derived from negative speech sample $\chi = 11.7$, $P < 0.05$. The results of the pairwise comparisons can be seen in Table 6.

*6.4. Dominance.* Means and SEMs for the ratings of the stimulus dominance are presented in Figure 10. Varying

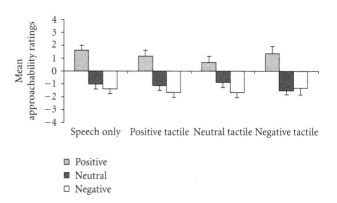

FIGURE 9: Means and SEMs for the ratings of the stimulus approachability.

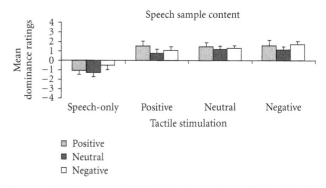

FIGURE 10: Means and SEMs for the ratings of the stimulus dominance.

the congruency of the tactile stimulation had a statistically significant effects to the ratings of the stimuli when the emotional content of the speech sample was positive $\chi = 19.8$, $P < 0.001$, when the emotional content of the speech sample was neutral $\chi = 14.8$, $P < 0.01$, and when the emotional content of the speech sample was negative $\chi = 20.4$, $P < 0.001$. Varying the emotional content of the speech had no statistically significant effects to the ratings. The results of the pairwise comparisons can be seen in Table 7.

TABLE 4: Pairwise comparisons between the speech samples within the four concurrent tactile stimulation categories. In each cell there is Wilcoxon's $T$ value, stars to indicate the $P$ value, the emotional content of the speech sample rated as more pleasant, and Cohen's $D$ value.

| Concurrent tactile stimulation | Emotional content of the speech sample | | |
| --- | --- | --- | --- |
| | Positive versus neutral | Positive versus negative | Neutral versus negative |
| Speech only | $T = 3.0**$ Positive $d = 1.13$ | $T = 2.9**$ Positive $d = 1.21$ | ns |
| Derived from positive speech sample | ns | ns | ns |
| Static vibration | $T = 2.5*$ Positive $d = 0.97$ | $T = 2.4*$ Positive $d = 0.98$ | ns |
| Derived from negative speech sample | ns | ns | ns |

$*P < 0.05$, $**P < 0.01$, $***P < 0.001$, and ns: non-significant.

TABLE 5: Pairwise comparisons between the concurrent tactile stimulation categories within each of the speech samples used. In the table the tactile stimulation derived from positive speech sample is referred as pos and the tactile stimulation derived from negative speech sample as neg.

| Emotional content of the speech sample | Concurrent tactile stimulation | | | | | |
| --- | --- | --- | --- | --- | --- | --- |
| | speech-only versus pos | speech-only versus static vibration | speech-only versus neg | pos versus static vibration | pos versus neg | static vibration versus neg |
| Positive | $T = 2.60**$ pos $d = 1.22$ | $T = 2.59*$ static vibration $d = 1.03$ | $T = 2.68**$ neg $d = 1.18$ | ns | ns | ns |
| Neutral | $T = 3.10**$ pos $d = 1.44$ | $T = 3.55***$ static vibration $d = 2.10$ | $T = 3.39***$ neg $d = 1.56$ | ns | ns | ns |
| Negative | $T = 3.14**$ pos $d = 1.56$ | $T = 3.32***$ static vibration $d = 2.28$ | $T = 3.29***$ neg $d = 1.65$ | $T = 1.98*$ static vibration $d = 0.43$ | ns | $T = 1.98*$ static vibration $d = 0.41$ |

$*P < 0.05$, $**P < 0.01$, $***P < 0.001$, and ns: non-significant.

TABLE 6: Pairwise comparisons between the speech samples within the four concurrent tactile stimulation categories.

| Concurrent tactile stimulation | Emotional content of the speech sample | | |
| --- | --- | --- | --- |
| | positive versus neutral | positive versus negative | neutral versus negative |
| Speech-only | $T = 3.43***$ positive $d = 1.71$ | $T = 3.46***$ positive $d = 2.02$ | ns |
| Derived from positive speech sample | $T = 3.11**$ positive $d = 1.38$ | $T = 3.28***$ positive $d = 1.56$ | ns |
| Static vibration | $T = 2.26*$ positive $d = 0.93$ | $T = 3.04*$ positive $d = 1.44$ | $T = 2.21*$ neutral $d = 0.56$ |
| Derived from negative speech sample | $T = 3.23***$ positive $d = 1.64$ | $T = 2.77**$ positive $d = 1.28$ | ns |

$*P < 0.05$, $**P < 0.01$, $***P < 0.001$, and ns: non-significant.

TABLE 7: Pairwise comparisons between the concurrent tactile stimulation categories within each of the speech samples used.

| Emotional content of the speech sample | Concurrent tactile stimulation | | | | | |
|---|---|---|---|---|---|---|
| | speech-only versus pos | speech-only versus static vibration | speech-only versus neg | pos versus static vibration | pos versus neg | static vibration versus neg |
| Positive | $T = 3.11$** pos $d = 1.61$ | $T = 2.74$* static vibration $d = 1.55$ | $T = 3.0$** neg $d = 1.42$ | ns | ns | ns |
| Neutral | $T = 2.84$** pos $d = 1.12$ | $T = 3.0$** static vibration $d = 1.42$ | $T = 2.95$** neg $d = 1.44$ | ns | ns | ns |
| Negative | $T = 2.03$* pos $d = 0.90$ | $T = 3.0$** static vibration $d = 1.29$ | $T = 2.93$** neg $d = 1.48$ | ns | ns | ns |

$*P < 0.05$, $**P < 0.01$, $***P < 0.001$, and ns: non-significant.

## 7. Summary

Varying the tactile stimulation had the following effects to the results. In general, all the speech tactile stimuli were rated as significantly more dominant and arousing than the speech only stimuli. In addition, the speech tactile stimuli where the tactile stimulation was static vibration were in some cases rated as more arousing than the speech tactile stimuli where the tactile stimulation was derived from positive or negative speech samples. This effect, however, was independent of the congruency of the tactile signal and speech. The effect of the stimulus congruency became relevant for the ratings of the pleasantness. Congruent speech tactile stimuli were rated as less pleasant than the speech only stimuli when the emotional content of the speech was positive. Varying the tactile stimulation had no statistically significant effects for the ratings of approachability.

Varying the emotional content of the speech affected the ratings of pleasantness, but only when the stimulus was speech only or when the concurrent tactile stimulation was static vibration. In those cases the stimuli were rated adequately in respect to their emotional content. In addition, the results showed that all the stimuli with positive emotional content were rated as more approachable than the stimuli with negative or neutral emotional content. Interestingly, when the concurrent tactile stimulation was static vibration also the speech stimulus with neutral content was rated as more approachable than the stimulus with negative emotional content. The emotional content of the speech had no statistically significant effects for the ratings of the arousal or dominance.

## 8. Discussion

The results of both experiments showed that the speech tactile stimuli were rated as more arousing and dominant than speech only stimuli. This result, however, was not fully independent of the form of the tactile stimulation. The results of Experiment 2 showed that when the concurrent tactile stimulation was static vibration, the speech tactile stimuli were experienced as more arousing than other speech tactile stimuli. In addition, in Experiment 1 the speech tactile stimuli were rated as less approachable than the speech only stimuli but in Experiment 2 the concurrent tactile stimulation had no effect on the ratings of approachability. However, the results of Experiment 2 suggested that congruent speech tactile stimuli were in some cases rated as less pleasant than speech only or incongruent speech tactile stimuli.

Then, the results of both experiments showed that the emotional content of the speech affected mostly the ratings of pleasantness and approachability. The stimuli with positive emotional content were in general rated as more pleasant and approachable than the stimuli with neutral or negative emotional contents. Further, the results of Experiment 2 showed that when static vibration was provided during speech the emotional content of the speech affected the pleasantness and approachability ratings more efficiently than when the stimulus was speech only or when the tactile stimulation was derived from positive or negative speech sample.

Previous studies [15, 18] suggest that by providing synchronous audiotactile or speech tactile signals the cognitive performance can be affected so that people, for example, can detect stimuli more accurately than when the signal is asynchronous. From this perspective it was reasonable to assume that temporal synchrony in amplitude variations of tactile and speech signals may have an effect on the emotion-related ratings of the stimuli as well. However, when looking at the ratings of congruent and incongruent speech tactile stimuli one can find only minor differences between the stimuli. Interestingly, they also show that at least with the current set of stimuli congruent speech tactile samples were in some cases rated as less pleasant than incongruent speech tactile samples. At this point, the reasons behind this result can only be speculated. As it can be seen from the results, both congruent and incongruent speech tactile stimuli were rated as rather neutral in respect to the pleasantness and approachability. This result was also at least partly independent of the content of the speech despite the fact that the speech only samples were in general rated adequately in respect to their emotional content (e.g., negative speech samples were rated as unpleasant). Therefore, it seems possible that the amplitude changes used in the current study redirected the participant's attention away from the emotional message conveyed by the content of the speech sample, thus, making the experience neutral.

Then, even though the ratings of the congruent and incongruent speech tactile stimuli were rather similar, the form of the speech tactile signal did affect the ratings of the speech tactile stimuli. Speech-tactile stimuli with static vibrations were rated as more arousing than stimuli with congruent or incongruent tactile vibrations. They also had a clear effect on the ratings of the pleasantness and approachability of the speech unlike congruent and incongruent tactile vibrations. As both incongruent and congruent stimuli were rated rather similarly, it seems likely that the absence of amplitude (e.g., rhythm) changes in speech tactile stimuli with static vibrations caused the differences in the ratings. Intuitively it seems that the continuous static vibration elevated the level of arousal. From a theoretical framework [21–23] valence and arousal represent motivational parameters related to the general disposition to approach or avoid stimulation and the vigor of that tendency. Therefore, by elevating the level of arousal static vibration also activated the motivational system related to the general disposition to approach or avoid stimulation, and this way affected the experienced approachability of the speech sample. Thus, by providing static vibration simultaneously with speech we were able to create more arousing experience therefore intensifying the effects of the content of the speech sample to the experienced pleasantness and approachability of the stimulus.

There were also some similarities in the results when compared with previous studies. One previous study showed that in person-to-person communication participants used tactile stimulation to emphasize the content of the speech [10]. The current results show that tactile stimulation can modulate emotion-related responses to speech as the speech tactile stimuli were experienced as more arousing and as more dominant than speech only stimuli. This is in line with the results of the earlier studies. A novel finding in the current study was that with concurrent static tactile signal the pleasantness and approachability ratings of the content of the speech were clearly affected. This result as far as we know has not been obtained earlier. It suggests that by offering carefully selected tactile signal simultaneously with speech also other emotion-related dimensions than arousal can be affected.

One central difference emerged in the stimulus ratings between the two experiments. In Experiment 1 the participants rated the speech tactile stimuli as less approachable than the speech only stimuli. However, in Experiment 2 there were no differences between the approachability ratings of the speech tactile and speech only stimuli. This result seems to reflect observations from our previous studies [28, 29] in which the continuity of the stimuli has had an effect on the ratings of stimulus pleasantness and approachability. In general, continuous stimuli have been rated as less pleasant

and as less approachable than discontinuous stimuli. In Experiment 1 the prototype device was vibrating during the whole stimulus presentation while in Experiment 2 the prototype device vibrated only in the beginning of the stimulus. Hence, in Experiment 1 the tactile stimulation was continuous while in Experiment 2 the stimulation can be regarded as discontinuous. The results of the current study can, thus, be seen supporting the idea that the continuity of the vibrotactile stimulation is an important factor effecting the experienced pleasantness and approachability of the tactile stimulation.

From the interface design perspective the obtained results can be used to enrich emotion-related speech communication relatively easily. The static vibration was related to the elevated level of arousal and dominance as well as experiences of pleasantness and approachability. Therefore, at this point it seems that there is no need for a special algorithm detecting the emotional state of the user during conversation. Instead, the user can just send a static vibration whenever necessary simultaneously with emotional speech, for example, by squeezing the device or pushing a button. In general, the speech tactile stimuli shifted the experienced level of arousal and dominance. From a theoretical point of view [21–23] the enhancement in the subjective level of arousal can be easily seen as means to elevate the level of attentive behavior. Therefore, from application point of view, the results suggest that tactile cues can be used in mobile contexts to catch the attention during a conversation if wanted. Similarly, the static vibration cues can also be used to enhance the effect of the emotional content of the speech to the receiver. So, if one wants to make, for example, pleasant message more pleasant and approachable to the listener, static vibration works well for this purpose.

There were some restrictions in the current study. The experiment was conducted in a laboratory with a special prototype device. However, to maintain ecological validity the position of participant's hand mimicked accurately the position of a hand when a person is holding a mobile phone (i.e., the dominant hand's thumb was touching the actuators on the other side of the device, and the tips of the dominant hand's other fingers were touching the device on the other side). Therefore, all the participants received the tactile stimulation in the same parts of the hand. In addition, the vibrotactile actuators used to produce the tactile signal in the current study are similar as the vibrotactile actuators currently used in mobile phones. So, the amplitude changes varied in the study are reproducible with commercial products. Finally, it should be noted that the prototype was not capable of producing both tactile and auditory stimulation simultaneously. During the experiment the speech samples were presented to the participant via headphones. This may have some effects to the results. In real use cases, however, people often use headphones or a loudspeaker with mobile devices, for example, when walking and listening music or driving. Therefore, it seems that in future studies different user scenarios could be taken into account when studying the modulation of emotional speech with tactile stimulation.

Next it would be possible to study in a laboratory how people use vibrotactile cues during longer conversations. Also, studies outside laboratory could provide an insight on how the users would use the tactile modulation of speech during their daily activities. In addition, it would be interesting to study how other than vibrotactile haptic cues (e.g., thermal stimulation or electrotactile stimulation) could modulate emotional responses related to speech.

In summary, our current results suggest that any concurrent tactile stimulation has an effect on the ratings of arousal and dominance of speech and that this effect is independent of the emotional content of the speech. Further, the results suggest that both the experienced arousal and approachability of a spoken message can be affected by concurrent static vibration. In addition, the continuity of the tactile stimulation had an effect on the ratings of approachability. The results suggest that discontinuous or brief static tactile stimulation should be used especially in the case one wants to create speech tactile stimuli experienced as approachable and pleasant.

## Acknowledgments

This paper was a part of Mobile Immersion project funded by the Finnish Funding Agency for Technology and Innovation, TEKES and steered by Nokia Research Center. The author would also like to thank the volunteers who took part in the experiment.

## References

[1] H. F. Harlow, "The nature of love," *American Psychologist*, vol. 13, no. 2, pp. 673–685, 1958.

[2] H. F. Harlow, *Learning to Love*, Albion, San Francisco, Calif, USA, 1971.

[3] H. F. Harlow, R. O. Dodsworth, and M. K. Harlow, "Total social isolation in monkeys," *Proceedings of the National Academy of Sciences of the United States of America*, vol. 54, no. 1, pp. 90–97, 1965.

[4] S. E. Jones and A. E. Yarbrough, "A naturalistic study of the meanings of touch," *Communication Monographs*, vol. 52, pp. 19–56, 1985.

[5] M. J. Hertenstein, D. Keltner, B. App, B. A. Bulleit, and A. R. Jaskolka, "Touch communicates distinct emotions," *Emotion*, vol. 6, no. 3, pp. 528–533, 2006.

[6] J. Smith and K. MacLean, "Communicating emotion through a haptic link: design space and methodology," *International Journal of Human Computer Studies*, vol. 65, no. 4, pp. 376–387, 2007.

[7] J. N. Bailenson, N. Yee, S. Brave, D. Merget, and D. Koslow, "Virtual interpersonal touch: expressing and recognizing emotions through haptic devices," *Human-Computer Interaction*, vol. 22, no. 3, pp. 325–353, 2007.

[8] M. Ilves and V. Surakka, "Emotions, anthropomorphism of speech synthesis, and psychophysiology," in *Emotions in the Human Voice. Volume III: Culture and Perception*, K. Izdebski, Ed., pp. 137–152, Plural Publishing, San Diego, Calif, USA, 2009.

[9] M. Ilves, V. Surakka, and T. Vanhala, "The effects of emotionally worded synthesized speech on the ratings of emotions and voice quality," in *Proceedings of the Affective Computing and Intelligent Interfaces (ACII '11)*, pp. 588–598, October 2011.

[10] A. Chang, S. O'Modhrain, R. Jacob, E. Gunther, and H. Ishii, "ComTouch: design of a vibrotactile communication device," in *Proceedings of the 4th Conference on Designing Interactive Systems: Processes, Practices, Methods, and Techniques (DIS '02)*, pp. 312–320, June 2002.

[11] M. S. Beauchamp, "See me, hear me, touch me: multisensory integration in lateral occipital-temporal cortex," *Current Opinion in Neurobiology*, vol. 15, no. 2, pp. 145–153, 2005.

[12] J. Driver and T. Noesselt, "Multisensory interplay reveals crossmodal influences on "Sensory-Specific" brain regions, neural responses, and judgments," *Neuron*, vol. 57, no. 1, pp. 11–23, 2008.

[13] J. J. Foxe, I. A. Morocz, M. M. Murray, B. A. Higgins, D. C. Javitt, and C. E. Schroeder, "Multisensory auditory-somatosensory interactions in early cortical processing revealed by high-density electrical mapping," *Cognitive Brain Research*, vol. 10, no. 1-2, pp. 77–83, 2000.

[14] J. J. Foxe, G. R. Wylie, A. Martinez et al., "Auditory-somatosensory multisensory processing in auditory association cortex: an fMRI study," *Journal of Neurophysiology*, vol. 88, no. 1, pp. 540–543, 2002.

[15] J. P. Bresciani, M. O. Ernst, K. Drewing, G. Bouyer, V. Maury, and A. Kheddar, "Feeling what you hear: auditory signals can modulate tactile tap perception," *Experimental Brain Research*, vol. 162, no. 2, pp. 172–180, 2005.

[16] T. Ro, J. Hsu, N. E. Yasar, L. Caitlin Elmore, and M. S. Beauchamp, "Sound enhances touch perception," *Experimental Brain Research*, vol. 195, no. 1, pp. 135–143, 2009.

[17] J. Vroomen and M. Keetels, "Perception of intersensory synchrony: a tutorial review," *Attention, Perception, and Psychophysics*, vol. 72, no. 4, pp. 871–884, 2010.

[18] H. Gillmeister and M. Eimer, "Tactile enhancement of auditory detection and perceived loudness," *Brain Research*, vol. 1160, no. 30, pp. 58–68, 2007.

[19] E. C. Wilson, C. M. Reed, and L. D. Braida, "Integration of auditory and vibrotactile stimuli: effects of phase and stimulus-onset asynchrony," *Journal of the Acoustical Society of America*, vol. 126, no. 4, pp. 1960–1974, 2009.

[20] M. Sato, C. Cavé, L. Ménard, and A. Brasseur, "Auditory-tactile speech perception in congenitally blind and sighted adults," *Neuropsychologia*, vol. 48, no. 12, pp. 3683–3686, 2010.

[21] M. M. Bradley, "Measuring emotion: the self-assessment manikin and the semantic differential," *Journal of Behavior Therapy and Experimental Psychiatry*, vol. 25, no. 1, pp. 49–59, 1994.

[22] M. M. Bradley and P. J. Lang, "Affective reactions to acoustic stimuli," *Psychophysiology*, vol. 37, no. 2, pp. 204–215, 2000.

[23] P. J. Lang, M. K. Greenwald, M. M. Bradley, and A. O. Hamm, "Looking at pictures: affective, facial, visceral, and behavioral reactions," *Psychophysiology*, vol. 30, no. 3, pp. 261–273, 1993.

[24] H. Schlosberg, "Three dimensions of emotion," *Psychological Review*, vol. 61, no. 2, pp. 81–88, 1954.

[25] J. Anttonen and V. Surakka, "Emotions and heart rate while sitting on a chair," in *Proceedings of the SIGCHI Conference on Human Factors in Computing Systems (CHI '05)*, pp. 491–499, April 2005.

[26] R. J. Davidson, "Cerebral asymmetry, emotion and affective style," in *Brain Asymmetry*, R. J. Davidson and K. Hugdahl, Eds., pp. 361–387, The MIT Press, Cambridge, Mass, USA, 1995.

[27] V. Surakka, *Contagion and modulation of human emotions [Ph.D. thesis]*, Department of Psychology, Acta Universitatis Tamperensis, 1998.

[28] K. Salminen, V. Surakka, J. Lylykangas et al., "Emotional and behavioral responses to haptic stimulation," in *Proceedings of the SIGCHI Conference on Human Factors in Computing Systems (CHI '08)*, pp. 1555–1562, April 2008.

[29] K. Salminen, V. Surakka, J. Rantala, J. Lylykangas, P. Laitinen, and R. Raisamo, "Emotional responses to haptic stimuli in laboratory versus travelling by bus contexts," in *Proceedings of the Affective Computing and Intelligent Interaction (ACII '09)*, pp. 1–7, September 2009.

[30] J. Rantala, R. Raisamo, J. Lylykangas et al., "The role of gesture types and spatial feedback in haptic communication," *IEEE Transactions on Haptics*, vol. 4, no. 4, pp. 295–306, 2011.

# 6

# Length and Roughness Perception in a Moving-Plateau Touch Display

**Junji Watanabe,[1] Yusuke Godai,[2,3] and Hideyuki Ando[4]**

[1] *NTT Communication Science Laboratories, Nippon Telegraph and Telephone Corporation, 3-1, Morinosato-Wakamiya, Atsugi, Kanagawa 243-0198, Japan*
[2] *Graduate School of Electro-Communications, University of Electro-Communications, 1-5-1, Chofugaoka, Chofu, Tokyo 182-8585, Japan*
[3] *Machinetool Division, Mayekawa Electric. Co., Ltd., 2000, Tatsuzawa, Moriya, Ibaraki 302-0118, Japan*
[4] *Graduate School of Information Science and Technology, Osaka University, 2-1, Yamadaoka, Suita, Osaka 565-0871, Japan*

Correspondence should be addressed to Junji Watanabe, watanabe.junji@lab.ntt.co.jp

Academic Editor: Arun Kumar Tripathi

We have proposed a tactile geometry display technique based on active finger movement. The technique uses a perceptual feature that, during finger movement, the length of a touched object is perceived to increase when the object is moved in the same direction as the finger movement or to decrease when it is moved in the opposite direction. With this display technique, a wide range of tactile shapes can be presented with realistic rigid edges and continuous surfaces. In this work, to further develop our technique, we performed psychophysical experiments to study perceptions of length and roughness under this presentation technique. The results indicated that the elongation (shrinkage) of the object can be observed regardless of the roughness of the touched object and that the perceived roughness of the object slightly changes but the changes are much smaller than those theoretically expected.

## 1. Introduction

*1.1. Moving-Plateau Touch Display.* When we touch an object in a space, we actively move our fingers across its surface. Since the cutaneous signals sequentially presented to the fingertips are integrated with proprioceptive signals of the finger and arm, we can perceive the shape and texture of the object, even if it is larger than the fingertips. The interplay of the cutaneous and proprioceptive sensations is essential for developing touch displays, and we have proposed a novel touch display technique for presenting tactile geometry based on the perceptual features of the two sensory processes [1–3]. Touched objects do not usually move during exploratory finger movements, but if the object moves during the finger movement, an illusory shape of the object can be perceived. As shown in Figure 1(a), when the object moves in the same direction as the finger, the length of the object is perceived to increase. Conversely, when the object moves in the opposite direction as in Figure 1(b), its length is perceived to decrease. This is because the human

tactile system judges the length based on the initial and final positions of the moving edges, even if the information about the object's movement exists on the fingertip. In this touch display technique, called the Moving-Plateau Touch Display (MPTD), the extent of the change in the perceived length can be controlled by manipulating the velocity of the object during the finger movement. In this paper, we verify the generality of our display technique from the results of psychophysical experiments on the perceptions of length and roughness under the MPTD presentation.

*1.2. Related Touch Displays and Characteristics of MPTD.* To clarify the characteristics of the MPTD, here we briefly introduce previous touch displays for presenting tactile surfaces and shapes. In a pin array display, pins are arranged as a matrix on a two-dimensional plane and the pins independently rise and fall [4–7]. Although a high-density pin matrix display has been developed [8], pin-based displays cannot present a smooth continuous surface,

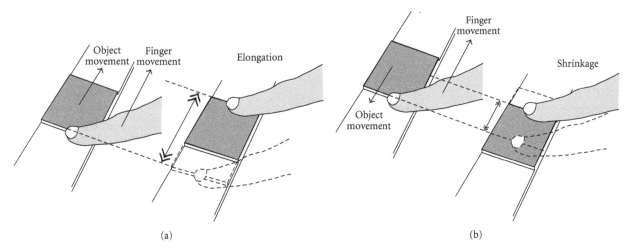

FIGURE 1: The principle of MPTD. (a) When the object moves in the same direction as the finger, the length is perceived to increase. (b) When it moves in the opposite direction, the length is perceived to decrease.

which is essential for achieving natural tactile information presentation. In probe-based displays, such as Phantom [9] and Spider [10], the contact point is a pen or sphere connected to force generator. These displays can present smooth proprioceptive sensation, but can not present a cutaneous one. In an encounter-type display [11, 12], the display stays at the location of a virtual object and waits for the user to encounter it. With such devices, there is no need to prepare the whole surface in the environment, but contact situations are limited or mechanical probes have to be used to present the object's surface. As an extension of the encountered-type displays, a plate [13], rotating drum [14], or moving centroid [15] has been used to present local orientation or slips at the location of the contact point with the fingertip, which can produce both proprioceptive and cutaneous sensations and significantly enhance perception of shape and surface.

The MPTD is another variation of the encounter-type display. The MPTD was implemented by using a linear slider, an object attached to the slider, and a laser distance sensor for measuring finger movements. When the user touches an object on the slider, the MPTD can change the position of the object according to the finger movements measured with the distance sensor and thereby present tactile geometric information. The MPTD can present not only realistically rigid edges but also continuous surfaces, which are difficult for prior tactile displays. In addition, this technique can easily be extended to a two-dimensional shape by moving the object along two orthogonal axes (see Figure 2 and video on the website [3]).

In the MPTD presentation, it has been demonstrated that perceived length is changed by moving the object on the slider during finger movements [1–3]. However, the relationship between the effect of the MPTD and roughness of the object remains unclear. In this work, we tested the gene-rality and effectiveness of the MPTD by conducting psychophysical experiments to determine (i) whether the perceived length changes with the roughness of the object

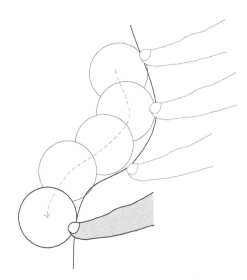

FIGURE 2: Principle for presenting smooth two-dimensional shapes in the MPTD presentation. The touched object is moved on the two orthogonal axes according to the finger movements.

and (ii) whether perceived roughness changes when the length is modulated by the MPTD.

## 2. Materials and Methods

*2.1. Participants.* Six people (one male author, three naïve males, and two naïve females, who were all right handed and in their twenties) participated in all experiments. The participants, excluding the author, were volunteers unaware of the purpose of the experiments. They had no known abnormalities of their tactile sensory systems. Informed consent was obtained from the naïve participants before the experiment started. Recruitment of the participants and experimental procedures were conducted in accordance with the Declaration of Helsinki.

*2.2. Apparatus.* The participant traced an object placed on a linear slider (KBA-10E-ST-M20N-20A, CKD Inc.), whose motor had been replaced with a high-response motor (MSMD041S1A, Panasonic Inc.). The finger position of the participant was measured with a laser range finder (LK-500, KEYENCE Corp.), and its information was sent to a PC. The data were collected with the PC using an AD board (PCI-3523A, Interface Corp.), and the finger velocity was calculated. The liner slider was driven by a DA board (PCI-3523A, Interface Corp.) of the PC at a 1-kHz cycle.

*2.3. Stimuli.* Past tactile experiments used a variety of roughness samples, such as abrasive surfaces (e.g., [16, 17]), one-dimensional gratings (e.g., [18, 19]), and two-dimensional dot patterns (e.g., [20, 21]). However, the randomness of the roughness parameters makes it difficult to quantitatively evaluate the experimental results. Our solution is to use original plastic samples. As illustrated in Figure 3(a), we wrapped nylon string around a flawless round bar and made a casting mold of the string-wrapped bar with silicon. Figure 3(b) is an example of the casting molds. Using the casting mold, we made a roughness sample of a one-dimensional grating with casting resin. A photograph of the roughness sample and its cross-section are shown in Figure 4(a) and 4(b), respectively. In our experiments, the roughness is expressed by the diameter of the nylon string (e.g., 1.0-mm diameter (mm-d)). A smooth surface (0 mm-d) was made from the mold of a bare round bar. The length of roughness surface was adjusted by covering flanking areas with masking tapes.

*2.4. Length and Roughness Configuration.* The velocity of the object on the linear slider $V_o$, the expected length $L_e$, the expected roughness $R_e$ expressed in mm-d, and their ratio to the original ones $X$ are calculated by

$$V_o = \alpha V_f (\alpha < 1), \tag{1}$$

$$L_e = \frac{V_f}{V_f - V_o} \times L, \tag{2}$$

$$R_e = \frac{V_f}{V_f - V_o} \times R, \tag{3}$$

$$X = \frac{1}{(1 - \alpha)}, \tag{4}$$

where $V_f$ is the velocity of the finger movement, $\alpha$ is the ratio of object's velocity to finger's velocity, and $L$ and $R$ are the original length and roughness of the touched object, respectively. If the object does not move, that is, $\alpha = 0$, the veridical length and roughness can be perceived ($X = 1.0$). If the object moves in the same direction as the finger at half the speed of the finger movement, that is, $\alpha = 0.5$, since the number of bumps on the object is constant, twice the original length and roughness can be perceived ($X = 2.0$). If the object moves at the same speed in the opposite direction, that is, $\alpha = -1.0$, half of the original length and roughness can be perceived ($X = 0.5$).

## 3. Perceived Lengths with Varied Roughness

*3.1. Procedure.* A participant sat in front of the linear slider. A standard length sample (length of 40 mm, and roughness of 0.00, 0.14, 0.40, or 1.00 mm-d) was put on the forward side of the linear slider. A test length sample (32 samples, length of 16- to 90-mm-length at 2-mm interval, and the same roughness as the standard sample) was put on the interior side of the linear slider. First, the participant traced the test length sample from the left starting position to the right end position once as in Figure 5(a). At this time, the linear slider did not move. Then, the participant traced the standard length sample from the left starting position to the right end position once as in Figure 5(b). At this time, the linear slider moved at a relative velocity rate $\alpha$ defined in (1). Then, the participant verbally indicated which of length samples he/she perceived to be longer by an alternative forced choice task (2AFC). Next, another test length sample was set up based on the answer. We selected the test length sample using the simple up-and-down method. For example, a test sample reported as longer was replaced with one whose length was 2 mm shorter. Then, the shorter test sample was presented until the participant reported that it was shorter. This procedure was repeated until the answer changed three times. We regarded the length of the last test sample as the point of subjective equality (PSE) of perceived length. We selected five velocity ratios ($\alpha = -0.67, -0.25, 0.00, 0.20$, and $0.50$) of the linear slider at random. The expected values of perceived length calculated from (2), their differences from the original lengths, and their ratios to the original ones calculated from (4) for the five velocity ratios are shown in Table 1. The participant tried the simple up-and-down method four times at each velocity ratio (total of 20 times). In addition, we conducted experiments with four roughness conditions (0.00, 0.14, 0.40, and 1.00 mm-d).

To eliminate any distraction caused by sound noise (motor noise and tracing sounds), the participants wore both earplugs (ear putty, KOKEN) and ear muffs (Leightning L3, Bilsom). Participants' eyes were always closed. The participants practiced before the experiment to attain a constant finger movement velocity of 30 mm/sec and constant finger pressure of 50 g. In order to keep the regular speed of the finger movement, they moved their finger according to metronome (120 beats per minute). When the participants were aware of a failure in the finger movement, they were asked to report it, and the trial was performed again.

*3.2. Results.* The experimental results for the four roughness conditions (0.00, 0.14, 0.40, and 1.00 mm-d) are shown in Figure 6. The horizontal axis represents the velocity ratio of the liner slider $\alpha$ and the vertical axis represents the differences of the PSE of perceived length from the original length. Averages of perceived lengths across all participants and their standard errors are shown. Dotted lines show theoretical values calculated from (2).

The results for the four roughness conditions showed similar tendencies. In order to evaluate the statistical difference

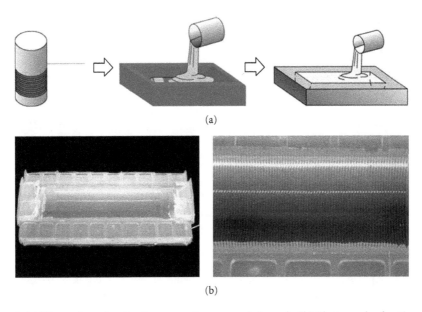

(a)

(b)

Figure 3: (a) Illustrations showing how a roughness sample is made. (b) Photograph of casting mold.

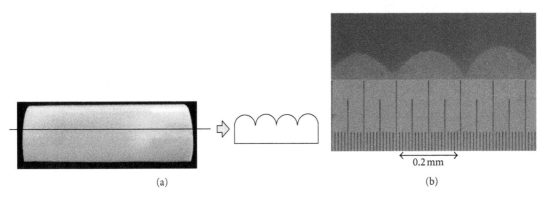

0.2 mm

(a)

(b)

Figure 4: (a) Photograph of roughness sample. (b) Photograph of cross-sectional surface of the roughness sample (0.20 mm-d). This sample was cut with a band saw.

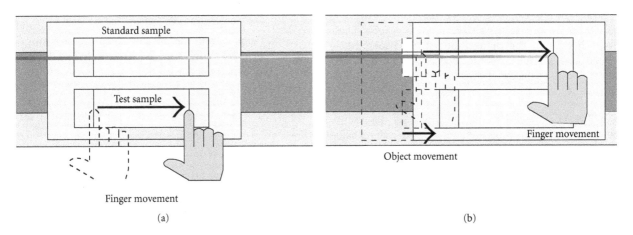

(a)

(b)

Figure 5: Experimental procedures. (a) The participant traced the test length sample while the linear slider was static. (b) The participant traced the standard length sample while the linear slider was moved at a relative velocity rate $\alpha$.

TABLE 1: Theoretically expected length $L_e$ (mm), difference of $L_e$ from original length (40 mm), and its ratio $X$ to original according to velocity ratio $\alpha$.

| Velocity ratio $\alpha$ | −0.67 | −0.25 | 0.00 | 0.20 | 0.50 |
|---|---|---|---|---|---|
| Expected length $L_e$ (mm) | 24 | 32 | 40 | 50 | 80 |
| Difference of $L_e$ from original length (mm) | −16 | −8 | 0 | +10 | +40 |
| Ratio to original $X$ | 0.60 | 0.80 | 1.00 | 1.25 | 2.00 |

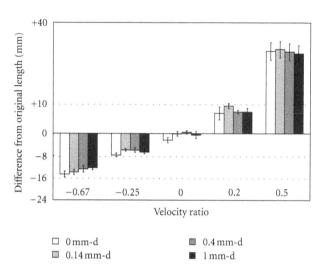

FIGURE 6: Differences in the PSEs of perceived length from the original length in 0.00, 0.14, 0.40, and 1.00- mm-d roughness conditions. Dotted lines show theoretical values calculated from (2).

in the PSEs, we first performed a two-way repeated measures ANOVA with the roughness condition and velocity ratio as factors, and the PSE of perceived length as the dependent variable. The statistical results showed a nonsignificant difference between roughness conditions ($F$ (3, 15) = 1.13, $P$ = 0.37) and a significant difference between velocity ratios ($F$ (4, 20) = 155.26, $P$ < .01). The interaction between them was not significant ($F$ (12, 60) = 1.06, $P$ = 0.41). The post hoc multiple comparisons (Ryan's method, significant level = 0.05) showed significant differences between all combinations of velocity ratios (see Remark 1 for the statistical analyses excluding the author's data). These results suggest that the perceived lengths change according to the velocity ratios and that the roughness of the traced object does not influence the perceived length under the MPTD presentation.

Since a significant difference was not observed in the roughness conditions, we use all data of the four roughness conditions without distinction for the following analyses. When the velocity ratio was zero (the standard length sample did not move), almost veridical length was perceived (average 39.3 mm), and the value was not significantly different from the theoretical one (40 mm) ($t$ (23) = 1.34, $P$ = 0.19), suggesting that the participants could judge the length correctly. In order to avoid artifacts due to the presentation order of standard and test samples, we subtracted the value of velocity ratio $\alpha$ = 0.00 from those of the rest and then made comparisons with the theoretical values. When the object was moved during a finger movement, the magnitudes of elongation or shrinkage fell short of the theoretical ones: theoretical value of 79.9% for $\alpha$ = −0.67, 74.1% for $\alpha$ = −0.25, 88.7% for $\alpha$ = 0.20, and 75.5% for $\alpha$ = 0.50. These results indicate that the changes in perceived lengths are associated with the velocity ratios and that the magnitudes of elongation or shrinkage of them are slightly smaller than the theoretical ones.

*Remark 1.* The statistical results remained the same even when the author's data were excluded. A two-way repeated measures ANOVA showed a nonsignificant difference between roughness conditions ($F$ (3, 12) = 0.76, $P$ = 0.54) and a significant difference between velocity ratios ($F$ (4, 16) = 113.44, $P$ < .01). The interaction between them was not significant ($F$ (12, 48) = 0.97, $P$ = 0.50). The post hoc multiple comparisons (Ryan's method, significant level = 0.05) showed significant differences between all combinations of velocity ratios.

## 4. Perceived Roughness under MPTD Presentation

*4.1. Procedure.* In this experiment, we investigated the roughness perception under the MPTD presentation. The apparatuses were the same as in the previous experiment. The standard roughness sample (length of 40 mm, and roughness of 0.4 or 0.6 mm-d) was put on the forward side of the linear slider. The test roughness sample (15 samples, length of 40 mm, and roughness of 0.20- to 0.90-mm-d at a 0.05-mm-d interval) was put on the interior side of the linear slider. First, the participant traced the test roughness sample once. At this time, the linear slider was stationary. Then, the participant traced the standard roughness sample once. At this time, the linear slider moved at a relative velocity ratio $\alpha$. The participant verbally indicated which sample he/she perceived to be rougher by 2AFC. Next, another test sample was set on the linear slider using the same up-and-down method as in the previous experiment. We regarded the roughness of the last test sample as the PSE of perceived roughness. We used the five velocity ratios ($\alpha$ = −0.67, −0.25, 0.00, 0.20, and 0.50) of the linear slider at random. The participant tried the up-and-down method four times at each velocity ratio (total of 20 times). In addition, we conducted experiments with two roughness conditions (0.40 and 0.60 mm-d). The theoretically expected roughness for 0.40 and 0.60 mm-d calculated from (3), and their ratios to the original ones calculated from (4) for the five velocity ratios are shown in Table 2.

*4.2. Results.* Figure 7 shows the averages of the PSEs of perceived roughness across all participants and their standard errors for the two roughness conditions (0.4 and 0.6 mm-d). The horizontal axis represents the velocity ratio of the linear slider $\alpha$, and the vertical axis represents the PSE of perceived roughness. Perceived roughness (solid line) and theoretically expected values (dotted line) are plotted.

TABLE 2: Theoretically expected roughness $R_e$ (mm-d) and its ratio $X$ to the original roughness (0.40 and 0.60 mm-d) according to velocity ratio $\alpha$

| Velocity ratio $\alpha$ | −0.67 | −0.25 | 0.00 | 0.20 | 0.50 |
|---|---|---|---|---|---|
| Expected roughness $R_e$ (mm-d) for 0.40 mm-d | 0.24 | 0.32 | 0.40 | 0.50 | 0.80 |
| Expected roughness $R_e$ (mm-d) for 0.60 mm-d | 0.36 | 0.48 | 0.60 | 0.75 | 1.20 |
| Ratio to original $X$ | 0.60 | 0.80 | 1.00 | 1.25 | 2.00 |

The same trend was observed in the two roughness conditions that when the velocity ratio increased, the PSEs of perceived roughness were slightly increased. In order to evaluate the statistical difference in the PSEs, we first performed a two-way repeated measures ANOVA with the roughness condition and velocity ratio as factors, and the PSE of perceived roughness as the dependent variable. The statistical results showed significant differences between roughness conditions ($F$ (1, 5) = 58.93, $P$ < .01) and between velocity ratios ($F$ (4, 20) = 7.02, $P$ < .01). The interaction between them was not significant ($F$ (4, 20) = 0.58, $P$ = 0.68). The post hoc multiple comparisons (Ryan's method, significant level = 0.05) showed that there were significant differences between following combinations of velocity ratios: [$\alpha$ = −0.67 and 0.20], [$\alpha$ = −0.67 and 0.50], and [$\alpha$ = −0.25 and 0.50] (see Remark 2 for the statistical analyses excluding the author's data).

To evaluate the magnitude of the change in roughness with the changes in velocity ratios, we subtracted the value of velocity ratio $\alpha$ = 0.00 from those of the rest, and then compared the differences with the theoretical values. When the object was moved during a finger movement, the changes in perceived roughness were smaller than the theoretical ones in all velocity ratios in the two roughness conditions. The proportions to the theoretical ones were 41.5% for $\alpha$ = −0.67, 38.2% for $\alpha$ = −0.25, 15.3% for $\alpha$ = 0.20, and 17.0% for $\alpha$ = 0.50 in 0.4 mm-d roughness condition, and 26.8% for $\alpha$ = −0.67, 26.0% for $\alpha$ = −0.25, 42.1% for $\alpha$ = 0.20, and 11.2% for $\alpha$ = 0.50 in 0.6 mm-d roughness condition. These results suggest that, although the perceived roughness could be changed according to the changes in velocity ratios, the changes were much smaller than those expected by theory (less than half in all velocity ratios).

Remark 2. When the author's data were excluded, we found less effect of the velocity ratios on the perceived roughness than when the data were included. A two-way repeated measures ANOVA showed significant differences between roughness conditions ($F$ (1, 4) = 40.44, $P$ < .01) and between velocity ratios ($F$ (4, 16) = 4.57, $P$ < .05). The interaction between them was not significant ($F$ (4, 16) = 0.59, $P$ = 0.67). The post hoc multiple comparisons (Ryan's method, significant level = 0.05) showed that there was a significant difference only between the combination of velocity ratios: [$\alpha$ = −0.67 and 0.50].

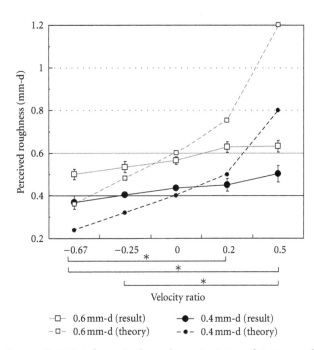

FIGURE 7: PSEs of perceived roughness in 0.40 and 0.60-mm-d roughness conditions. The theoretical values calculated from (3) are plotted with dotted lines. The significant differences between velocity ratios are also shown (*$P$ < .05).

## 5. Discussion

5.1. Principle Findings. In the current paper, two psychophysical experiments were performed under the MPTD presentation. The first experiment examined length perception with varied roughness of touch objects, and the results demonstrated that the perceived length could be changed systematically according to the velocity ratios of object's movement and that this trend was observed regardless of the roughness of the touched object. This means that the MPTD can effectively work regardless of presented texture. The second experiment examined roughness perception when the perceived length was changed, and the result indicated that, although the perceived roughness was modulated by the movements of the touched object, the changes in perceived roughness were much smaller than theoretically expected values. This suggests that the texture of touched object might be modulated but not dramatically changed when the MPTD is used for presenting geometric information.

5.2. Perceptions of Length and Roughness under MPTD. Since our experiments were performed without visual guidance, only the proprioceptive signal of the finger movement and the cutaneous signal on the fingertip were available for perceiving the information about touched object. In the first experiment, the systematic increase/decrease of perceived length was observed regardless of a variety of relative movements between the skin on the fingertip and object, which were caused by the movements of the finger and touched object. In addition, the perceived length of the touched object was comparable to the travel distance of the finger even when the physical roughness of the object was changed. These results suggest that the proprioceptive signals of finger locations at the initiation and end of finger movement are dominant determinants for judging the length of an object in our experimental condition, where the direction and velocity of the finger movement were constant. Considering that the perceived length could be changed depending on the direction [22] and velocity [23, 24] of the finger movement, their roles under the MPTD presentation would be an issue awaiting further investigation.

The results of second experiment indicated that the difference in the relative velocity between the skin and object had little influence on the perceived roughness. This trend agrees with the previous findings with active exploration of one-dimensional gratings [18], two-dimensional raised-dot patterns of truncated cones [25] and textured material surfaces [26], and with passive touch of two-dimensional raised-dot patterns [27]. In our experiment, the participant could not perceive the roughness before or after the finger movement, since the flanking areas of the roughness surface were covered with masking tapes, suggesting that the roughness was not judged when the finger was static. Meanwhile how the participant judged the roughness during the finger movement was not clear. The participant could judge the roughness during any period of the finger movement. It is also known that the sensitivity could be somehow degraded during a finger movement [28]. How the surface roughness is perceived under the MPTD remains for a future study.

The computational mechanisms of the interplay between proprioceptive and cutaneous sensory signals are currently attracting attention in scientific studies of touch (e.g., studies on temporal processing [29, 30], motion processing [31, 32], thermal processing [33], and time course of the interplay [34]), and the MPTD might be an interesting display system for psychophysically investigating mechanisms underlying these sensory processing.

*5.3. Future Prospect of MPTD.* As mentioned in the introduction, the MPTD can easily be extended to a two-dimensional shape display by moving the object along two orthogonal axes. In addition to this tactile function, a visual image presentation function can be integrated (see also video on the website [3]). For example, as shown in Figure 8, when a piece of transparent material is placed on a transparent screen and the image is projected from the back of the screen, the edge of the tactile object on the screen can align with the edge of the visual image. When the user moves his/her finger on the static visual image, the transparent tactile material is moved synchronously according to the shape of the visual image. Then, the visual and tactile edges of the object can overlap.

# 6. Conclusion

To clarify the effectiveness of the MPTD with objects of different roughness, we conducted two psychophysical experiments. In the first experiment, we examined the relationship between physical roughness of the object and its perceived length and found that the roughness of the touched

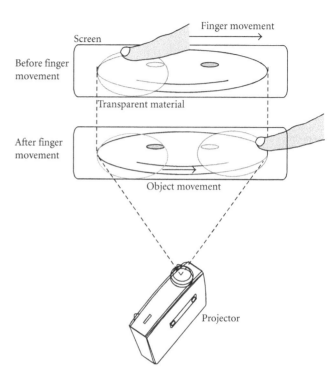

FIGURE 8: Principle for achieving a visual-tactile function with the MPTD.

object does not influence perceived length. In the second experiment, we examined perceived roughness when the length is presented by the MPTD and found that the MPTD influences the perception of the object's roughness, but the changes in perceived roughness are much smaller than those theoretically expected. From these experiments, we can conclude that the MPTD can present geometric information for a wide range of object, and that, when the MPTD is used, the information can be presented without a drastic distortion of its roughness.

# References

[1] H. Ando, T. Amemiya, T. Maeda, J. Watanabe, and M. Nakatani, "Embossed touch display: illusory elongation and shrinking of tactile objects," in *Proceedings of the International Conference on Computer Graphics and Interactive Techniques, Emerging Technologies (SIGGRAPH '06)*, Boston, Mass, USA, July 2006.

[2] H. Ando, J. Watanabe, T. Amemiya, and T. Maeda, "The two dimension outline shape display device using active touch," in *Proceedings of the 16th International Conference on Artificial Reality and Telexistence (ICAT)*, Special Workshop, p. 3A1-1, Hangzhou, China, December 2006.

[3] http://www.junji.org/mptd/.

[4] H. Iwata, H. Yano, F. Nakaizumi, and R. Kawamura, "Project FEELEX: adding haptic surface to graphics," in *Proceedings of the Computer Graphics Annual Conference (SIGGRAPH '01)*, pp. 469–475, Los Angels, Calif, USA, August 2001.

[5] P. S. Wellman, W. J. Peine, G. Favalora, and R. D. Howe, "Mechanical design and control of a high-bandwidth shape

memory alloy tactile display," in *Proceedings of the 5th International Symposium on Experimental Robotics V*, vol. 232, pp. 56–66, Barcelona, Spain, June 1997.

[6] J. Lee, I. Ahn, and J. Park, "Design and implementation of tactile feedback device using electromagnetic type," in *Proceedings of the Intelligent Robots and Systems (IROS '99)*, vol. 3, pp. 1549–1554, Kyongju, Korea, October 1999.

[7] C. R. Wagner, R. D. Howe, and S. J. Lederman, "A tactile shape display using RC servomotors," in *Proceedings of the 10th Symposium on Haptic Interfaces for Virtual Environment and Teleoperator Systems*, p. 354, Orlando, Fla, USA, March 2002.

[8] M. Shimojo, M. Shinohara, and Y. Fukui, "Human shape recognition performance and pin-matrix density in a 3 dimensional tactile display," in *Proceedings of the 5th IEEE International Workshop on Robot and Human Communication*, pp. 513–518, Tsukuba, Japan, November 1996.

[9] J. K. Salisbury and M. A. Srinivasan, "Phantom-based haptic interaction with virtual objects," *IEEE Computer Graphics and Applications*, vol. 17, no. 5, pp. 6–10, 1997.

[10] M. Ishii, M. Nakata, and M. Sato, "Networked SPIDAR: a networked virtual environment with visual, auditory, and haptic interactions," *Presence*, vol. 3, no. 4, pp. 351–359, 1994.

[11] S. Tachi, T. Maeda, R. Hirata, and H. Hoshino, "A construction method of virtual haptic space," in *Proceedings of the 4th International Conference on Artificial Reality and Tele-existence (ICAT '94)*, pp. 131–138, Tokyo, Japan, July1994.

[12] Y. Yokokohji, N. Muramori, Y. Sato, and T. Yoshikawa, "Designing an encountered-type haptic display for multiple fingertip contacts based on the observation of human grasping behavior," in *Proceedings of the 12th International Symposium on Haptic Interfaces for Virtual Environment and Teleoperator Systems (HAPTICS '04)*, pp. 66–73, Chicago, Ill, USA, March 2004.

[13] A. Frisoli, M. Solazzi, F. Salsedo, and M. Bergamasco, "A fingertip haptic display for improving curvature discrimination," *Presence*, vol. 17, no. 6, pp. 550–561, 2008.

[14] M. A. Salada, J. E. Colgate, M. V. Lee, and P. M. Vishton, "Fingertip haptics: a novel direction in haptic display," in *Proceedings of the 8th Mechatronics Forum International Conference*, pp. 1211–1220, Enschede, The Netherlands, June 2002.

[15] W. R. Provancher, M. R. Cutkosky, K. J. Kuchenbecker, and G. Niemeyer, "Contact location display for haptic perception of curvature and object motion," *International Journal of Robotics Research*, vol. 24, no. 9, pp. 691–702, 2005.

[16] M. Hollins and S. R. Risner, "Evidence for the duplex theory of tactile texture perception," *Perception and Psychophysics*, vol. 62, no. 4, pp. 695–705, 2000.

[17] T. Miyaoka, T. Mano, and M. Ohka, "Mechanisms of fine-surface-texture discrimination in human tactile sensation," *Journal of the Acoustical Society of America*, vol. 105, no. 4, pp. 2485–2492, 1999.

[18] S. J. Lederman, "Tactual roughness perception: spatial and temporal determinants," *Canadian Journal of Psychology*, vol. 37, no. 4, pp. 498–511, 1983.

[19] M. Hollins, S. J. Bensmaïa, and S. Washburn, "Vibrotactile adaptation impairs discrimination of fine, but not coarse, textures," *Somatosensory and Motor Research*, vol. 18, no. 4, pp. 253–262, 2001.

[20] C. E. Connor and K. O. Johnson, "Neural coding of tactile texture: comparison of spatial and temporal mechanisms for roughness perception," *Journal of Neuroscience*, vol. 12, no. 9, pp. 3414–3426, 1992.

[21] M. Kahrimanovic, W. M. Bergmann Tiest, and A. M. L. Kappers, "Context effects in haptic perception of roughness," *Experimental Brain Research*, vol. 194, no. 2, pp. 287–297, 2009.

[22] M. A. Heller and T. D. Joyner, "Mechanisms in the haptic horizontal-vertical illusion: evidence from sighted and blind subjects," *Perception and Psychophysics*, vol. 53, no. 4, pp. 422–428, 1993.

[23] M. Hollins and A. K. Goble, "Perception of the length of voluntary movements," *Somatosensory Research*, vol. 5, no. 4, pp. 335–348, 1988.

[24] B. L. Whitsel, O. Franzen, D. A. Dreyer et al., "Dependence of subjective traverse length on velocity of moving tactile stimuli," *Somatosensory Research*, vol. 3, no. 3, pp. 185–196, 1986.

[25] A. M. Smith, C. E. Chapman, M. Deslandes, J. S. Langlais, and M. P. Thibodeau, "Role of friction and tangential force variation in the subjective scaling of tactile roughness," *Experimental Brain Research*, vol. 144, no. 2, pp. 211–223, 2002.

[26] T. Yoshioka, J. C. Craig, G. C. Beck, and S. S. Hsiao, "Perceptual constancy of texture roughness in the tactile system," *Journal of Neuroscience*, vol. 31, no. 48, pp. 17603–17611, 2011.

[27] E. M. Meftah, L. Belingard, and C. E. Chapman, "Relative effects of the spatial and temporal characteristics of scanned surfaces on human perception of tactile roughness using passive touch," *Experimental Brain Research*, vol. 132, no. 3, pp. 351–361, 2000.

[28] M. P. Vitello, M. O. Ernst, and M. Fritschi, "An instance of tactile suppression: active exploration impairs tactile sensitivity for the direction of lateral movement," in *Proceedings of the The EuroHaptics Conference*, pp. 351–355, Paris, France, July 2006.

[29] S. Yamamoto and S. Kitazawa, "Reversal of subjective temporal order due to arm crossing," *Nature Neuroscience*, vol. 4, no. 7, pp. 759–765, 2001.

[30] S. Kuroki, J. Watanabe, N. Kawakami, S. Tachi, and S. Nishida, "Somatotopic dominance in tactile temporal processing," *Experimental Brain Research*, vol. 203, no. 1, pp. 51–62, 2010.

[31] J. C. Craig, "The effect of hand position and pattern motion on temporal order judgments," *Perception and Psychophysics*, vol. 65, no. 5, pp. 779–788, 2003.

[32] S. Kuroki, J. Watanabe, K. Mabuchi, S. Tachi, and S. Nishida, "Directional remapping in tactile inter-finger apparent motion: a motion aftereffect study," *Experimental Brain Research*, vol. 216, no. 2, pp. 311–320, 2011.

[33] H. N. Ho, J. Watanabe, H. Ando, and M. Kashino, "Somatotopic or spatiotopic? Frame of reference for localizing thermal sensations under thermo-tactile interactions," *Attention, Perception, and Psychophysics*, vol. 72, no. 6, pp. 1666–1675, 2010.

[34] E. Azanon and S. Soto-Faraco, "Changing Reference Frames during the Encoding of Tactile Events," *Current Biology*, vol. 18, no. 14, pp. 1044–1049, 2008.

# 7

# Haptic Addition to a Visual Menu Selection Interface Controlled by an In-Vehicle Rotary Device

**Camilla Grane and Peter Bengtsson**

*Division of Human Work Science, Department of Business Administration, Technology and Social Sciences, Luleå University of Technology, 97187 Luleå, Sweden*

Correspondence should be addressed to Camilla Grane, camgra@ltu.se

Academic Editor: Ian Oakley

Today, several vehicles are equipped with a visual display combined with a haptic rotary device for handling in-vehicle information system tasks while driving. This experimental study investigates whether a haptic addition to a visual interface interferes with or supports secondary task performance and whether haptic information could be used without taking eyes off road. Four interfaces were compared during simulated driving: visual only, partly corresponding visual-haptic, fully corresponding visual-haptic, and haptic only. Secondary task performance and subjective mental workload were measured. Additionally, the participants were interviewed. It was found that some haptic support improved performance. However, when more haptic information was used, the results diverged in terms of task completion time and interface comprehension. Some participants did not sense all haptics provided, some did not comprehend the correspondence between the haptic and visual interfaces, and some did. Interestingly, the participants managed to complete the tasks when using haptic-only information.

## 1. Introduction

As complexity in vehicles increases, new techniques are being developed to reduce the demands on a driver's attention [1–5]. Because driving is mainly a visual task [6], many new systems have been developed to reduce visual load by providing supporting auditory or haptic information. For example, a haptic rotary device can provide haptic information intended to support interaction with a visual user interface. In this paper, we focus on this type of haptic information.

Today, several cars are outfitted with haptic rotary devices to help the driver handle secondary tasks [7]. This type of haptic information includes kinaesthetic and tactile sensations [8] provided through active touch [9]. An exploratory procedure of repeated hand movement [10], in this case turning the rotary device back and forth, is required to perceive the haptic information. Haptic information includes the placement of a ridge between menu items [7] and special haptic effects for scrolling through a list or searching for radio stations. These kinds of haptic effects could help a driver if designed to extend or correlate with the visual information. That is, the haptic interface provides similar information as the visual interface. This redundant information may help drivers perform actions without looking at the visual display. If the driver knows that a desired function is three steps to the right in the menu, the driver can select the correct function by simply counting the haptic ridges, a strategy that allows the driver to keep focus on the road. In principle, this ability to multitask while maintaining one's main visual attention on the task of driving might be a positive outcome of the new multimodal techniques developed for in-vehicle use. However, the effects of complementary haptic information are not fully understood. For example, it is unclear whether the mental resources required to operate haptic devices make such devices unsafe. Many studies have shown that high mental workload negatively impacts driving [11–17]. Hence, the challenge with the new visual-haptic techniques is to find a way of communicating information that supports rather than burdens or confuses the driver.

These new multimodal techniques use more than one sense, a strategy addressed in multiple resources and time-sharing theories. According to Wickens [18], multiple resource theory concludes that sometimes it is better to divide information across modalities instead of presenting all information through the same modality. Although this assumption is somewhat vague, Wickens [18] argues that the effectiveness of multiple modalities could be due to the fact that different senses use different resources. Furthermore, the multiple resource theory [18] states that some information is better suited for one modality even though that modality is time-shared with another task using the same modality. Moreover, the model refers to the visual and auditory modalities, but it is not clear if the same holds for the visual and haptic modality. Therefore, it is difficult to predict the relationship between vision and haptics, especially in highly demanding tasks such as driving a vehicle. Nevertheless, some studies have shown that using a combination of visual and haptic information can be beneficial [19, 20], a conclusion that suggests similar multimodal effects concerning secondary tasks might be expected while driving.

Few studies comprise haptic interfaces for in-vehicle use, and typically these studies deal with force feedback or vibrotactile information. Force feedback provided through a haptic gas pedal was found promising when a car was closely following other cars [21]. Moreover, vibrotactile information has proven effective for directing a driver's attention and for presenting direction information [22, 23]. According to Van Erp and Van Veen [23], visual direction information induced a higher workload than vibrotactile information. Furthermore, the fastest reaction time was found with multimodal visual-vibrotactile information. Van Erp and Van Veen's study [23] implies that drivers may benefit from haptic information. However, vibrations are primarily for on/off information; more complex content is difficult to present through vibrations. New haptic devices, providing haptic cues in different ways, are constantly being developed to ease handling of in-vehicle secondary tasks [24–27]. These haptic devices usually do not evoke actions rather they support driver-initiated activities.

Rydström et al. [28] studied the use of a haptic rotary device providing specific haptic cues as a complement to an in-vehicle visual interface. For example, a haptic cue marked where a radio station could be found with an attraction force. The haptic cues were compared to a reference interface with more common haptic effects, such as ridges placed between different alternatives. One of five haptic cues improved performance in terms of task completion time and reduced the number of glances off road. It was not clear whether the lack of improvement for the other haptic cues was due to design issues, unfamiliarity, or something else such as mental overload. However, since the reference interface also included haptic information, the results do not exclude haptics as a positive complement for in-vehicle design. Lederman and Abbott [29] presented an interesting theory about ecological validity that might explain the somewhat negative results for haptic cues in the study by Rydström et al. [28]. Lederman and Abbott [29] concluded that, since early computers mainly presented information visually, users are more sensitive and open to visual stimuli in computer interfaces even when haptic cues are provided; that is, because users expect visual information, visual information overpowers information provided by the other senses. On the other hand, when a haptic rotary device is used, the interface has similarities with a traditional mechanical knob that commonly provides inflexible haptic steps. Consequently, based on Lederman and Abbott [29], haptic effects that resemble mechanical knobs could be expected to have higher ecological value than new and unexpected haptic cues, such as those used by Rydström et al. [28]. According to Hayward et al. [8], haptic effects do not need to imitate reality; they need only to be suggestive. Hence, haptic cues may be more accepted and easily sensed if simultaneously presented with visual cues.

A haptic rotary device was also used in a study by Grane and Bengtsson [30]. Instead of complementing haptic cues, as used by Rydström et al. [28], the study by Grane and Bengtsson [30] comprised a fully corresponding haptic and visual interface that provided the same information through both channels. This could be done using different textures as menu items instead of functions. Because textures can effectively be perceived both haptically and visually [31–33]; textures were considered suitable for modality comparisons. Additionally, the textures made it possible to investigate if the participants could learn to choose between menu items in an interface with haptic-only information. It was thought that experienced users would be able to find and select frequently used functions without taking their eyes off road if the interface provided effective haptics. Grane and Bengtsson [30] found it possible to use a haptic-only interface even though the visual-haptic interfaces in the study resulted in better performance. Furthermore, a fully corresponding visual-haptic interface induced significantly less mental workload and fewer turn errors, that is, when a target was passed without being selected, than a more common interface with visual information supported by haptic ridges placed between menu items. Based on these results, a fully corresponding interface was predicted to have benefits in high-workload environments; however, this needs to be studied further by including a driving task. A haptic addition to a visual interface could help drivers keep their eyes on the road. However, since driving is a highly demanding cognitive task, there is a risk that added information could confuse rather than help drivers.

This study investigates the use of a visual interface combined with a haptic rotary device for solving menu selection tasks during simulated driving. The purpose was to determine whether a haptic interface that corresponds well to a visual interface interferes with or supports secondary task performance and whether the haptic interface could be used without drivers taking their eyes off the road. Four interfaces were compared during simulated driving: visual only, partly corresponding visual-haptic, fully corresponding visual-haptic, and haptic only. The interfaces were experimentally compared in terms of task completion time and error rate. In addition, mental workload was measured and the participants were interviewed. Interviews were used to provide a deeper understanding of the statistical data and to capture the participants' comprehension and interpretation of the interfaces.

Three hypotheses were made in the experimental study. First, a haptic addition was expected to improve secondary task performance. Second, a fully corresponding visual-haptic interface was expected to produce better performance results than a partly corresponding interface. Third, it was expected that a haptic-only interface would allow tasks to be completed successfully although generating lower performance than interfaces that also provided visual information.

## 2. Experiment Method

*2.1. Participants.* Forty first-year engineering students (27 men and 13 women) participated in the study as part of an academic course. The participants were between 19 and 25 years old ($M = 20.4$, SD $= 1.5$). None of the participants had experience with the haptic rotary device or the simulator environment used in the study.

*2.2. Equipment.* A simple desktop simulator was set up in accordance with the equipment specified in the Lane Change Test User Guide 1.2 [34]. Figure 1 shows the driving environment with a 20′ LCD monitor (2) and a Logitech Momo Racing steering wheel (1) placed in front of the participant. The figure also shows the equipment for solving a menu selection task: a haptic rotary device (3), a laptop computer (4), and a 6.4′ display (5). The haptic rotary device (Alps Haptic Commander) is a knob (Ø 3.5 cm) that could be turned and pushed. The equipment for the menu selection task was placed in the imagined centre stack with the haptic rotary device placed about a forearm's distance from the participant and approximately 30 degrees from the participant's right side. The laptop computer was also placed on a 30-degree angle from the participant's centreline, and the 6.4′ display was placed just under the monitor associated with the primary task. All equipment was fixed, but the participant's chair was adjustable. All the participants could position themselves at a comfortable distance from the steering wheel and haptic rotary device.

*2.3. Simulated Driving.* The Lane Change Test (LCT) method was chosen as the primary task since it is a simulated driving task with a high level of control and reliability [35] suitable for comparing different conditions. The driving scene and driving task was simple and the same for all participants. When using the LCT, the participant drove for about three minutes on a straight three-lane road on which no other cars or obstacles were present. The driving task was to keep the car inside a driving lane and change lanes when directed by signs. Eighteen signs were placed along the road to show which lane to choose. There were different tracks available in the LCT method, and a variation of tracks was recommended to avoid learning effects. The tracks only differed in which order the signs were placed. The signs were placed the same distance apart. In this study, tracks one through five were used once for each participant and the order of the tracks

FIGURE 1: The figure shows the experimental setup: a steering wheel (1), a screen with a simulated highway (2), a haptic rotary device (3), a laptop used for the menu selection task (4), and a 6.4′ display (5).

was consistent. The driving speed was controlled by the test leader and fixed to 60 km/h.

*2.4. Haptic and Visual Interface Design.* The experimental task was a simple menu selection task programmed in and controlled by Macromedia Director 8.5. Textures were used as menu items instead of letters or functions, which are more common in these types of studies. The textures made it possible to create a fully corresponding visual-haptic interface. Moreover, textures were necessary to investigate whether a haptic interface could be used alone. Four textures—A, B, C, and D—were presented to the participants as visual images on the laptop screen and/or perceived as haptic effects through the haptic rotary device (presented in alphabetical order in Figure 2). The textures were designed using ergonomic policies developed by Ivergård [36] and results from user tests. The visual interface was created in Adobe Illustrator CS5 and the haptic interface with Alps Rotary Haptic Editor. Repeated click effects with a linearly changing torque were used to create the haptic textures (Table 1).

The rotation angle for a whole menu was 150 degrees; the rotation angle for each menu item was 30 degrees with 10 degrees in between. For some experimental conditions, a haptic ridge separated the menu items. A ridge was made by a single click effect with a linearly changing torque of 5 mN m/deg, a maximum torque of 50 mN m, and a traction force of 30%. A traction force makes the click effect more distinct. Haptic walls were placed at the menu borders as end stops with a steep incline (50 mN m/deg) and a maximum torque set at 90 mN m. A damper effect, that is, a friction proportional to the knob velocity, was added over the whole menu to reduce unwanted vibrations. The damper coefficient (d) was set to 30 mN m s. The damper torque can be calculated as $-d^*$ the velocity (rad/s).

*2.5. Experimental Conditions.* The interface had four menu fields with different textures. The menus and textures were either presented visually and/or haptically. Figure 2 presents the experimental conditions compared in the study:

  (i) interface V: visual only,

  (ii) interface pVH: partly corresponding visual-haptic,

TABLE 1: Specification of the haptic effects used in the experiment.

| Texture | Length (deg) | Repetition | Max. torque (mN m) | Torque/deg (mN m/deg) | Traction force (%) |
|---------|-------------|------------|---------------------|------------------------|---------------------|
| A | 1 | 30 | 0 | 0 | 0 |
| B | 15 | 2 | 10 | 3 | 30 |
| C | 5 | 6 | 10 | 9 | 30 |
| D | 1 | 30 | 10 | 40 | 30 |

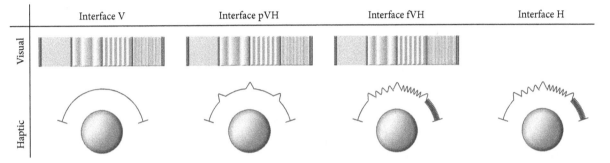

FIGURE 2: The visual and haptic information provided in the four different interfaces (V, pVH, fVH, and H). The haptic information is represented visually around the haptic rotary device. The visual and haptic textures are placed in alphabetic order (A, B, C, and D).

(iii) interface fVH: fully corresponding visual-haptic, and

(iv) interface H: haptic only.

The visual-only interface (V) had no haptic support other than end stops, that is, haptic walls at the beginning and at the end of a menu. Similar end stops were also found in the other three interfaces. The partly corresponding visual-haptic interface (pVH) used the same visual interface as V with an addition of sensible menu field boarders, that is, haptic ridges placed in between the menu fields. In the fully corresponding interface (fVH), the visual interface information was also presented haptically; that is, both menu field boarders and textures were presented visually and haptically. In the haptic-only interface (H), the menu field boarders and textures could be felt, as in fVH, but no visual information was provided.

*2.6. Experimental Design.* The experiment used an intersubjects design as Rydström and Bengtsson [37] found asymmetric learning effects in a similar study. Ten participants were randomly assigned to each experimental condition.

*2.7. Procedure.* An experimental session lasted about one hour, and the test leader gave all participants the same instructions. Each session started with the simulated driving. The participants drove on two practice tracks, one immediately after the other. Thereafter, the menu selection task was explained and the participants practiced the task during two training trials. The first training trial presented the textures in alphabetic order with the label "A," "B," "C," or "D" displayed on the laptop monitor. In this trial, the participants learned the textures, noting when they felt they were ready to continue. The second training trial resembled the experimental trial. The participants were asked to find and select one of four textures identified as the target.

The texture to select, for example, "Locate A," was given through headphones by a computer voice as well as displayed on the 6.4′ display. The start position was always on the left most texture, and the active texture was marked blue. The participants turned the haptic rotary device to the appropriate texture and selected it by pressing the device. If they selected the right texture, a tone was played, the textures changed order, and a new target texture was given. If they selected a wrong texture, nothing happened. To proceed, they had to select the right texture. This training phase continued until 12 correct selections were made in a sequence. That is, the training phase required them to select each texture correctly at least two times. The length of a practice trial differed between participants, but at the beginning of the experimental trials all of the participants had reached the threshold level of proficiency. In the experimental trial, the participants drove three tracks in the LCT and carried out tasks with the rotary device at the same time. The order of textures and target textures were counterbalanced and did not change between participants. Twelve textures were selected during a driving round, which took approximately three minutes. The experimental tasks occurred once every 13 seconds throughout the whole round except for a small pause at the beginning and end. The time (13 seconds) was selected to reduce a floor effect and was based on results from a prestudy. To ensure that selections were based on visual and haptic perception only, pink noise was provided through the headphones. At the end of each experiment, the participants completed one questionnaire that asked them to provide information about themselves (e.g., their level of computer experience) and completed two NASA-TLX forms [38].

*2.8. Measurements and Analysis.* Performance was measured as the time it took to complete a task and the number of errors made. Two types of errors were measured: push errors and turn errors. A push error was registered when the participants selected a texture that was not a target. When the participants went past the right texture without selecting it, a turn error was registered. In the analysis, the number of push errors was divided by the total number of tasks for each participant. This did not change the data or the results but made the results more informative. The same was done for the turn errors. If the participants did not manage to select a texture within 13 seconds, the task was logged as a missing value and given the highest possible time in the analysis, 13 seconds. NASA-TLX [38] was used to measure the participants' experienced mental workload. After the experimental trials, the participants completed two NASA-TLX forms: the rating scale form and the pair-wise comparison form. In addition to descriptive statistics, the results from the menu selection task and the NASA-TLX forms were analysed with the Kruskal-Wallis tests. The interfaces were also compared pair-wise with the Mann-Whitney tests to answer the hypothesis. Nonparametric tests were used due to nonnormally distributed data and nonhomogeneity. To answer the third hypothesis, the total amount of push errors made by each participant was analysed using binomial distribution (the Bernoulli trial). The $\alpha$ level was set to 0.05.

## 3. Experiment Results

*3.1. Task Completion Time.* Figure 3 shows a boxplot of the mean task completion time (s) for each interface. The box-plot shows a larger spread for the fully corresponding visual-haptic interface (fVH) compared to the other interfaces. A significant difference was found between the interfaces with the Kruskal-Wallis test (H (3) = 18.76, $P < .001$). To test the first hypothesis, the visual-only interface (V) was compared to the two interfaces with a haptic addition (pVH and fVH) with the Mann-Whitney tests. The menu selection tasks were completed significantly faster with the partly corresponding interface (pVH) ($U = 11.00$, $P = .003$, $r = -.66$). However, no difference was found between V and fVH ($U = 39.00$, $P = .406$, $r = -.19$). To test the second hypothesis, the partly corresponding interface (pVH) was compared to the fully corresponding interface (fVH), revealing no difference ($U = 39.50$, $P = .427$, $r = -.18$). To test the third hypothesis, the haptic-only interface (H) was compared with the interfaces with visual information. The haptic-only interface needed significantly longer time to complete a task than the other interfaces: H-V ($U = 10.00$, $P = .002$, $r = -.68$), H-pVH ($U = .00$, $P = .000$, $r = -.85$), and H-fVH ($U = 19.00$, $P = .019$, $r = -.52$).

*3.2. Turn Errors.* The spread of turn errors (%) in each interface is visualised with a boxplot (Figure 4). The Kruskal-Wallis test revealed a significant difference between the interfaces (H (3) = 19.32, $P < .001$). The first hypothesis, tested with the Mann-Whitney tests, revealed that significantly more turn errors were made with only visual information (V) compared to the partly corresponding visual-haptic

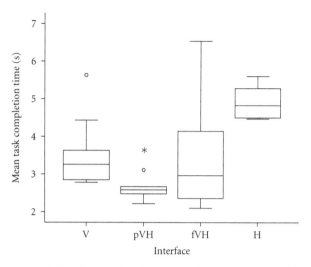

FIGURE 3: Boxplot showing the mean task completion time (s).

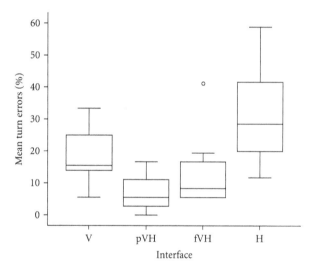

FIGURE 4: Boxplot showing the turn errors (%).

interface (pVH) ($U = 16.00$, $P = .010$, $r = -.58$). However, no difference was found between V and fVH ($U = 29.50$, $P = .118$, $r = -.35$). When the second hypothesis was tested, no difference between the partly and fully corresponding interfaces was found ($U = 31.00$, $P = .146$, $r = -.33$). In addition, the test of the third hypothesis revealed that significantly more turn errors were made with the haptic-only interface than the interfaces with visual information: H-V ($U = 22.00$, $P = .034$, $r = -.47$), H-pVH ($U = 2.00$, $P = .000$, $r = -.81$), and H-fVH ($U = 9.50$, $P = .002$, $r = -.69$).

*3.3. Push Errors.* No significant differences were found with the Kruskal-Wallis test for push errors (H (3) = 7.56, $P = .056$). The Mann-Whitney tests were used to answer the three hypotheses. Significantly more push errors were made with the haptic-only interface (H) than with the partly corresponding interface (pVH) ($U = 18.50$, $P = .015$, $r = -.55$). No other differences were found. Table 2 presents the median values and ranges of push errors for each interface.

The third hypothesis was tested with the Bernouilli trial. The largest number of push errors made by a participant using the haptic-only interface was used in the analyses, that is, 13 push errors out of 36 selections. With the probability of selecting a nontarget set to .75, the probability of making 13 or fewer push errors out of 36 selections by chance was less than .05 ($P = 9.47E - 07$).

*3.4. Mental Workload.* No significant differences were found with the Kruskal-Wallis test for mental workload (H (3) = .89, $P = .828$). The Mann-Whitney tests were used to answer the three hypotheses. No differences were found. Table 2 presents the median values and ranges of mental workload for each interface.

## 4. Interview Method

*4.1. Respondents.* Every participant attending the experiment was also interviewed at the end of each experimental session.

*4.2. Interview Design and Questions.* Interviews were used to provide a deeper understanding of the statistical data by capturing the participants' experiences and comprehension of the different interface conditions. The interviews were semistructured since we wished to compare the answers between different interface conditions. Every participant was asked the same questions, but the questions were sometimes explained, followed up, or adjusted to suit the type of interface they had used. The questions were all open ended since we were interested in the participants' thoughts, experiences, and difficulties with the different interfaces. We did not know what to expect and could therefore not ask specific questions with predetermined answer alternatives. The interviews all began with questions concerning the menu selection task: "How did it feel to use the rotary device and the user interface you used for solving the tasks?" and "What did you find good and bad?" All participants were asked how they experienced their performance: "How do you think you managed to drive and carry out tasks at the same time?" The participants were also asked more specific questions about the information presented in their interface related to other information. These questions were different according to the interfaces used. For example, the participants from the visual-only interface were asked the following questions: "How do you think it would have been if you were able to feel ridges between the menu alternatives?", "How do you think it would have been if you also could sense the textures when you were moving pass them?", and "How do you think it would have been if you could sense the textures but not see them?". The participants that experienced the fully corresponding visual-haptic interface were also asked more specific questions about their comprehension of the information: "You could both see and feel the four textures. Which information did you use the most?" and "Was any information unnecessary?" The interviews lasted about ten minutes and were conducted in Swedish, the participants' native language. Each interview was, with permission from the participants, recorded on tape.

TABLE 2: Median and range of push errors and mental workload for each interface.

| Interface | Push errors (%) | | Mental workload | |
|---|---|---|---|---|
| | Median | Range | Median | Range |
| V | 2.78 | 13.89 | 736.50 | 891.00 |
| pVH | 1.39 | 8.33 | 682.75 | 441.50 |
| fVH | 4.17 | 11.76 | 635.75 | 683.50 |
| H | 10.13 | 36.11 | 678.25 | 595.00 |

*4.3. Analysis.* A method similar to the sequential analyses described by Miles and Huberman [39] was used for the analyses. At first, the interviews were transcribed verbatim and reduced to individual case synopses. Since the interview material was short, the next step in the analyses was to make matrices with key terms and key phrases. Thereafter, the phrases were reduced or labelled as quotations. The material was further analysed by creating clusters and attaching labels, such as plus or minus signs. The matrices made it possible to produce an overview of the material and to compare answers between the interface conditions. The data was not analysed with statistical methods since open-ended questions were used. If some participants identified a specific feature as important, it did not mean that the other participants would have agreed or disagreed. However, those comments could still help explain the statistical data. Therefore, the answers were summarized in text form describing key incidents as "the majority," "some," or "a few" and similar. The actual answer incidences can be found in Tables 3–5 and, for some parts, directly in the text. The key words and quotations used in the results section have been translated into English.

## 5. Interview Results

*5.1. Spontaneous Remarks.* At the opening of the interviews, the participants were asked how it felt to use the interface for the menu selection task and what they considered good and bad about the interface. The spontaneous answers differed depending on which interface was used (Table 3). However, participants from the same interface group often used similar expressions and mentioned the same problems. To describe their user interfaces, many participants from V and pVH used the phrases "easy to use," "easy to learn," and "it felt good." Some participants from fVH also described the user interface "as easy to use." The participants from H were least satisfied with the user interface. Some of them described the only-haptic interface as "quite easy" or "fairly easy" to use. They thought it was troublesome in the beginning, but after a while they got used to it. Almost all participants from the haptic-only interface (H) mentioned difficulties differentiating a pair of the textures. However, the participants did not find the same textures similar. For example, some participants had problems with texture A and B while others mentioned C and D. Only a few from the interfaces with visual information mentioned problems differentiating or finding textures. Some participants from interface V mentioned problems with turn errors. The marker sometimes moved passed the target when they tried

Table 3: Answer incidences for spontaneous remarks.

| | Interface V | Interface pVH | Interface fVH | Interface H |
|---|---|---|---|---|
| Easy to use | 6 | 5 | 3 | 0 |
| Fairly easy | 0 | 0 | 1 | 6 |
| No label | 4 | 5 | 6 | 4 |
| Differentiation problems | 2 | 2 | 2 | 9 |
| No label | 8 | 8 | 8 | 1 |
| Turn errors | 3 | 0 | 0 | 0 |
| No label | 7 | 10 | 10 | 10 |

Table 4: Answer incidences for experienced performance.

| | Interface V | Interface pVH | Interface fVH | Interface H |
|---|---|---|---|---|
| Good | 1 | 6 | 3 | 1 |
| Fairly good | 6 | 3 | 5 | 2 |
| Passable | 3 | 0 | 1 | 7 |
| No label | 0 | 1 | 1 | 0 |

to select it, or they turned too far since there were no ridges between the menu items. No participants from the other interfaces mentioned the same problem.

*5.1.1. Interface V.* Two participants from interface V spontaneously said that they had preferred a user interface with haptic ridges provided from the rotary device. This was expressed from one participant as "I would like to see that it had some form of response when turning it… it may perhaps be some ridge or so."

*5.1.2. Interface pVH.* Two participants spontaneously remarked that the haptic ridges were positive. One of them said, "It was good that there were ridges… because I looked at the display and then I saw where it (the target) was and could sort of count out were [sic] it was with the ridges".

*5.1.3. Interface fVH.* The opinions of interface fVH diverged. Two participants described the haptics as non-congruent: they found no correlation between what they felt and saw. Two other participants spontaneously said they had preferred haptic ridges instead of haptic ridges and textures. One participant expressed it as "(y)ou could not really feel where you were… you felt these structures instead. I had probably thought it was better if there were only four positions". Another participant had the opposite opinion: "I liked it (the haptic textures); it is better than merely ridges."

*5.1.4. Interface H.* Two participants from interface H spontaneously said they would have preferred more visual feedback. Two others wanted more pronounced ridges and larger space for the textures or in-between textures. One wanted the textures to differ more and another wanted an addition of auditory information.

*5.2. Experienced Performance.* The participants explained their performance differently depending on which interface they had used (Table 4). The majority of participants who used interface pVH described their performance as "good," whereas most of the participants who used interfaces V and fVH expressed their performance as "fairly good." The participants who used interface H were least satisfied with their performance. One participant said, "(i)t was more

difficult than I thought; you got a bit stressed when you did not really find the right texture".

*5.3. Interface Preferences.* The participants had a relatively clear idea of how it would have been to have other types of information, although they occasionally thought it hard to imagine. Table 5 presents the positive and negative responses to different types of information. The information discussed was similar to the different interfaces compared in the experimental study, and the results are therefore grouped accordingly.

*5.3.1. Interface V.* Almost all participants from interface pVH and fVH wanted more than just visual information. A participant from interface pVH feared that "(t)he risk is… that you, when you push, happen to move it (the cursor) to another menu item." Six participants from pVH and five from fVH specifically explained that without haptic information they would have taken their eyes off the road more often. With respect to the haptic information, they said they could watch the road while performing the task by counting the ridges. Many participants from interface H were negative about only visual information. One participant would have preferred to have only visual information instead of haptic-only, and two participants said they would rather have had haptic-only information than visual-only information. One participant who preferred haptic-only information argued that it was "(b)etter to use the perception of touch so that you will not need to look off the road."

*5.3.2. Interface pVH.* When interface pVH was discussed, the tone was different. Almost all of the comments about this interface were positive. The arguments for interface pVH were very much the same independent of which interface the participant had used. A participant from interface V expressed the common argument for visual information with ridges: "(i)t would probably be much easier because… then it is only to turn without looking at the display because you know how many clicks there should be".

*5.3.3. Interface fVH.* When interface fVH was discussed, the responses were more positive than negative from participants that used interface V and H, whereas the number of negative and positive responses from participants who used interface pVH were similar. Participants from interface V and pVH had similar arguments for and against an addition of haptic textures. A typical positive response came from one participant from interface V: "It had possibly been better because then you would not need to look on that (the visual

TABLE 5: Answer incidences for interface preferences.

| | Opinions about visual-only information (V) | | | |
| --- | --- | --- | --- | --- |
| | Positive | Fairly positive | Negative | No label |
| Interface pVH | 0 | 0 | 9 | 1 |
| Interface fVH | 0 | 0 | 9 | 1 |
| Interface H | 1 | 1 | 5 | 3 |
| | Opinions about visual information and haptic ridges (pVH) | | | |
| | Positive | Fairly positive | Negative | No label |
| Interface V | 7 | 2 | 1 | 0 |
| Interface fVH | 5 | 2 | 1 | 2 |
| Interface H | 4 | 0 | 0 | 6 |
| | Opinions about fully corresp. visual-haptic information (fVH) | | | |
| | Positive | Fairly positive | Negative | No label |
| Interface V | 5 | 1 | 2 | 2 |
| Interface pVH | 5 | 0 | 5 | 0 |
| Interface H | 5 | 0 | 3 | 2 |
| | Opinions about haptic-only information (H) | | | |
| | Positive | Fairly positive | Negative | No label |
| Interface V | 1 | 3 | 5 | 1 |
| Interface pVH | 0 | 3 | 7 | 0 |
| Interface fVH | 1 | 4 | 1 | 4 |

interface); you could concentrate on watching the road and just feel". Another participant from interface V gave a typical negative response: "Then you would get more to think on. I would think it could have been a bit laborious". Several participants from interface H thought a visual addition would make the task easier and that it would speed up their responses. However, some feared that it would be too much information and that they would look too much at the display and miss the road.

*5.3.4. Interface H.* The two visual interfaces V and pVH generated mostly negative responses to having haptic information only, as in interface H. One participant from interface V described it in the following way: "It can probably be quite comfortable to have something that you can look at in case you get insecure. It feels as if you trust vision more than the perception of touch". However, not all participants were negative. Some participants from interface V and fVH were fairly positive. For example, one participant from interface fVH chose to use the haptic information only even though he had visual information available.

*5.4. Perception of Interface fVH.* The perception of the fully corresponding visual-haptic interface differed among the participants. Three categories were found: only ridges, ridges and textures—not correlated, and ridges and textures—correlated.

*5.4.1. Only Ridges.* Three participants did not perceive the haptic texture information; they only felt the ridges between menu items, as in pVH. The user interface included haptic texture information; that is, the participants excluded the information by themselves. One of the participants

perceived the textures during training, but not while driving. The participant explained it as "(t)he clicks had different characters for different positions in the beginning (during training), which it never was during the test. Perhaps my brain fooled me, but I thought it felt as if there was one distinct and identical click between every position in the test."

*5.4.2. Ridges and Textures: Not Correlated.* The other participants all perceived the textures, but two of them did not understand the correlation between the visual and haptic information: "It was a bit bumpy, there were ridges or something but when you turned, it did not jump on every step. I saw that I was two steps away, but it was not really only two steps".

*5.4.3. Ridges and Textures: Correlated.* Five of the participants who perceived the textures also understood their purpose. Three of those participants chose not to use the textures. One of them explained it this way: "I think it was a bit odd that you should feel.... It would demand more exercise to use the sense of touch, so now I mostly thought it was a bit disturbing.... I had thought it would be better if there were only four positions". However, two participants deliberately used the haptic textures. One of them did not use the visual information at all: "While I was driving, I did not look at this (the visual interface); you did not have to".

## 6. Discussion

When driving, the eyes and mind need to be focused on the road. Secondary tasks should therefore be carefully designed. Haptic addition to a visual interface could ease interaction or could provide too much information to process. In this study, different amounts of haptic information were studied and both advantages and disadvantages were found. All interfaces were studied while concurrently performing a simulated driving task that needed both visual and cognitive attention. Different results could be found for these types of visual-haptic interfaces in different human-computer situations.

### 6.1. First Hypothesis.

The first hypothesis in this paper was accepted: haptic additions to a visual interface improved performance. Both task completion time and error rate, in terms of turn errors, were significantly lower when haptic ridges were added to the visual interface (pVH). The fully corresponding interface with haptic ridges and texture information did not result in the same positive results and responses. This issue will be addressed and discussed more thoroughly later. The turn error result means that the target was more often passed over without being selected when the interface lacked haptic information. This suggests that the haptic ridges made it easier to stop at a certain position and stay in that position during selection. This suggestion is also evident in the interviews: some participants using interface V spontaneously mentioned these kinds of problems. The positive results for the visual-haptic interface (pVH) in comparison to the visual-only interface (V) agree with Wickens' [18] theory of multiple resources. The addition of a haptic interface reduces the visual load and makes effective multitasking possible. According to the interviews, the haptic ridges were important. Because of the ridges, the participants did not have to look away from the road to find a target. Many participants using interface pVH mentioned they could count the ridges to be sure of their position while watching the road. With only visual information, the participants needed to look away from the road throughout the task. The interview answers indicate that the participants looked off the road less often with the partly corresponding visual-haptic interface (pVH) than with the visual-only interface (V), which is good from a driving and safety perspective. Furthermore, the interview answers revealed that almost all participants who received only visual information preferred haptic ridges and thought the knobs lacked such ridges. This agrees with Lederman and Abbott's [29] theory about ecological validity. The haptic rotary device resembles a mechanical knob that usually provides ridges. This might be expected by the participants and explain why they thought they were lacking. If they had used a nonhaptic computer mouse instead, they might not have thought of haptic ridges as a possible improvement.

### 6.2. Second Hypothesis.

The second hypothesis in the paper was rejected: a fully corresponding interface with haptic textures (fVH) did not produce higher performance results than an interface with haptic ridges (pVH). The haptic rotary device's full potential was used in the fully corresponding visual-haptic interface (fVH) with the intention to ease driver demand and facilitate use. Redundant information was expected to aid decision making. The expectations were based on results from a study by Grane and Bengtsson [30]

where a fully corresponding visual-haptic interface generated fewer turn errors and less mental demand than a partly corresponding interface. In this paper, however, no differences between the interfaces were found, and consequently the results do not correspond with Grane and Bengtsson's [30] findings. The main difference between the two studies is that this study comprised a simulated driving task and the Grane and Bengtsson's [30] study did not. Accordingly, a fully corresponding interface that normally induces low mental demand cannot be expected to give the same positive results in a driving situation. The interviews revealed an inconsistent comprehension of the fully corresponding interface. A few participants reported that the haptic textures were useful while some described them as unnecessary. Apparently, there is a risk that haptic information intended to facilitate the use of a visual menu selection interface is confusing rather than helpful.

### 6.3. The Fully Corresponding Interface.

According to the interviews, the perception and comprehension of the fully corresponding interface varied and three different groups were found. A few participants did not perceive the haptic textures, only the haptic ridges separating the menu items. Guest and Spence [40] point out that there is no evidence for enhanced discrimination performance with visual-haptic texture perception. Rather, the two senses seem to act independently and divided attention between the modalities reduces each senses' ability to discriminate. In highly demanding environments, such as driving a vehicle, this effect could be further augmented. This may explain why some of the participants using the fully corresponding visual-haptic interface only sensed a part of the haptics provided, the haptic ridges. The ridges stood out more since they had a higher torque than the haptic textures and therefore were easier to discriminate.

Some of the participants using the fully corresponding visual-haptic interface (fVH) sensed more haptic information than ridges but did not comprehend the correspondence with the visual information provided. According to Ernst and Bülthoff [41], information from different modalities has to be efficiently merged to form a coherent percept. If visual and haptic information are to be integrated, it should be clear that the information comes from the same object. Wall and Harwin [42] remarked that visual and haptic exploration through probes and monitors provides approximations rather than exact models of natural surfaces. Even if an interface is designed to be corresponding, it is unclear whether users will merge the information as in real life. Exactly how the brain decides to interpret information as a whole is not known. According to Ernst and Bülthoff [41], signals should most likely not differ too much spatially. In the study described in this paper, the information that meets the eye and the hand are separated spatially. It could be difficult for the brain to build a whole from those obvious separated information bearers even though the signals match in time and have a similar design. This may explain why some of the participants using the fully corresponding interface did not interpret it as coherent. However, in a study by Grane and Bengtsson [30], a fully corresponding interface with a similar spatial separation as found in this paper proved better than a partly corresponding interface. The main difference between the study described in this paper and Grane and Bengtsson's study [30] is that Grane and Bengtsson's study [30] lacked a simulated driving task. Therefore, the problem with integrating the haptic and visual information might be an effect of rational resource utilization due to mental overload. According to Ernst and Bülthoff [41], the brain is not willing to wait for an accurate answer if it can deliver a quick, uncertain response. If it is easier to grasp the visual information describing the textures, some of the participants may have responded based on that information only without spending time on the haptic textures. As concluded by Wickens [18] and Lederman and Abbott [29], some tasks are more appropriate for one modality than another. When drivers want to find a target in a menu as quickly as possible, it is naturally more effective to visually scan a menu than to serially turn through a haptic menu. If the textures already are perceived visually, it may seem unnecessary to use mental resources to merge the haptic information with the visual information. The perceived noncorrespondence between the haptic and visual information could also be explained by Lederman and Abbott's [29] theory of ecological validity. It is possible that the participants used a familiar behaviour. Visual menu selection interfaces are more commonly found in daily life without informative haptics. As a result, the participants might have expected the visual information, perhaps accompanied with haptic ridges and consequently would have been more open to the visual stimuli and confused by the haptic textures. With more contact with these types of systems, it might be easier to take in and process the haptic information. More experienced users might learn new interaction strategies that use the haptic information in a resource-effective manner.

Interestingly, some participants using the fully corresponding visual-haptic interface (fVH) had no problems sensing the haptic information and interpreted it as corresponding with the visual interface. According to their interview answers, some still considered the haptic textures as unnecessary although two participants considered them useful. One of those two participants said he did not need the visual information and chose to use only the haptics so he could pay more attention to the road. Why did he do that if the available visual information was more efficient to process? Could it be that the haptic modality dominates over visual for some people? Visual information is traditionally said to dominate haptic information in multimodal tasks. This was shown by Rock and Victor [43] and has been proven by others. Interestingly, in the Rock and Victor [43] study, two out of ten participants mainly used the haptic information, indicating a haptic dominance for those two. Lederman et al. [44] question vision as the dominant modality; they found vision to be important when spatial density was judged and tactile cues important when roughness was judged. Furthermore, McDonnell and Duffett [45] found a clear individual difference in modality dominance. If haptic dominates vision for some people, it could possibly explain why the haptic information was interpreted as

corresponding for some of the participants in the study even though they never had used a similar interface. Accordingly, when designing interfaces for demanding situations such as driving, the designer should not trust that users will use the most efficient information.

*6.4. Third Hypothesis.* In the third hypothesis, the haptic information was expected to be useful even though it would induce lower performance results than when visual information was used concurrently. This hypothesis was tested by including an interface with haptic-only information. By removing the visual interface, the participants were forced to rely on their haptic sense. The third hypothesis was accepted since the participants managed to complete the tasks with this interface. Furthermore, as expected the haptic-only interface demanded more time and resulted in more turn errors than the other interfaces with visual information. In addition, more push errors were made with the haptic-only interface when compared to the partly redundant interface (pVH). For clarification, a turn error was registered when a target was passed without being selected and a push error when the wrong target was selected. Other studies also have found haptic exploration of objects to be more time consuming than visual exploration [30, 31]. This could be expected since a haptic search using a rotary device is restricted to serial and requires repeated hand movements back and forth in a menu field to sense the textures [46]. Moreover, the menu items could easily be compared visually, while a haptic comparison required a hand movement. Haptic comparison of textures while searching for the target could also explain the increased turn errors. If the participants were uncertain about a target and wanted to compare it with other textures, the target sometimes needed to be passed over without being selected, resulting in a turn error. According to the interview answers, the participants using the haptic-only interface had problems differentiating the textures. This explains the increased number of turn errors and the increased number of push errors. It is clear that the haptic information did not provide sufficient support for making quick selections. Most participants using the haptic-only interface described it as difficult to use and would rather use an interface with visual support. Nevertheless, many participants were negative toward visual-only information, a common setup in many vehicles today. Since the interfaces used in this study were developed for this study only, the novelty was high. With more interaction, performance might improve. Furthermore, the interfaces were developed primarily for modality comparison. Other types of haptic effects, developed with a focus on usability, might be more easily comprehended and used, especially after some training.

*6.5. Further Research.* This study focused on secondary task performance. An interesting continuation of this study would be to analyse driving data. Secondary task performance does not necessarily correlate with driver performance. Moreover, the primary task in this study was constituted by a simple desktop simulator. It would be interesting to increase validity by further investigating haptic-visual interfaces with more advanced driving simulators or real driving.

## 7. Conclusions

As expected in the first hypothesis, a multimodal approach that adds haptic information to an in-vehicle visual interface for solving menu selection tasks supported the participants' performance. However, this applied for a visual-haptic interface with marked menu boarders and not for a fully corresponding visual-haptic interface. Consequently, the second hypothesis was rejected. Interestingly, the fully corresponding visual-haptic interface, expected to ease interaction by providing redundant visual-haptic information, was interpreted and comprehended differently by the users. Some participants did not sense all haptics provided, and some did not comprehend the correspondence between the senses. This study makes clear that a haptic interface that correlates well with an in-vehicle visual interface could confuse rather than support some drivers. Furthermore, this study clarifies the importance of including some form of driving task when testing in-vehicle interfaces. The results in this study did not correspond with the findings in a similar study with no driving task [30]. A fully corresponding visual-haptic interface proved better when no driving task was included. Moreover, an informative haptic interface could be used without any visual information, as expected in the third hypothesis. Finally, this study does not present a fully developed solution, but it does provide a step towards an explanation to why haptic interfaces sometime confuse rather than support drivers using in-vehicle interfaces.

## References

[1] P. Bengtsson, C. Grane, and J. Isaksson, "Haptic/graphic interface for in-vehicle comfort functions—a simulator study and an experimental study," in *Proceedings of the 2nd IEEE International Workshop on Haptic, Audio and Visual Environments and their Applications*, pp. 25–29, Ottawa, Canada, September 2003.

[2] G. E. Burnett and J. M. Porter, "Ubiquitous computing within cars: designing controls for non-visual use," *International Journal of Human Computer Studies*, vol. 55, no. 4, pp. 521–531, 2001.

[3] K. Prynne, "Tactile controls," *Automotive Interiors international*, pp. 30–36, 1995.

[4] C. Spence and C. Ho, "Multisensory interface design for drivers: past, present and future," *Ergonomics*, vol. 51, no. 1, pp. 65–70, 2008.

[5] W. W. Wierwille, "Demands on driver resources associated with introducing advanced technology into the vehicle," *Transportation Research Part C*, vol. 1, no. 2, pp. 133–142, 1993.

[6] M. Sivak, "The information that drivers use: is it indeed 90% visual?" *Perception*, vol. 25, no. 9, pp. 1081–1089, 1996.

[7] D. Grant, "Two new commercial haptic rotary controllers," in *Proceedings of the EuroHaptics*, pp. 451–455, Munich, Germany, June 2004.

[8] V. Hayward, O. R. Astley, M. Cruz-Hernandez, D. Grant, and G. Robles-De-La-Torre, "Haptic interfaces and devices," *Sensor Review*, vol. 24, no. 1, pp. 16–29, 2004.

[9] J. J. Gibson, "Observations on active touch," *Psychological Review*, vol. 69, no. 6, pp. 477–491, 1962.

[10] R. L. Klatzky, S. J. Lederman, and D. E. Matula, "Haptic exploration in the presence of vision," *Journal of Experimental Psychology*, vol. 19, no. 4, pp. 726–743, 1993.

[11] H. Alm and L. Nilsson, "The effects of a mobile telephone task on driver behaviour in a car following situation," *Accident Analysis and Prevention*, vol. 27, no. 5, pp. 707–715, 1995.

[12] C. Collet, A. Guillot, and C. Petit, "Phoning while driving I: a review of epidemiological, psychological, behavioural and physiological studies," *Ergonomics*, vol. 53, no. 5, pp. 589–601, 2010.

[13] C. Collet, A. Guillot, and C. Petit, "Phoning while driving II: a review of driving conditions influence," *Ergonomics*, vol. 53, no. 5, pp. 602–616, 2010.

[14] J. Engström, E. Johansson, and J. Östlund, "Effects of visual and cognitive load in real and simulated motorway driving," *Transportation Research Part F*, vol. 8, no. 2, pp. 97–120, 2005.

[15] D. Lamble, T. Kauranen, M. Laakso, and H. Summala, "Cognitive load and detection thresholds in car following situations: safety implications for using mobile (cellular) telephones while driving," *Accident Analysis and Prevention*, vol. 31, no. 6, pp. 617–623, 1999.

[16] T. C. Lansdown, N. Brook-Carter, and T. Kersloot, "Distraction from multiple in-vehicle secondary tasks: vehicle performance and mental workload implications," *Ergonomics*, vol. 47, no. 1, pp. 91–104, 2004.

[17] D. L. Strayer and W. A. Johnston, "Driven to distraction: dual-task studies of simulated driving and conversing on a cellular telephone," *Psychological Science*, vol. 12, no. 6, pp. 462–466, 2001.

[18] C. D. Wickens, "Multiple resources and performance prediction," *Theoretical Issues in Ergonomic Science*, vol. 3, no. 2, pp. 159–177, 2002.

[19] M. S. Prewett, L. Yang, F. R. B. Stilson et al., "The benefits of multimodal information: a meta-analysis comparing visual and visual-tactile feedback," in *Proceedings of the 8th International Conference on Multimodal Interfaces*, pp. 333–338, ACM Press, Alberta, Canada, November 2006.

[20] H. S. Vitense, J. A. Jacko, and V. K. Emery, "Multimodal feedback: an assessment of performance and mental workload," *Ergonomics*, vol. 46, no. 1–3, pp. 68–87, 2003.

[21] M. Mulder, M. Mulder, M. M. van Paassen, and D. A. Abbink, "Haptic gas pedal feedback," *Ergonomics*, vol. 51, no. 11, pp. 1710–1720, 2008.

[22] C. Ho, H. Z. Tan, and C. Spence, "Using spatial vibrotactile cues to direct visual attention in driving scenes," *Transportation Research Part F*, vol. 8, no. 6, pp. 397–412, 2005.

[23] J. B. F. Van Erp and H. A. H. C. Van Veen, "Vibrotactile in-vehicle navigation system," *Transportation Research Part F*, vol. 7, no. 4-5, pp. 247–256, 2004.

[24] F. Asif, J. Vinayakamoorthy, J. Ren, and M. Green, "Haptic controls in cars for making driving more safe," in *Proceedings of the IEEE International Conference on Robotics and Biomimetics (ROBIO '09)*, pp. 2023–2028, Guilin, China, 2009.

[25] G. Costagliola, S. Di Martino, F. Ferrucci, G. Oliviero, U. Montemurro, and A. Paliotti, "Handy: a new interaction device for vehicular information systems," in *Proceedings of the Mobile Human-Computer Interaction (Mobile HCI '04)*, S. Brewster and M. Dunlop, Eds., vol. 3160 of *Lecture Notes in Computer Science*, pp. 264–275, Springer, Glasgow, UK, 2004.

[26] J. Mark Porter, S. Summerskill, G. Burnett, and K. Prynne, "BIONIC – 'eyes-free' design of secondary driving controls," in *Proceedings of the Accessible Design in the Digital World Conference 2005*, Dundee, Scotland, August 2005.

[27] A. Tang, P. McLachlan, K. Lowe, C. R. Saka, and K. MacLean, "Perceiving ordinal data haptically under workload," in *Proceedings of the 7th International Conference on Multimodal Interfaces (ICMI '05)*, pp. 317–324, ACM, Trento, Italy, October 2005.

[28] A. Rydström, R. Broström, and P. Bengtsson, "Can haptics facilitate interaction with an in-vehicle multifunctional interface?" *IEEE Transactions on Haptics*, vol. 2, no. 3, pp. 141–147, 2009.

[29] S. J. Lederman and S. G. Abbott, "Texture perception: studies of intersensory organization using a discrepancy paradigm, and visual versus tactual psychophysics," *Journal of Experimental Psychology*, vol. 7, no. 4, pp. 902–915, 1981.

[30] C. Grane and P. Bengtsson, "Menu selection based on haptic and/or graphic information," in *Proceedings of the 11th International Conference on Human-Computer Interaction*, G. Salvendy, Ed., Las Vegas, Nev, USA, July 2005.

[31] W. M. Bergmann Tiest and A. M. L. Kappers, "Haptic and visual perception of roughness," *Acta Psychologica*, vol. 124, no. 2, pp. 177–189, 2007.

[32] E. Gentaz and Y. Hatwell, "Haptic processing of spatial and material object properties," in *Touching for Knowing: Cognitive Psychology of Haptic Manual Perception*, Y. Hatwell, A. Strieri, and E. Gentaz, Eds., pp. 123–159, J. Benjamins, Amsterdam, The Netherlands, 2003.

[33] M. A. Heller, "Visual and tactual texture perception: intersensory cooperation," *Perception and Psychophysics*, vol. 31, no. 4, pp. 339–344, 1982.

[34] A. G. DaimlerChrysler, Lane Change Test—User Guide 1.2. Stuttgart: DaimlerChrysler AG, Research and Technology, 2004, http://people.usd.edu/~schieber/pdf/LCT-UserGuide.pdf.

[35] S. Mattes, "The lane-change-task as a tool for driver distraction evaluation," in *Quality of Work and Products in Enterprises of the Future*, H. Strasser, K. Kluth, H. Rausch, and H. Bubb, Eds., pp. 57–60, Ergonomia, Stuttgart, Germany, 2003.

[36] T. Ivergård, *Handbook of Control Room Design and Ergonomics*, Taylor and Francis, London, Uk, 1989.

[37] A. Rydström and P. Bengtsson, "Haptic, visual and cross-modal perception of interface information," in *Proceedings of the Human Factors Issues in Complex System Performance*, D. de Waard, G. R. J. Hockey, P. Nickel, and K. A. Brookhuis, Eds., pp. 399–409, Shaker Publishing, Maastricht, The Netherlands, 2007.

[38] S. G. Hart and L. E. Staveland, "Development of NASA-TLX (Task Load Index): results of empirical and theoretical research," in *Human Mental Workload*, P. A. Hancock and N. Meshkati, Eds., pp. 139–183, North-Holland, Amsterdam, The Netherlands, 1988.

[39] M. B. Miles and A. M. Huberman, *Qualitative Data Analysis*, SAGE, Thousand Oaks, Calif, USA, 1994.

[40] S. Guest and C. Spence, "What role does multisensory integration play in the visuotactile perception of texture?" *International Journal of Psychophysiology*, vol. 50, no. 1-2, pp. 63–80, 2003.

[41] M. O. Ernst and H. H. Bülthoff, "Merging the senses into a robust percept," *Trends in Cognitive Sciences*, vol. 8, no. 4, pp. 162–169, 2004.

[42] S. A. Wall and W. S. Harwin, "Interaction of visual and haptic information in simulated environments: texture perception," in *Proceedings of the Haptic Human-Computer Interaction 2000*, S. Brewster and R. Murray-Smith, Eds., pp. 108–117, Springer, Glasgow, UK, August-September 2000.

[43] I. Rock and J. Victor, "Vision and touch: an experimentally created conflict between the two senses," *Science*, vol. 143, no. 3606, pp. 594–596, 1964.

[44] S. J. Lederman, G. Thorne, and B. Jones, "Perception of texture by vision and touch. Multidimensionality and intersensory integration," *Journal of Experimental Psychology*, vol. 12, no. 2, pp. 169–180, 1986.

[45] P. M. McDonnell and J. Duffett, "Vision and touch: a reconsideration of conflict between the two senses," *Canadian Journal of Psychology*, vol. 26, no. 2, pp. 171–180, 1972.

[46] C. Grane and P. Bengtsson, "Serial or parallel search with a multi-modal rotary device for in-vehicle use," in *Proceedings of the 2nd International Conference on Applied Human Factors and Ergonomics (AHFE '08)*, W. Karwowski and G. Salvendy, Eds., USA Publishing, 2008.

# 8

# Getting Real: A Naturalistic Methodology for Using Smartphones to Collect Mediated Communications

**Chad C. Tossell,[1] Philip Kortum,[1] Clayton W. Shepard,[2] Ahmad Rahmati,[2] and Lin Zhong[2]**

[1] *Department of Psychology, Rice University, 6100 Main Street, MS-25, Houston, TX 77005, USA*
[2] *Department of Electrical and Computer Engineering, Rice University, 6100 Main Street, MS-25, Houston, TX 77005, USA*

Correspondence should be addressed to Chad C. Tossell, chad.tossell@rice.edu

Academic Editor: Eva Cerezo

This paper contributes an intentionally naturalistic methodology using smartphone logging technology to study communications in the wild. Smartphone logging can provide tremendous access to communications data from real environments. However, researchers must consider how it is employed to preserve naturalistic behaviors. Nine considerations are presented to this end. We also provide a description of a naturalistic logging approach that has been applied successfully to collecting mediated communications from iPhones. The methodology was designed to intentionally decrease reactivity and resulted in data that were more accurate than self-reports. Example analyses are also provided to show how data collected can be analyzed to establish empirical patterns and identify user differences. Smartphone logging technologies offer flexible capabilities to enhance access to real communications data, but methodologies employing these techniques must be designed appropriately to avoid provoking naturally occurring behaviors. Functionally, this methodology can be applied to establish empirical patterns and test specific hypotheses within the field of HCI research. Topically, this methodology can be applied to domains interested in understanding mediated communications such as mobile content and systems design, teamwork, and social networks.

## 1. Introduction

Smartphones have provided ubiquitous computing and communication resources to a growing number of users. The International Telecommunication Union [1] recently reported over 940 million smartphone service subscriptions worldwide and that this number is growing exponentially. These devices have transformed the mobile phone into a technological companion [2] that is completely portable, connected, available, and powerful. Researchers can now leverage logging technology available through these devices to access real communications data from real environments [3].

However, those employing this technology must guard against the implicit assumption that logging does not affect the behavior of participants [4]. Similar to traditional field methodologies, reactivity (i.e., a modification in behavior as a consequence of being measured [5]) can occur if careful steps are not taken to plan for the "selection, provocation, recording and encoding of behaviors and settings" [6] in a way that preserves naturally occurring behaviors [7]. This could seriously impact both internal and external validity of the data collected via these devices [7]. We submit, with careful design, smartphone logging can be used for enhanced naturalistic studies to better establish empirical patterns, develop theories, and test specific hypotheses in communications research [8]. This technique seems ripe for human factors (HFs) domains such as interface design, teamwork, and social networks to collect and analyze an enormous amount of mediated communications data from real settings.

The present work contributes a naturalistic use of smartphone logging to preserve realistic behaviors. To this end, we begin with a review of relevant literature to demonstrate some of the capabilities and applications of the emerging technique. Second, we describe the method in detail and include some of the important constraints that must be considered when implementing the methodology. Third, we describe some of the specific benefits and limitations of the methodology by way of examples. We conclude with a discussion of how the methodology fits into HCI research in general.

## 2. Background

Smartphones are used in diverse settings [9] to share information within and across teams [10], maintain social relationships [11], and develop social networks [12] among a number of other things. To understand communications through these devices, traditional research methods (e.g., laboratory, field) are commonly used or adapted to fit mobile environments [13]. Each of these methods offers several benefits and limitations [14, 15]. For instance, laboratory studies are highly controlled and can provide data high in internal validity [16]. The potential drawback, however, in many laboratory studies is the lack of ecological validity due to the artificial setting [17].

When studying interactions with smartphones, traditional field methodologies (e.g., diary studies, ethnography, observation) seem to be a more natural fit to enhance ecological validity [18, 19]. However, field studies have met challenges when applied to studying communications outside of the lab; two are briefly described here. Observer effects are a primary concern. For example, Eagle and Pentland [20] described several examples where invasiveness adversely impacted the validity of communications data. These field studies required researchers to view confidential meetings, teenagers in their bedroom, and the communication of lovers. Second, traditional data collection techniques have largely required user inputs which may adversely influence accuracy. Diary studies, for example, often interrupt users from their main task, place a burden on participants to report, and rely on their memory of events [21].

Logging methodologies have addressed many of these concerns by allocating observations to technology. These methodologies provide access to data that can be collected without an observer present or a requirement for users to provide self-reports [3]. Tasks do not have to be constructed by the experimenter. Instead, data can be pulled from participants' daily activities on familiar interfaces within normal contexts [22]. Thus, data collected from loggers are typically considered more objective, accurate, and realistic [20, 23].

Using logs to understand realistic behaviors with technology is not a new approach [15, 24]. More recently, researchers in HCI have used Web logs to better understand browsing strategies [25], search behaviors [26], revisitation of websites [27], and usage differences between groups (e.g., novice-expert [28]). These studies have characterized interaction behaviors for enhanced design of interfaces [29]. For instance, website revisitation rates have been analyzed in multiple studies [25, 30] and applied to the design of history interfaces for internet browsers.

In research on teams, communications data have been collected and analyzed via automated methods to assess performance, develop training, and reduce errors [31]. Both physical communication data and the content of communications have been analyzed to understand team cognition [32] and performance [33]. Much of the work conducted in this domain has collected communications content relevant to team tasks on dedicated systems (e.g., the radio on an airplane [33]) and applied to training development and the design of communication systems. Smartphones, in contrast, are used across tasks for both personal and professional communications [10].

Smartphone logging of communications data is a recent trend. Most notably, authors of [20] installed logging capabilities on first-generation smartphones to passively collect data from participants in two academic departments. These data have been used to understand the development of social networks [12, 34, 35], predict smartphone usage [36], classify behavioral patterns [37], and study the role of location [20] and temporal patterns [38] in communication behaviors.

More intrusive and controlled studies have also been conducted using smartphone logging. Authors of [39] sent messages to participants at various times and asked participants to take pictures of their current setting and describe their information needs. These responses were logged and analyzed for technology design. Authors of [40] used a within-subjects experimental design to assess the effects of a novel interface on decreasing missed phone calls. This study used a longitudinal approach and collected a large amount of data via smartphones to convincingly show the effectiveness of the new system. Clearly, smartphone logging has been employed in a number of diverse ways.

Although logging has been applied effectively to a number of research aims, the technology has not been advantageously employed in a systematic manner to preserve naturalistic behaviors. For instance, many of the previous logging studies mentioned above have reminded participants they are being measured by requiring them to report data, introducing novel interfaces, or collecting data considered private. Similar to other research methodologies, using logger technology involves planned constraints to improve accuracy [6]. We submit that employing loggers can be more naturalistic by reducing the potential for provoking normal behaviors due to measurement. Removing this unwanted variance is clearly important for all research applications. Below we describe the constraints involved with implementing smartphone logging and how we employed a more naturalistic approach to study communications.

## 3. Collecting Naturalistic Communications

One of the central tenets in Human-Computer Interaction (HCI) is to understand user differences based on demographics, experience, or other characteristics [41]. To date, there is a lack of studies using naturalistic and longitudinal methodologies to assess these user differences for enhanced mobile systems design. Because smartphones are becoming more ubiquitous, we think such methodologies could be beneficial for the future design of mobile systems and content. This section considers a number of factors important to implement a naturalistic approach to logging smartphone usage. Decisions on each of these factors can influence the level of realism of data collected. Our methodology requires the researcher to address nine considerations in the design of the mobile-logging-based studies (Table 1). These

TABLE 1: Nine constraints for designing a study using logger technology.

| Label | Consideration |
| --- | --- |
| Variables | What variables are needed? Logging is selective and intentional regarding what is collected and what is ignored. For instance, researchers can collect a large number of contextual and demographic variables to a small number (e.g., just time and type of searches). Common dependent variables include physical data alone (e.g., call frequency & duration) to physical and content data (e.g., SMS message). |
| Privacy | Are data required potentially sensitive to participants? Many actions performed on smartphones are considered private. |
| Obtrusiveness | How do I collect the data? This can range from fully automated (low interruptions) to requiring participants to report (e.g., experience sampling with logger). |
| Interface | What interface(s) will participants use? New interfaces can be introduced or logging can be embedded and run as a background process on current interfaces. |
| Tasks | What tasks will participants perform? These tasks can be completely naturalistic (i.e., participant constructed) or experimenters can construct artificial tasks. |
| Technology | What technology is used? Logs can be pulled from public files (e.g., search databases) which would allow participants to use familiar technology. On the other end of the spectrum, researchers can provide new instrumented technologies to participants. |
| Participants | Who are the participants? Subjects may consist of a random population of people that are totally unaware they are being studied to individuals within an academic department or domain of interest (e.g., pilots) that are highly aware of the measurement. |
| Setting | Where will the study take place? One benefit of smartphone logging is that communication data can be collected in real environments (instead of a laboratory). |
| Study duration | How long to measure usage? This could range from one task of interest to longitudinal measurements over a period of months or years. |

considerations are not necessarily unique to smartphone logging. Some are shared by other methodologies, while others apply more directly to smartphones. We describe each consideration in turn and how decisions can impact reactivity. Of course, many of the factors are not mutually exclusive (e.g., privacy).

*Variables.* As with any research endeavor, the variables of interest highly influence the nature of the methodology. A naturalistic approach to logging must take several precautions in selecting data to be collected. Foremost, mediated communications, such as text messages, are considered more private than mail [42]. By collecting data such as these, participants could change their normal communications behaviors. Researchers implementing a naturalistic logging methodology can, however, record physical data from communications such as word count. Additionally, researchers that have a particular interest can collect a select amount of content. For instance, in one study, we hashed all communications data except emoticons. Table 2 is an example of some of the data that have been collected through naturalistic smartphone logging.

*Privacy.* Privacy must be considered at multiple levels in a naturalistic logging methodology. Smartphone loggers can collect the content of communications including from people outside of the study [43]. Collecting these data, however, can adversely impact user behavior because users may be reluctant to engage in highly personal communications if their privacy is not guaranteed [24], even though they may adapt [44]. Capturing communications content may not be considered invasive for dedicated professional systems [31]; however, communications data on smartphones are highly private in nature [42].

Several privacy constraints should be implemented throughout a study in order to conform to the methodology. First, we submit that participants should be aware of how their data are to be used. The rationale of the study and anonymization process should be explained to participants in detail before the study begins. This process at the beginning of the study has also been noted as an important step to minimize reactivity [44]. Second, participants should be assigned participant numbers to keep user interactions anonymous and researchers must be intentional about avoiding linking usage data with names. This can

TABLE 2: Example of data that can be collected through logging.

| SMS and e-mail | Phone | Web | Apps |
|---|---|---|---|
| Contact | Contact | URL | Name |
| Date/time | Date/time | Date/time | Date/time |
| Duration | Duration | Duration | Duration |
| Launches | Outgoing or ingoing | Referring URL URLs | |
| Sent or received | | | |
| Word count | | | |
| Type of emoticons | | | |
| Number of Emoticons | | | |

be particularly challenging when the study is longitudinal due to concerns such as phone malfunctions. For instance, in one implementation of the methodology, constraints were designed beforehand to maintain privacy for times when researcher-participant interactions were required (e.g., phone malfunctions). Only one researcher, who did not have access to data directly from the iPhones or the server, interacted with participants. Because this researcher did not have knowledge about their participant numbers, no data could be linked to the malfunctioning device. The technical issues were passed to other researchers along with the phones without any information that could identify the participant. Only phones were matched to user IDs in order to prevent any linkages between user IDs and names.

At another level, the logging technology can be designed to help preserve users' privacy. For example, participant numbers should be automatically associated with usage data on the phone and an encrypted tunnel should be used to transfer the collected data, in order to prevent unauthorized eavesdropping. The logger should not allow researchers or participants to view the actual content and contact information of emails, text messages, phone calls, and the address book. Instead, researchers can employ other methods to retain research critical data without collecting sensitive data. Contact information (i.e., phone numbers, names, and e-mail addresses) can be automatically assigned unique alphanumeric codes by the logger before it reaches any human. Similarly, text analysis, performed on the device, can extract relevant information from communication content (e.g., word count) and return only that information, not the specific content. By employing these measures, no potentially sensitive information ever leaves the phone, but important data can be linked together for analyses. For example, in a study where a participant sends a text message to her mother and then calls her mother later, the same code should be assigned to the contact for both transactions. Although content information could have been captured, this can negatively influence the realism of user behaviors. Steps such as these can enhance user privacy, and, subsequently, more naturalistic data can be collected because participants' normal behaviors are not disrupted because of privacy concerns.

*Participants.* A small number of HCI studies have reported data from users unaware that they were being recorded. Many times these include data from a cookies log that were recorded from websites, such as search engines. To implement the current methodology, participants should be fully informed of the data being collected from their phones. Though this may increase reactivity (at least initially), research ethics should also be taken into account and considered in the design of the methodology. Careful selection of experimental participants is also important. For instance, researchers should avoid recruiting subjects with previous relationships to the experimenters or the design of the study. It is also important to limit the potential reinforcement that the participants are being measured by minimizing or eliminating non-study-related meetings. Additionally, other participant behaviors, such as international travel, should be considered. If cost is not an issue in the administration of the study, then travel may not be an issue. If cost is an issue, then selecting participants who do not have extensive overseas travel planned would be important to maintaining the completeness of the data.

*Study Duration.* Longer studies allow the effects of being measured to wear off [45, 46]. Additionally, some events are by their very nature of low frequency. Small time frames might miss key events. Further, longer data collection efforts have the potential to yield richer information about cycles and trends that might not be obvious in shorter studies. Although there are no strict suggestions for the duration of smartphone logging in order to apply this naturalistic methodology, longer is generally considered better. We suggest that researchers also consider other factors such as familiarity with the device when choosing the study duration.

*Obtrusiveness.* Similarly, measurement obtrusiveness increases participant reactivity [5]. There are a number of ways researchers or logging technology can intrude and remind participants they are being watched or impede on normal behavior. For instance, requiring users to respond to text messages or perform a data upload procedure to collect data (e.g., performing an online action) can increase subject reactivity. While these kinds of activities can provide valuable information such as the immediate context where users are using their device and other self-report information, they come at the cost of interrupting normal activities. In addition to interrupting normal behaviors, constant requirements for users to perform any study-related actions are both unnatural actions by nature and may residually lead to additional activities that might not normally occur. A naturalistic logging methodology should not require *any* user actions to record data.

Beyond the technical design of the logger, a minimum number of participant contact meetings should be scheduled with participants to collect self-report data once the study has commenced, if at all. An optimal implementation of the current methodology is for research-related meetings to be scheduled before logging begins and then after logging ends. Any meetings during usage data collection could again remind users they are being measured and this provocation could lead to reactivity.

*Interface.* Another factor important to consider in preserving realistic and generalizable behaviors is the types of interfaces implemented on the technology being used in the HCI study. For instance, employing novel interfaces (e.g., a custom browser) or changing technologies over the course of the study (e.g., phone swapping) can adversely affect data validity by producing false rates of behaviors, increased variability and result in numerous other problems [45]. Users habituate to being measured over time with a stable interface [46]. Constant reminders that the technology is being logged simply reinforce the feeling of being observed, much like a live observer can adversely impact subject behaviors [47].

As with most of these considerations, tradeoffs must be made. In web logging studies it has become common to require users to install and use a different browser with a unique interface, in order to capture interactions such as button clicks (e.g., the back arrow) and use of history systems (e.g., bookmarks). The down side, of course, is that the ability to generalize these results may be problematic because interactive behaviors may have been driven by the novel interface and not what the users would have normally done on their usual browsers.

*Tasks.* The tasks users perform can range from self-constructed tasks in ecologically valid environments to researcher-constructed tasks in controlled laboratory environments. Of course, there is value to each approach. The latter approach applied to smartphones can be used to achieve statistical control and assess specific HCI problems (e.g., usability for common tasks [48]). The external validity of such studies, though, may be questionable due to the highly contextual nature of smartphone use. A naturalistic approach allows users to perform the tasks they might usually do with their smartphone. To apply the current methodology, researchers should avoid influencing what users do with their smartphone.

*Technology.* One challenge in smartphone logging is the design of constraints to encourage participants to use the instrumented technology as if it was their own. This can be difficult because smartphones are not typically used in isolation of other technologies (i.e., "on an island" [49]). Many actions that can be performed on smartphones can also be performed on other technologies such as a laptop or

another flip phone. For the current methodology, we suggest researchers require their participants to use the instrumented smartphone as their primary device and provide incentives to encourage this behavior. Thus, researchers should provide smartphones that represent the latest commercial offerings to promote this transition or work with phones previously purchased by the participants. Further incentives, such as unlimited data, texting and copious nationwide phone minutes, can further entice participants to use the experimental equipment exclusively.

## 4. Applications

Clearly, two of the primary benefits of naturalistic logging are the tremendous amount of data that can be collected and access to data not meant for the public eye. This section describes how these data differ from self-reports, provides evidence of preserving realistic behavior, and details several example applications of a naturalistic smartphone logging methodology applied to research problems in HCI.

*4.1. Example Applications.* Data sets obtained from logging smartphones can be extremely large. Indeed, in studies conducted by our lab using this methodology [50, 51] the amount of data gathered was enormous. For example, for a population of 24 participants over 18,000 hours of iPhone usage was captured. This included over 650,000 application launches, 460,000 sent and received text messages, and 42,000 phone calls. Although providing new smartphones along with free service may seem costly, the amount of data received in return is large.

A naturalistic smartphone logging methodology can be applied to a number of research problems. We briefly provide two examples of studies that leveraged the proposed methodology. In the first, we examined gender differences in emotive expressions online [50]. The second example is a snapshot of data collected over a period of one year to characterize communications through SMS and voice phone channels.

*4.1.1. Emoticon Use.* In [50], we had a particular interest in emoticon use through text messages (SMS). We obfuscated the content of the text messages and the contact information between users. However, we recorded both the number and type of emoticons sent and received by our participants. We used these data to examine differences between genders in their use of emoticons. Our naturalistic logging approach examined a smaller number of users over a period of six months. Still, reliable differences were found between genders. Contrary to previous studies that suggested technology closes the gender gap, our results showed that females more frequently used emoticons within text messages. The number of emoticons sent via participants' phones was adjusted by number of messages and verbosity. On all counts, females sent and received more emoticons. Surprisingly, however, emoticon vocabulary ratios calculated for each participant (number of unique emoticons sent/total number of emoticons sent) revealed that males sent out a wider range of emoticons compared to females.

TABLE 3: Percentages of time spent on iPhone applications from both self-reports and actual usage.

| | Duration | | Frequency | |
|---|---|---|---|---|
| | Self-report mean % | Actual usage mean % | Self-report mean % | Actual usage mean % |
| SMS | 26% | 14% | 32% | 27% |
| Phone | 17% | 16% | 11% | 14% |
| Email | 19% | 4% | 21% | 10% |
| Web | 18% | 6% | 19% | 6% |
| Other | 20% | 61% | 17% | 43% |

Previous studies that analyzed emoticon differences were mixed. All of these data, however, were from public content (e.g., listservs, blogs, etc.). When private data were analyzed (after gaining full consent from participants), stable gender differences were found. These results could be applied to the design of future smartphone communications systems, for instance, providing easier ways to personalize smartphone keyboards to allow some users (e.g., females) to surface frequently used characters (e.g., happy face emoticons).

*4.1.2. Characterizing Communications in Social Networks.* In another study, we explored how text messaging (SMS) and voice phone mediums were employed to encounter contacts in participants' social networks. Over 42,000 phone calls and 346,000 text messages were collected between 5,291 participant-nonparticipant dyads that made up our dataset for this analysis. Zipf-like distributions were found within each of these modalities. Thus, a small number of contacts were encountered very frequently via text messaging and voice phone calls and a long tail of contacts were contacted once or twice.

To understand empirical patterns associated with how both communication modalities were used, we examined longitudinal patterns. 24% of the contacts were encountered by our participants via both modalities (these contacts are referred to as "intermodal contacts" hereafter). 57% of contacts were encountered on voice phone only. The remaining 19% were encountered on SMS only. We also observed high stability of contacts encountered across both modalities. 96% of intermodal contacts were encountered across at least two months. 71% were encountered over 7 months. Thus, many of these intermodal contacts were likely more strongly tied to our participants.

Findings in communication patterns with each of these contacts revealed optimization trends that cannot be captured in any other way. The number of messages sent to intermodal contacts increased over time. These messages were shorter in length compared to messages sent to other contacts. Conversely, the number of phone calls made to these same intermodal contacts decreased over time. The duration of these calls was generally higher than phone calls made to other contacts. Future interfaces could be designed to better integrate aspects of these two modes of communication. For instance, a more intelligent linkage between the two modes might show an integrated history of communications with contacts. Another potential improvement would be

for SMS applications to better transfer draft messages that require higher data entry as the interface on smartphones seems to afford shorter messages.

*4.2. Assessments of the Methodology.* Studies conducted using logging technology result in the enhanced accuracy of the resulting data compared to other methods [20]. This has been corroborated in our own studies using the methodology. Participants were asked to report the relative proportions of usage in terms of both frequency and duration for five categories (Table 3). We found that users were fairly accurate at ranking how much they used various communication applications. However, they were not precise at estimating the relative amounts. Participants significantly underreported the amount of time spent on other applications. This is a vivid demonstration that smartphone logging can be used to collect data that cannot be collected accurately via other means (e.g., self-reports [53]).

One of our studies that applied the above methodology has also indicated that continuous measurements do not influence participants' normal behaviors. Participants responded on a Likert Scale (1 = strongly disagree to 5 = strongly agree) to the following statement: "The fact that my iPhone use was being measured changed my normal behaviors." 89% of the participants strongly disagreed and no one responded with a 4 or 5 ($M = 1.17$). A similar open-ended question was also answered and 86% indicated no change in behavior, 8% indicated that measurements initially changed their behavior, but that the effect quickly faded, and 8% indicated that it affected specific behaviors such as application downloads.

## 5. Discussion

Logging is a flexible approach that has addressed many of the challenges associated with traditional research methods [3, 13, 20]. However, researchers must take great care in designing these kinds of studies to preserve realism and minimize the potential adverse effects of measurement on behavior. We introduced nine important dimensions to consider in this regard: privacy, variables, interface stability, technology selection, nature of the task(s), participant selection, setting, and duration of the study. Decisions on these elements contribute to the overall realism of behaviors captured. The overall level of realism is important because it allows researchers to collect data without provoking normal behaviors.

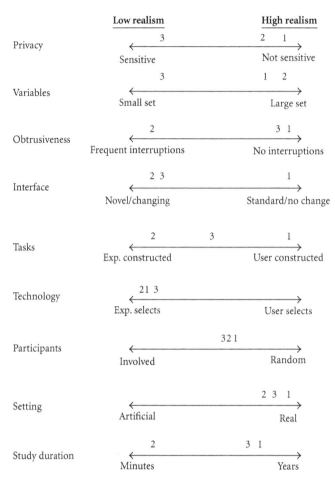

FIGURE 1: Three studies (1-current study, 2-experience sampling [52], 3-experimental [40]) that used smartphone logging to collect data and the approximate placements on each of the nine considerations.

Of course, many of these dimensions have trade-offs. Striking a balance between collecting relevant data and impacting real behaviors can be challenging (similar to other methodologies). The pursuit of specific research goals may mean that it is not always necessary to have the highest level of realism. For example, if the goal is to understand the role of location on smartphone usage that uses semantic analysis of messages [43], then privacy constraints could be relaxed in order to accomplish this goal. And if novel interfaces are the subject of the research [40], then the importance of the stability of the interface would need to be relaxed to assess the effects of the interface. Logging can also be employed in an obtrusive way (e.g., experience sampling [39]) to get more qualitative information (e.g., pictures of current location).

The primary strengths of the methodology introduced in this report are the commitment to naturalistic data collection and longitudinal nature of the study. Figure 1 shows where three different studies (including the current one) roughly fall along the dimensions introduced above in Table 1. The first study is the current methodology described in detail in this paper. The second study was conducted by Jönsson et al. [52] and used SMS probes to collect information on learning environments for development of distributed pedagogical tools. These probes were sent everyday to students' mobile

phones at an unpredictable time with instructions. These instructions were in the form of a game or request and had students use their provided phones to collect information (e.g., take a picture of your surroundings). This is similar to other studies that used smartphone logging for participatory design (e.g., [39]). The third study conducted by Oulasvirta et al. [40] used a repeated-measures approach combined with unobtrusive logging to understand communications via smartphones. A combination of experimental control using a standard A-B intervention, a longitudinal collection period (265 days), and the collection of a host of contextual and usage variables truly demonstrates the innovative methods that can be employed with logging [3]. They also recorded voice phone communications for qualitative analyses. Decisions on each consideration can vary widely across studies, confirming that smartphone logging is a flexible tool that can be leveraged in a number of ways based on research goals. The current approach rates high on most of the dimensions, as seen in Figure 1 suggesting that the behaviors measured were more realistic.

Of course, although logging in a highly realistic fashion can yield a wealth of information, there are limitations. For example, the technology cannot directly capture user intent or the immediate context of use. These could be collected, however, from complementary methods (e.g., surveys, ethnography).

More innovative naturalistic approaches that leverage smartphone technologies can also be pursued. For example, we [54] used the above methodology to collect data from iPod Touch users. A quasi-experimental design was employed and uncovered differences in usage between socioeconomic status (SES) groups. In particular, we found that lower SES groups used these handheld mobile computers much more and for a wider range of tasks compared to their higher SES peers. This information can be leveraged by designers to accommodate users of different backgrounds (e.g., income level) which, of course, is a central tenet of HF [41]. Other domains could apply a similar approach to other groups of interest (e.g., novice-expert).

Regardless of the topical application, a more naturalistic approach to implementing this technology can better leverage its strengths and uncover real behaviors. These include enhanced access to mediated communications in ecologically valid settings, accuracy in capturing real behaviors, and noninvasive data collection which does not rely on participants or reinforce the fact they are being measured. Other strengths of particular relevance to the study of communications can be inferred as well. For instance, it allows researchers to quantitatively assess the influences of the social, physical, and temporal environment on communications in an integrated way.

## 6. Conclusion

Clearly, naturalistic studies can be beneficial to the field of communications research to establish empirical patterns and test hypotheses. We argue that researchers in HCI are in a unique position to leverage emerging logging technologies to this end. Many researchers in our field often have the technical background that is necessary for working with the technology as well as the psychological research experience necessary to design, analyze, and apply behavioral data appropriately.

Data gathered from logging methodologies can be useful in understanding communications in ways that standard observational and self-report methodologies cannot. We do not argue that logging should completely replace traditional methodologies. However, we do believe that it is an important method to complement these techniques by providing more accurate, longitudinal, and objective data that cannot be obtained in other ways. The design and implementation of logging studies can be more time consuming and challenging for HCI researchers. However, these enhanced insights into user behaviors can more effectively inform theories, empirical patterns of behaviors, and the next generation of highly usable communications systems.

## Acknowledgments

This work was supported in part by the National Science Foundation Award IIS/HCC 0803556. Additionally, the authors acknowledge the fantastic efforts of Amy Buxbaum, Beth Herlin, Wen Xing, and Dhevi Rajendran for their assistance on this project.

## References

[1] ITU, 2010, http://www.itu.int/ITU-D/ict/material/FactsFigures2010.pdf.

[2] R. Ling, *The Mobile Connection*, Elsevier, Dresden, Germany, 2004.

[3] M. Raento, A. Oulasvirta, and N. Eagle, "Smartphones: an emerging tool for social scientists," *Sociological Methods and Research*, vol. 37, no. 3, pp. 426–454, 2009.

[4] D. R. Dubey, R. N. Kent, and S. G. O'Leary, "Reactions of children and teachers to classroom observers: a series of controlled investigations," *Behavior Therapy*, vol. 8, no. 5, pp. 887–897, 1977.

[5] R. E. Sykes, "Toward a theory of observer effect in systematic field observation," *Human Organization*, vol. 37, pp. 148–156, 1978.

[6] K. E. Weick, "Systematic observational methods," in *Handbook of Social Psychology*, G. Lindzey and E. Aronson, Eds., 1968.

[7] F. C. Harris and B. B. Lahey, "Subject reactivity in direct observational assessment: a review and critical analysis," *Clinical Psychology Review*, vol. 2, no. 4, pp. 523–538, 1982.

[8] J. G. Kelly, "Naturalistic observations and theory confirmation: an example," *Human Development*, vol. 10, no. 3, pp. 212–222, 1967.

[9] J. Kjeldskov and C. Graham, "A review of mobile HCI research methods," in *Proceedings of the International Conference on Human-Computer Interaction*, Udine, Italy, 2003.

[10] B. Beurer-Zuellig and M. Meckel, "Smartphones enabling mobile collaboration," in *Proceedings of the 41st Annual Hawaii International Conference on System Sciences (HICSS '08)*, January 2008.

[11] R. E. Grinter and M. A. Eldridge, "Y do tngrs luv 2 txt msg?" in *Proceedings of the Computer Supported Cooperative Work (CSCW '01)*, pp. 219–239, 2001.

[12] N. Eagle, A. Pentland, and D. Lazer, "Inferring friendship network structure by using mobile phone data," *Proceedings of the National Academy of Sciences of the United States of America*, vol. 106, no. 36, pp. 15274–15278, 2009.

[13] P. Hagen, T. Robertson, M. Kan, and K. Sadler, "Emerging research methods for understanding mobile technology use," in *Proceedings of the Australasian Computer-Human Interaction Conference (OZCHI '05)*, Canberra, Australia, 2005.

[14] J. Kjeldskov and J. Stage, "New techniques for usability evaluation of mobile systems," *International Journal of Human Computer Studies*, vol. 60, no. 5-6, pp. 599–620, 2004.

[15] C. D. Wickens and J. G. Hollands, *Engineering Psychology and Human Performance*, Prentice Hall, New Jersey, NJ, USA, 3rd edition, 2000.

[16] J. Rubin, *Handbook of Usability Testing*, John Wiley & Sons, New York, NY, USA, 1994.

[17] J. E. Driskell and E. Salas, "Collective behavior and team performance," *Human Factors*, vol. 34, no. 3, pp. 277–288, 1992.

[18] J. Grudin, "Why groupware applications fail: problems in design and evaluation," *Office: Technology and People*, vol. 4, pp. 245–264, 1988.

[19] R. K. Merton, *Social Theory and Social Structure*, The Free Press, Glencoe, Ill, USA, 1949.

[20] N. Eagle and A. Pentland, "Reality mining: sensing complex social systems," *Personal and Ubiquitous Computing*, vol. 10, no. 4, pp. 255–268, 2006.

[21] S. Carter and J. Mankoff, When participants do the capturing: The role of media in diary studies. *Human-computer interaction institute*, 2005, http://repository.cmu.edu/hcii/123/.

[22] M. Kamvar, M. Kellar, R. Pater, and Y. Xu, "Computers and iPhones and mobile phones, oh my! A logs-based comparison of search users on different devices," in *Proceedings of the WWW: International World Wide Web Conference*, Madrid, Spain, April 2009.

[23] A. Kivi, "Measuring mobile user behavior and service usage: methods, measurement points, and future outlook," in *Proceedings of the 6th Global Mobility Roundtable*, Los Angeles, Calif, USA, 2007.

[24] K. Purcell and K. Brady, "Adaptation to the invasion of privacy: monitoring behavior with a miniature radio transmitter," *Merrill-Palmer Quarterly*, vol. 12, pp. 242–254, 1965.

[25] L. D. Catledge and J. E. Pitkow, "Characterizing browsing strategies in the world wide web," in *Proceedings of the 3rd International World Wide Web Conference*, Darmstadt, Germany, 1995.

[26] B. J. Jansen, A. Spink, and T. Saracevic, "Real life, real users, and real needs: a study and analysis of user queries on the Web," *Information Processing and Management*, vol. 36, no. 2, pp. 207–227, 2000.

[27] L. Tauscher and S. Greenberg, "Revisitation patterns in World Wide Web navigation," in *Proceedings of the 1997 Conference on Human Factors in Computing Systems (CHI '97)*, pp. 399–406, March 1997.

[28] V. Cothey, "A longitudinal study of World Wide Web users' information-searching behavior," *Journal of the American Society for Information Science and Technology*, vol. 53, no. 2, pp. 67–78, 2002.

[29] M. C. Burton and J. B. Walther, "The value of web log data in use-based design and testing," *Journal of Computer-Mediated Communication*, vol. 6, no. 3, 2001.

[30] B. McKenzie and A. Cockburn, "An empirical analysis of web page revisitation," in *Proceedings of the 34th Annual Hawaii International Conference on System Sciences (HICSS '01)*, January 2001.

[31] P. W. Foltz and M. J. Martin, "Automated communication analysis of teams," in *Team Effectiveness in Complex Organizations*, E. Salas, G. F. Goodwin, and S. Burke, Eds., Taylor Francis, New York, NY, USA, 2008.

[32] P. A. Kiekel, N. J. Cooke, P. W. Foltz, and S. M. Shope, Automating, 2001.

[33] C. A. Bowers, F. Jentsch, E. Salas, and C. C. Braun, "Analyzing communication sequences for team training needs assessment," *Human Factors*, vol. 40, no. 4, pp. 672–679, 1998.

[34] A. G. Miklas, K. K. Gollu, K. K. W. Chan, S. Saroiu, K. P. Gummadi, and E. De Lara, "Exploiting social interactions in mobile systems," *Lecture Notes in Computer Science*, vol. 4717, pp. 409–428, 2007.

[35] E. Yoneki, "Visualizing communities and centralities from encounter traces," in *Proceedings of the 3rd ACM Workshop on Challenged Networks (CHANTS '08)*, pp. 129–131, September 2008.

[36] K. Farrahi and D. Gatica-Perez, "What did you do today? Discovering daily routines from large-scale mobile data," in *Proceedings of the 16th ACM International Conference on Multimedia (MM '08)*, pp. 849–852, October 2008.

[37] N. Eagle and A. S. Pentland, "Eigenbehaviors: identifying structure in routine," *Behavioral Ecology and Sociobiology*, vol. 63, no. 7, pp. 1057–1066, 2009.

[38] L. Hossain, K. Chung, and S. Murshed, "Exploring temporal communication through social networks," in *Proceedings of the 11th IFIP TC 13 International Conference on Human-Computer Interaction (Interact '07)*, Springer, 2007.

[39] S. Hulkko, T. Mattelmäki, K. Virtanen, and T. Keinonen, "Mobile probes," in *Proceedings of the 3rd Nordic Conference on Human-Computer Interaction (NordiCHI '04)*, pp. 43–51, Tampere, Finland, October 2004.

[40] A. Oulasvirta, R. Petit, M. Raento, and S. Tiitta, "Interpreting and acting on mobile awareness cues," *Human-Computer Interaction*, vol. 22, no. 1-2, pp. 97–135, 2007.

[41] B. Shneiderman, "Universal usability," *Communications of the ACM*, vol. 43, no. 5, pp. 85–91, 2000.

[42] J. Häkkilä and C. Chatfield, "'It's Like if you opened someone else's letter"user perceived privacy and social practices with SMS communication," in *Proceedings of the 7th International Conference on Human Computer Interaction with Mobile Devices and Services (MobileHCI '05)*, pp. 219–222, September 2005.

[43] M. Raento, A. Oulasvirta, R. Petit, and H. Toivonen, "ContextPhone: a prototyping platform for context-aware mobile applications," *IEEE Pervasive Computing*, vol. 4, no. 2, pp. 51–59, 2005.

[44] S. M. Johnson and O. D. Bolstad, "Reactivity to home observation: a comparison of audio recorded behavior with observers present or absent," *Applied Behavioral Analysis*, vol. 8, pp. 181–185, 1975.

[45] S. N. Haynes and W. F. Horn, "Reactivity in behavioral observation: a review," *Behavioral Assessment*, vol. 4, no. 4, pp. 369–385, 1982.

[46] S. M. Johnson and O. D. Bolstad, "Methodological issues in naturalistic observation: some problems and solutions for field research," in *Behavior Change: Methodology, Concepts, and Practice*, L. A. Hamerlynck, L. C. Handy, and E. J. Mash, Eds., Research, Champaign, Ill, USA, 1973.

[47] P. A. Adler and P. Adler, "Observational techniques," in *Collecting and Interpreting Qualitative Materials*, N. K. Denzin and Y. S. Lincoln, Eds., Sage, Thousand Oaks, Calif, USA, 1988.

[48] C. C. Tossell, P. T. Kortum, C. W. Shepard, A. Rahmati, and L. Zhong, "Assessing the performance of common tasks on handheld mobile computers," in *Proceedings of the 54th Human Factors and Ergonomics Society Annual Meeting (HFES '10)*, pp. 542–546, October 2010.

[49] T. Matthews, J. Pierce, and J. Tang, "No smartphone is an island: the impact of places, situations, and other devices on smartphone use," IBM RJ10452, 2009.

[50] C. C. Tossell, P. Kortum, C. Shepard, L. H. Barg-Walkow, A. Rahmati, and L. Zhong, "A longitudinal study of emoticon use in text messaging from smartphones," *Computers in Human Behavior*, vol. 28, pp. 659–663, 2012.

[51] C. C. Tossell, P. Kortum, A. Rahmati, C. Shepard, and L. Zhong, "Characterizing web use on smartphones," in *Proceedings of the Human Factors in Computing Systems (CHI '12)*, ACM, 2012.

[52] B. Jönsson, A. Svensk, D. Cuartielles, L. Malmborg, and P. Schlaucher, "Mobility and learning environments—engaging people in design of their everyday environments," Tech. Rep., 2002.

[53] P. M. Podsakoff, S. B. MacKenzie, J. Y. Lee, and N. P. Podsakoff, "Common method biases in behavioral research: a critical review of the literature and recommended remedies," *Journal of Applied Psychology*, vol. 88, no. 5, pp. 879–903, 2003.

[54] C. C. Tossell, J. Jardina, P. Kortum et al., "Effects of socioeconomic diversity on iPod touch device use in real-world environments," in *Proceedings of the 56th Annual Meeting of the Human Factors & Ergonomics Society*, Las Vegas, Nev, USA, 2011.

# 9

# Accuracy and Coordination of Spatial Frames of Reference during the Exploration of Virtual Maps: Interest for Orientation and Mobility of Blind People?

## Mathieu Simonnet[1] and Stéphane Vieilledent[2]

[1] CNRS UMR 6285 LabSTICC-IHSEV/HAAL, Telecom Bretagne, Technopôle Brest-Iroise,
CS 83818-29238 Brest Cedex 3, France
[2] LaTIM-Inserm U 1101, Université de Brest (UEB), Brest, France

Correspondence should be addressed to Mathieu Simonnet, mathieu.simonnet@telecom-bretagne.eu

Academic Editor: Antonio Krüger

Even if their spatial reasoning capabilities remain quite similar to those of sighted people, blind people encounter difficulties in getting distant information from their surroundings. Thus, whole body displacements, tactile map consultations, or auditory solutions are needed to establish physical contacts with their environment. Therefore, the accuracy of nonvisual spatial representations heavily relies upon the efficiency of exploration strategies and the ability to coordinate egocentric and allocentric spatial frames of reference. This study aims to better understand the mechanisms of this coordination without vision by analyzing cartographic exploration strategies and assessing their influence on mental spatial representations. Six blind sailors were immersed within a virtual haptic and auditory maritime environment. They were required to learn the layout of the map. Their movements were recorded and we identified some exploration strategies. Then they had to estimate the directions of six particular seamarks in aligned and misaligned situations. Better accuracy and coordination were obtained when participants used the "central point of reference" strategy. Our discussion relative to the articulation between geometric enduring representations and salient transient perceptions provides implications on map reading techniques and on mobility and orientation programs for blind people.

## 1. Introduction

Movement plays a major role in the acquisition of environmental knowledge since it is the only way we have of interacting with the world [1]. Therefore movements performed when people explore a novel environment may influence their performance in spatial tasks. As a consequence, understanding the relationships between exploratory movement patterns and environmental knowledge remains crucial in particular for blind people who can never get direct visual information. Thus the main goal of this study is to identify efficient cartographic exploration strategies in order to propose their inclusion in teaching programs devoted to mobility and orientation of blind people facing navigation tasks.

Navigation in the physical environment consists in whole body displacements to reach a spatial goal which can be directly perceived or located beyond the immediate perceptual field. Even if certain objects can be considered as attractors or repellers that trigger guidance mechanisms of the participant through the environment [2], navigation remains possible when these particular landmarks are unavailable to the participant. In this latter case, other much more complex mechanisms involving geometrical features [3] or salient axes within the environment [4] for example are involved in orientation [5]. They play a major role in the choice of spatial information to be used and emphasize the amount of memory resources devoted to the task. Although the notion of spatial cognitive map, considered as a form of cartographic mental field [6], is still widely debated, it is used as a concept to provide a framework to better understand mental spatial processes [7].

For navigation efficiency the cognitive coordination between an egocentric system within which the self-to-objects spatial relations is systematically updated as soon as the participant moves and an allocentric one within which the participant builds a representation based on the objects-to-objects relations remains crucial [8]. This coordination depends both on the geometry of the environmental configuration and on the activity of the participant. Shelton and McNamara [9] and Mou et al. [5] showed that encoding an intrinsic reference, that is, a salient axis, within the objects configuration favors the coordination and integration of the egocentric and allocentric systems. During a disorientation episode triggering the feeling of being lost Wang and Spelke [3] and Waller and Hodgson [10] pointed out that this occurs when none of the elements of the transient egocentric point of view belongs to a more enduring allocentric representation of the environment. As proposed by Thinus-Blanc and Gaunet [11], in order to get reoriented, one has to extract spatial invariants defined as the properties of the surrounding world which remain perceptually and mentally salient in both the egocentric and allocentric systems despite the tremendous variability of the sensory inputs during the displacement of the participant. Thus becoming lost and subsequently actively working to be reoriented may constitute a valuable opportunity to facilitate the improvement of the overall spatial knowledge. Solving this problem, and especially without vision, requires the participant to find a way to explore the environment with appropriate strategies.

Given the scenario that the spatial reasoning capabilities of blind individuals remain similar those of sighted people [12], blind people encounter difficulties in obtaining distal information from their surroundings. Accurately localizing objects solely with audition remains difficult [13]. The mechanism for resolving this problem is more complex for individuals without vision due to their inability to perceive directly distal information. Even if it has been shown that nonvisual spatial representation could be built from auditory cues [14], blind people often need whole body displacements (e.g., walking) or consultations of tactile maps to establish a physical contact with the surrounding objects [15]. Therefore, the accuracy of nonvisual spatial representations heavily relies upon the efficiency of exploration strategies. Hill and Ponder [16] and Hill and Rieser [17] have documented two types of processes to explore novel spaces without vision. The investigation phase consists in looking for the salient features of the environment using predominantly two exploration strategies to facilitate the location of objects. Firstly, the "perimeter" pattern is implemented by moving around the "perimeter" of the area in a constant direction until returning to the starting point. Secondly, the "grid" pattern is a series of straight-line movements systematically crossing the area. Then, the memorization phase aims at encoding the relationship of the important objects in the layout. Encoding strategies have been studied in locomotor [18] and in manipulatory [19] tasks leading to the identification of two main patterns of movement observed in both kinds of tasks. The "cyclic" strategy consists in successive visits to all the different objects, the same object being visited at the beginning and at the end of the sequence. This strategy involves the egocentric system. Though the "back-and-forth" strategy consists in repeated movements between the same two objects and, as such, involves the allocentric system, it leads to a better learning of the objects layout. The congruence of the observed behaviors in small manipulatory and large-locomotor-scaled spaces lead us to assume that extracting spatial invariants may be grounded on high-level mental processes consisting in using numerous route-like representations in order to identify their shared landmarks, connect them and construct map-like knowledge. This theory is consistent with the nature of the "reference point" strategy identified by Tellevik [20] as a pattern of movements in which subjects related their exploration to a salient landmark. The author showed that this strategy helped participants to obtain directional and angular information to locate objects and places.

Virtual reality has emerged as a powerful and flexible tool for simulation of real environments with both ecological validity and experimental control [21]. Researchers have created specific multimodal environments and assessed their efficiency in providing more responsive and salient spatial information for blind individuals [22]. For example, Lahav and Mioduser [23] studied nonvisual exploration strategies in virtual environment (VE) by recording movement patterns produced by blind people via a haptic interface in a virtual classroom. In line with previous results obtained in real environments [19], they confirmed that VE provided blind people with reliable access to spatial knowledge. The potential gains offered by nonvisual VE are also revealed in spatialized auditory environment [24] and spatial performances obtained in VE were more accurate when participants used allocentric strategies than egocentric ones. Furthermore, Delogu et al. [25] showed that combination of haptic and sonification allows blind people to explore a virtual map and recognize it among different tactile maps and seems particularly interesting in the understanding of cognitive mechanisms allowing blind people to acquire spatial knowledge [24]. By this respect, works such as those of Brock et al. [26] investigating tactile maps exploration in a mixed real and virtual environment using a kinect device open new opportunities to systematically analyze the efficiency of different exploration strategies.

If spatial efficiency is considered as the capability to coordinate egocentric and allocentric spatial frames of reference the aim of the present study consists in assessing the accuracy of mental representations of blind sailors learning the representation of a large geographical maritime space via a haptic and auditory VE. Blind sailors are expert users of tactile maps because they use them much more often than sighted people. We expect to identify some efficient exploration strategies that could be transferred to less spatially skilled people. Thus, haptic exploration strategies are analyzed to assess their influence on spatial performances. The main goal of this research is to identify and correlate haptic strategies and spatial performances in order to detect efficient patterns of exploration. This could lead to set up new geographic learning methods in the future.

TABLE 1: Gender, current age, age of onset of blindness, and education level of the participants.

|  | Gender | Current age | Age of blindness | Education level |
| --- | --- | --- | --- | --- |
| Participant 1 | M | 27 | 24 | Baccalaureate |
| Participant 2 | M | 27 | 18 | Baccalaureate |
| Participant 3 | M | 45 | 23 | Masters Degree |
| Participant 4 | M | 47 | 42 | Baccalaureate |
| Participant 5 | F | 44 | 0 | Baccalaureate |
| Participant 6 | M | 36 | 0 | Baccalaureate |

For the purpose of the present study blind sailors constitute an interesting population because they are accustomed to manipulate tactile maps. Indeed, contrary to urban environments, maritime environments contain very few predefined itineraries and do not allow blind sailors to rely on street directions to update their positions. Consequently, they need to efficiently explore maps and build their route by themselves.

By this respect, we attempt to answer the three following questions.

(i) Can blind sailors be accurate when learning haptic and auditory maritime VE?

(ii) Can particular kinematics features and specific strategies be identified within the exploration patterns?

(iii) What are the relationships between the spatial performances and haptic exploration patterns?

## 2. Method

*2.1. Participants.* Six blind adults (38 ± 9 years) volunteered for the experiment, one woman and five men. The experiment had been approved by the local ethics committee and respected the declaration of Helsinki. Participants gave their informed consent prior to their inclusion in the study. Due to the wide variability of blindness, ranging from a visual impairment with a high degree of light perception, to complete blindness with no light perception, the six participants met the physiological definition of blindness [27, 28]. Two participants were congenitally blind and the four others lost vision later in life (Table 1). None of the participants had any kind of visual perceptions.

The participants were recruited from a blind sailing association in Brest (France). All participants are familiar with maritime maps and use their own personal computers with text-to-speech software on a daily basis.

*2.2. Apparatus.* In this study, we used a 40 cm wide and 30 cm high virtual map (Figure 1) comprised of a homogeneous land mass (25% of the map area), the sea and six salient landmark objects within the ocean. In maritime terms these landmarks were referred to as beacons. The map was generated by SeaTouch, a haptic and auditory JAVA application developed in the European Centre for Virtual Reality for the

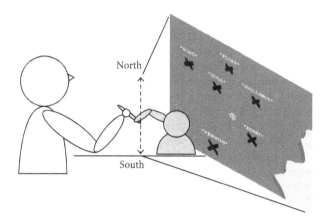

FIGURE 1: Experimental apparatus. The blind participant holds the force feed-back device and touches the virtual map of SeaTouch. The dark part of the map is the sea and the light one is the land. The crosses are the beacons and the white translucent sphere is the position of the haptic cursor. The virtual map is rendered in the vertical plane providing the implicit assumption that the workspace is aligned north up.

navigational training of blind sailors. The haptic interaction between the participant and the virtual map was provided by a Phantom Omni device (Sensable Technologies). We chose this device for its force feedback and its wide three-dimensional workspace (30 × 40 cm). Indeed, force feedback allows participants to feel clearly the tactile-kinesthetic information rendered when a beacon is touched. Eventually, three-dimensional workspace allows users to explore the sea area and jump over coastlines and land areas with the phantom cursor. Within the VE, the rendering of the sea was soft and sounds of waves were played when the participants touched it. The rendering of the earth was rough and extruded by one centimeter from the surface of the sea. When the haptic cursor came into contact with the land the sound of song of birds that are found inland were played. Between the land and the sea, the coastline was rendered as a vertical cliff that could be touched and followed. In this case, the sounds of sea birds were played. The salient objects, the six beacons, were generated by a spring effect, an attractor field analogous to a small magnet of 1 centimeter in diameter. When the haptic cursor contacted with them a synthetic voice announced the name of each object (Boat, Gull, Float, Penguin, Guillemot and Egret).

*2.2.1. Procedure.* The experimental protocol has been sequentially conducted in three different phases: training, exploration, and evaluation.

*2.2.2. Training.* To ensure that the participants mastered the haptic and auditory interactions with the virtual map, they trained until they were able to easily follow the coastline, move over the surface of the sea, and locate beacons with the stylus of the haptic device. The training phase ended when these abilities were verbally self reported by the participants.

*2.2.3. Exploration.* Before beginning any movement, the blind participants were informed that the ultimate purpose of the exploration was to obtain enough spatial knowledge to prepare for the questions phase during which the relative directions between different beacons would be estimated without any tangible or virtual map. Exploring the virtual map consisted in displacing the stylus of the haptic device within the haptic, vocal, and auditory environment, and the exploration stopped when the participant could remember the names of the six beacons and localize them on the map without confusion.

*2.2.4. Questions and Data Collection.* After the exploration phase the participants pointed from each beacon's location to three others in each of the two proposed alignment situations. So, they answered eighteen questions in the so-called aligned situation and replicated eighteen new questions in the so-called misaligned situation.

In the aligned situation, we posed the following kind of questions: "You are at the Gull and you are facing the north, what is the direction of the Egret?" Here, the axes of the participant and the north were aligned. To estimate this direction, the participant was presumably evaluating it primarily from an egocentric frame of reference.

In the misaligned situation, the following kinds of question were posed: "You are at the Gull and facing the Penguin, what is the direction of the Egret?" Here, the axes of the participant and the north were different. The participant had to process a mental rotation to combine these two axes and estimate the required direction. In other words participants were forced to coordinate egocentric and allocentric directions and frames of reference by themselves.

The questions were only answered by means of the tangible pointer of a real protractor that was fixed to the table in front of participants. This protractor allowed participants to point naturally toward a particular direction. They did not feel any graduation with this tool and were able to indicate angles like they would have done with fingers. Then we read the angle values and reported the results.

Angular data was collected to the nearest degree (Figure 2).

Small circles represent beacons. Arrows represent the axes of the participant, the north and the pointer of the protractor. The direction estimations were read on the protractor.

*2.3. Data Analysis.* To assess spatial knowledge of the participants, estimated directions between beacons were used and

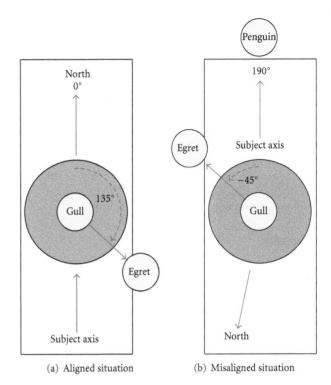

Figure 2: The use of a tactile protractor in aligned (a) and misaligned (b) situations.

the kinematics of participants' movements were analyzed to characterize the spatial activity involved in spatial encoding processes.

Firstly, the angular response to each directional question was used to compute the unsigned angular error (AE) that is the difference, expressed in degrees between the estimated and the correct directions of the beacon. 6 (subjects) × 6 (beacons) × 3 (questions) × 2 (alignments) led to the collection of 216 analyzed AE.

Secondly, the exploration pattern, that is the spatial trajectories of the stylus of the haptic device were analyzed as follows. The trajectories were considered as a whole from the beginning to the very end of the movement. Within these entire sequences, we measured the elapsed duration time (ED), the travelled distance (TD), and the parallelism index (PI). PI indicates how parallel is a given direction of the cursor's single movement in comparison to the direction of its previous one [29]. Remaining totally independent from the TD, PI was calculated as the average cosine between the current and previous directions of the movement. Thus, PI is potentially comprised between −1 and 1, from back and forth movements to strictly straight movements performed in the same direction with intermediate values obtained for variously pronounced zigzag movements. Following the proposal of Hill and Ponder [16] and Hill and Rieser [17], two phases were identified within the exploratory time, investigation and memorization. For each of these phases, we computed the same variables (ED, TD, and PI). The investigation phase was characterized by the participant discovering the environment and consequently this phase ended when the haptic cursor contacted each beacon at least once. Then, during the memorization phase, the participant displaced the haptic cursor between the different beacons in order to encode their position in memory. As mentioned above, the memorization phase ended when the participant said that he could localize the six beacons without confusion.

In addition, we also attempted to characterize the exploration strategy, that is, the spatiotemporal order in which blind sailors explored and touched the six different beacons in the maritime VE. We wanted to determine if some of these patterns of movement may be more effective than others to gain an efficient spatial knowledge and if they were the same for all the participants or specific to each individual.

## 3. Results

AE, ED, and TD did not follow a normal distribution (Lilliefors test, $P > .05$). Thus, statistical paired comparisons were performed on both alignment situations (aligned and misaligned) by means of the nonparametric Wilcoxon test. Conversely, since PI followed a normal distribution (Lilliefors test, $P < .05$) we used a nonpaired Student's $t$-test.

*3.1. Responses to the Questions.* For the entire set of responses, AE mean was equal to 21.6 (SD 21.3) deg with values ranging from 0.2 (for best responses) deg to 89.2 deg (for worst responses). This distribution was characterized by an equal number of responses on both sides of a threshold value of 15.2 deg. All the participants self-reported that they encountered more difficulties in answering the questions in the misaligned than in the aligned situation and commented that these additional problems stemmed from the necessity to mentally rotate the map they had memorized in order to update their orientation before pointing with the protractor.

Evidence of these difficulties is quantitatively clear. Mean AE was equal to 14.7 (SD 14.0) deg with values spread from 0.2 deg to 87.5 deg in the aligned situation, whereas mean AE was equal to 28.4 (SD 24.9) deg with values spread from 0.4 deg to 89.2 deg in misaligned situation. These values not only indicate that the mean value almost doubled when the axes of the participant and the north were different (14.7 deg to 28.4) but we also noticed specific data distribution in each situation (Figure 3). Half of the data remained below 12.0 deg in aligned situation and 95% of the direction estimates did not exceed 35 deg. In nonaligned situation half of the responses remained below 21.7 deg 95% of responses were within AE values below 80 deg. In summary, the distribution of the responses was more homogenous across the different clusters in this later case with a better balance between accurate and inaccurate responses, but overall this last result reinforces the idea that the accuracy of the participants responses tended to decrease in misaligned situation compared to aligned one. The observed AE differences between the two situations were significant (Wilcoxon test, $z = 4.95$, $P < .0001$) and confirmed the existence of an alignment effect [30]. This researcher asked participants to learn a building configuration from maps and demonstrated that performances were better when the orientation of the map matched the participant orientation to the view of the building.

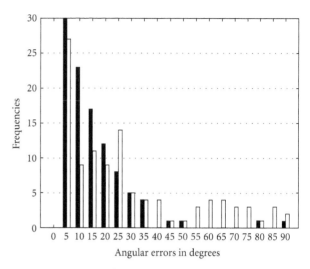

FIGURE 3: Frequencies of angular errors (deg) performed in aligned (black) and misaligned (white) situations.

This effect could potentially originate from specific biases when answering questions concerning the different beacons to be pointed or from individual answering strategies for each participant. Indeed, even if we did not notice any AE difference between the beacons either in aligned (Wilcoxon test, $z$ ranging from 0.21 to 1.7, $P > .05$) nor in misaligned situation (Wilcoxon test, $z$ ranging from 0.10 to 0.87, $P > .05$) with mean values spread from 12.2 (SD 18.8) deg to 18.1 (SD 19.1) deg and from 21.8 (SD. 23.3) deg to 35.5 (SD 23.3) deg, respectively, we observed that AE tended to augment in misaligned situation for four of the six beacons (Wilcoxon test, $z$ ranging from 2.39 to 2.89, $P < .05$).

At the individual level, participants performed differently from each other according to the alignment situation (Table 2). When confronted with aligned situations, three subgroups of participants emerged from the responses to the questions. Participants 1, 2, and 3 whose results were similar (Wilcoxon test, $z$ ranging from 0.12 to 0.54, $P > .05$) made up the first subgroup and their results were significantly better (Wilcoxon test, $z$ ranging from 2.11 to 3.29, $P < .05$) than those obtained by participants 4 and 5 (Wilcoxon test, $z = 0.35$, $P > .05$) who made up the second subgroup. Participant 6 remained alone in the third subgroup with intermediate responses that were not significantly different from those of the first two subgroups. Although the pattern of individual responses appeared to be more complex when the participants were confronted with misaligned situations, two main subgroups could be distinguished with participants 2 and 3 obtaining similar (Wilcoxon test, $z = 0.37$, $P > .05$) and better (Wilcoxon test, $z$ ranging from 2.85 to 3.64, $P < .05$) responses than those, also similar (Wilcoxon test, $z = 0.61$, $P > .05$) obtained by participants 4 and 5.

In addition, the observed differences between both alignment situations were not identically organized for each participant (details are shown in Table 2) since the comparison of AE obtained in aligned and misaligned situations did not reach a significant level for three participants

Accuracy and Coordination of Spatial Frames of Reference during the Exploration of Virtual Maps: Interest for Orientation and Mobility of Blind People?

99

TABLE 2: Averages and standard deviations of AE (deg). The comparisons between aligned and misaligned direction estimations were performed by means of the Wilcoxon test.

| Participants | Aligned | Misaligned | Wilcoxon test ($P > .05$) |
|---|---|---|---|
| 1 | 10° (±6°) | 26° (±18°) | $P = .003$ |
| 2 | **10° (±11°)** | **14° (±11°)** | $P = .199$ |
| 3 | **9° (±8°)** | **12° (±9°)** | $P = .384$ |
| 4 | 22° (±17°) | 42° (±30°) | $P = .043$ |
| 5 | 21° (±20°) | 46° (±23°) | $P = .003$ |
| 6 | **16° (±13°)** | **30° (±30°)** | $P = .122$ |

(P2, P3, and P6), whereas significantly better performances occurred for the three others (P1, P4, and P5) in aligned situation.

*3.2. Movements of the Haptic Cursor during Exploration.* Qualitatively the movements of the haptic cursor had different shapes depending on the participant but also on the experimental phase (Tables 3 and 4).

A large elliptical shape (the extent of the physical workspace of the haptic device) has not been systematically followed by all the participants (e.g., P4) even if some of them displaced the cursor along at least one subpart of this border either during the investigation phase (e.g., P3 and P5) or, more rarely, also during the memorization phase (e.g., P6).

In addition to the physical limits of the workspace, the participants had to determine the position of the coastline in order to clearly identify a functional area within which the six beacons were located. The coastline was carefully followed by participants 1, 3, and 5 during the investigation phase and, overall, very few movements went above the land portion of the virtual map. These movements performed along the maritime borders of the virtual space or along the virtual coastline allowed the participants to calibrate the amplitude of their arm movements in the actual space and to match those with the displacements of the virtual cursor.

Since the participants also had to discover and memorize the positions of the six beacons, the cursor movements did not only consist in following the maritime or terrestrial edges of the virtual space. Covering central part of the virtual sea, these trajectories have three main characteristics. Firstly, for each participant, the movements performed during the memorization phase could not be considered as the reproduction of those performed during the investigation phase indicating that participants estimated by themselves that touching the entire set of beacons only once during the investigation phase was not enough and that they needed additional experiences of sensorimotor interactions with the environment to improve their spatial knowledge. Secondly, as expected, the spatial density of trajectories was not identical between participants. Whereas some of them (P1 and P2) briefly swept the virtual sea letting large unexplored portions either during the investigation phase (P1) or during the memorization one (P2), others preferred to systematically displace their cursor until almost all the portions of space were explored (P3 and P6 during investigation, P4 and P6

during memorization). Thirdly, differences in the way participants reached the beacons also appeared between the two exploration phases. With the knowledge that each beacon was touched at least once during the investigation phase, it remains difficult to identify specific searching patterns of movement during the investigation phase since the cursor often stayed far away from the beacons (P1, P2, P3, and P6). Reaching patterns remained difficult to identify for some participants during the memorization phase (P1 and P6), but they seemed to be very well organized for others who established systematic links between stabilized series of beacons (P2, P3, P4, and P5).

Quantitatively at the global level, that is considering the entire exploration phase which lasted 573.7 (SD 281.6) sec, TD was equal to 315.8 (SD 179.5) km after conversion of the cursor displacements to the map scale. These values correspond to movements performed at a mean velocity of 0.564 (SD 0.157) km per sec (still expressed in the map scale), but large differences could be observed between participants concerning ED ranging from 254 to 989 sec for participants 1 and 6, respectively, TD ranging from 131.5 to 629.4 km for the same participants and velocity ranging from 0.293 to 0.721 km per sec for participants 4 and 2.

PI values (0.532 SD 0.686) indicate that, while travelling across the map, participants mainly produced curved trajectories. Indeed the average deviation from the straight line computed over three consecutive samples was about 58 deg despite some differences between participants (from 48 deg to 65 deg for P4 and P2). Finally, their movements allowed participants to touch about a hundred of beacons (102.8, SD 42.8) even if P1 touched four times less beacons (46) than P5 (179).

At the phase level, that is, considering investigation and memorization separately, some differences also appeared (Table 5). Indeed, the number of touched beacons was always lower during the investigation phase than during the memorization one (Wilcoxon test, $z = 2.20$, $P < .05$) and this was accompanied by differences for TD (Wilcoxon test, $z = 1.99$, $P < .05$) and ED (Wilcoxon test, $z = 2.20$, $P < .05$). Nevertheless, since the ratios between investigation (about 1/3) and memorization (about 2/3) were simultaneously maintained for TD and ED, movement velocity remained unchanged (Wilcoxon test, $z = 1.57$, $P > .05$) during both phases despite differences in the curvature of the trajectories reflected by PI values ($t = 25.67$, $P < .0001$). Those were higher during the investigation phase (0.650 SD 0.611) corresponding to

TABLE 3: (from (a–f)) Investigation and memorization phases tracks of participants 1, 2, and 3. Virtual map (land area in pale yellow, sea in blue and beacons in dark yellow circles) and exploration trajectories (thin red lines) during the investigation (left) and memorization (right) phases for each participant.

TABLE 4: (from (g–l)) Investigation and memorization phases tracks of participants 4, 5, and 6.

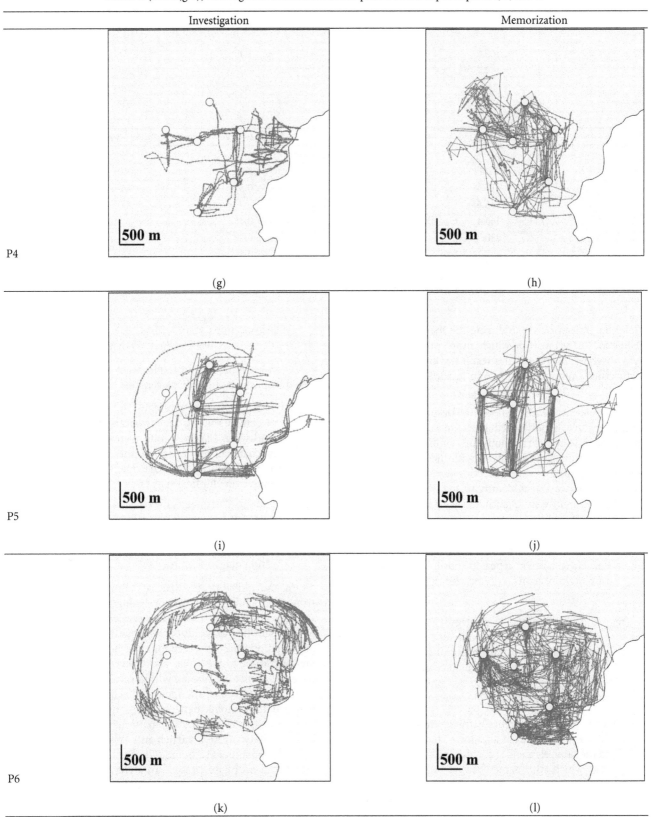

TABLE 5: Travelled distance (TD in km after conversion of the cursor displacements to the map scale), elapsed duration (ED in sec), velocity (km/sec), number of touched beacons, and parallelism index (PI) for each participant during the investigation and memorization phases.

| | TD | ED | Velocity | Beacons | PI |
|---|---|---|---|---|---|
| | | | Investigation | | |
| P1 | 49.0 | 77 | 0.6 | 9 | 0.688 |
| P2 | 105.6 | 96 | 1.1 | 32 | 0.562 |
| P3 | 140.7 | 205 | 0.7 | 21 | 0.628 |
| P4 | 61.1 | 224 | 0.3 | 24 | 0.785 |
| P5 | 175.9 | 254 | 0.7 | 61 | 0.61 |
| P6 | 199.3 | 293 | 0.7 | 11 | 0.604 |
| Mean (±s.d.) | 121.9 (±60.9) | 192 (±87) | 0.7 (±0.3) | 26.3 (±19.0) | |
| | | | Memorization | | |
| P1 | 82.4 | 177 | 0.5 | 37 | 0.414 |
| P2 | 111.4 | 206 | 0.5 | 64 | 0.259 |
| P3 | 136.6 | 322 | 0.4 | 83 | 0.436 |
| P4 | 166.4 | 553 | 0.3 | 71 | 0.543 |
| P5 | 230.8 | 333 | 0.7 | 118 | 0.217 |
| P6 | 430.1 | 696 | 0.6 | 86 | 0.422 |
| Mean (±s.d.) | 192.9 (±126.8) | 381 (±203) | 0.5 (±0.1) | 76.5 (±26.8) | |

straighter trajectories than during the memorization phase (0.405 SD 0.736) within which more pronounced curves were observed. Moreover, this result was confirmed for each participant ($t$ ranging from 7.96 to 15.53, $P < .0001$).

*3.3. Strategies for Reaching Beacons.* Despite their apparent complexity, we hypothesized that the movements of the haptic cursor were not randomly distributed and that, in particular, the sequences of contacts with the different beacons obeyed some specific rules reflecting exploration strategies. In this section, we aim at identifying five of these strategies.

Three of them were quantitatively assessed by means of appropriate algorithms.

(i) The "back-and-forth" strategy [18, 19], as mentioned earlier, consists in repeated movements between the same two beacons (e.g., beacon A-beacon B-beacon A).

(ii) Although the "cyclic" strategy [18, 19] consists in successive visits of all the different objects, the same object being visited at the beginning and at the end of the sequence, we also took into account the successive visits of three, four, or five beacons before touching the first one again.

(iii) The "point of reference" strategy has been depicted [20] as a set of "back-and-forth" patterns converging to the same element. It corresponds to sequences during which the same beacon was systematically touched after each contact with the other ones leading to star-shaped patterns. Owing to the fact that six beacons were displayed in the VE, we could potentially observe stars with five branches at most (e.g., beacons A-B-A-C-A-D-A-E-A-F-A), but we also took

into account stars with 4, 3, and 2 branches only. These latter were named "V-shapes".

The two remaining strategies were assessed by means of visual inspection of the displacements of the haptic cursor.

(i) The "perimeter" strategy [16] corresponds to displacements along the physical limits of the virtual workspace. These limits were determined by the mechanical properties of the haptic device to be manipulated by the participants. In our case, they offered an elliptical shape.

(ii) The "grid" strategy [16] consists in repeated displacements of the cursor along straight parallel lines followed by displacements still along straight parallel lines, the second series of displacements being perpendicular to the first one.

At the global level, that is, considering all kinds of strategies mentioned above, we distinguished 117 individual strategies. Our analysis clearly revealed that whereas 37% of the identified exploration strategies occurred during the investigation phase, the remaining 63% occurred during the memorization phase (Figure 4). Nevertheless, all of them were not evenly distributed within each of these two phases. Indeed, with 39% of the identified sequences consisting in repeated movements between the same two beacons, the "back-and-forth" exploration pattern was widely involved in the activity of the 6 participants (Figure 4) but with different proportions (12% and 27% for the investigation and memorization phases, resp.). In a complementary way, we observed that the "point of reference" pattern represented 25% of the total number of strategies with only 7% appearing during the investigation phase and 18% taking place during the memorization phase. The "cyclic" strategy appeared less often than the two previous strategies, but it still represented

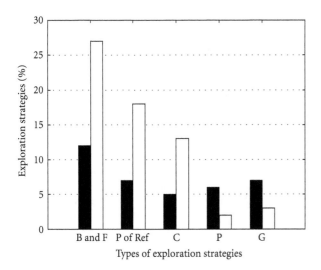

FIGURE 4: Frequencies of each exploration pattern during the investigation (black) and memorization (white) phases. (B & F = "back-and-forth"; P of Ref = "point of reference"; C = "cyclic"; P = "perimeter"; G = "grid").

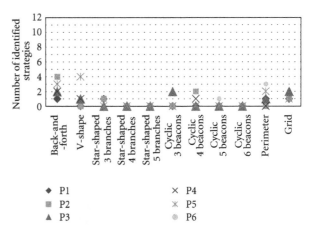

FIGURE 5: Number of exploration strategies for each participant during the investigation phase.

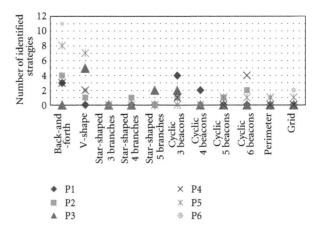

FIGURE 6: Number of exploration strategies for each participant during the memorization phase.

18% of the total number with 5% during the investigation phase and 13% during the memorization one. Taken together, these three first results revealed that the "back-and-forth", "point of reference", and "cyclic" patterns were used almost twice as frequently during memorization phase than during investigation phase. Conversely, the "perimeter" (8% of the total number) and the "grid" (10%) strategies were used more often during the investigation phase (6% and 7% of the total number, resp.) than during the memorization one (2% and 3% of the total number, resp.).

Individually, participants presented different sequences of exploration strategies when learning the configuration (Figures 5 and 6). Indeed, it appears that P1 was expected to learn the beacons layout by means of short "cyclic" strategies whereas P2 tried to memorize the beacons configuration by means of short "point of reference" strategies and long "cyclic" strategies and P3 combined a lot of short and long "point of reference" strategies. P4 and P5 clearly focused on long "cyclic" strategies to encode the beacons configuration. Finally, P6 mainly used "back-and-forth" and (less often) "cyclic" patterns even if he continued to employ "perimeter" and "grid" strategies during the investigation phase.

In summary, two main characteristics emerge from these analysis performed at the individual level. On the one hand, it appears that even if the different versions of the "cyclic" strategy were not much used during the investigation phase, they were systematically employed by each participant during the memorization phase. However, only participants 2, 4, and 5 performed six points' cycle. On the other hand, results revealed that each participant except the first one used at least one version of the "point of reference" strategies. Finally, only the participants 2 and 3 used the "point of reference" strategies with four and five branches, that is, on almost the whole configuration.

## 4. Discussion

In this experiment, we immersed six blind participants in a haptic and auditory maritime VE and asked them to learn the spatial location of a set of six beacons. Then, without reference to the VE the participants had to answer two series of questions. In the first series the axes of the participant was north oriented with respect to the map (aligned situation) whereas, in the second series, the north and the participant axes were always different (misaligned situation). In this latter case, participants were forced to mentally rotate their own position within the map in order to coordinate egocentric and allocentric frames of reference.

In the perspective of map reading techniques improvement for blind people, the aims of our study were to assess how accurate blind sailors could be when they were constrained to coordinate both spatial frames of reference by themselves as it is the case when they have to read a map, determine their current location, and plan displacements. Understanding the cognitive processes involved in reading a map necessitated to analyze their spatial performances (AE), the kinematics of their haptic exploration patterns, and the relationships between both of them. These three points are used to explain the results of the present experimentation.

*4.1. Can Blind Sailors Be Accurate When Learning Haptic and Auditory Maritime VE?* Even if we cannot exclude that the results obtained by Warren [30] may be task dependant, 15 degrees appear to be the minimal threshold to distinguish accurate estimated directions from inaccurate ones. Following this information and looking at the AE, we found that three of our participants were accurate in aligned situation and two of these three (P2 and P3) were also accurate in misaligned situation. Moreover, they did not present any significant difference between AE in aligned and misaligned situations. This leads to the inference that they did not encounter major difficulties in coordinating egocentric and allocentric spatial frames of reference. Fulfilling these two criteria (i.e., accuracy and coordination) appears to be the key condition for navigation efficiency [31] since only two of our participants met them. Neither accuracy nor coordination was obtained by P4 and P5, whereas P1 was only accurate in aligned situation indicating that he could not coordinate egocentric and allocentric frames of reference. Otherwise, despite the lack of difference between aligned and misaligned results, one can not consider that P6 coordinated both frames of reference since his accuracy level remained mediocre.

Thus, our results suggest that only P2 and P3 could perceive the salient features of the layout, encode relevant landmarks in long-term memory, and recall appropriate information in working memory in order to master spatial tasks and facilitate future navigation. Here, the coordination of egocentric and allocentric spatial frames of reference requires the ability to use a mental representation remaining independent of the individual orientation [4] but provides the participant with a more or less distorted geometric shape of the whole configuration [32]. Supporting the findings of Thinus-Blanc and Gaunet [11], this coordination mechanism implies to extract psychological invariants which are the connections between well-known schemata considered as typical geometric shapes elaborated from an allocentric frame of reference and a shape extracted from the environment encoded in an egocentric point of view (or haptic view).

Since movements performed during the exploration phase are the only way for participants to interact with VE and gain spatial knowledge, we wondered if the characteristics of the exploration patterns could explain how efficient invariants were extracted.

*4.2. Can Particular Kinematics Features and Specific Strategies Be Identified within the Exploration Patterns?* The fact that every participant spent one-third of the time and traveled distance during the investigation phase, and the remaining two-thirds during the memorization phase without modifying their average velocity leads us to think that participants produced twice effort to encode beacons positions than to discover them. It is therefore likely that, at least in this experiment, time and distance employed during the investigation phase constitutes valuable predicators of the amount of resources needed to achieve the memorization phase. This "one-third–two-third ratio" also appeared in the number of exploration strategies we identified whereas, only a quarter of the total beacons was touched during the investigation phase and three quarters during the memorization phase. This shows that the frequency of touched beacons increased during the memorization phase. Conversely, the index of parallelism decreased during this phase. Taken together these latter results indicate that during the memorization phase strategies were longer in terms of touched beacons and mostly consisted in abrupt direction changes as soon as a beacon was touched in order to reach another one. Doing so participants elaborated specific polygons whose vertices were the beacons and which could be assimilated to already known geometric shapes and thus favor the extraction of spatial invariants [11].

All participants used typical exploration patterns during the investigation phase ("back-and-forth", "perimeter", "grid"). During the memorization phase some of them mainly used the "reference point" strategy, whereas some others rather used the "cyclic" one. This leads to the idea that they built different mental geometric shapes probably encoded in distinct spatial frame of reference. According to previous works [18, 20, 33], the "reference point" strategy implies the allocentric spatial frame of reference, whilst the "cyclic" strategy rather involves the egocentric one. Indeed, Klatzky [34] proposed that an "object-centered representation" is necessary to perform efficient mental rotations (misaligned situation), whereas a "body centered representation" allows individuals to carry out mental translations (aligned situation). Looking at our results, one could suggest that only P2 and P3 were able to efficiently rotate and translate their mental beacons configuration because they obtained equivalent angular errors in both situations. This finding raises the question of whether specific exploration strategies could improve spatial performance.

*4.3. What Are the Relationships between the Spatial Performances and Haptic Exploration Patterns?* Participants 1 and 6 mainly used sequential "back-and-forth" patterns and thus probably only stored multiple discontinuous pieces of the layout. Doing so, they could encounter difficulties to connect them in a coherent and global manner. Conversely, the four other participants used long "object-to-object" strategies containing contacts with every beacon ("point of reference" and "cyclic") and could rapidly construct a complete geometric representation of the beacons configuration. But, among them, one can wonder why only P2 and P3 maintained a high level of accuracy and could still coordinate both spatial frames of reference.

Focusing on their exploration patterns, it appears that P2 and P3 are the only ones who used long "point of reference" strategies. They produced star-shaped patterns with four and five branches, respectively, whereas the other participants never exceeded two branches (V-shape). The case of P2 is particularly interesting since he has been the only participant who combined a star-shaped strategy with four branches with two "cyclic" patterns containing all the beacons of

Accuracy and Coordination of Spatial Frames of Reference during the Exploration of Virtual Maps: Interest for Orientation and Mobility of Blind People?

105

the configuration and one could pose the question of the role played by each of those strategies. Looking at other participants, we can observe that four complete "cyclic" without "point of reference" strategies led to poor performances (P4), whereas two full "point of reference" without any "cyclic" strategies were strongly efficient (P3).

Several reasons may explain the poor performances elicited by the "cyclic" strategy. The series of beacons to be touched are reached in a given order that can be referred as unidirectional. Consequently, inferring directions between beacons can potentially require the participant to mentally follow the course in the same direction and provoke the accumulation of angular errors when turning each stored beacon. This mechanism can be compared to the well-known path integration process used by blind and sighted humans to displace their whole body in the absence of external cues [35].

Conversely, many reasons explain the advantages of the "point of reference" strategy. Using this strategy, one takes care to establish direct bidirectional connections between a stabilized beacon in the center of the layout and each of the other beacons. In such a case, we propose to name this pattern the "central point of reference" strategy which balances the whole configuration in terms of angles and distances around the most salient landmark. In other words, participant builds a mental star shape composed of many incomplete triangles that share the same vertex (central point) and can have a common edge. This network facilitates the mental completion of triangles [34] and thus allows participants to reduce the number of inferences needed to deduce shortcuts between two nonpreviously connected beacons. Moreover, from a path integration perspective, the efficiency of the process is also enhanced since the amount of cumulated angular errors is systematically reset each time the participant touches the central point.

Referring to previous findings [11], this particular beacon constitutes an invariant which favors the cognitive coordination between egocentric and allocentric spatial frames of reference. Indeed, the "central point of reference" strategy combines two well-known strategies already identified in the locomotor domain: the allocentric "reference point" strategy depicted by Tellevik [20] as a set of "back-and-forth" patterns converging toward the same element and the egocentric "home-base-to-objects" strategy [16, 17] which is a set of "back-and-forth" patterns between the initial position of the participant and the position of other elements.

## 5. Conclusion

Given that allocentric representation is encoded in long-term memory and that egocentric system is required to interact within the environment [36], we suggest that when using the "central point of reference" strategy, participants memorized the star-shaped geometric schemata in an enduring representation and mentally projected their whole body in the center of the configuration to link this representation with imagined egocentric perceptions. Being immersed within the VE could certainly facilitate the articulation between top-down processes which organize spatial knowledge and bottom-up

mechanisms which extract salient sensory information in order to construct a single functional representation that is allowing to efficiently manage spatial tasks. This suggests that using the complete version of the "point of reference" exploration strategy remains a powerful way to learn a beacon configuration in a VE. However, it raises the question whether explicit instructions to use the "central point of reference" pattern could provide participants with a solution to accurately combine egocentric and allocentric spatial frames of reference. If it was the case, new perspectives could be proposed in learning methods and programs devoted to help blind people and the organization of their spatial knowledge.

Such an approach would deserve new experimentations to know whether exploration strategies are the cause or the consequence of a particular level of spatial skills. One could think that both play a role in a circular process within which performing new exploration strategies could improve the spatial skill level but also within which performing a particular strategy might be impossible unless a specific skill level is reached. This is can be considered as a hypothesis for future researches addressing the question of the influence of the spatial layouts. Indeed, even if our study showed that the central point of reference strategy appears to be the more efficient, when conceiving virtual environments devoted to human learning, it remains important to determine which parameters of the layouts are the best levers to improve spatial knowledge. Nevertheless, this could lead to find important individual differences, and one cannot exclude that certain exploration strategies could be better for some blind participants than for others depending on the way they have built their spatial mental representations.

Eventually, we emphasize that our results concern complete blind people. We notice that congenitally blind (participants 5 and 6) do not use the most efficient strategy and do not obtain the best results (participants 2 and 3). Even if all participants were used to manipulate tactile geographic maps and thus our results concern experts rather than beginners, our sample remains probably too small to propose a definitive conclusion about visual experience. Moreover, the strategy of the central point of reference is efficient when participants use our "single finger system" on a configuration with 6 elements in a 30 cm × 40 cm workspace, but it has not been validated in other conditions or after a long lasting training program. For all these reasons, we remain very cautious about the extrapolation of our results until other complementary modalities have been tested.

## Conflict of Interests

The authors report no conflict of interests. The authors alone are responsible for the content and writing of the paper.

## Acknowledgments

The authors would like to express their gratitude to all those who gave us the possibility to complete this study. The authors want to thank the blind sailors of Orion association which accepted to perform experiments but also CECIAA society for funds and the master graduate students in computer science in the European Center for Virtual Reality (http://www.cerv.fr/) for helping with the implementation of SeaTouch.

# References

[1] D. M. Wolpert, Z. Ghahramani, and J. R. Flanagan, "Perspectives and problems in motor learning," *Trends in Cognitive Sciences*, vol. 5, no. 11, pp. 487–494, 2001.

[2] W. H. Warren, "The dynamics of perception and action," *Psychological Review*, vol. 113, no. 2, pp. 358–389, 2006.

[3] R. F. Wang and E. S. Spelke, "Human spatial representation: insights from animals," *Trends in Cognitive Sciences*, vol. 6, no. 9, pp. 376–382, 2002.

[4] D. Waller, D. R. Montello, A. E. Richardson, and M. Hegarty, "Orientation specificity and spatial updating of memories for layouts," *Journal of Experimental Psychology*, vol. 28, no. 6, pp. 1051–1063, 2002.

[5] W. Mou, Y. Fan, T. P. McNamara, and C. B. Owen, "Intrinsic frames of reference and egocentric viewpoints in scene recognition," *Cognition*, vol. 106, no. 2, pp. 750–769, 2008.

[6] E. C. Tolman, "Cognitive maps in rats and men," *Psychological Review*, vol. 55, no. 4, pp. 189–208, 1948.

[7] N. Burgess, "Spatial memory: how egocentric and allocentric combine," *Trends in Cognitive Sciences*, vol. 10, no. 12, pp. 551–557, 2006.

[8] M. J. Sholl, "Cognitive maps as orienting schemata," *Journal of Experimental Psychology*, vol. 13, no. 4, pp. 615–628, 1987.

[9] A. L. Shelton and T. P. McNamara, "Systems of spatial reference in human memory," *Cognitive Psychology*, vol. 43, no. 4, pp. 274–310, 2001.

[10] D. Waller and E. Hodgson, "Transient and enduring spatial representations under disorientation and self-rotation," *Journal of Experimental Psychology*, vol. 32, no. 4, pp. 867–882, 2006.

[11] C. Thinus-Blanc and F. Gaunet, "Representation of space in blind persons: vision as a spatial sense?" *Psychological Bulletin*, vol. 121, no. 1, pp. 20–42, 1997.

[12] R. G. Golledge, R. D. Jacobson, R. Kitchin, and M. Blades, "Cognitive maps, spatial abilities and human wayfinding," *Geographical Review of Japan B*, vol. 73, no. 2, pp. 93–104, 2000.

[13] J. M. Loomis, R. L. Klatzky, R. G. Golledge, J. G. Cicinelli, J. W. Pellegrino, and P. A. Fry, "Non visual navigation by blind and sighted: assessment of path integration ability," *Journal of Experimental Psychology*, vol. 122, no. 1, pp. 73–91, 1993.

[14] W. Heuten, D. Wichmann, and S. Boll, "Interactive 3D sonification for the exploration of city maps," in *Proceedings of the 4th Nordic Conference on Human-Computer Interaction: Changing Roles (NordiCHI '06)*, M. Anders, K. Morgan, T. Bratteteig, G. Ghosh, and D. Svanaes, Eds., pp. 155–164, ACM, New York, NY, USA, 2006.

[15] M. A. Espinosa, S. Ungar, E. Ochaíta, M. Blades, and C. Spencer, "Comparing methods for introducing blind and visually impaired people to unfamiliar urban environments," *Journal of Environmental Psychology*, vol. 18, no. 3, pp. 277–287, 1998.

[16] E. Hill and P. Ponder, *Orientation and Mobility Techniques: A Guide for the Practitioner*, American Foundation for the Blind, New York, NY, USA, 1998.

[17] E. Hill and J. Rieser, "How persons with visual impairments explore novel spaces: strategies of good and poor performers," *Journal of Visual Impairment and Blindness*, vol. 87, pp. 8–15, 1998.

[18] F. Gaunet and C. Thinus-Blanc, "Early-blind subjects' spatial abilities in the locomotor space: exploratory strategies and reaction-to-change performance," *Perception*, vol. 25, no. 8, pp. 967–981, 1996.

[19] F. Gaunet, J. L. Martinez, and C. Thinus-Blanc, "Early-blind subjects' spatial representation of manipulatory space: exploratory strategies and reaction to change," *Perception*, vol. 26, no. 3, pp. 345–366, 1997.

[20] J. M. Tellevik, "Influence of spatial exploration patterns on cognitive mapping by blindfolded sighted persons," *Journal of Visual Impairment and Blindness*, vol. 86, no. 5, pp. 221–224, 1992.

[21] J. M. Loomis, J. J. Blascovich, and A. C. Beall, "Immersive virtual environment technology as a basic research tool in psychology," *Behavior Research Methods, Instruments, & Computers*, vol. 31, no. 4, pp. 557–564, 1999.

[22] R. Golledge, M. Rice, and D. Jacobson, "Multimodal interfaces for representing and accessing geospatial information," in *Frontiers of Geographic Information Technology*, S. Rana and J. Sharma, Eds., pp. 181–208, Springer, Berlin, Germany, 2006.

[23] O. Lahav and D. Mioduser, "Haptic-feedback support for cognitive mapping of unknown spaces by people who are blind," *International Journal of Human-Computer Studies*, vol. 66, no. 1, pp. 23–35, 2008.

[24] W. Heuten, *Non-Visual Support for Navigation in Urban Environments*, vol. 4 of *Oldenburg Computer Science Series*, OLWIR, 2008.

[25] F. Delogu, M. Palmiero, S. Federici, C. Plaisant, H. Zhao, and O. Belardinelli, "Non-visual exploration of geographic maps: does sonification help?" *Disability and Rehabilitation*, vol. 5, no. 3, pp. 164–174, 2010.

[26] A. Brock, S. Lebaz, B. Oriola, D. Picard, C. Jouffrais, and P. Truillet, "Kin'touch: understanding how visually impaired people explore tactile maps," in *Proceedings of the ACM Annual Conference Extended Abstracts on Human Factors in Computing Systems Extended Abstracts*, pp. 2471–2476, 2012.

[27] J. A. Leonard and R. C. Newman, "Spatial orientation in the blind," *Nature*, vol. 215, no. 5108, pp. 1413–1414, 1967.

[28] Y. Hatwell, A. Streri, and E. Gentaz, *Touching for Knowing: Cognitive Psychology of Haptic Manual Perception*, John Benjamins, Philadelphia, Pa, USA, 2003.

[29] S. M. Brudzynski and S. Krol, "Analysis of locomotor activity in the rat: parallelism index, a new measure of locomotor exploratory pattern," *Physiology and Behavior*, vol. 62, no. 3, pp. 635–642, 1997.

[30] D. Warren, "Perception of map-environment correspondence: the roles of features and alignment," *Ecological Psychology*, vol. 2, pp. 131–150, 1990.

[31] C. Gallistel, *The Organization of Learning*, The MIT Press, Cambridge, Mass, USA, 1990.

[32] M. D. Giraudo and J. Pailhous, "Distortions and fluctuations in topographic memory," *Memory and Cognition*, vol. 22, no. 1, pp. 14–26, 1994.

[33] S. Millar, "The utilization of external and movement cues in simple spatial tasks by blind and sighted children," *Perception*, vol. 8, no. 1, pp. 11–20, 1979.

[34] R. L. Klatzky, "Path completion after haptic exploration without vision: implications for haptic spatial representations," *Perception and Psychophysics*, vol. 61, no. 2, pp. 220–235, 1999.

[35] M. L. Mittelstaedt and H. Mittelstaedt, "Idiothetic navigation in humans: estimation of path length," *Experimental Brain Research*, vol. 139, no. 4, pp. 318–332, 2001.

[36] N. Burgess, S. Becker, J. A. King, and J. O'Keefe, "Memory for events and their spatial context: models and experiments," *Philosophical Transactions of the Royal Society B*, vol. 356, no. 1413, pp. 1493–1503, 2001.

# 10

# Psychophysiology to Assess Impact of Varying Levels of Simulation Fidelity in a Threat Environment

**Thomas D. Parsons,[1] Albert A. Rizzo,[2] Christopher G. Courtney,[2,3] and Michael E. Dawson[3]**

[1] Clinical Neuropsychology and Simulation (CNS) Lab, Department of Psychology, University of North Texas,
   Denton, TX 76203, USA
[2] Institute for Creative Technologies, University of Southern California, Playa Vista, Los Angeles, CA 90094, USA
[3] Department of Psychology, University of Southern California, Los Angeles, CA 90089, USA

Correspondence should be addressed to Thomas D. Parsons, thomas.parsons@unt.edu

Academic Editor: Pablo Moreno-Ger

There are many virtual environments found in the serious game community that simulate real world scenarios. There is a broad range of fidelity and experimental controls among these serious games. An important component to most evaluations is the extent to which level of fidelity impacts the persons immersed in the serious game. While a great deal of virtual environment and serious game research has assessed the subjective state or feeling of the participant (e.g., the participant's sense of presence) through the use of questionnaires, the current study examines participant experience by examining psychophysiological responses of participants to their surroundings. The primary goal in this study was evaluative: will a virtual environment with arousing contents result in increased sensory arousal if it is presented in a highly immersive configuration? A secondary goal of this study was to investigate the utility of our environment to offer varying levels of stimulus threat to impact the user's experience of the virtual environment. Increased simulation fidelity in an arousing environment resulted in faster heart rates and increased startle eyeblink amplitudes, suggesting that higher fidelity scenarios had great efficacy related to sensory arousal.

## 1. Psychophysiology to Assess Impact of Varying Levels of Simulation Fidelity in a Threat Environment

Virtual environments (VEs) and serious games offer the potential to stimulate and measure changes in the users' emotion, neurocognition, and motivation processes. The value in using simulation technology to produce serious games targeting such processes has been acknowledged by an encouraging body of research. Some of the work in this area has addressed affective processes: anxiety disorders, pain distraction, and posttraumatic stress disorder [1–3]. Other work has assessed neuropsychological processes [4, 5]. Further, psychophysiology is increasingly being incorporated into research using virtual reality environments [6–8]. The use of psychophysiological measures in affective and neurocognitive studies of persons immersed in VE scenarios offers the potential to develop current physiological computing approaches [9] into affective computing [10] scenarios.

The incorporation of simulation technology into neuroergonomic and psychophysiological research is advancing at a steady rate [11]. New discoveries and techniques are demanding a more rapid and advanced paradigm. In response to the demands, a wide variety of simulations have been developed. The range and depth of these simulations cover a large domain, from simple low fidelity task environments to complex high fidelity full immersion simulators. All of these simulators rely on some type of representation of the real world. An important issue for research into simulation for social and behavioral sciences is the determination of how advanced the simulator needs to be to adequately assess and/or train a particular individual or team. While high-end simulations can train a variety of user types, the cost associated with these devices can be difficult to justify [12].

In this paper, we attempt to build on earlier work that used psychophysiology to assess the propensity of users to respond to virtually generated sensory data as if they were real [13]. We aim to assess the propensity of users to respond to virtually generated sensory data as if they were real [14]. In the same way people experience physiological responses to stimuli in the real world, researchers seek to quantify participant experience by measuring responses evoked by stimuli in a VE. A low fidelity VE may be preferable in studies where a maximal amount of experimental control is desired because such environments may increase psychometric rigor through limiting the number of sensory variables available to the user [15]. Contrariwise, high fidelity environments are preferable for studies desiring increased ecological validity because they recreate more of the real world environment—better capture the participant's performance as it would occur in a real world setting [16].

Discussions of the level of fidelity and experimental control needed for a VE often go beyond simple discussions of the "immersive" qualities of the environment to discussions of the impact upon the perceived feeling of "presence" of the individual while immersed in the environment [17]. A number of discussions of the distinction between the terms "immersion" and "presence" can be found in the literature [18–22]. This distinction is important for the current study because issues of fidelity tend to reflect levels of immersion, while levels of presence reflect the user's experience relative to the level of fidelity/immersion. For the current study, we focus on fidelity and levels of immersion. We also feel that it is important to differentiate between immersion and presence. By immersion, we follow Slater and Wilburs [21] delineation, in which immersion is seen as an objective description of aspects of the system—that which the overall VE can deliver (e.g., the level of fidelity in representing the real world; the field of view, the number of sensory systems it simulates, the frame-rate, and latency [14]). Hence, the level of immersion is an objective property of a VE that in principle can be measured independently of the human experience that it engenders. We view presence as a subjective phenomenon (e.g., sensation of being in a VE).

Knowledge of the user-state during exposure to the VE is imperative for development and assessment of VE design. A number of presence studies have researched such issues using questionnaires [23–25]. Subjective measures tend to rely on post-test assessments of the user's feelings during the exposure to the VE, which is dependent on memory of the event [26]. Self-report data, when used in isolation, are highly susceptible to influences outside the subject's own targeted attitudes [21]. The item's wording, context, and format are all factors that may affect self-report responses. A limitation of questionnaire measures is that they can only be administered following a participant's immersion in a VE, but in order to assess participant experience during the actual immersion in a VE, researchers have sought a more objective measure. Online assessment of participant experience is difficult when using subjective measures, in that the very existence of subjective questions during immersion serves to break the continuity of the participant's conscious awareness currently being experienced. As a result, a quite different view seems to be emerging, in which presence is treated as something rooted in physiological and behavioral activity [14, 22] and there is a growing emphasis upon physiological and behavioral assessment [27], as well as the

relation between immersion and emotion [28, 29]. Further, there has been increased use of neuroscience techniques for presence measurement, such as EEG [30], transcranial Doppler [31], and fMRI [32].

Up until this point, VE studies have typically relied on self-report and behavioral measures to assess levels of fear and arousal [33, 34]. Some studies however, have moved toward using more objective psychophysiological measures. Jang et al. [35] measured psychophysiological responses including skin resistance and heart rate variability to assess arousal levels in normal subjects exposed to fear of driving and fear of flying VEs. Subjects showed lowered levels of skin resistance compared to baseline, indicating higher levels of arousal, especially during the first 7 to 8 minutes of exposure to the VE. Other studies have also found VEs to be physiologically arousing [36–38].

Meehan et al. [39] sought to uncover a more objective, valid, and reliable measure of presence through psychophysiological metrics. Because psychophysiological responses can be made without consciousness of the response, the experience of the virtual environment, and feelings of presence, need not be interrupted. Meehan and colleagues found that heart rate and skin conductance increased along with increased feelings of presence. They conclude that psychophysiological measures may be utilized as an objective and reliable measure of presence, though they note that additional research using different environments and stressors is necessary to further elucidate these findings.

Psychophysiological metrics proffer the advantage of an objective measure of response that can be recorded in real-time as the environment is experienced, providing a continuous measure of presence. Indeed, highly immersive presentations are thought to not only increase subjective ratings, but also result in increased physiological responses [18]. As such, researchers may study the impact of VEs on participants by looking at the psychophysiological responses of participants to their surroundings [6, 39, 40]. The recording of psychophysiological variables while participants operate within VEs has produced useful results in studies examining presence and immersion [41–44]. As such, the VE assets that allow for precise stimulus delivery within ecologically enhanced scenarios appears well matched for this research.

*1.1. Current Study.* In the current study, we aimed to look at the psychophysiological responses of participants experiencing "high" versus "low" levels of immersion into a virtual Iraqi scenario that had varying levels of stimulus intensity. Further, these psychophysiological responses may aid researchers in their development of VEs that balance fidelity and experimental control.

The primary goal in this study was evaluative: will a virtual environment with arousing contents result in increased sensory arousal if it is presented in a highly immersive configuration? To assess this, we looked at subjects immersed in a VE on two separate experimental runs consisting of both a "high" immersion condition and a "low" immersion condition. A secondary goal of this study was to investigate the utility of our environment to offer varying levels of stimulus threat to impact the user's experience of the VE.

Within each of the immersion conditions (high and low), arousal was manipulated by presenting participants with differing "safe" and "ambush" zones. Safe (low threat) zones consisted of little activity aside from driving down a desert road, while the more stressful ambush (high threat) zones included gunfire, explosions, and shouting amongst other stressors.

In the current study, startle eyeblink and heart rate were measured to assess psychophysiological differences in response to varying degrees of immersion and levels of arousal in a virtual Iraqi environment. Participants encountered a highly immersive VE while wearing a head mounted display (HMD) that used two OLED microdisplays with onboard 3D frame sequential video processors to deliver flicker-free motion. Together with the integrated $X$, $Y$, and $Z$-axis head-tracker, the participant was able to look around the VE by turning his or her head left or right, up or down, and leaning forward or back. Also in the high immersion condition, to increase the potential for sensory immersion, the participant was seated on a tactile transducer. Although participants experienced the same VE content in the low immersion condition, the VE was presented on a computer screen. It was expected that the highly immersive condition would lead to an increased sensory arousal, thus resulting in augmented levels of psychophysiological responding.

*1.2. Hypotheses.* We hypothesized that the highly immersive condition would elicit a more intense physiological response to the stressful high threat zones due to the higher-fidelity environment. It is important to note that the volume levels in both the high and low immersion conditions were held constant in order to increase experimental control of the arousal manipulation in this study and to limit changes in arousal to changes brought on by increased levels of fidelity, rather than changes in volume level. It is our hope that this research will (1) proffer a greater understanding of the psychophysiological correlates of immersion in an arousing VE and (2) act as an initial validation (ecological validation) of the intended impact of varying degrees of stimulus intensity programmed into our virtual Iraqi city.

*1.3. Serious Games and Clinical Psychology.* Serious game researchers are increasingly interested in working with clinicians to better understand a military service member's ability to return to active duty. Recent conflicts have increased the prevalence of blast injuries to the head. Many of these brain injuries may have no external marker of injury. As a result, there is need for the serious games community to research innovative assessment methods. Currently, clinicians make "Return-to-Duty" assessments that are based upon the "Return-to-Play" guidelines found in Sports Medicine. Both have incorporated two dimensional cognitive assessments to aid in decisions related to resuming activities following a concussion. Unfortunately, these two dimensional computerized assessments were not developed with the intention of tapping into everyday behaviors like driving through a Middle Eastern city.

Serious gaming environments can increase the ecological validity of neurocognitive batteries through the use of simulation technologies for assessment and treatment planning. The success of such serious games may lead to a psychophysiological computing approach, in which such data gleaned from persons interacting within a military relevant simulation may be used to develop adaptive virtual environments for training and rehabilitation. A beginning step is the identification of the level of immersion needed for a serious game to proffer the appropriate level of arousal. This is the overarching goal of this study.

## 2. Methods

*2.1. Participants.* A total of 50 healthy college aged students (males: $N = 23$, mean age = 20.4, mean years of education = 14.6; females: $N = 27$, mean age = 19.8, mean years of education = 14.1) participated in this experiment. An interview with a psychologist and a mental health history form were completed with each participant in order to allow for the following of strict exclusion criteria to minimize the possible confounding effects of additional factors known to adversely impact a person's ability to process information, including psychiatric (e.g., mental retardation, psychotic disorders, diagnosed learning disabilities, attention-deficit/hyperactivity disorder, and bipolar disorders, as well as substance-related disorders within two years of evaluation) and neurologic (e.g., seizure disorders, closed head injuries with loss of consciousness greater than 15 minutes, and neoplastic diseases) conditions.

*2.2. Apparatus*

*2.2.1. Hardware.* The apparatus used for the virtual humvee (i.e., a high mobility multipurpose wheeled vehicle) included a Pentium 4 desktop computer with a 3 GHz Processor; 3 GB of RAM; and an nVidia GeForce 6800. Two monitors were used: (1) one for displaying the Launcher application which is used by the Examiner and (2) another for displaying the participant's view of the VE in the HMD. Participants wore an eMagin Z800 head mounted display, and an InterSense InteriaCube 2+ attached for enhanced tracking. A Logitech Driving Force steering wheel was clamped on to the edge of a table in front of the monitors. A separate module consisting of the gas and brake pedals was positioned under the table. To increase the potential for sensory immersion, we built a tactile transducer using a three foot square platform with six Aura bass shaker speakers (AST-2B-04, 4 Ω 50 W Bass Shaker) attached. The tactile transducer was powered by a Sherwood RX-4105 amplifier with 100 Watts per Channel ×2 in Stereo Mode.

*2.2.2. Virtual Environment.* The software was designed using Virtual Battle Space 2 (VBS2). The VBS2 engine was used due to its robust fidelity simulation, ease of modification, and the fact that many military forces have adopted it. The VBS2 engine offers enhanced capability for interoperability and compatibility with existing standards for simulation. We designed the scenarios using a visual scenario editor and VBS2's own scripting language. To implement the scenario we used VBS2-engine specific script language and the built-in Finite State Machine (FSM) functionality.

### 2.2.3. Neuroscience and Simulation Interface.
The application uses the Neuroscience and Simulation Interface (NSI) developed in the Neuroscience and Simulation Laboratory (NeuroSim) at the University of Southern California [45]. The NSI was used for data acquisition, stimulus presentation, psychophysiological monitoring, and communication between the psychophysiological system and the VE. Parameters were saved to files using the NSI and automatically loaded through its control module. The NSI allowed our system to switch between parameter files, or executables modules, in order to perform specific experimental sequences. The NSI enabled the sending of event markers from the stimulus presentation computer to a recording device. Matlab scripts were executed in real-time from within NSI and filters were compiled to execute as stand-alone programs. The software runs on Windows XP 32-bit, and requires 5 Gb of free hard drive space for installation and storage of user data.

### 2.3. Stimuli and Design.
The University of Southern California's Institutional Review Board approved the study. After informed consent was obtained, basic demographic information was obtained. Next, participants were immersed in a VE on two separate experimental runs consisting of both a "high" immersion condition and a "low" immersion condition. In the high immersion condition, participants wore a head mounted display (HMD) with full tracking capabilities and were free to explore their environment visually. The high immersion condition also made use of headphones and a tactile transducer floor to simulate the experience of a large vehicle. The low immersion condition consisted of the same virtual Iraqi scenario presented on a 17 inch laptop screen while wearing headphones. Stimuli within the virtual environment experienced in both immersion conditions were identical. The only differences between conditions were due to the inclusion of the enhanced presentation quality of the high immersion condition. The presentation order of high and low immersion conditions was counterbalanced across subjects.

The VE used in both immersion conditions was comprised of a series of low threat and high threat zones in a virtual Iraqi city. In both the high immersion and low immersion conditions, participants experienced the VE from the perspective of the driver of a Humvee. The speed of the vehicle was kept constant as it followed a predefined trajectory to control for time spent in each zone of the VE and to keep that time consistent across participants. Participants were given a basic 10° steering wheel to limit the trajectory, though they were instructed to stay on the road. This allowed for some level of control of the environment without sacrificing experimental control of the stimuli experienced. Low threat zones consisted mainly of a road surrounded by a desert landscape and were free of gunfire and other loud noises (see Figure 1). The high threat zones included improvised explosive devices (IEDs), gunfire, insurgents, and screaming voices (see Figure 2). The

Figure 1: Serious gaming environment: low threat zone.

Figure 2: Serious gaming environment: high threat zone.

auditory background levels associated with the low threat and high threat zones were identical in both the high and low immersion conditions. Participants passed through three low threat and three high threat zones in an alternating sequence in both immersion conditions. Low threat zones were always experienced first and were used to allow the participant to habituate to the novelty of the virtual environment. High and low threat zones also varied in length, with low threat zones consistently lasting longer than high threat zones. High threat zones averaged 20 seconds in duration, while low threat zones averaged 50 seconds. This was to ensure that zone lengths were not predictable, and so that participants had ample time to return to low levels of responding after experiencing the highly arousing high threat zones. The total length of each run was 210 seconds.

An acoustic startle stimulus was used to elicit startle eyeblink responses. Following accepted guidelines for human startle eyeblink electromyographic studies [46], the startle stimulus was a 110 dB white noise burst 50 ms in duration with a near instantaneous rise/fall time presented binaurally through Telephonics TDH-50P headphones. Decibel levels were measured with a Realistic sound level meter using a Quest Electronics earphone coupler. Startle stimuli were experienced intermittently throughout the experimental runs. A total of four startle stimuli were experienced in both the low threat and high threat zones in each run.

### 2.4. Dependent Variables.
Psychophysiological assessment included: startle eyeblink amplitude and heart rate, which were recorded simultaneously throughout the experiment using Contact Precision Instruments equipment and a computer running SAM1 software.

*2.4.1. Startle Eyeblink Response.* One psychophysiological measure employed in the current study, and that is widely used as an index of valence (e.g., emotional positive or negative reactions), is electromyographic (EMG) recording of the startle eyeblink reflex. This reflex is often elicited by a burst of loud white noise with a nearly immediate rise and fall time presented at very high decibel levels (e.g., 110 dB) for a brief duration (e.g., 50 ms). Vrana et al. [47] found that startle responses are facilitated when startle stimuli are presented in conjunction with a negative stimulus, and inhibited when presented with a positive stimulus relative to startle presentations with neutral stimuli. It is important to note that the positive and negative stimuli used in the Vrana et al. study were matched on subjective ratings of arousal, meaning the startle reflex can be a sensitive measure of valence. Relevant to the measurement of eyeblink responses during exposure to VEs, these findings have been replicated with moving film clips [48, 49].

Startle eyeblink responses were recorded as electromyographic activity using two small (4 mm in diameter) silver-silver chloride electrodes placed over the orbicularis oculi muscle of the left eye and an 8 mm silver-silver chloride electrode placed behind the left ear to serve as a ground. One 4 mm electrode was placed directly below the pupil in forward gaze while the other was placed about 1 cm lateral to the first. The electrodes were placed as close to the eye as possible while still allowing the participant to open and close his or her eyes comfortably. Impedance between the two electrodes was measured and deemed acceptable if below 10 kΩ.

*2.4.2. Heart Rate.* A second psychophysiological measure employed in the current study was the electrocardiographic (ECG) recording. Heart rate is a psychophysiological measure that is useful in differentiating between orienting and defensive responses. A person's heart rate will accelerate during a defensive response and decelerate when orienting occurs [50]. Numerous studies have found that phobic participants will exhibit an accelerated heart rate when viewing feared images, while control participants will respond with a deceleration to the same images [51]. Thus, cardiovascular responding can be an informative measure when differentiating between the effectiveness of fear elicitation in VEs. An increase in heart rate during the high threat zones would thus likely be indicative of a defensive response caused by increased levels of fear experienced by the participant.

ECG was recorded with use of a Lead 1 electrode placement, with one 8 mm silver-silver chloride electrode placed on the right inner forearm about 2 cm below the elbow and another placed in the same position on the left inner forearm. Electrode sites were cleaned with rubbing alcohol in order to improve contact.

*2.5. Data Analytics*

*2.5.1. Startle Eyeblink Response.* The raw EMG signal was recorded at a rate of 1000 Hz throughout the experiment using a 10 Hz high pass and 200 Hz low pass filter. Raw signals were stored and exported for analysis in microvolt

(μV) values. The raw EMG signal was rectified and integrated for analysis. In order to qualify for scoring, the eyeblink response had to begin within a window of 20 to 100 ms following the offset of the startle stimulus and reach peak activity within a window of 20 to 150 ms following the startle stimulus [46]. Blinks occurring at longer latencies were not considered to be the result of the startle stimulus. Amplitudes were recorded as the difference between the peak activity value and the baseline level present immediately preceding onset of the blink response. If the participant was blinking during the onset of the startle stimulus, that blink response was removed from further analysis due to artifact. Participants who failed to reach 1 μV amplitudes on greater than 50% of startled trials were considered nonresponders and were dropped from further EMG analyses. One participant reached this criterion, leaving 49 participants to be included in EMG analyses.

Due to the high levels of variability between participants in EMG responses, all blink amplitude values were standardized by taking the difference between each participant's raw EMG amplitude value on each trial and that participant's mean value across all trials and dividing by the standard deviation of all values. Scores were then subjected to a linear transformation resulting in a mean of 50 and a standard deviation of 10 for display purposes. This helped to ensure that all participants contributed to group means equally, minimizing the influence that one participant could have on the outcome of the subsequent analyses.

*2.5.2. Heart Rate.* Interbeat intervals (IBIs) were scored as the time difference in milliseconds between successive R waves in the ECG signal. IBIs across a period of 5 seconds during each high threat and low threat zone were analyzed. The 5 second period occurred at least 10 seconds following any startle stimulus or large explosion, and no startle stimuli or explosions occurred during the period. A mean IBI score was recorded for each 5 second period and analyzed.

For each dependent variable, a 2 (immersion level) by 2 (zone type) repeated measures analysis of variance (ANOVA) was utilized to determine whether the high immersion setting was effective in increasing psychophysiological responding in general and whether it affected participants differently in low threat versus high threat zones.

All significant main effects and interactions were followed with paired samples *t*-tests in order to identify the precise nature of these effects. All reported significant *t*-test results are corrected using a sequentially rejective test procedure based on a modified Bonferroni inequality to prevent inflation of type 1 error rates [52].

## 3. Results

*3.1. Startle Eyeblink Results.* A significant immersion level main effect was uncovered, and was the result of increased blink amplitudes when participants were in the high immersion setting, $F(1,48) = 16.34$, $MSE_{immersion} = 0.49$, $MSE_{zone\ type} = 0.38$, $MSE_{immersion\ *\ zone\ type} = 0.33$, $P < 0.001$. Zone type did not yield a significant main effect. The interaction between zone type and immersion level also

TABLE 1: Distribution statistics for EMG eyeblink results.

| Immersion level | Median safe zone | Median ambush zone | 25% quartile | 75% quartile | Minimum | Maximum |
| --- | --- | --- | --- | --- | --- | --- |
| High | 50.6 | 52.3 | 40.7 | 58.5 | 36.3 | 65.4 |
| Low | 47.8 | 47.1 | 38.2 | 55.7 | 32.4 | 62.4 |

Quartile and range data are given for the entire sample, while separate median values are given for both the safe and ambush zones.

TABLE 2: Distribution statistics for heart rate results.

| Immersion level | Median safe zone | Median ambush zone | 25% quartile | 75% quartile | Minimum | Maximum |
| --- | --- | --- | --- | --- | --- | --- |
| High | 67.5 | 68.2 | 60.2 | 83.5 | 52.3 | 95.4 |
| Low | 66.3 | 66.4 | 59.2 | 80.8 | 49.9 | 90.2 |

Quartile and range data are given for the entire sample, while separate median values are given for both the safe and ambush zones.

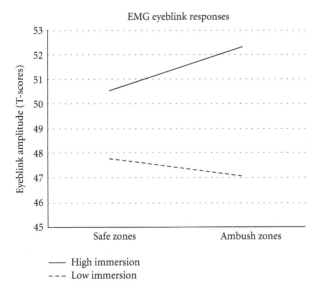

FIGURE 3: EMG eyeblink response amplitudes for high and low immersion conditions. All amplitudes are reported as T-scores.

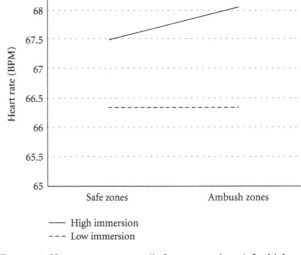

FIGURE 4: Heart rate responses (in beats per minute) for high and low immersion conditions.

failed to reach significance. However, a post hoc paired samples t-test revealed that the difference between the high and low immersion was only significant while participants experienced the high threat zones, $t(48) = 3.82$, $P < 0.001$. As can be seen in Figure 3 and Table 1, eyeblink amplitudes increased in the high threat zone only in the high immersion setting. Responses in the high threat zone of the high immersion setting were large enough to account for most of the immersion level main effect as differences between high and low immersion in the low threat zones were not significant after Rom correction.

*3.2. Heart Rate Results.* In general, ECG results were in agreement with EMG results. Again, a significant main effect of immersion level was found, $F(1, 49) = 10.78$, $MSE_{immersion} = 0.06$, $MSE_{zone\ type} = 0.03$, $MSE_{immersion * zone\ type} = 0.03$, $P < 0.01$. This immersion level effect was the result of faster heart rates when participants were in the high immersion setting. As can be seen in Figure 4 and Table 2, participants were again evidencing increased responding during the high threat zones only when in the high immersion setting, although this

increase in heart rate was not significant. No significant zone type main effect or interaction between immersion level and zone type existed. There was again a significant difference between the high and low immersion presentations only during the high threat zones, $t(49) = 3.42$, $P < 0.001$, as was the case in regards to the eyeblink results.

## 4. Discussion

*4.1. Primary Analysis: Effects of Immersion Level.* For our primary analysis in this study we sought to evaluate whether a highly immersive environment results in increased sensory arousal as measured by psychophysiological responses. Immersion effects were consistent with each measure. Participants consistently had faster heart rates when in the high immersion setting, suggesting that highly immersive VEs are more arousing than experiencing the same presentation on a computer screen. Participants also had larger startle eyeblinks when highly immersed, especially during the high threat zones, which suggests that the high immersion format facilitated startle eyeblinks.

Although on first reading these results appear to reflect the possibility that highly immersive VEs are more effective for eliciting increased arousal and producing fear responses than are low immersion VEs, this conclusion cannot be generalized given that there are restorative virtual environments that decrease arousal [53, 54]. The fact is that this VE was a warzone simulation with varying levels of threat stimuli. Both of the dependent measures were shown to mainly vary with immersion, not threat.

Another area that may put our results at odds with those reported by others is the issue that our study was for neuroscientific assessment of varying levels of fidelity and threat in a nonclinical sample of healthy college age students. Clinical populations tend to have significantly greater responding to threat stimuli presented in VEs when compared to nonclinical populations. For example, virtual stimuli that are relevant to a given phobia (e.g., phobics respond with more anxiety to phobogenic stimuli) will have more robust reactions to threatening stimuli. Further, it also seems intuitively clear that participants in the current study would react less to the threatening zones than would persons sensitive to the content of the virtual Iraq (e.g., soldiers returning from a rotation in Iraq, suffering from PTSD, or having been in a war zone) [55].

*4.2. Secondary Analysis: Effects of Zone Type.* A secondary goal of this study was to investigate the utility of our environment to offer varying levels of stimulus threat to impact the user's experience of the VE. Our analysis revealed that high threat zones were ineffective in creating statistically significant increases in arousal levels compared to the low threat zones, according to eyeblink and heart rate responses. However, participants appeared to show the appropriate directional trend toward increased heart rate and eyeblink responding in the high immersion setting, lending credence to the notion that the high immersion setting may be more effective in creating differential responding between the two zone types. However, these trends in response did not lead to significant interactions between immersion level and zone type.

*4.3. Enhancing the Virtual Environment.* The lack of differential responding in the high threat and low threat zones may have been due to the fixed order of presentation. While the presentation of the low and high immersion settings was counterbalanced across participants, the order of the zones was not. This meant that in each pair of low threat and high threat zones, the low threat zone was experienced first. While it is impossible to know what the exact effects of a counterbalanced presentation order would have on psychophysiological response, one possible explanation for the lack of differential responding may have been caused by habituation that led to a general decrease in responding during the high threat zones in comparison to the low threat zones that always preceded them. Had the high threat zones occurred prior to the low threat zones, a greater difference between the different types of zones may have been revealed, especially in the high immersion setting.

Additionally, the low threat zones were generally longer in duration than the high threat zones. This may have led to greater habituation taking place during the low threat zones, and created an additional confound that is difficult to account for in participant responses. Moreover, the low threat zones would transition into the high threat zones unpredictably and without warning, making the low threat zones potentially threatening.

The presentation of startle stimuli may also have added to the lack of differential responding in the low threat and high threat zones. In order to make the startle stimuli stand out from the background noise in the environment enough to elicit a startle response, the maximum capacity of the environmental noises were reduced to ten percent of the startle stimulus volume, greatly lowering the potentially arousing effects of gunshots and explosions experienced in the high threat zones.

It is important to note that there is parallel research on the restorative effects of nature that has explored the relationship between presence/immersion, psychophysiological measurements, and virtual reality. Previous research examining whether immersion in a VE simulated nature setting could produce restorative effects found that immersion in virtual nature settings has similar beneficial effects as exposure to surrogate nature. These results also suggest that VR can be used as a tool to study and understand restorative effects [53, 54].

*4.4. Future Directions.* Future studies using this VE may be enhanced through counterbalancing of the order of zones experienced in the VE. Counterbalancing across participants to allow for half to experience low threat zones first and half to experience high threat zones first should help to alleviate the possible order effects that occurred in the present study. In order to better understand which particular zone is the most effective in increasing arousal, it is important that the high and low immersion conditions can begin with any zone. We can then counterbalance whether a low threat zone or a high threat zone is experienced first, and which particular low threat or high threat zone is experienced first. A uniform amount of time spent in each zone will also help to control the effects of habituation from zone to zone. Furthermore, in order to make the low threat zones more clearly perceived as being safe, a cue could be given to warn the user of the impending high threat zone. This way, the low threat zones are clearly separated from the high threat zones.

The removal of startle stimuli to allow background environmental noises to be played at one hundred percent capacity may also be beneficial in creating more arousing high threat zones. Eyeblink responses will no longer be an option as a psychophysiological measure of valence in a noisy background environment, but facial corrugator EMG recording can be used as an index of perceived valence in its stead. Other metrics such as electrodermal activity, respiration, and blood pressure may also be useful measures of arousal, and responses would most likely be enhanced by the increased volume levels.

A further enhancement for future studies would be the addition of subjective evaluations. Having both subjective and objective information would strengthen the validity of the results and allow combining them for the conclusions [56]. The inclusion of the subjective data may have aided this study through greater explanatory power for the nonsignificant but apparent difference between low/high threat in the eyeblink responses found in low immersion.

*4.5. Conclusions.* One of the main goals of the present research was to assess whether a VE with arousing contents would result in increased sensory arousal if it is presented in a highly immersive configuration. A secondary goal of this study was to investigate the utility of our environment to offer varying levels of stimulus threat to impact the user's experience of the VE. Increased simulation fidelity in an arousing VE resulted in faster heart rates and increased startle eyeblink amplitudes, suggesting that higher fidelity scenarios with threatening contents were related to sensory arousal. Hence, highly immersive VEs appear to be more effective for eliciting increased arousal and producing fear responses than are low immersion VEs.

## Conflict of Interests

No financial Conflict of interests exist for any of the authors of this paper.

## Acknowledgment

This research is partially supported by the US Army Research Laboratory, Human Research & Engineering Directorate, Translational Neuroscience Branch (Aberdeen Proving Ground, MD).

## References

[1] A. Gorini and G. Riva, "Virtual reality in anxiety disorders: the past and the future," *Expert Review of Neurotherapeutics*, vol. 8, no. 2, pp. 215–233, 2008.

[2] T. D. Parsons and A. A. Rizzo, "Affective outcomes of virtual reality exposure therapy for anxiety and specific phobias: a meta-analysis," *Journal of Behavior Therapy and Experimental Psychiatry*, vol. 39, no. 3, pp. 250–261, 2008.

[3] M. B. Powers and P. M. G. Emmelkamp, "Virtual reality exposure therapy for anxiety disorders: a meta-analysis," *Journal of Anxiety Disorders*, vol. 22, no. 3, pp. 561–569, 2008.

[4] T. D. Parsons, "Neuropsychological assessment using virtual environments: enhanced assessment technology for improved ecological validity," in *Advanced Computational Intelligence Paradigms in Healthcare: Virtual Reality in Psychotherapy, Rehabilitation, and Assessment*, S. Brahnam, Ed., pp. 271–289, Springer, Germany, 2011.

[5] T. D. Parsons, A. A. Rizzo, S. Rogers, and P. York, "Virtual reality in paediatric rehabilitation: a review," *Developmental Neurorehabilitation*, vol. 12, no. 4, pp. 224–238, 2009.

[6] L. Pugnetti, M. Meehan, and L. Mendozzi, "Psychophysiological correlates of virtual reality: a review," *Presence: Teleoperators and Virtual Environments*, vol. 10, no. 4, pp. 384–400, 2001.

[7] C. G. Courtney, M. E. Dawson, A. M. Schell, A. Iyer, and T. D. Parsons, "Better than the real thing: eliciting fear with moving and static computer-generated stimuli," *International Journal of Psychophysiology*, vol. 78, no. 2, pp. 107–114, 2010.

[8] T. D. Parsons and J. Reinebold, "Adaptive virtual environments for neuropsychological assessment in serious games," *IEEE Transactions on Consumer Electronics*, vol. 58, pp. 197–204, 2012.

[9] J. Allanson and S. H. Fairclough, "A research agenda for physiological computing," *Interacting with Computers*, vol. 16, no. 5, pp. 857–878, 2004.

[10] R. W. Picard, *Affective Computing*, MIT Press, Cambridge, Mass, USA, 1997.

[11] R. Parasuraman and G. F. Wilson, "Putting the brain to work: neuroergonomics past, present, and future," *Human Factors*, vol. 50, no. 3, pp. 468–474, 2008.

[12] T. S. Langhan, "Simulation training for emergency medicine residents: time to move forward," *Canadian Journal of Emergency Medicine*, vol. 10, no. 5, pp. 467–469, 2008.

[13] M. Slater, P. Khanna, J. Mortensen, and I. Yu, "Visual realism enhances realistic response in an immersive virtual environment," *IEEE Computer Graphics and Applications*, vol. 29, no. 3, pp. 76–84, 2009.

[14] M. V. Sanchez-Vives and M. Slater, "From presence to consciousness through virtual reality," *Nature Reviews Neuroscience*, vol. 6, no. 4, pp. 332–339, 2005.

[15] M. R. Banaji and R. G. Crowder, "The bankruptcy of everyday memory," *American Psychologist*, vol. 44, no. 9, pp. 1185–1193, 1989.

[16] T. D. Parsons, T. Bowerly, J. G. Buckwalter, and A. A. Rizzo, "A controlled clinical comparison of attention performance in children with ADHD in a virtual reality classroom compared to standard neuropsychological methods," *Child Neuropsychology*, vol. 13, no. 4, pp. 363–381, 2007.

[17] M. Slater, "Presence 2005," in *Proceedings of the 8th International Workshop on Presence*, Department of Computer Science, University College London, London, UK, 2005.

[18] C. Dillon, E. Keough, J. Freeman, and J. Davidoff, "Aroused and immersed: the psychophysiology of presence," in *Proceedings of the 3rd International Workshop on Presence*, pp. 27–28, Delft University of Technology, Delft, The Netherlands, 2000.

[19] J. V. Draper, D. B. Kaber, and J. M. Usher, "Telepresence," *Human Factors*, vol. 40, no. 3, pp. 354–375, 1998.

[20] N. Schwarz, "How the questions shape the answers," *American Psychologist*, vol. 54, no. 2, pp. 93–105, 1999.

[21] M. Slater and S. Wilbur, "A framework for immersive virtual environments (FIVE): speculations on the role of presence in virtual environments," *Presence: Teleoperators and Virtual Environments*, vol. 6, no. 6, pp. 603–616, 1997.

[22] M. Slater, "Measuring presence: a response to the Witmer and Singer presence questionnaire," *Presence-Teleoperators and Virtual Environments*, vol. 8, pp. 560–565, 1999.

[23] R. M. Baños, C. Botella, A. Garcia-Palacios, H. Villa, C. Perpiña, and M. Alcañiz, "Presence and reality judgment in virtual environments: a unitary construct?" *Cyberpsychology and Behavior*, vol. 3, no. 3, pp. 327–335, 2000.

[24] J. Lessiter, J. Freeman, E. Keogh, and J. Davidoff, "A cross-media presence questionnaire: the ITC-sense of presence inventory," *Presence: Teleoperators and Virtual Environments*, vol. 10, no. 3, pp. 282–297, 2001.

[25] M. Usoh, E. Catena, S. Arman, and M. Slater, "Using presence questionnaires in reality," *Presence: Teleoperators and Virtual Environments*, vol. 9, no. 5, pp. 497–503, 2000.

[26] B. G. Witmer and M. J. Singer, "Measuring presence in virtual environments: a presence questionnaire," *Presence: Teleoperators and Virtual Environments*, vol. 7, no. 3, pp. 225–240, 1998.

[27] M. Gordon, R. A. Barkley, and B. J. Lovett, "Tests and observational measures," in *Attention-Deficit Hyperactivity Disorder: A Handbook for Diagnosis and Treatment*, R. A. Barkley, Ed., pp. 369–388, Guilford, New York, NY, USA, 3rd edition, 2006.

[28] R. M. Baños, C. Botella, M. Alcañiz, V. Liaño, B. Guerrero, and B. Rey, "Immersion and emotion: their impact on the sense of presence," *Cyberpsychology and Behavior*, vol. 7, no. 6, pp. 734–741, 2004.

[29] M. Meehan, S. Razzaque, B. Insko, M. Whitton, and F. P. Brooks, "Review of four studies on the use of physiological reaction as a measure of presence in stressful virtual environments," *Applied Psychophysiology Biofeedback*, vol. 30, no. 3, pp. 239–258, 2005.

[30] T. Baumgartner, L. Valko, M. Esslen, and L. Jäncke, "Neural correlate of spatial presence in an arousing and noninteractive virtual reality: an EEG and psychophysiology study," *Cyberpsychology and Behavior*, vol. 9, no. 1, pp. 30–45, 2006.

[31] M. Alcañiz, B. Rey, J. Tembl, and V. Parkhutik, "A neuroscience approach to virtual reality experience using transcranial Doppler monitoring," *Presence: Teleoperators and Virtual Environments*, vol. 18, no. 2, pp. 97–111, 2009.

[32] T. Baumgartner, D. Speck, D. Wettstein, O. Masnari, G. Beeli, and L. Jäncke, "Feeling present in arousing virtual reality worlds: Prefrontal brain regions differentially orchestrate presence experience in adults and children," *Frontiers in Human Neuroscience*, vol. 2, article 8, 2008.

[33] S. L. Calvert and S. L. Tan, "Impact of virtual reality on young adults' physiological arousal and aggressive thoughts: interaction versus observation," *Journal of Applied Developmental Psychology*, vol. 15, no. 1, pp. 125–139, 1994.

[34] B. R. Cornwell, L. Johnson, L. Berardi, and C. Grillon, "Anticipation of public speaking in virtual reality reveals a relationship between trait social anxiety and startle reactivity," *Biological Psychiatry*, vol. 59, no. 7, pp. 664–666, 2006.

[35] D. P. Jang, I. Y. Kim, S. W. Nam, B. K. Wiederhold, M. D. Wiederhold, and S. I. Kim, "Analysis of physiological response to two virtual environments: driving and flying simulation," *Cyberpsychology and Behavior*, vol. 5, no. 1, pp. 11–18, 2002.

[36] K. Elsesser, I. Heuschen, I. Pundt, and G. Sartory, "Attentional bias and evoked heart-rate response in specific phobia," *Cognition and Emotion*, vol. 20, no. 8, pp. 1092–1107, 2006.

[37] F. K. Graham and R. K. Clifton, "Heart-rate change as a component of the orienting response," *Psychological Bulletin*, vol. 65, no. 5, pp. 305–320, 1966.

[38] H. Kaviani, J. A. Gray, S. A. Checkley, Veena Kumari, and G. D. Wilson, "Modulation of the acoustic startle reflex by emotionally-toned film- clips," *International Journal of Psychophysiology*, vol. 32, no. 1, pp. 47–54, 1999.

[39] M. Meehan, B. Insko, M. Whitton, and F. P. Brooks, "Physiological measures of presence in stressful virtual environments," *Acm Transactions on Graphics*, vol. 21, pp. 645–652, 2002.

[40] J. M. Flach and J. G. Holden, "The reality of experience: Gibson's way," *Presence: Teleoperators and Virtual Environments*, vol. 7, no. 1, pp. 90–95, 1998.

[41] L. W. Jerome and P. J. Jordan, "Psychophysiological perspective on presence: the implications of mediated environments on relationships, behavioral health and social construction," *Psychological Services*, vol. 4, no. 2, pp. 75–84, 2007.

[42] M. F. Macedonio, T. D. Parsons, R. A. Digiuseppe, B. K. Weiderhold, and A. A. Rizzo, "Immersiveness and physiological arousal within panoramic video-based virtual reality," *Cyberpsychology and Behavior*, vol. 10, no. 4, pp. 508–515, 2007.

[43] T. D. Parsons, A. Iyer, L. Cosand, C. Courtney, and A. A. Rizzo, "Neurocognitive and psychophysiological analysis of human performance within virtual reality environments," *Studies in Health Technology and Informatics*, vol. 142, pp. 247–252, 2009.

[44] B. K. Wiederhold and A. Rizzo, "Virtual reality and applied psychophysiology," *Applied Psychophysiology Biofeedback*, vol. 30, no. 3, pp. 183–185, 2005.

[45] T. D. Parsons and C. Courtney, "Neurocognitive and Psychophysiological Interfaces for Adaptive Virtual Environments," in *Human Centered Design of E-Health Technologies*, C. Röcker T and M. Ziefle, Eds., pp. 208–233, IGI Global, Hershey, Pa, USA, 2011.

[46] T. D. Blumenthal, B. N. Cuthbert, D. L. Filion, S. Hackley, O. V. Lipp, and A. Van Boxtel, "Committee report: guidelines for human startle eyeblink electromyographic studies," *Psychophysiology*, vol. 42, no. 1, pp. 1–15, 2005.

[47] S. R. Vrana, E. L. Spence, and P. J. Lang, "The startle probe response: a new measure of emotion?" *Journal of Abnormal Psychology*, vol. 97, no. 4, pp. 487–491, 1988.

[48] P. M. G. Emmelkamp, M. Krijn, A. M. Hulsbosch, S. De Vries, M. J. Schuemie, and C. A. P. G. Van der Mast, "Virtual reality treatment versus exposure in vivo: a comparative evaluation in acrophobia," *Behaviour Research and Therapy*, vol. 40, no. 5, pp. 509–516, 2002.

[49] D. M. Jansen and N. H. Frijda, "Modulation of the acoustic startle response by film-induced fear and sexual arousal," *Psychophysiology*, vol. 31, no. 6, pp. 565–571, 1994.

[50] A. S. Carlin, H. G. Hoffman, and S. Weghorst, "Virtual reality and tactile augmentation in the treatment of spider phobia: a case report," *Behaviour Research and Therapy*, vol. 35, no. 2, pp. 153–158, 1997.

[51] L. F. Hodges, B. A. Watson, G. D. Kessler, B. O. Rothbaum, and D. Opdyke, "Virtually conquering fear of flying," *IEEE Computer Graphics and Applications*, vol. 16, no. 6, pp. 42–49, 1996.

[52] D. M. Rom, "A sequentially rejective test procedure based on a modified bonferroni inequality," *Biometrika*, vol. 77, no. 3, pp. 663–665, 1990.

[53] Y. A. W. de Kort, A. L. Meijnders, A. A. G. Sponselee, and W. A. IJsselsteijn, "What's wrong with virtual trees? Restoring from stress in a mediated environment," *Journal of Environmental Psychology*, vol. 26, no. 4, pp. 309–320, 2006.

[54] D. Valtchanov, K. R. Barton, and C. Ellard, "Restorative effects of virtual nature settings," *Cyberpsychology, Behavior, and Social Networking*, vol. 13, no. 5, pp. 503–512, 2010.

[55] A. A. Rizzo, K. Graap, K. Perlman et al., "Virtual Iraq: initial results from a VR exposure therapy application for combat-related PTSD," *Studies in health technology and informatics*, vol. 132, pp. 420–425, 2008.

[56] L. L. Di Stasi, L. L. Di Stasi, R. Renner et al., "Saccadic peak velocity sensitivity to variations in mental workload," *Aviation Space and Environmental Medicine*, vol. 81, no. 4, pp. 413–417, 2010.

# 11

# Decision Aiding to Overcome Biases in Object Identification

**Mary Fendley and S. Narayanan**

*College of Engineering and Computer Science, Wright State University, Dayton, OH 45435, USA*

Correspondence should be addressed to Mary Fendley, mary.fendley@wright.edu

Academic Editor: Kerstin S. Eklundh

Human decision makers typically use heuristics under time-pressured situations. These heuristics can potentially degrade task performance through the impact of their associated biases. Using object identification in image analysis as the context, this paper identifies cognitive biases that play a role in decision making. We propose a decision support system to help overcome these biases in this context. Results show that the decision support system improved human decision making in object identification, including metrics such as time taken to identify targets in an image set, accuracy of target identification, accuracy of target classification, and quantity of false positive identification.

## 1. Introduction

As the growth of sensor technology outpaces the analyst's ability to process captured images, object identification within the military image analysis task has become an increasingly time-critical human problem-solving task [1]. Intuitively, in this information-rich domain, the pressure associated with time-critical decision making can lead human operators to deploy a variety of techniques to alleviate the time pressure. When this time pressure persists, the decision maker often changes their cognitive processing methods, leading to the use of cognitive heuristics and their resulting biases.

Cognitive heuristics are rules-of-thumb employed during decision making that can lead to biases that degrade the quality of decisions. Huey and Wickens [2] identify how heuristics and biases impact decision making through the distortion of hypothesis formulation and situation awareness. They also conclude that this distortion, which can degrade decision making, can occur during information processing.

Pioneering work by Tversky and Kahneman [3] and others in the judgmental decision making field [4–8] identifies several heuristics and biases that commonly appear during decision-making tasks. Although much research has been done on the effects of biases in judgmental decision making tasks, there has been little work done that specifically identifies cognitive biases within a time-critical task such as object identification. Thus there is a need to understand potential biases and develop support systems to mitigate their negative impacts, thereby aiding the analyst [9]. While decision support tools such as algorithms are currently being developed, they are presently not employed extensively by image analysts (IAs) in field settings [10]. Clearly, the dearth of tools indicates further work is needed to develop effective decision support methods to relieve the cognitive demands of the IAs task. This paper presents a study to identify the impact of cognitive biases that occur during object identification and describes how a decision support framework was designed, implemented, and empirically evaluated, which aids the human analyst in information processing.

## 2. Biases in Object Identification

A recent work by Arnott [11] contributes an exhaustive taxonomy of cognitive biases identified by decision theory researchers. This taxonomy of biases is divided into six broad categories. They are described as follows.

> (i) *Memory.* Biases involving the storage and recall of information.

(ii) *Statistical.* Biases referring to the decision maker going against normative principles of probability theory during information processing.

(iii) *Confidence.* Biases serving to increase the decision maker's confidence in their ability to make good decisions.

(iv) *Presentation.* Biases skewing the way decision makers perceive and process information.

(v) *Situation.* Biases concerning the manner in which people respond to the overall decision making environment.

(vi) *Adjustment.* Biases affecting the way decision makers make adjustments from a given position.

To have the knowledge necessary to understand which biases potentially occur during the decision-making task, where in the decision making process they occur, and the types of errors produced, a combination of a pilot study, similar to the study described in this paper, and interviews with subject matter experts was conducted. This information was integrated to get a better picture of the participants' cognitive processes. These results were used to determine which cognitive biases potentially affect the analyst during the decision-making task. These biases, shown in Table 1, fit into four of the categories listed in the work of Arnott [11].

The participants were asked to identify their rationale for choosing an object as a target. The choices given to the participants were (1) I saw a similar target in the same area in previous images, (2) it made sense that the target was in this location because of its type, (3) there are similar targets in the image about which I was confident (easily detectible), (4) this target was located near another target in a previous image, and (5) I am unsure of the type of target, but do not remember seeing any other type in this area in previous images. These responses, along with data gathered through concurrent protocol and a tracer to record mouse clicks and keystrokes as they interacted with the computerized system, were integrated to determine which biases were potentially occurring and at what time.

Decision points were chosen to determine the presence of a particular bias. An example of one of these decision points is the influence of the order bias. In one of the sequences, errors were made in identifying a target in the tenth image. Figure 1 shows the first (shown on left) and the tenth image (shown on right). The plane can easily be seen in the lower right of the image (on the tarmac) in the image on the left. In the image on the right, only a white mark is there. Seventeen percent of the participants incorrectly identified this as a plane. The identification of the bias was supported by the rationale the participants chose, stating that they saw the "targets" in the first two images.

Object identification, is at its core, an information-processing task. The extension of this relationship between object identification and information processing suggests that the biases present in one task related to information processing have the potential to exist in any task where information processing is central to its execution. This assertion is bolstered by the command and control research of Duvall [12],

TABLE 1: Potential biases in object identification.

| Bias category | Cognitive bias | |
| --- | --- | --- |
| Memory biases | Imaginability | An event that is easily imagined is judged to be more probable |
| | Recall | An event may seem more probable if an instance is easily recalled |
| | Search | An effective search strategy may make an event seem more frequent |
| Statistical biases | Correlation | Probability of the co-occurrenceof events may be overestimated due to previous cooccurrence |
| Confidence biases | Confirmation | Confirming, rather than disconfirming, evidence is sought |
| | Redundancy | Redundant data may cause undue confidence in its accuracy and importance |
| | Selectivity | Expectation of the nature of an event influences what information is thought to be relevant |
| Presentation biases | Order | Undue importance may be placed on the first or last data point |

FIGURE 1: Sample images showing bias.

which mapped the Observe, Orient, Decide, and Act model to Huey and Wickens' information-processing model and denoted the presence of several biases. Some of these biases were also present in this object identification task.

The research literature suggests that the very nature of the image analyst's object identification task makes it highly likely that biases will be present. Biederman's theory on human recognition of objects in two-dimensional images suggests that humans completing such a task are easily susceptible to cognitive biases, and he proposes their presence, as the final identification of the object is done by matching the human's perception of the object with what is held in their memory [13].

## 3. Decision Support System Development

Decision support systems are designed to improve decision making by enhancing cognitive decision-making capabilities and should be integrated with the decision process of the operator. The comments regarding the negative perceived

FIGURE 2: Display of example smages of SCUD.

impact of time constraints verify the existing body of literature [14–16] which suggests that by having to search faster, the human changes their cognitive strategies to the heuristics that lead to biases. To design an effective decision support system, it is imperative to accurately match the expressed bias with the well-established debiasing strategy, cognitive forcing, visualization, feedback, memory reliance, and task complexity, which has the best chance to mitigate the expressed bias. This will need to be considered in the development of the decision support to address each of the cognitive biases.

The decision support system (DSS) includes three separate artifacts that, together, were intended to enhance overall performance through both debiasing and enabling the productive use of heuristics. These three artifacts include a repository of sample snapshots of the targets taken from different angles and under different conditions, a message board relaying potentially useful information regarding the area where the sets of images were taken, and a marking aid used to draw attention to specific areas/entities in the images. The image repository was designed to mitigate specific biases through visual cues and aiding the decision making without relying solely on their memory. The message board intended to help mitigate specific biases through providing feedback and cognitive forcing, aiding in selecting a strategy to optimize decision making [17], and aiding with task complexity. The marking aid serves to mitigate the specific biases shown by attempting to reduce task complexity, cognitive forcing, and aiding with memory reliance. The following sections describe each of these in greater detail.

*3.1. Image Repository.* An image repository serves as the first component of the DSS. The image repository serves as a debiasing method by decreasing the decision maker's reliance on memory, decreasing the level of task complexity, and increasing the ability to visualize. These sample snapshots of the targets were taken from images similar to those presented to the participants in these trials. The repository was designed to show the analyst instances of each target without having to scroll through a menu. Therefore, each of the targets was presented under five different conditions (one image for each condition for each target) within one viewing window. These images showed the target from the front or top view, side view, black and white, partially occluded, and mostly occluded or in busy surroundings. A menu of the

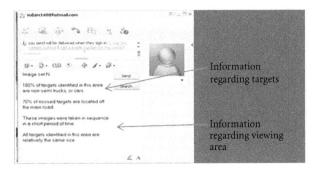

FIGURE 3: Message board.

available targets is located above the view windows for the analyst to select the target they wish to see. Figure 2 shows an example of what the participants would see when pulling up the snapshots of a target.

The images in the repository were chosen to make the decision maker aware of the different possible appearances of the targets and help them make faster, more accurate decisions by having these constantly available while performing the task. This represents a small sample of what could be expanded to become a very useful tool for the image analyst under real working conditions.

*3.2. Message Board.* A message board is the second component of the DSS. The message board functions as a debiasing method by serving as a cognitive forcing strategy and by providing reliable feedback to the decision maker. The message board provided information regarding the area where the trial images were taken. Five distinct pieces of information were provided for each of the image sets. This information was presented as the likelihood of a given type of target being present and the percentage of targets previously found in specific areas of the terrain (e.g., on roads, near hangar, around wooded areas). Figure 3 shows a screenshot of how the message board appeared to the participants.

The messages were available to the participants throughout the trial set and were used to help them look beyond the obvious areas of interest in the image and to give them an idea of whether their use of heuristics was going to lead them in the right direction. As image analysts look at

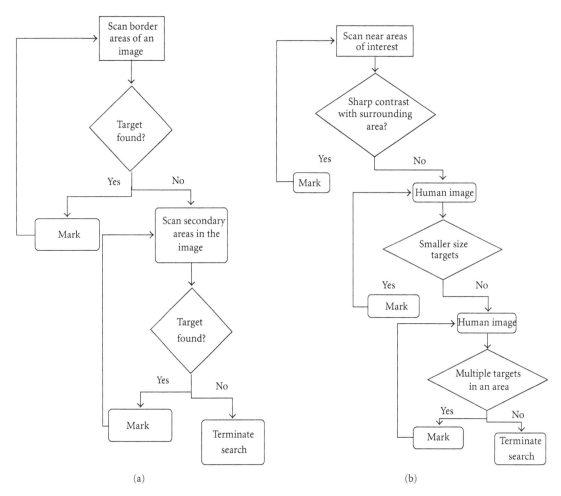

(a)                                                                                    (b)

FIGURE 4: Marking aid processes.

multitudes of images taken in the same area, this concept could be expanded to develop an automatic calculation of these figures for real time use.

*3.3. Marking Aid.* The marking aid is the third component of the DSS. The marking on the images from the algorithm serve as debiasing support as a cognitive forcing strategy that also decreases reliance on memory. Markings were done in MATLAB according to two location-based criteria discussed below.

(i) Results from the condition without decision support showed that targets were frequently and consistently missed around the perimeter of an image, and when there was a primary and secondary area in the image. An example of this is where there is a main road with several targets and a smaller road, which may or may not have targets (Figure 4(a)).

(ii) Targets were also frequently missed when they were smaller (due to location or type) than other targets in the image, when they blended with an adjacent, man-made object, or there was more than one target in a similar area (Figure 4(b)).

The images sets using the algorithm were presented in the same format as those without the aid's assistance. Figure 5 shows a sample image with the markings.

While performing the task with decision support, the participant could have an image with markings like the one seen above, and at the same time was shown the message board and had access to the image repository.

## 4. Empirical Evaluation

*4.1. Hypotheses.* The first hypothesis is that it will take less time to analyze the image sets with the decision support tool. The second hypothesis is that target identifications will be more accurate with the decision support tool. The third hypothesis is that target classifications will be more accurate with the decision support tool. The fourth hypothesis is that there will be fewer false positives while identifying targets with the decision support tool. The next section describes the study conducted to determine the role of the decision support system in terms of how biases impacted the identification and classification task.

*4.2. Design of Experiment.* A between-subjects experiment was designed and conducted to test the impact of the design

FIGURE 5: Image with markings.

support tools on the cognitive biases impacting object identification.

4.2.1. *Participants.* Forty-six participants were recruited from the university community and consisted mainly of graduate students with some classroom or field experience working with images. All participants were asked if they were color blind, as not being color blind is a requirement for military image analysts.

4.2.2. *Apparatus and Stimuli.* The experiment was conducted on an office environment on a 17-in and display monitor, and the input device was a mouse. The participants viewed images through an interface that allowed them to move from image to image and zoom in on the image. The relevant information displayed on the left-hand side includes the coordinates of the cursor over the image and a top drop-down menu showing the file name of the image being viewed. The remaining buttons are used for listing, viewing, and saving the images. The right-hand side lists the file names of all the images in the system. The number listed to the left of the filename reflects the number of detected targets. The file names will appear in descending priority order once the images have been viewed. The images used for the experiment were series of frames taken from infrared movies, similar to what an analyst might view from sensor data. A sample of the interface with an image displayed can be seen in Figure 1.

4.2.3. *Procedure.* Five sequences of ten images were shown to the participants in random order. The images were modified to extract the biases already shown to potentially be present in the decision-making task. Once the participant selects an image to view, a new window appears showing the image with a box that allows them to zoom in on a particular area of the image. Figure 3 shows a screenshot of a sample image being viewed.

The participant uses the mouse to draw a box around areas they determine to be a target. They are then asked to classify the type of target and choose their confidence in

selecting this object as a target. The participants were then tasked with determining target location and classification by type. They were also instructed to rate their confidence level in their classification.

The result of this exercise is a set of images marked with the location of the targets. During the experiment they were asked to explain their decision-making processes out loud. This was followed up by a questionnaire designed to extract additional information on the participant's cognitive processes during the completion of the task. Data were collected through the use of concurrent protocol and a tracer within the system, collecting information regarding where in the image the participant spent time examining, how many times they returned to view a specific area, and so forth.

## 5. Results

Information gathered from the concurrent protocol and the tracer was used to empirically evaluate the decision support. For the quantitative variable, time, a $t$-test was used to compare the time taken to identify the targets. For the variables accuracy of target identifications, accuracy of target classifications, and number of false positives identified, a Pearson's chi-squared test was used to compare the analysis process with and without the decision support. $P$ values less than 0.05 were considered significant. The decision support system was evaluated on four quantitative aspects measured by the tracer (time taken to identify targets in an image set, accuracy of target identification, accuracy of target classification, and quantity of false positive identifications). The quantitative results are shown in Figures 6, 7, 8, and 9.

5.1. *Time to Identify Targets.* The times taken to identify targets without decision support and with decision support were analyzed. A significant difference ($t(45) = -2.983, P < 0.0046$) was shown for time to identify targets between the two trials, indicating the decision aid was able to reduce the time taken to identify targets overall. We are 95% confident that the average difference in time to identify targets lies between $-3.69$ and $-0.72$.

5.2. *Accuracy of Target Identification.* The accuracy of identifying targets without decision support and with decision support was analyzed. The percentage of correctly identified targets differed with the use of decision support, $\chi^2(1, N = 14283) = 673.08, P < 0.0001$, indicating the decision aid was able to increase the accuracy of target identification.

5.3. *Accuracy of Target Classification.* The accuracy of correctly classifying targets without decision support and with decision support was analyzed. The percentage of correctly classified targets differed with use of decision support, $\chi^2(1, N = 14283) = 554.06, P < 0.0001$, indicating the decision aid was able to increase the accuracy of target classification.

5.4. *Identifications of False Positives.* The number of false positives identified without decision support and with decision support was analyzed. The percentage of identified false

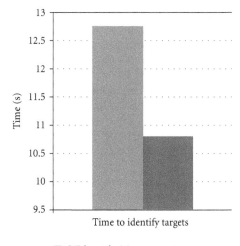

FIGURE 6: Time for identifications.

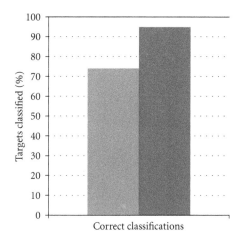

FIGURE 8: Accuracy of classifications.

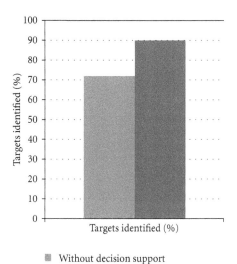

FIGURE 7: Targets identified.

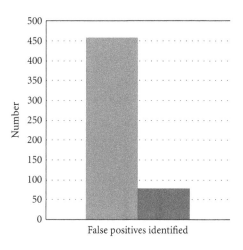

FIGURE 9: Number of false positives.

positives differed with use of decision support, $\chi^2(1, N = 535) = 268.49$, $P < 0.0001$, indicating the decision aid was able to reduce the number of false positives identified.

## 6. Summary and Conclusions

Employment of the decision support system produced a statistically significant improvement in the participant's ability to both accurately identify targets and accurately classify targets by type. The statistically significant improvement was present in each similar image set pair, as well as the aggregated experimental comparison. Employment of the decision support produced a statistically significant reduction in the number of false positives identified by the subjects.

Clearly these results indicated that the combination of artifacts selected as part of the decision support was good choice. Interestingly, the concurrent protocol found that the

participants felt that the image repository was the most helpful decision support artifact. This was followed closely by the message board artifact. The least helpful artifact was the marking aid, which ironically would be the most likely artifact to be automated.

Further analysis was done to determine the types of biases the decision support was successful in mitigating. Examining Arnott's [11] broad bias categorizations (memory, statistical, confidence, presentation), the decision support showed improvement across each one. Looking at the individual biases, each shows improvement, most notably in the redundancy bias, which was completely eliminated. Imaginability, correlation, and order were also nearly eliminated. This was likely due to the fundamental nature of the object identification task.

These results indicate that the artifacts used in this decision support system work together to mitigate several of the biases very nicely, but that there is still room for significant improvement. It would seem most likely that the decision support could be further refined to lower the presence of biases that were not mitigated well by the current version, but at some point tradeoffs will have to be made as not all biases will be mitigated 100% of the time, and attempts to mitigate some biases may have the opposite effect on others by causing an increase in their influence.

The work done with this research can be applicable across many different domains. As previously discussed, there is a lack of research in the area of aiding image analysts. This work provides a foundation for developing systems based on sound cognitive engineering principles to aid the image analyst. The next step for improving the performance of the decision support system is to automate the information provided by the decision support so that real-time feedback can be reported and to examine the interaction of the automated system and the human image analyst to ensure accurate cognitive coupling for improved performance.

## References

[1] A. C. Muller and S. Narayanan, "Cognitively-engineered multisensor image fusion for military applications," *Information Fusion*, vol. 10, no. 2, pp. 137–149, 2009.

[2] B. M. Huey and C. D. Wickens, *Workload Transition: Implications for Individuals and Team Performance*, National Academy Press, Washington, DC, USA, 1993.

[3] A. Tversky and D. Kahneman, "Judgment under uncertainty: heuristics and Biases," in *Judgment and Decision Making*, T. Connolly, H. R. Arkes, and K. R. Hammond, Eds., pp. 35–52, Cambridge University Press, New York, NY, USA, 2nd edition, 2000.

[4] I. K. Ash, "Surprise, memory, and retrospective judgment mak-ing: testing cognitive reconstruction theories of the hindsight Bias effect," *Journal of Experimental Psychology*, vol. 35, no. 4, pp. 916–933, 2009.

[5] M. B. Cook and H. S. Smallman, "Human factors of the confirmation bias in intelligence analysis: decision support from graphical evidence landscapes," *Human Factors*, vol. 50, no. 5, pp. 745–754, 2008.

[6] S. Hayibor and D. M. Wasieleski, "Effects of the use of the availability heuristic on ethical decision-making in organizations," *Journal of Business Ethics*, vol. 84, no. 1, pp. 151–165, 2009.

[7] M. A. McCann, "SSRN-It's Not About the Money: The Role of Preferences, Cognitive Biases and Heuristics Among Professional Athletes by Michael," 2007, http://papers.ssrn.com/sol3/papers.cfm?abstract_id=822864.

[8] R. F. West, M. E. Toplak, and K. E. Stanovich, "Heuristics and Biases as measures of critical thinking: associations with cognitive ability and thinking dispositions," *Journal of Educational Psychology*, vol. 100, no. 4, pp. 930–941, 2008.

[9] S. Swift and M. Minardi, "Target recognition," *The Journal of Net-Centric Warfare*, vol. 5, no. 5, pp. 38–40, 2006.

[10] S. Swift, "Personal communication," in *Phone Interview with Steve Swift, Jim Morgan, and Jim Leonard*, M. E. Fendley, Ed., Dayton, Ohio, USA, 2006.

[11] D. Arnott, "Cognitive biases and decision support systems development: a design science approach," *Information Systems Journal*, vol. 16, no. 1, pp. 55–78, 2006.

[12] L. M. Duvall, *Accounting for Human Information Processing: A Critical Element for Future United States Air Force Command and Control Systems*, Air University, Maxwell Air Force Base, Ala, USA, 2005.

[13] I. Biederman, "Recognition-by-components: a theory of human image understanding," *Psychological Review*, vol. 94, no. 2, pp. 115–147, 1987.

[14] A. J. Maule, "Strategies for adapting to time pressure," in *Decision Making under Stress: Emerging Themes and Applications*, R. Flin, E. Salas, M. Stub, and L. Martin, Eds., pp. 271–279, Ashgate Publishing Company, Brookfield, Vt, USA, 1997.

[15] J. W. Payne, J. R. Bettman, and E. J. Johnson, "The adaptive decision maker: effort and accuracy in choice," in *Insights in Decision Making: A Tribute to Hillel J. Einhorn*, R. M. Hogarth, Ed., pp. 129–153, The University of Chicago Press, Chicago, Ill, USA, 1990.

[16] W. W. Zachary, "Decision support systems: designing to extend the cognitive limits," in *Handbook of Human-Computer Interaction*, M. Helander, Ed., Elsevier Science, 1988.

[17] P. Croskerry, "Achieving quality in clinical decision making: cognitive strategies and detection of bias," *Academic Emergency Medicine*, vol. 9, no. 11, pp. 1184–1204, 2002.

# 12

# Collaborative Exploration with a Micro Aerial Vehicle: A Novel Interaction Method for Controlling a MAV with a Hand-Held Device

**David Pitman and Mary L. Cummings**

*Humans and Automation Lab, Massachusetts Institute of Technology, 77 Massachusetts Avenue, Cambridge, MA 02139, USA*

Correspondence should be addressed to David Pitman, dpitman@mit.edu

Academic Editor: Kerstin S. Eklundh

In order to collaboratively explore an environment with a Micro Aerial Vehicle (MAV), an operator needs a mobile interface, which can support the operator's divided attention. To this end, we developed the Micro Aerial Vehicle Exploration of an Unknown Environment (MAV-VUE) interface, which allows operators with minimal training the ability to remotely explore their environment with a MAV. MAV-VUE employs a concept we term Perceived First-Order (PFO) control, which allows an operator to effectively "fly" a MAV with no risk to the vehicle. PFO control utilizes a position feedback control loop to fly the MAV while presenting rate feedback to the operator. A usability study was conducted to evaluate MAV-VUE. This interface was connected remotely to an actual MAV to explore a GPS-simulated urban environment.

## 1. Introduction

Field personnel, such as emergency first responders, police, specialists (e.g., building inspectors or bomb technicians), or dismounted, forward-deployed soldiers, often rely on satellite-based maps to gain information prior to or during field operations. All of these groups operate in hazardous environments, which may contain hostile, armed people, unstable structures, or environmental disasters. Satellite maps, currently the standard for performing Intelligence, Surveillance and Reconnaissance (ISR) of an outdoor environment, have many inherent flaws. As a flat image, these maps give no elevation information, and often, due to shadows and shading, give false impressions of elevation. For example, while it can be safely assumed that roads approximate a level plane, the rest of an urban environment is often closer to a series of blocks of varying heights or depths with shadows cast by adjacent buildings. Building entrances and exits are hidden due to the birds-eye view of a satellite image, with little to no information about a building's exterior. Moreover, this imagery is often outdated or relevant only to the season in which the image was taken. Combined, these flaws often give field personnel a false mental model of their environment.

Many of these flaws and dangers could be remedied by having field personnel operate a robot to locally explore and map their environment. Given the need of these personnel to simultaneously perform another primary task, such as looking out for snipers, an autonomous robot (i.e., an Unmanned Vehicle (UV)) would allow these groups to better perform ISR and improve their Situational Awareness (SA) in real time by reducing attention needed from operating the robot. However, performing an ISR mission aided by a UV requires an interface, which allows the user to easily transition between a low workload, high-level control of the robot (e.g., moving to locations of interest) and low-level, fine-grained control to align the robot for obtaining the best view.

Recent advances in several fields have led to a new type of unmanned autonomous vehicle, known as Micro Aerial Vehicles (MAVs). Given their compact size, low cost, and flight capabilities, MAVs are primarily marketed and designed for ISR-type missions in commercial and military applications. Rotorcraft MAVs may have two, four, or six rotors, are typically less than two feet across, and can carry payloads of up to a kilogram, which are typically digital cameras. Rotorcraft MAVs are capable of Vertical Take-Off and

Landing (VTOL), which allows them to be launched and recovered in confined spaces or urban environments which may not have the physical space to allow for a traditional takeoff/landing. These MAVs are able to precisely hover and move to a fixed point in the air. This allows them to easily survey from a fixed vantage point without the need to make repeated passes of an Area of Interest (AOI), a capability referred to as "perch and stare." To support these capabilities, MAVs range from semi- to fully autonomous. Even the most basic MAVs have complex flight dynamics, which require a low level of automation to maintain vehicle stability in-flight. More advanced MAVs are fully autonomous and capable of flying a route of Global Positioning System (GPS) waypoints with no human intervention [1].

MAVs are currently controlled via computer interfaces known as Ground Control Stations (GCSs). Typically a ruggedized laptop display, GCSs, may incorporate specialized controls such as miniature joysticks or pen styli and range from a hand-held device to a large briefcase in size. If an operator is required to assume the role of a traditional pilot, that is, having command authority over velocity and yaw, roll, and pitch, this aid comes at the cost of increased training requirements, dividing the operator's attention and possibly diminishing his or her SA. The problem of divided attention currently makes MAVs effectively unusable by personnel who already have demanding tasks they cannot afford to ignore, such as navigating hostile environments.

Current operational MAV interfaces are constrained in that the operator's primary task is to operate the MAV, which includes both flying the vehicle and searching imagery from the vehicle concerning targets of interest. These design choices appear to be the extension of larger Unmanned Aerial Vehicle (UAV) ground stations (e.g., the Predator GCS). Other design choices have confusing rationale when considering the needs and divided attention of a field operator in a hostile environment. As a consequence, current GCSs and interfaces have a number of design decisions, which require extensive and costly training, and preclude them from being used effectively by field operators, who almost universally have other, more urgent primary tasks to accomplish.

From a human-centered view, MAVs performing local ISR missions could report directly to personnel in the field and even collaborate together to discover an unexplored environment. Creating a high-level interface on a truly mobile device will mitigate many of the existing flaws in present-day MAV interfaces. This interface must appropriately balance the need to support intermittent interaction from a user and having safe, intuitive flight controls that allow fine-grained control over the MAV's position and orientation, such as peering in a window or over a high wall.

## 2. Background

*2.1. Human Supervisory Control.* MAV interfaces embody a form of Human Supervisory Control (HSC), where a human supervisor executes control of a complex system by acting through an intermediate agent, such as a computer. This interaction is performed on an intermittent basis, which may be periodic or in response to changing conditions of the system [2].

HSC of a UAV relies upon a set of hierarchical control loops [3]. If an operator is required to manually perform the inner control loops within this hierarchy, such as piloting a MAV, his attention is divided between the original task (i.e., looking for victims) and lower level functions (i.e., keeping the MAV airborne and free from obstacles). Introducing automation into the inner control loops of basic flight control and navigation allows an operator to effectively execute higher level mission-related goals. To this end, in a later section we will describe a control architecture and user interface that allows a field operator the ability to use a MAV to explore an environment without having to spend critical cognitive resources on low level control and navigation tasks.

*2.2. Related Work.* Teleoperation was first introduced by Sheridan in his work on Levels of Automation (LOA) and HSC [4]. Teleoperation refers to the concept of a human operator controlling a robot (or autonomous vehicle) without being present. Teleoperation is often performed via manual control (i.e., increase forward velocity by 1 m/s through the use of a joystick or other interface), which requires the constant attention of the operator. This drastically increases the cognitive workload of the operator, and in turn leaves less time to perform other tasks. As such, teleoperation is viewed as a difficult problem, especially when compounded with the practical constraints encountered such as time delays in communications and low bandwidth for information, among others.

A large body of literature exists on teleoperation. Chen et al. distilled existing research into a set of constraints common to many teleoperation interactions including Field of View (FOV), orientation and attitude of the robot, frame rate, and time delays [5]. Many of these constraints are still relevant in the case of an autonomous MAV, which delivers live imagery to the operator.

Several researchers [6–10] have investigated using an interface to control a robot from a hand-held device. Many of these interfaces use classical What-You-See-Is-What-You-Get (WYSIWYG) controls and widgets (i.e., sliders, buttons, scroll bars). Multitouch hand-held devices with high-fidelity displays for Human-Robot Interaction (HRI), such as an iPod Touch, have been designed by Gutierrez and Craighead, and O'Brien et al., although neither group conducted user studies [9, 10]. O'Brien et al. implemented a multitouch interface with on-screen joysticks for teleoperation of a Unmanned Ground Vehicle (UGV). However, they note that these controls are small and difficult to use, with the additional problem of the user's thumbs covering the display during operation. Both of these interfaces are for the ground-based PacBot and do not accommodate changes in altitude.

Murphy and Burke performed a qualitative survey of Unmanned Search and Rescue (USAR) operator's interaction with robots in search and rescue missions, which led to a specific list of lessons learned [11]. Based on real-world emergency situations and several live exercises, they found the major hurdle to adoption and use of robots in USAR is not due to current robotic capabilities, but the interaction between the robot and operator. Foremost among their findings were that operators often did not have enough SA to operate the robot or interpret information from the robot's sensors. They also state that the interaction between operator and robot in a USAR domain should be based on consuming information from the robot's sensors rather than operating the robot. Murphy and Burke make a convincing argument for an interface where the primary focus is to facilitate and enhance operator SA through consuming information rather than operating the robot.

Very little research exists specifically on operator interaction with MAV. Durlach et al. completed a study in 2008 which examined training MAVs operators to perform ISR missions in a simulated environment [12]. Operators were taught to fly a simulated Honeywell RQ-16 MAV with either a mouse or game controller. Although Durlach et al. state that they limited the simulated MAV to a maximum velocity of six kilometers/second (km/s), the vehicle was fly-by-wire, with stabilized yaw, pitch, and roll axes to maintain balanced flight, which participants could only crash by colliding with other objects in the simulation. No mention was made as to the incorporation of video/communication delay. The study specifically looked at whether discrete or continuous input teleoperation controls yielded better performance using two different two interfaces.

To evaluate these displays and controls, Durlach et al. trained and tested 72 participants. During these flights, the operators manually flew the MAV, with no higher-level automation such as waypoint guidance. For training, participants flew seven practice missions, navigating slalom and oblong race tracks and were allowed five attempts per mission. No information was provided on why participants needed seven practice missions and five attempts per mission. If the participants successfully completed the practice missions, they were given two ISR missions to perform (with additional practice missions in between the two ISR missions). Both missions involved identifying Persons of Interest (POIs) and Objects of Interest (OOIs) in a simulated outdoor urban environment. During the mission, the participant had to orient the MAV to take reconnaissance photos of the POIs/OOIs with the MAV's fixed cameras. Twenty-four participants were excluded from post hoc analysis of the first mission by the researchers due to their inability to identify all POIs.

By the end of the experiment, each participant had received approximately two hours of training in addition to the primary missions. The first primary mission had no time limit, while the second had a seven minute time limit. While there were significant interaction effects between the controller and input methods (discrete versus continuous) in some circumstances, participants using a game controller with a continuous input teleoperation control performed statistically significantly better overall. Durlach et al. also identified a common strategy of participants using gross control movements to approach a target, then hovering and switching to fine-grained teleoperations controls to obtain the necessary ISR imagery. With both of these interfaces, over half of the participants collided with an obstacle at least once during the primary ISR missions.

The generalizability of Durlach et al.'s results is limited because their controls and displays were simulated, with no time delay, or lag, between imagery received by the MAV and displayed to the user and vice versa, inherent in real-world interactions. As shown by Sheridan, a time delay over 0.5 Second (sec) within a teleoperation interface significantly affects the operator's performance [13], so these results are preliminary but provide important lessons learned for user strategies and preferences.

## 3. Interface Design

A Cognitive Task Analysis (CTA) was performed to gain a better understanding of how potential field operators would use hand-held devices to operate a MAV during an ISR mission. While the details of the CTA are provided elsewhere [14], it was found that operators would intermittently use a MAV during their mission. However, there may be points during the mission when the operator would need to take a more active role and teleoperate the MAV to explore in more detail, such as obtaining a particular view of the environment. Finally, at other times the operator may not be actively interacting but fully focused on consuming information delivered by sensors hard mounted on the MAV. The resulting interface, the Micro Aerial Vehicle Exploration of an Unknown Environment (MAV-VUE), is outlined in the following sections along with a discussion of the theory and rationale behind the design.

*3.1. MAV-VUE Displays and Interaction.* MAV-VUE is a hand-held application that supports an operator collaboratively exploring an environment with a MAV. While MAV-VUE is implemented on the iPhone OS, the interface is platform agnostic and could be implemented on many other hand-held devices. Although MAV-VUE is designed to interact with any ground-based or in-air UV, our implementation used a small quad-rotor helicopter, which is capable of VTOL and hovering at a fixed position and heading. MAV-VUE allows the operator to interact with the MAV in two different modes, appropriate to different tasks. The first, Navigation mode, allows the operator to direct the MAV to autonomously fly between specified waypoints. In the second flight mode, also known as Nudge Control, operators can fly the MAV to perform fine-tuned adjustments for adjusting the position and orientation of the MAV for imagery analysis.

*3.2. Navigation Mode: Map and Waypoints.* In the Navigation Mode, a map (Figure 1) of the environment occupies the entire iPhone display, which is $320 \times 480$ pixels (px). The map displays relevant features of the environment, as well as the location of the MAV and waypoints.

Given the small display size of the iPhone, the user may zoom in and out of the map by using pinching and stretching gestures, as well as scroll the map display along the $x$ or $y$ axis by dragging the display with a single touch. Both actions are established User Interaction (UI) conventions for the iPhone interface. The MAV is represented by an icon typically used in command and control environments.

Collaborative Exploration with a Micro Aerial Vehicle: A Novel Interaction Method for Controlling a MAV with a
Hand-Held Device

127

FIGURE 1: The map display and general interface of MAV-VUE.

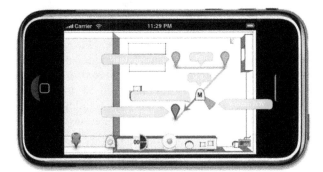

FIGURE 2: Details of the MAV-VUE map display.

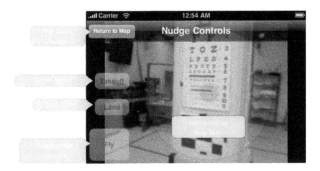

FIGURE 3: Overview of nudge control interface.

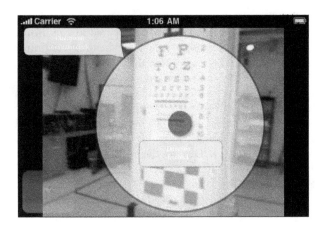

FIGURE 4: Details of nudge control directional interface.

As seen in Figure 2, the MAV's direction and velocity are represented by a red vector originating from the center of the MAV. The length of the vector indicates the speed of the MAV. Likewise, a blue arc shows the current orientation of the MAV's camera. The spread of this arc is an accurate representation of the FOV of the on-board camera. Additionally, users may toggle a small inset view of the MAV's camera. A tool bar along the bottom of the display provides the ability to switch to Nudge Control or show other interface components, such as Health and Status monitoring, or the MAV camera's view.

The map is intended mainly for gross location movements of the MAV, while the Nudge Control mode (Section 3.3) is intended for more precise movements while viewing imagery from the MAV's camera. As such, the map allows the user to construct a high-level flight plan using waypoints. Users double-tap on the map display to create a waypoint at the location of their taps (Figure 2). This waypoint is then added to the queue of waypoints and transmitted to the MAV. Acting autonomously, the MAV plans a path between all of the given waypoints with no human intervention, avoiding known or detected obstacles.

### 3.3. Nudge Control Flight Mode.
Nudge Control (Figures 3 and 4) allows an operator fine-grained control over the MAV, which is not possible in the more general navigation mode (Section 3.2). A user has the ability to more precisely position the camera (and thus, the MAV) both longitudinally and vertically, in order to better see some object or person of interest. Within the Nudge Control display, users are shown

feedback from the MAV's webcam, which is discussed in more detail in the next section.

### 3.4. Order Reduction of Operator Controls.
Control of systems, which incorporate one or more closed feedback loops, is defined as a $N$th-order system, where $N$ refers to the derivative of the differential equation which describes the feedback loop in the controls used by the human operator. For example, a first-order feedback loop responds to changes in the first derivative of the system (i.e., velocity-derived from position). Error, the difference between the output of the controls and the desired state of the system, is fed back to the input in an attempt to bring the output closer to the desired state. First-order and higher control systems are commonly known as rate-based control due to the operator manipulating the rate of change of an aspect of the system. In contrast, zero-order control systems are often referred to as position based because operators only provide position coordinates as an input to the system [15]. As an example, changing the heading of a vehicle from 30° to 60° via a 1st order feedback loop requires constantly changing the robot's rate of yaw (how fast the vehicle is turning) until the desired heading is reached. For first-order order systems, operators typically perform a pulsed control input, which has, at least, two distinct actions: first starting the turn at 30°, then ending the turn as the vehicle approaches 60°. In contrast, with a zero-order control loop, the operator simply gives a command of 60° and the vehicle autonomously turns to

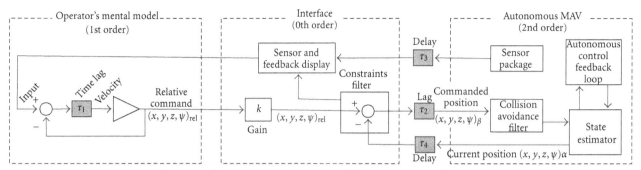

FIGURE 5: Diagram of perceived first-order control. Delays and lags are represented by $\tau$, gains represented by $k$.

this heading. A 1st order system (changing velocity) requires more attention by the operator as compared to a zero-order system (changing position) since he or she must continually monitor the turn in order to stop the robot at the right time.

A second order control loop relies on changing the acceleration of the system. It is generally recognized that humans have significant difficulty controlling 2nd-order and higher systems as they typically use an incorrect cognitive model of a 1st order feedback loop for any higher-order rate-based controls [15]. Due to the increased complexity of the feedback loops and number of actions required to successfully complete a maneuver, an operator's cognitive workload is significantly higher for 2nd order systems than when operating zero- or 1st order controls, leading to lower performance as shown in a number of studies [4, 13, 16].

Teleoperation only exacerbates these problems because additional time latencies are introduced into the system, which increases the effect of error in the feedback loop and prevents immediate responses by the operator. In addition, the lack of sensory perception on the part of the operator, who is not physically present at the location of the vehicle, reduces SA which may otherwise allow the operator to compensate for these hindrances. All UAVs use teleoperated 2nd order, or higher, control loops and as a result, have some form of flight control stabilization (i.e., fly-by-wire) to autonomously augment the operator's controls [17, 18].

While human pilots are thought to be effective 1st order controllers, due to their capability to form a working cognitive model of 1st order feedback loops [15], it is doubtful whether UAV pilots can effectively use 1st order controls. One-third of all US Air Force Predator UAV accidents have occurred in the landing phase of flight, when human pilots have 1st order control of the vehicles. As a result, the US Air Force will be upgrading their fleet of UAVs to autonomously land [19], effectively reducing the pilot's control to zero-order. System communication delays, the lack of critical perceptual cues, and the need for extensive training, which result in pilot-induced oscillations and inappropriate control responses, suggest 1st order control loops will result in poor operator performance for any type of UAV. This problem would likely be more serious for MAV operators who are not, by the nature of their presence in the field, able to devote the cognitive resources needed to fully attend to the MAV's control dynamics.

For field personnel, it is imperative to reduce the complexity of operating a robot, such as a MAV, which is used primarily for the purpose of exploring an unknown environment. Operators are under high workload, with their attention divided between many tasks, and their goal is to obtain imagery (i.e., ISR missions), not to fly the vehicle. A solution is to make the control system simpler by reducing the order of the feedback loop to a position-based, zero-order control system, which require less attention and SA than higher-order systems, as well as significantly less training. However, for the precision positioning and orientation required to obtain effective imagery in an ISR mission, position-based, zero-order control systems can be cumbersome and difficult to use. While, in theory, they are safer and less prone to error, unwieldy zero-order control interfaces have impaired many teams at USAR competitions [20] and participants in Durlach et al.'s study [12]. Unfortunately, providing a velocity-based, 1st-order interface to a MAV operator can cause operator control instabilities (e.g., pilot-induced oscillations), as also demonstrated by the Durlach et al. study [12]. In addition, for field personnel controlling a MAV, the environmental pressures of a hostile setting, the need for formal and extensive training, and the issue of divided attention suggest that any type of rate-control systems are not appropriate [11]. As such, some balance between using position-based, zero-order and rate-based, higher-order control is warranted in these scenarios to optimize an operator's performance.

*3.5. Perceived First-Order Control.* Perceived First-Order (PFO) control can provide a stable and safe zero-order control system, while at the same time presenting 1st-order controls to improve the usability of the operator's interface. We propose that this approach will allow users to achieve effective control of an ISR MAV with minimal training. The intention is to provide a design compromise that increases performance and safety by using different levels of feedback loops which are appropriate to each aspect of the system (including the human). Users perceive that they are operating the robot via a velocity-based, 1st order control interface, which matches their mental model of rate-based controls. However, PFO control converts the user's rate-based 1st order commands (relative velocity changes), into a position-based, zero-order control system (Figure 5). By working in a zero-order control loop that uses absolute position coordinates, commands are time invariant, unlike velocity or acceleration commands. This time invariance eliminates the problem of over/undershooting a target inherent to 1st

Collaborative Exploration with a Micro Aerial Vehicle: A Novel Interaction Method for Controlling a MAV with a
Hand-Held Device

129

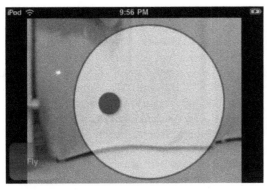 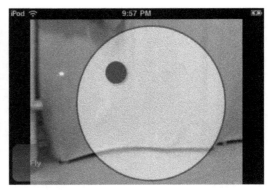

(a) Tilting the interface to the left, which commands the MAV
to move to the left

(b) Tilting the device forward and to the left, which commands
the MAV to move forward and left

FIGURE 6: Interface feedback as a result of the operator performing a tilt gesture with the device.

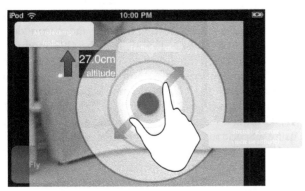 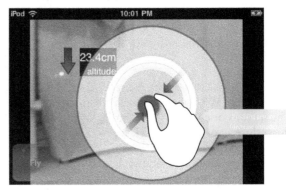

(a) Increase the MAV's altitude 27 cm by making a stretch gesture

(b) Decrease the MAV's altitude 23.4 cm by making a pinch gesture

FIGURE 7: Gestures to change the $z$ coordinate (altitude) of the MAV.

or 2nd order control systems when operators issue a "bang-bang" set of commands (e.g., a discrete forward command followed by a discrete stop/slow down command) [15]. This hybrid approach allows the user to more accurately and easily predict the movement of a remotely operated robot, such as a MAV, as well as easily formulate plans without sacrificing safety.

In MAV-VUE, users are given visual feedback (Figure 6) of their rate commands by a red dot on the display in the Nudge Control Flight Mode (Section 3.3), which is overlaid on top of sensor imagery. An operator changes the $x$ and $y$ location of the MAV by tilting the hand-held device in the relative direction he or she intends the UV to travel (Figure 4). A tilt gesture has the benefit of leaving the imagery display unobstructed while the user is maneuvering the MAV, unlike a corresponding touch gesture which will obstruct an operator's view of the displayed imagery. The Two-Dimensional (2D) tilt vector of the hand-held device defines the relative distance along the $x$-$y$ axes from the MAV's existing location (which is considered the origin).

The angle and direction of tilt is calculated by the orientation sensors (e.g., accelerometers) of the device. A discrete-time high-pass filter is used to clean the device's orientation data in order to provide a stable tilt vector [21]. Additionally, a "dead zone" was implemented which ignored tilt gestures

that were within $\pm 14.5°$ in the horizontal $x$ and $y$ plane. This value was empirically chosen based on the testing apparatus and the research of Rahman et al. [22]. The user may also control the heading ($\theta$) and altitude ($z$) of the MAV.

This interface allows users to feel like they have greater control over the robot's movements and orientation through what appears to be direct control of the robot. Internally, PFO control translates a user's inputs into a position-based, zero-order control loop to prevent the user from putting the robot in jeopardy. This approach also helps to mitigate known problems with time lag, caused by both human decision-making and system latencies. This blend of rate and position control loops drastically decrease the training required to effectively use an interface for an ISR mission. PFO control achieves the best of both position and velocity control while giving users enough control such that they feel they can effectively perform their mission without risking the vehicle's safety.

3.5.1. *Altitude Mode.* Performing a pinch or stretch gesture on the flight control interface will cause the device to issue a new position command with a change in the $z$-axis. A stretch gesture results in a relative increment of the $z$ coordinate, while a pinch gesture causes a relative decrement (Figures 7(a) and 7(b)).

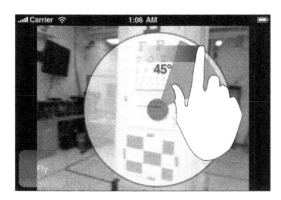

FIGURE 8: Swiping a finger across the screen causes the device to rotate (yaw) right or left.

As the operator performs these gestures, a set of circular rings provides feedback on the direction and magnitude of the gesture. Additionally, the proposed altitude change is shown on-screen along with an arrow indicating the direction of travel.

*3.5.2. Heading Control.* Operators indirectly control the yaw and pitch of the MAV's sensors through natural touch gestures. The sensor's orientation is determined by performing a swiping gesture across the screen (Figure 8).

The magnitude and direction (left or right) of the swipe corresponds to the magnitude and direction of the relative yaw command, which corresponds to an angle, $\theta$, in polar coordinates which is used to change the yaw. Internally, the device performs the appropriate calculations to use either the sensor's independent abilities to rotate, or, if necessary, the vehicle's propulsion system to rotate the entire MAV, moving the sensor to the desired orientation. This device, therefore, leverages existing automated flight control algorithms to adjust yaw, pitch, and roll given the position updates that are translated via the user's interactions.

## 4. Usability Evaluation

A usability study was conducted to assess the MAV-VUE interface with untrained users, who completed a short MAV ISR task requiring navigation in an artificial urban environment. Performance was compared with a model of an "ideal" human, who performed this task perfectly to understand how well the interface aided users with no specialized training in gaining SA and performing supervisory control of a MAV. The objective of this study was to ascertain the usability of hand-held interfaces for supervisory control of an autonomous MAV.

To achieve these objectives, four research questions were investigated. First, do users find the interface intuitive and supportive of their assigned tasks? Second, can the user effectively manipulate the position and orientation of the MAV to obtain information about the environment? Third, how well does a casual user perform the navigation and identification tasks compared to the model of a "perfect" participant? Fourth, can the user find and accurately identify an OOI and/or a POI using the interface?

The study was conducted using one of two second-generation iPod Touches running MAV-VUE. Each had a screen resolution of $320 \times 480$ px and 16-bit color-depth. Both iPod Touches were fitted with an antiglare film over the screens. The MAVServer was run on an Apple MacBook, using OS X 10.5 with a 2 Gigahertz (GHz) Intel Core 2 Duo and 4 Gigabytes (GB) of memory. Wireless communication occurred over one of two 802.11 g (set at 54 Megabytes (Mb)) Linksys 54 G access point/routers, running either DDWRT firmware or Linksys firmware. The MacBook communicated with the Real-Time indoor Automation Vehicle test Environment (RAVEN) motion-capture network over a 100 Mb ethernet connection. The RAVEN facility [1] was used to control the MAV and simulate a GPS environment. Custom gains were implemented to control the MAV based upon the final vehicle weight.

An Ascending Technologies Hummingbird AutoPilot (v2) quad rotor was used for the MAV. This Hummingbird was customized with foam bumpers and Vicon dots to function in the RAVEN facility, and the GPS module was removed. 3-Cell Thunderpower lithium polymer batteries (1,350 milli-Amperes (mA) and 2,100 mA capacity) were used to power the MAV. Communication with the MAV was conducted over 72 Megahertz (MHz), channels (ch) 41, 42, 45 using a Futurba transmitter and a DSM2 transmitter using a Specktrum transmitter to enable the Hummingbird serial interface. The computer-command interface occurred over the XBee protocol operating at 2.4 GHz, ch 1. The MAV was controlled at all times through its serial computer-command interface and the RAVEN control software, which autonomously flew the MAV between given waypoints.

A Gumstix Overo Fire COM (4 GB, 600 MHz ARM Cortex-A8 CPU, 802.11 g wireless adapter, Gumstix OE OS) with a Summit Expansion Board was mounted on top of the MAV in a custom-built enclosure along with a Logitech C95 webcam, with a maximum resolution of $1024 \times 768$ px and a 60° FOV. The webcam was configured with auto-white balance disabled, focus at infinity, resolution at $480 \times 360$ px, and connected to the Summit Expansion board via a Universal Serial Bus (USB) 1.0. Webcam images were captured and transmitted in JPEG format, quality 90, via wireless using User Datagram Protocol (UDP) and a custom script based on the uvccapture software from Logitech limited to a maximum rate of 15 frames per second (FPS), although the frame rate experienced by the user was lower due to network conditions and the speed of the network stack and processor on the iPod. The Gumstix and webcam were powered using 4 AAA 1,000 mA batteries. The total weight of the webcam, Gumstix, batteries, and mounting hardware was 215 grams.

Testing before and during the experiment indicated there was approximately a 1–3 second delay (which varied due to network conditions) from when an image was captured by the webcam to when it appeared in MAV-VUE. Position updates and sending commands between MAV-VUE and the MAV (i.e., creating a waypoint or a nudge control movement) typically took between a few milliseconds and 300–500 ms, dependent on the calibration of the RAVEN system and the quality of the XBee radio link.

Collaborative Exploration with a Micro Aerial Vehicle: A Novel Interaction Method for Controlling a MAV with a
Hand-Held Device

131

A preexperiment survey identified each participant's familiarity with Remote Control (RC) vehicles, iPhones, and other relevant demographic information. A postexperiment usability survey was given to judge participants' perceptions of their performance during the flights and of the interface. Participants were also interviewed after the experiment about their experience to gain further feedback.

Since participants' spatial reasoning abilities may be critical in their ability to use the MAV-VUE interface for exploring an unknown environment, participants were given two written tests to assess their spatial reasoning capabilities. The first was the Vandenberg and Kuse Mental Rotation Test (MRT) [23], which is a pencil and paper test used to establish a participant's aptitude for spatial visualization by comparing drawings of objects from different perspectives. The original test has largely been lost and a reconstructed version from 2004 was used [24–26].

The second was the Perspective Taking and Spatial Orientation Test (PTSOT) [27, 28], which is a pencil and paper perspective-taking test shown to predict a participant's ability for spatial orientation and reorientation. Both of these tests were chosen because they have been shown to be a statistically valid predictor of a participant's spatial reasoning skills [26, 28].

### 4.1. Participants and Procedure.

Fourteen participants (8 men and 6 women) were recruited from the MIT community. All participants were between the ages of 18 and 29, with an average age of 22 years (standard deviation (sd) 2.93 years). All had self-reported corrected vision within 20/25, and no color blindness. Nine participants were undergraduate students, three were graduate students, and two were working professionals. Each participant performed the experiment individually. Participants signed an informed consent/video consent form and completed a background questionnaire, which asked about experiences with computers, the military, iPhones, and video games. After finishing the demographic survey, the two spatial reasoning tests were administered.

Following these tests, the experiment and interfaces were explained in detail to the participant. Participants were in a separate room from the MAV and never saw the MAV or environment until the experiment concluded. The experiment administrator demonstrated taking off, navigating via waypoints, flying using nudge controls to find a POI (represented as a headshot on a 8″ × 11″ sheet of paper) and landing the MAV once (on average, flying for two to three minutes). All flights were performed with the participant standing upright and holding the mobile device with two hands in front of them. Participants were allowed to ask questions about the interface during this demonstration flight.

Participants then completed a short training task to become acquainted with the interface and MAV. During this training task, participants were asked to create four waypoints and use nudge controls to identify the same headshot, which was shown during the demonstration flight. Participants were allowed to ask questions about the interface and were assisted by the demonstrator if they

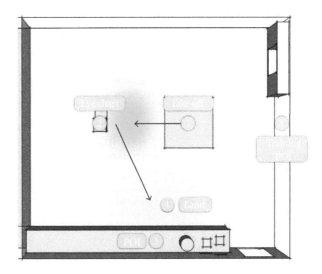

FIGURE 9: Annotated version of the map used in the study showing the layout of the environment.

became confused or incorrectly used the interface. Aside from the demonstration and a three-minute training flight, participants were given no other opportunities to practice with or ask questions about the interface before starting the primary experimental scored task.

Once a participant completed the training task, he or she was given an unannotated version of the supplementary map (Figure 9) on paper for the purposes of receiving instructions about their tasks and began the scored task, which was to search and perform identification tasks in an urban environment for five to six minutes. During this time, the experiment administrator provided no coaching to the participants and only reminded them of their objectives. Participants flew in the same area as the training exercise, with a new headshot and eye chart placed at different locations and heights in the room (Figure 9), with neither at the location used in training.

Participants were first instructed to fly to the green area (Figure 9, no. 2) indicated on the supplemental map using waypoints, and once there, to search for a Snellen eye chart in the vicinity, which was placed at a different height (1.67 m) than the default height the MAV reached after takeoff (0.5 m). After identifying the eye chart, participants read aloud the smallest line of letters they could accurately recognize. Upon completing this goal, participants were asked to fly to the yellow area (Figure 9, no. 4) of the supplementary map and to search the vicinity for a POI headshot, which was recessed into a box at location no. 3 in Figure 9, placed at a height of 1.47 m. After participants felt they could accurately identify the POI from a set of potential headshots, they were asked to land the MAV in place. Due to limited battery life, if the participant reached the five-minute mark without reaching the POI, the MAV was forced to land by the experiment staff. If the participant reached the POI with less than 30 seconds of flight time remaining, the staff allowed the participant up to an extra minute of flight before landing.

After finishing the task, each participant was asked to fill out a survey selecting the POI he or she recognized during the flight from a photo contact sheet. Participants concluded the experiment by taking a usability survey and answering questions for a debriefing interview conducted by the experiment administrator. Each experiment took approximately 75 minutes.

Participants' navigation and flight commands were logged to a data file. The webcam imagery from each flight was also recorded, along with relevant parameters of the MAV's location, orientation, and velocity. Interface use was recorded on digital video. Field notes were taken during the experiment to record any emerging patterns or other matters of interest. The results are presented in the next section.

## 5. Results and Discussion

Participants and the interface were evaluated using a combination of qualitative and quantitative metrics. One participant's times and Nudge Control command data was not used due to the MAV crashing, which occurred as a result of network interference and was not caused by the participant's actions. However, the participant's eye chart, POI, and demographic data were still used. Another participant's scored task was interrupted due to a faulty battery, forcing the MAV to land prematurely. The participant's overall time was adjusted to compensate for time lost to the landing, takeoff, and time needed to reorient after take-off.

During the study, participants completed a scored task, which had two main objectives: (1) to find and read the smallest line of letters they could identify on an eye chart and (2) to find a POI which they were asked to identify after the eye chart task. Given the small sample size, much of the focus of this section is on the qualitative evaluation of the interface. Nonparametric tests were used to analyze quantitative metrics when appropriate. An $\alpha$ of 0.05 was used for determining the significance of all statistical tests.

*5.1. Overall Performance.* Participants, on average, took 308 s (sd 52.76 s) to complete the scored task (measured as the time from takeoff to the time a land command was issued). For the scored task (Figure 9), the participants flew a path, on average, 13.00 m long (sd 10.57 m), and created between one and six waypoints (median 3) in the Navigation Mode. Further descriptive statistics on participants' performance is shown in the appendix. Participants' times to complete the scored task were compared to that of a hypothetical "perfect" human who performed the same task with no errors. Given the optimal course path of 4.77 m (Figure 9), it was empirically determined that a perfect human participant would take approximately 83 s to complete the scored task. The time of 83 s was based on the speed of the MAV, the minimum number of inputs required to perfectly align the MAV to find and identify the eye chart and POI, and also incorporated the delay of receiving imagery from the quad. During the experiment, it was observed that this delay was typically between one and two seconds, with a maximum of three seconds. Therefore, the maximum time delay of three seconds was used in this calculation.

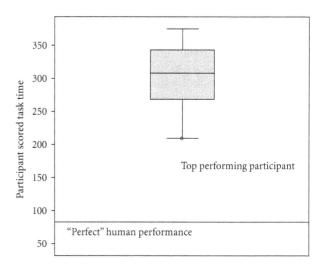

FIGURE 10: Box plot of participants' times to complete the scored task.

This ideal time was compared to the mean of the participants' flight time using a single-point comparison (two-tailed, one sample student's $t$-test), with $t(13) = 15.09$ and $P < 0.0001$. In comparison, the top performing participant, who completed the task the fastest and accurately identified the POI and all letters on the fourth line of the eye chart, completed the scored task in 209 s, approximately 1.87 standard deviations below the mean time (Figure 10).

*5.2. Eye Chart Identification.* During the scored task, participants' first objective was to move to the green area near the eye chart (no. 2 in Figure 9) using the Navigation Mode, then switch to Nudge Control to find the eye chart and identify the smallest line of letters they could read. All participants successfully found the eye chart. Participants were able to read between lines 2 and 6 of the eye chart, with a median of line 4. Participants' PTSOT scores were positively correlated with their time to find the eye chart using Nudge Control (Pearson, $r = 0.545$, $P = 0.044$, $N = 14$). A lower PTSOT score is better, so participants with superior spatial orientation abilities found the eye chart faster. Example images from participants' flights are shown in Figure 11. As a comparison, a person with 20/20 vision could read line 4 from 30 foot (ft) away, although this number is not directly applicable because the imagery shown to the participant was degraded by a variety of factors including the webcam lens, focus, image resolution, and jpeg compression.

Although participants were successful at identifying a line of the eye chart, it was not without difficulty. While hovering, the MAV is not perfectly still, but constantly compensating for drift and atmospheric instabilities. This motion caused the webcam image to blur at times, which often prevented participants from immediately obtaining clear imagery. The line of the eye chart that participants were able to read was negatively correlated with the number of yaw commands issued (Spearman Rho, $\rho = -0.586$, $P = 0.035$, $N = 13$). This correlation indicates that participants who rotated the MAV less were more likely to identify a lower line of the

(a) Image from a task in which the participant successfully identified line 4 of the eye chart

(b) Image from a task in which the participant successfully identified line 6 of the eye chart

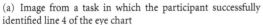

FIGURE 11: Images obtained by the MAV's camera that participants viewed while trying to read a line of the eye chart.

eye chart. The two participants who were best at eye chart identification correctly identified line 6 of the eye chart, although both participants took much longer than other participants to examine the eye chart after it was found (58.5 s and 42.5 s longer than the mean, 1.86 and 1.35 sd above the mean, resp.).

*5.3. Person of Interest Identification.* Once participants finished reading a line of the eye chart, their next objective was to fly to the yellow area of the map (no. 3 in Figure 9) using the Navigation Mode, then switch to Nudge Control to find the headshot of a POI. They examined the POI, until they felt they could identify the headshot again after finishing the task. Nearly all of the participants, 13 of 14, successfully found the POI. Of those 13 participants who found the POI, 12 correctly identified the POI from the photo contact sheet shown to them after the experiment. Using Nudge Control, participants took, on average, 98.1 s (sd 41.2 s) to find and identify the POI.

During this time, participants spent an average of 27.7 s (sd 18.2 s) searching for the POI. Once they initially found the POI, participants used, on average, 70.5 s (sd 38.2 s) repositioning the MAV to obtain better imagery or examine the POI. Example imagery from participants' flights can be seen in Figure 12.

Three participants tied for being the fastest to find the POI in 10 s, which was 17.7 s faster than the mean time (0.96 sd below the mean), but they had no strategy in common nor did they find the POI from similar locations. The time participants spent finding and identifying the eye chart was negatively correlated with the time spent finding and identifying the POI (Pearson, $r = -0.593$, $P = 0.033$, $N = 13$), indicating a learning effect, that is, participants who took longer to initially find the eye chart then took less time to find the POI.

*5.4. Participants' Navigation Strategies.* Three participants' waypoint and Nudge Control commands were reconstructed from logged data, which represent the worst, average, and best performance. This provides insight into strategies used by participants during the scored task. The paths shown in Figures 13(a), 13(b), and 13(c) outline the participants' flight paths when they used waypoints and Nudge Control. Each participant's path is shown in gray. Navigation mode waypoints are shown as large numbered yellow circles, and Nudge Control movements are shown as smaller red dots. The orientation of the MAV's webcam is shown as a blue arc, which, to prevent visual clutter, does not represent the full 60° width of the FOV. The takeoff location is shown as a large black circle in the center of the figures. The location of the scored task POI and eye chart are shown as labeled gray boxes.

Participant A had the worst performance in the experiment, with a time of 373 s (1.34 sd above the mean), six Navigation waypoints, and 241 Nudge Control commands. Participant B, who represents participants with average performance, took 268.6 s (0.67 sd below the mean) to complete the scored task, using three Navigation waypoints and 45 Nudge Control commands. Participant C performed the best overall by being the fastest participant to accurately complete the scored task in 209.44 s (1.79 sd below average). Participant C used one Navigation waypoint and 35 Nudge Control commands to complete the task. Participant A, B, and C's flight paths are shown in Figures 13(a), 13(b), and 13(c), respectively. As shown by these flight paths, participants who issued the fewest commands, that is, more precisely controlled of the MAV to accomplish the same task at hand, had better performance.

*5.5. Subjective Responses.* After completing the tasks, participants answered a usability survey and were interviewed to gain general feedback on the interface. Participants generally felt confident about their performance using MAV-VUE, with 43% reporting that they were confident about the actions they took and 50% reporting that they felt very confident about their actions.

Participants found the Navigation Mode, consisting of the map and waypoints display, easy to use. A third (36%) felt

(a) A participant approaching the POI

(b) An example of imagery used by participants to identifying the POI

FIGURE 12: Examples of imagery seen by participants while finding and identifying the POI.

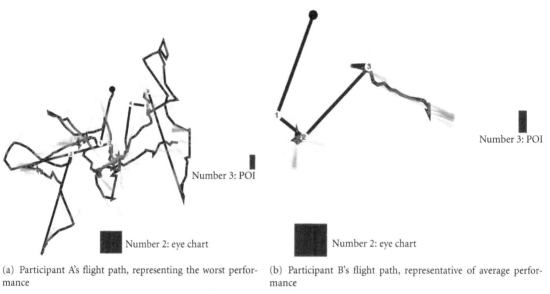

(a) Participant A's flight path, representing the worst performance

(b) Participant B's flight path, representative of average performance

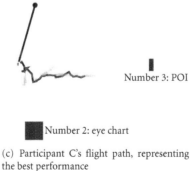

(c) Participant C's flight path, representing the best performance

FIGURE 13: Examples of participant flight paths.

very comfortable using waypoints, and 43% were comfortable using waypoints. All participants felt they understood adding a waypoint and using the webcam view very well. In the map display, 92% of participants rated that they understood the location of the MAV very well, with 79% understanding the orientation of the MAV very well. The MAV's direction of travel (the velocity vector in Figure 2) was understood very well by 86% of participants. Twelve participants wrote comments on the survey indicating they found the Navigation mode easy to use.

When asked about aspects of the interface they found confusing or easy to use, participants had conflicting

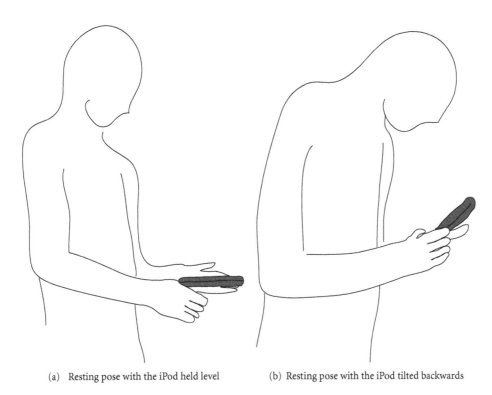

(a)   Resting pose with the iPod held level          (b)   Resting pose with the iPod tilted backwards

FIGURE 14: Resting poses observed while participants used the interface.

responses on a variety of topics. Four participants stated they found Nudge Control difficult due to the time lag between issuing commands and receiving webcam imagery back from the MAV. Other participants completely disassociated the delay in feedback, writing that they found Nudge Control easy to use, but felt that the MAV ignored their commands or did something different. Seven participants had positive feedback concerning Nudge Control, repeatedly expressing the same sentiments that Nudge Control was "easy," "straight-forward," or "very intuitive." However, every participant mentioned the time lag in their feedback. When further questioned about the time delay, several participants felt the delay was more annoying than an actual impediment to interacting with the MAV.

*5.6. Experiment Observations.* Upon reviewing video tape of participants during the study, several other trends in usage of the hand-held display and interface became apparent. Two of the most important findings that were not evident from other sources were the participant "rest" pose when using Nudge Control and usage of the Fly button. When using Nudge Control, it was observed that many participants' natural postures for holding the iPod were to have it tilted slightly towards them (Figure 14(b)) instead of the intended horizontal orientation (Figure 14(a)).

This appeared to be partly due to participants instinctively finding a viewing angle, which minimized glare, as well as the need for an ergonomically comfortable pose. However, this tilted "rest" pose corresponds to a command to move the MAV backwards since the neutral position was to have the

device almost level (small tilt values within a few degrees of zero were filtered out as neutral). Unfortunately, for many participants, the angle of their pose was subtle enough that they did not realize they were commanding the MAV to move backwards, and the MAV would slowly creep backwards as they focused on the identification tasks. While detected during pilot testing, which led to the development of the dead zone around the neutral point, the full experiment demonstrated the need for either a larger zone or individualized calibration.

## 6. Conclusions

Even with the availability of satellite imagery, many shortcomings prevent it from being a complete solution in helping field personnel such as soldiers, SWAT teams, and first responders to construct an accurate mental model of their environment. Collaboratively exploring a hostile environment with an autonomous MAV has many attractive advantages, which can help solve this problem. Field personnel are potentially kept out of immediate harm, while the MAV can navigate difficult terrain and environments, which may otherwise be inaccessible. Unfortunately, current interfaces for MAVs ignore the needs of an operator in such a hostile setting. These interfaces require the full, undivided attention of the operator, as well as physically requiring the operator to be completely engaged with a laptop or similar device. The U.S. Army has stated that they intend to begin issuing smart phones to recruits for use in the field, so leveraging such ubiquitous tools for MAV operation could reduce both equipment and training costs [29, 30].

TABLE 1: Performance descriptive statistics.

|  | N | Mean | Median | Mode | Std. dev. | Min. | Max. |
|---|---|---|---|---|---|---|---|
| MRT | 14 | 12.57 | 12.50 | 20 | 5.27 | 3 | 20 |
| PTSOT | 14 | 19.74 | 13.54 | 11.50 | 12.03 | 9.00 | 42.67 |
| Eye chart line | 14 | 4 | 4 | 4 | — | 2 | 6 |
| Eye chart line: % correct | 14 | 89.29% | 100% | 100% | 16.1 | 50% | 100% |
| Framerate | 13 | 8.38 | 7.74 | 6.98 | 1.93 | 6.98 | 13.41 |
| Path distance (m) | 13 | 13.00 | 10.57 | 5.26 | 10.73 | 5.26 | 47.17 |
| Num. waypoints | 13 | 3.23 | 3 | 2 | 1.59 | 1 | 6 |
| Num. nudge control commands | 13 | 62.92 | 45 | 45 | 56.47 | 28 | 241 |

TABLE 2: Times descriptive statistics (in seconds).

|  | N | Mean | Median | Mode | Std. dev. | Min. | Max. |
|---|---|---|---|---|---|---|---|
| Total time | 13 | 303.80 | 308.00 | 209.44 | 52.76 | 209.44 | 374.91 |
| Eye chart: total time | 13 | 141.5 | 136.5 | 71.00 | 40.3 | 71.0 | 213.0 |
| Eye chart: time to find | 13 | 84.0 | 71.5 | 36.0 | 32.5 | 36.0 | 150.0 |
| Eye chart: time identifying | 13 | 57.5 | 59.5 | 22.0 | 31.4 | 21.0 | 116.0 |
| POI: total time | 12 | 98.2 | 81.0 | 74.0 | 41.3 | 41.0 | 183.0 |
| POI: time to find | 12 | 27.7 | 27.0 | 10.0 | 18.2 | 10.0 | 73.0 |
| POI: time identifying | 12 | 70.5 | 58.0 | 71.0 | 38.2 | 33.0 | 150.0 |

TABLE 3: Descriptive statistics of nudge control commands performed by participants during the scored task.

|  | N | Mean | Median | Mode | Std. dev. | Min. | Max. |
|---|---|---|---|---|---|---|---|
| Num. $X$ commands | 13 | 23.92 | 15 | 2 | 30.56 | 2 | 119 |
| Num. $Y$ commands | 13 | 15.53 | 5 | 0 | 27.11 | 0 | 97 |
| Num. $Z$ commands | 13 | 10.15 | 7 | 5 | 13.37 | 3 | 54 |
| Num. Yaw commands | 13 | 18.62 | 16 | 8 | 10.60 | 8 | 44 |
| Mean distance of a participant's $X$ commands (m) | 13 | 0.138 | 0.141 | 0.090 | 0.023 | 0.090 | 0.170 |
| Mean distance of a participant's $Y$ commands (m) | 13 | 0.061 | 0.076 | 0.000 | 0.035 | 0.130 | 0.110 |
| Mean distance of a participant's $Z$ commands (m) | 13 | 0.227 | 0.239 | 0.130 | 0.055 | 0.130 | 0.300 |
| Mean distance of a participant's Yaw commands (rad) | 13 | 3.340 | 3.570 | 1.310 | 0.985 | 1.310 | 4.370 |
| Std. dev. of distance of a participant's $X$ commands (m) | 13 | 0.047 | 0.053 | 0.010 | 0.021 | 0.010 | 0.090 |
| Std. dev. of distance of a participant's $Y$ commands (m) | 13 | 0.035 | 0.037 | 0.000 | 0.028 | 0.000 | 0.090 |
| Std. dev. of distance of a participant's $Z$ Commands (m) | 13 | 0.086 | 0.750 | 0.040 | 0.032 | 0.040 | 0.160 |
| Std. dev. of distance of a participant's Yaw commands (rad) | 13 | 2.393 | 2.412 | 1.920 | 0.297 | 1.920 | 2.780 |

Combined, these factors demonstrate a clear need for a way to allow field personnel to collaboratively explore an unknown environment with a MAV, without requiring the operator's continual attention, additional bulky equipment, and specialized training. MAV-VUE is an interface that satisfies these demands while allowing novice users with minimal training to successfully control a MAV in a surveillance setting. Central to MAV-VUE is the invention of PFO Control, which allows an operator with minimal training to safely and precisely performed fine-tuned control of a MAV without the traditional human control problems found in teleoperation interfaces. Finally, to the best knowledge of the authors, this is the first time a formal study has examined using an HRI interface to control and work with a MAV in a real-world setting, and not a simulated environment and vehicle.

The results of this study unambiguously demonstrate the feasibility of a casual user controlling a MAV with a hand-held device to perform search and identify tasks in an unknown environment. With only three minutes of training, all participants successfully found and were able to read a line from an eye chart. Participants could easily manipulate the position and orientation of the MAV to obtain information about the environment. This demonstrates the suitability of using this type of interface for possibly performing detailed surveying and inspection tasks, such as structural inspections. Twelve of fourteen participants found and accurately identified a headshot of a POI, showing that this interface has real-world applications for ISR missions performed by soldiers and police SWAT teams. Equally important to the participants' success, the MAV never crashed or had a collision due to participants' actions. PTSOT scores were also

Collaborative Exploration with a Micro Aerial Vehicle: A Novel Interaction Method for Controlling a MAV with a Hand-Held Device

137

correlated with participant performance metrics, suggesting that this test can be used as a predictor of participants' performance with the interface. MAV-VUE extends the perception of an operator exploring an unknown environment. Unlike traditional teleoperated UVs though, MAV-VUE does not require that the operator devote their full attention to controlling the UV. Given the cooperative nature between the MAV and operator with MAV-VUE, where the UV intelligently traverses to an AOI and the operator uses Nudge Controls to perform fine-grained reconnaissance of an area, we view this interaction as a collaborative effort which utilizes the strengths of both autonomous robots and human intellect to better explore unknown environments.

# Appendix

## A. Scored Task Descriptive Statistics

For more details see Tables 1, 2, and 3.

# Disclosure

This paper is based on the M. Eng thesis of David Pitman. This research was funded by the Office of Naval Research Grant N00014-07-1-0230 and The Boeing Company.

# Conflict of Interests

The authors do not have any conflict of interests with the contents of this paper.

# References

[1] J. P. How, B. Bethke, A. Frank, D. Dale, and J. Vian, "Real-time indoor autonnomous vehicle test environment," *IEEE Control Systems Magazine*, vol. 28, no. 2, pp. 51–64, 2008.

[2] T. Sheridan, *Humans and Automation: System Design and Research Issues*, John Wiley & Sons, New York, NY, USA, 2002.

[3] M. L. Cummings, S. Bruni, S. Mercier, and P. J. Mitchell, "Automation architecture for single operator, multiple UAV command and control," *The International C2 Journal*, vol. 1, no. 2, pp. 1–24, 2007.

[4] T. Sheridan, *Telerobotics, Automation, and Human Supervisory Control*, MIT Press, Cambridge, Mass, USA, 1992.

[5] J. Y. C. Chen, E. C. Haas, and M. J. Barnes, "Human performance issues and user interface design for teleoperated robots," *IEEE Transactions on Systems, Man and Cybernetics C*, vol. 37, no. 6, pp. 1231–1245, 2007.

[6] T. Fong, N. Cabrol, C. Thorpe, and C. Baur, "A personal user interface for collaborative human-robot exploration," in *Proceedings of the International Symposium on Artificial Intelligence, Robotics, and Automation in Space*, Montréal, Canada, June 2001.

[7] H. K. Keskinpala, J. A. Adams, and K. Kawamura, "PDA-based human-robotic interface," in *System Security and Assurance*, vol. 4, pp. 3931–3936, October 2003.

[8] J. A. Adams and H. Kaymaz-Keskinpala, "Analysis of perceived workload when using a PDA for mobile robot teleoperation," in *Proceedings of the IEEE International Conference on Robotics and Automation (ICRA '04)*, vol. 4, pp. 4128–4133, May 2004.

[9] R. Gutierrez and J. Craighead, "A native iphone packbot OCU," in *Proceedings of the 4th ACM/IEEE International Conference on Human-Robot Interaction (HRI '09)*, pp. 193–194, ACM, La Jolla, Calif, USA, March 2009.

[10] B. J. O'Brien, C. Karan, and S. H. Young, "FOCUS—future operator control unit: soldier," in *Unmanned Systems Technology XI*, G. R. Gerhart, D. W. Gage, and C. M. Shoemaker, Eds., vol. 7332 of *Proceedings of SPIE*, p. 733, 2009.

[11] R. R. Murphy and J. L. Burke, "Up from the rubble: Lessons learned about HRI from search and rescue," in *Proceedings of the 49th Annual Meeting of the Human Factors and Ergonomics Society (HFES '05)*, vol. 49, pp. 437–441, September 2005.

[12] P. Durlach, J. Neumann, and D. Billings, "Training to operate a simulated micro-unmanned aerial vehicle with continuous or discrete manual control," Tech. Rep., U.S. Army Research Institute for the Behavioral and Social Sciences, January 2008.

[13] T. B. Sheridan, "Space teleoperation through time delay: review and prognosis," *IEEE Transactions on Robotics and Automation*, vol. 9, no. 5, pp. 592–606, 1993.

[14] D. Pitman, *Collaborative micro aerial vehicle exploration of outdoor environments [M.S. thesis]*, MIT, 2010.

[15] R. J. Jagacinski and J. M. Flach, *Control Theory for Humans: Quantitative Approaches to Modeling Performance*, Lawrence Erlbaum Associates, Mahwah, NJ, USA, 2003.

[16] T. Sheridan and W. Verplank, "Human and computer control of undersea teleoperators," Tech. Rep., Office of Naval Research, January 1978.

[17] S. Bouabdallah, A. Noth, and R. Siegwart, "PID vs LQ control techniques applied to an indoor micro Quadrotor," in *Proceedings of the IEEE/RSJ International Conference on Intelligent Robots and Systems (IROS '04)*, vol. 3, pp. 2451–2456, June 2004.

[18] M. Efe, "Robust low altitude behavior control of a quadrotor rotorcraft through sliding modes," in *Proceedings of the 15th Mediterranean Conference on Control and Automation (MED '07)*, pp. 1–6, July 2007.

[19] S. I. Erwin, "UAV Programs Illustrate DoD's Broken Procurement System," *National Defense*, vol. 2009, 2009.

[20] H. A. Yanco and J. L. Drury, "Rescuing interfaces: a multi-year study of human-robot interaction at the AAAI Robot Rescue Competition," *Autonomous Robots*, vol. 22, no. 4, pp. 333–352, 2007.

[21] I. Jang and W. Park, "Gesture-based user interfaces for handheld devices using accelerometer," in *Advances in Multimedia Information Processing*, vol. 3331, pp. 359–368, PCM, 2004.

[22] M. Rahman, S. Gustafson, P. Irani, and S. Subramanian, "Tilt Techniques: investigating the dexterity of wrist-based input," in *Proceedings of the 27th International Conference on Human Factors in Computing Systems (CHI '09)*, pp. 1943–1952, ACM, Boston, Mass, USA, April 2009.

[23] S. G. Vandenberg and A. R. Kuse, "Mental rotations, a group test of three-dimensional spatial visualization," *Perceptual and Motor Skills*, vol. 47, no. 2, pp. 599–604, 1978.

[24] M. Peters and C. Battista, "Applications of mental rotation figures of the Shepard and Metzler type and description of a mental rotation stimulus library," *Brain and Cognition*, vol. 66, no. 3, pp. 260–264, 2008.

[25] M. Peters, B. Laeng, K. Latham, and M. Jackson, "A redrawn vandenberg and kuse mental rotations test—different versions and factors that affect performance," *Brain and Cognition*, vol. 28, no. 1, pp. 39–58, 1995.

[26] M. Peters, J. T. Manning, and S. Reimers, "The effects of sex, sexual orientation, and digit ratio (2D : 4D) on mental

rotation performance," *Archives of Sexual Behavior*, vol. 36, no. 2, pp. 251–260, 2007.

[27] M. Kozhevnikov and M. Hegarty, "A dissociation between object manipulation spatial ability and spatial orientation ability," *Memory and Cognition*, vol. 29, no. 5, pp. 745–756, 2001.

[28] M. Hegarty and D. Waller, "A dissociation between mental rotation and perspective-taking spatial abilities," *Intelligence*, vol. 32, no. 2, pp. 175–191, 2004.

[29] A. N. Service, *Smartphones for All "Makes Sense in Long Run"*, U.S. Army News, 2011.

[30] C. Heininger, *Army Develops Smartphone Framework, Applications for the Front Lines*, U.S. Army News, 2011.

# 13

# Improving Interactions between a Power-Assist Robot System and Its Human User in Horizontal Transfer of Objects Using a Novel Adaptive Control Method

## S. M. Mizanoor Rahman[1] and Ryojun Ikeura[2]

[1] Institute for Media Innovation, Nanyang Technological University, 50 Nanyang Drive, Singapore 637553
[2] Division of Mechanical Engineering, Graduate School of Engineering, Mie University, Tsu, Mie 514-8507, Japan

Correspondence should be addressed to S. M. Mizanoor Rahman, mizansm@hotmail.com

Academic Editor: Cathy Bodine

Power assist systems are usually used for rehabilitation, healthcare, and so forth. This paper puts emphasis on the use of power assist systems for object transfer and thus brings a novelty in the power-assist applications. However, the interactions between the systems and the human users are usually not satisfactory because human features are not included in the control design. In this paper, we present the development of a 1-DOF power assist system for horizontal transfer of objects. We included human features such as weight perception in the system dynamics and control. We then simulated the system using MATLAB/Simulink for transferring objects with it and (i) determined the optimum maneuverability conditions for object transfer, (ii) determined psychophysical relationships between actual and perceived weights, and (iii) analyzed load forces and motion features. We then used the findings to design a novel adaptive control scheme to improve the interactions between the user and the system. We implemented the novel control (simulated the system again using the novel control), the subjects evaluated the system, and the results showed that the novel control reduced the excessive load forces and accelerations and thus improved the human-system interactions in terms of maneuverability, safety, and so forth. Finally, we proposed to use the findings to develop power assist systems for manipulating heavy objects in industries that may improve interactions between the systems and the users.

## 1. Introduction

Power assist system is a human-robot system that augments human's abilities and skills in performing tasks [1]. Breakthrough in power assist systems was conceived in early 1960s with "Man-amplifier" and "Hardiman", but the research on this promising field is not so satisfactory yet [1]. Currently, power assist systems are developed mainly for the sick, disabled and old people as rehabilitation and healthcare assistance [2, 3]. A few power assist devices have also been developed for other applications for example, lifting baby carriage [4], supporting agricultural works [5], hydraulic power-assist for automobiles [6], skill-assist in manufacturing [7], power-assisted slide doors for automobiles [8], power-assisted control for bicycle [9], power assistance for sports and horse training [10, 11], and so forth.

We think that handling heavy objects, which is common and necessary in industries, may be another potential field of application of the power assist systems [12, 13]. It is very necessary to move heavy objects in industries such as manufacturing and assembly, logistics and transport, construction, mining, disaster and rescue works, forestry, agriculture, and so forth. Manual handling of heavy objects is very tedious and it causes work-related disabilities and disorders such as back pain to the humans [14].

On the other hand, autonomous devices may not provide desired flexibility in object handling and positioning in many cases [15]. Hence, it is thought that the uses of suitable power assist systems may be appropriate for handling heavy objects in the aforementioned industries. However, such power assist systems are not found in the industries as their design has not got much attention yet [13].

Again, a power assist system reduces the perceived heaviness of an object handled with it [1], and hence, the load force (manipulative force tangential to grip surfaces) required to handle an object with power-assist should be lower than that required to handle the object manually. But, the limitations with the conventional power assist devices are that the human operator cannot perceive the heaviness of the object correctly before handling it with the assist system and eventually applies excessive load force, which results in faulty interactions between the system and the user such as sudden increase in acceleration, fearfulness of the user, lack of maneuverability and stability, fatal accident, and so forth [13]. However, the conventional assist devices for object manipulation do not consider this issue [16–19].

There are also other limitations in the conventional power assist devices for object manipulation as follows: human features are not included in control, the system is itself heavy, the amount of power assistance is unclear, the system is not evaluated properly for safety, maneuverability, efficiency, and so forth [16]. Again, the system may have the disadvantages of pneumatics, hydraulics, and so forth [16]. Operator's intention is not reflected in the control, and the system generates vibrations [17]. Human force is not measured directly and separately, the system restricts movement due to constraints, there are difficulties in path planning, the object handling speed is slow, and so forth [18]. Sometimes, the system generates excessive power [19]. Moreover, there are some common problems/issues with power assist devices such as actuator saturation, noises and disturbances, adjustment with human users, selection of appropriate control methods, accuracy, capacity and sensitivity of force sensors, number of force sensors, configuration of force sensors and of the entire system, number of degrees of freedom, stability, and so forth that should be addressed. However, the conventional power assist devices do not adopt any holistic approach to address these problems/issues to make the systems human-friendly.

In the industries, the workers need to manipulate objects in different directions such as vertical lifting (lifting objects from lower position to higher position) [13], vertical lowering (lowering objects from higher position to lower position), horizontal transfer [17], and so forth in order to fulfill the task requirements [13]. We assume that the maneuverability, heaviness perception, forces and motion features, task requirements, and so forth for manipulating objects with power-assist among these directions may be different from each other and these differences may affect the control and the system performances. Hence, it seems to be necessary to study the object manipulation with power-assist in all these directions, compare them to each other, and to reflect the differences in the control design. However, such study has also not been carried out yet.

We studied the lifting of objects in the vertical direction in our previous works [13], but transferring objects in the horizontal direction is still unaddressed though the horizontal transfer of objects is very necessary in many practical cases in the industries. A few researches studied the power assist devices for transferring objects in the horizontal direction [17, 20]. But, these devices are not designed targeting the

industrial applications and these devices have limitations in their performances as mentioned above because human features are not included in their controls, that is, the biomimetic approach of the control design is ignored.

Our pioneering research addresses the aforementioned issues holistically and aims to develop a model of power assist device to handle heavy objects that does not have the above limitations [12, 13]. This paper, as a part of the entire research, presents the design and evaluation of a novel adaptive control scheme for transferring objects with power-assist horizontally in cooperation with the humans based on human features that improves the human-system interactions. We developed a 1-DOF power assist system for transferring objects horizontally by the human subjects. We included weight perception in the system dynamics and control. We simulated the system and determined the optimum maneuverability conditions for transferring objects. We determined the psychophysical relationships between actual and perceived weights and analyzed the load forces and motion features for transferring objects with the system. We then used the human features to design, implement and evaluate a novel adaptive control scheme to reduce excessive load forces and accelerations, and thus to improve the performances of the human-robot system.

The results showed that the novel control improved the human-system interactions in terms of safety, maneuverability, naturalness, and so forth. We compared the findings for the horizontal transfer of objects with power-assist to that for the vertical lifting of objects [13]. Finally, we proposed to use the findings to develop human-friendly power assist devices for handling heavy objects in industries that may enhance interactions with human users in terms of maneuverability, safety, naturalness, and so forth.

## 2. The Experimental Human-Robot System

*2.1. System Configuration.* We developed a 1-DOF (horizontal translational motion) power assist robot system using a ball screw assembly actuated by an AC servomotor (Type: SGML-01BF12, made by Yaskawa, Japan). We coaxially fixed the ball screw and the servomotor on a metal plate and horizontally placed the plate on a table. We made three rectangular boxes by bending aluminum sheets (thickness: 0.5 mm). The boxes were horizontally transferred with the system by the human subjects and were called the power-assisted objects (PAOs). A PAO (box) could be tied to the ball nut through a force sensor (foil strain gauge type, NEC Ltd.) and be transferred by a subject. The dimensions (length × width × height) of the boxes were $16 \times 6 \times 5$ cm, $12 \times 6 \times 5$ cm and $8.6 \times 6 \times 5$ cm for the large, medium and small size respectively. The bottom, left and right sides of each PAO were kept open. The experimental setup of the system is shown in Figure 1.

*2.2. Human-Features-Based System Dynamics.* According to Figure 2, the targeted dynamics for transferring a PAO horizontally by a subject with the system is described by (1), where $F_o = mg$ If we include a hypothesis regarding weight

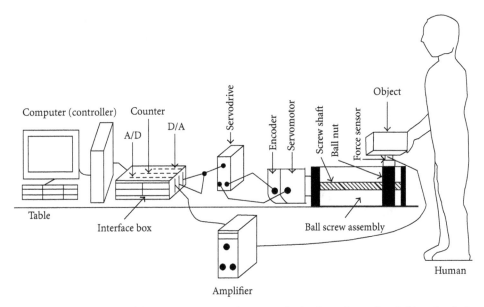

FIGURE 1: Experimental setup of the 1-DOF power assist system for horizontal transfer of objects by the human.

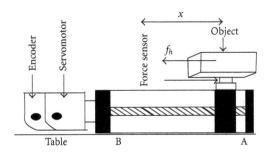

FIGURE 2: Dynamics of the 1-DOF power assist system for horizontal manipulation of objects. The PAO tied to the force sensor is transferred by the subject from position "A" to position "B".

perception in the dynamics, then (1) changes to (2). The hypothesis means that both $m_1$ and $m_2$ stand for mass, but $m_1$ forms inertia force and $m_2$ forms gravity force, and $m_1 \neq m_2 \neq m$, $m_1 \ll m$, $m_2 \ll m$, $|m_1\ddot{x}_d| \neq |m_2 g|$. A difference between $m_1$ and $m_2$ is considered due to the difference between human's perception and reality regarding the heaviness of the object transferred with the power assist system [1]. Consider

$$m\ddot{x}_d = f_h + F_0, \tag{1}$$

$$m_1\ddot{x}_d = f_h + m_2 g, \tag{2}$$

where, $m$ = actual mass of the PAO, $x_d$ = desired displacement of the PAO, $f_h$ = load force applied by the subject, $g$ = acceleration of gravity.

### 2.3. Control System Design.

We derived (3) from (2). We then diagrammed the control based on (3), which is shown in Figure 3. If the system is simulated using MAT-LAB/SIMULINK in velocity control mode of the servomotor, the commanded velocity ($\dot{x}_c$) to the servomotor is determined by (4), which is fed to the servomotor through a

D/A converter. During simulation, the servodrive determines the error displacement signal by comparing the actual displacement to the desired displacement. Consider

$$\ddot{x}_d = \frac{1}{m_1}(f_h + m_2 g), \tag{3}$$

$$\dot{x}_c = \dot{x}_d + G(x_d - x). \tag{4}$$

The control system in Figure 3 is designed for the especially developed 1-DOF power assist system (Figures 1 and 2) for understanding human characteristics and human's interactions with the system. We design the control system shown in Figure 3 following the position control method for controlling the robotic system. The displacement was used to feed-back as it is shown in the figure. Here, the input is the human force ($f_h$) and the output is the object's displacement. The choice between the position control and the force control is important. We think that the position control is a good choice where the motion path is repeated, well-structured, well-defined, certain, and the accuracy in the positional movement is desired. On the other hand, the force control may be a good choice where the environment is not well-defined, well-structured, uncertainty is high, motion

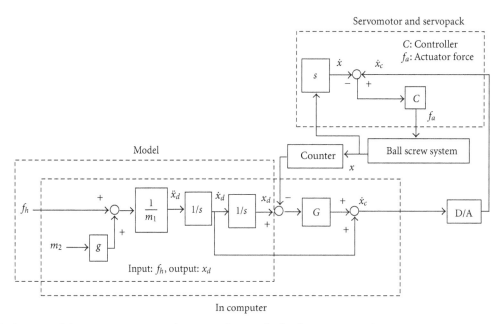

FIGURE 3: Block diagram of the power-assist control. Here, $G$ denotes feedback gain, D/A indicates D/A converter, and $x$ denotes actual displacement. Feedback position control was used with the servomotor in velocity control mode.

path or environment is changeable, and so forth [10, 11, 17, 21, 22]. We used the position control because:

(i) The position control significantly compensates the effects of friction, viscosity, inertia, and so forth. But, these effects need to be considered for the force control though it is very difficult to model and calculate the friction force. Again, the dynamic effects, nonlinear forces, and so forth, affect the system performances for the force control for the multi-degree of freedom systems.

(ii) The actuator force is less and the ball-screw gear ratio is high for the position control. But, the opposite is true for the force control.

(iii) For the position control with high gear ratio, it is easy to realize the real system. But, it is difficult to realize the real system for the force control.

## 3. Experiment 1: Analysis of the Human-System Interactions

We expressed the human's interactions with the system in terms of maneuverability, mobility, naturalness, safety, ease of use, comfort, weight perception, load force, object motion, and so forth, for the objects transferred with the power assist system.

*3.1. Experiment Procedures.* We nominated ten mechanical engineering male students aged between 23 and 31 years to voluntarily participate in the experiment. We simulated the system shown in Figure 3 using Matlab/Simulink (solver: ode4, Runge-Kutta; type: fixed-step; fundamental sample

TABLE 1: Values of variables for the simulation.

| $m_1$ (kg) | 2.0 | 1.5 | 1.0 | 0.5 |
|---|---|---|---|---|
| $m_2$ (kg) | 0.09 | 0.06 | 0.03 | |

time: 0.001 s) for twelve $m_1$ and $m_2$ sets (Table 1) separately. We chose the values of $m_1$ and $m_2$ based on our experiences.

Each subject transferred each size PAO with the assist system from "A" to "B" as shown in Figure 2 (distance between "A" and "B" was about 0.12 m) once for each $m_1$ and $m_2$ set separately. In each trial, the task required the subject to transfer the object from "A" to "B", maintain the object at "B" for 1-2 seconds and then release the object. We considered the subject's ease of use and comfort as the evaluation criteria for the maneuverability in transferring objects horizontally with the system [21]. For each trial (for each $m_1$ and $m_2$ set for each size object), the subject subjectively evaluated (scored) the system for maneuverability from the following alternatives.

(1) Very Easy and Comfortable (score: +2);

(2) Easy and Comfortable (score: +1);

(3) Borderline (score: 0);

(4) Uneasy and Uncomfortable (score: −1);

(5) Very Uneasy and Uncomfortable (score: −2).

All the subjects evaluated the system for maneuverability for the small, medium, and large size objects independently for each $m_1$ and $m_2$ set. The load force and motion (displacement, velocity, acceleration) data were recorded separately for each trial.

Each subject after each trial also manually transferred a reference-weight object (rectangular box made by bending aluminum sheet of thickness 0.5 mm) horizontally on a smooth table for about 0.12 m using the right hand alone for the reference weights. The weight of the reference-weight object could be changed by attaching extra masses inside the box. The subject thus compared the perceived weight of the PAO to that of the reference-weight object and estimated the magnitude of the perceived weight of the PAO following the psychophysical method "constant stimuli". The appearance and size of the PAO were same as that of the reference-weight object for each trial.

### 3.2. Experiment Results and Analyses

#### 3.2.1. Determining Optimum Maneuverability.
We determined the mean evaluation scores for the maneuverability for the twelve $m_1$ and $m_2$ sets for each size object separately. Table 2 shows the mean evaluation scores for the medium size object. We also determined similar scores for the large and small size objects. The results show that the maneuverability is not influenced by the visual object size. The reason may be that the subjects evaluate the maneuverability using their haptic senses where the visual size cues have no or less influence. However, the haptic size cues might influence the maneuverability [23, 24].

The results show that ten $m_1$ and $m_2$ sets got positive scores, but two sets got negative scores. We see that $m_1 = 0.5$ kg, $m_2 = 0.03$ kg and $m_1 = 1$ kg, $m_2 = 0.03$ kg got the highest scores. Hence, the optimum maneuverability is to be achieved at any one of these two conditions. A unique condition for the optimum maneuverability could be determined if we could use more values of $m_1$ and $m_2$ for the simulation.

The subjects felt very easy and comfortable to manipulate the objects only at $m_1 = 0.5$ kg, $m_2 = 0.03$ kg and $m_1 = 1$ kg, $m_2 = 0.03$ kg. Hence, we declared these two sets as the optimum conditions for the maneuverability. Here, the optimality/optimization was decided based on the human's feelings following the heuristics. The findings support our hypothesis that we could not identify the positive $m_1$ and $m_2$ sets (satisfactory maneuverability) from the negative $m_1$ and $m_2$ sets (unsatisfactory maneuverability) if we did not think $m_1 \neq m_2 \neq m$, $m_1 \ll m$, $m_2 \ll m$, $m_1 \ddot{x}_d \neq m_2 g$.

The results show that the optimum/best sets are also the sets of the smallest values of $m_1$ and $m_2$. Much smaller values of $m_1$ and $m_2$ may further reduce the perceived heaviness, but it needs to clarify whether or not this is suitable for human psychology. In zero-gravity or weightless condition when $m_2 = 0$, the object is supposed to be too light as it was found in [25] in actual environment and in [26] in virtual environment. But, we previously found that the zero-gravity is not feasible because the human loses some haptic information at zero-gravity that reduces human's weight perception ability [23].

#### 3.2.2. Determining Psychophysical Relationships between Actual and Perceived Weights.
We determined the mean perceived weight for each size object separately for $m_1 = 0.5$ kg, $m_2 = 0.03$ kg (condition 1) and $m_1 = 1$ kg, $m_2 = 0.03$ kg (condition 2) as presented in Figure 4. We assumed $m_2$ as the

TABLE 2: Mean maneuverability scores with standard deviations (in parentheses) for the medium size object.

| $m_1$ | $m_2$ | Mean maneuverability score |
| --- | --- | --- |
| 1 | 0.06 | +0.83 (0.04) |
| 2 | 0.06 | +0.33 (0.06) |
| *0.5* | *0.03* | *+2.0 (0)* |
| *1* | *0.03* | *+2.0 (0)* |
| 1.5 | 0.03 | +1.5 (0.05) |
| 2 | 0.09 | −0.17 (0.07) |
| 0.5 | 0.06 | +1.0 (0) |
| 1.5 | 0.09 | −0.17 (0.08) |
| 0.5 | 0.09 | +0.17 (0.05) |
| 1 | 0.09 | +1.0 (0.03) |
| 1.5 | 0.06 | +0.67 (0.08) |
| 2 | 0.03 | +1.17 (0.10) |

actual weight of the PAO that is, the actual weight was 0.03 kg or 0.2943 N for each size object for two $m_1$ and $m_2$ sets. We compared the perceived weights of Figure 4 to the actual weight (0.2943 N) for each size object for $m_1 = 0.5$ kg, $m_2 = 0.03$ kg and $m_1 = 1$ kg, $m_2 = 0.03$ kg. The figure shows (and we also found in our previous research) that $m_1$ does not affect weight perception, but $m_2$ does affect [13]. Again, we see that the visual object sizes do not affect weight perception [13, 24].

The results for analyses of variances, ANOVAs (visual object size, subject) separately analyzed on the perceived weights for two $m_1$ and $m_2$ sets showed that the variations due to the object sizes were insignificant ($F_{2,18} < 1$ for each $m_1$ and $m_2$ set). The reason may be that the subjects estimated the perceived weights using the haptic cues where the visual cues had no influences [24]. Variations between the subjects were found statistically insignificant ($F_{9,18} < 1$ for each $m_1$ and $m_2$ set).

The actual weight of the object was 0.2943 N, but the humans felt about 0.052 N (Figure 4) when the object was transferred with the system horizontally. Hence, the results show that the perceived weight was about 18% of the actual weight. Its physical meaning is that the perceived weight of an object transferred with power-assist in the horizontal direction is 18% of the perceived weight of the same object transferred in the horizontal direction manually. This happens because the power assist system reduces the perceived weight through its assistance to the humans [1, 13]. It is a known concept that a power assist system reduces the feeling of the weight; however, it was not quantified. This research quantified the weight attenuation for the horizontal transfer of objects with a power assist system. As we compare with our previous research, we find that the perceived weight reduces to 40% and 20% of the actual weight if the object is vertically lifted or lowered, respectively [13, 23]. Weight perception is less for the horizontal manipulation of objects because the gravity force is compensated.

#### 3.2.3. Analysis of Load Force.
The time trajectory of the load force for a typical trial is shown in Figure 5. We derived the

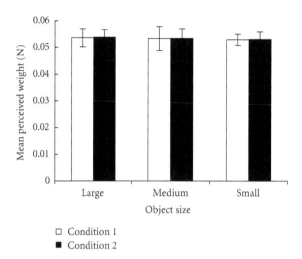

FIGURE 4: Mean ($n = 10$) perceived weights for different object sizes for conditions 1 ($m_1 = 0.5\,\text{kg}$, $m_2 = 0.03\,\text{kg}$) and 2 ($m_1 = 1\,\text{kg}$, $m_2 = 0.03\,\text{kg}$).

TABLE 3: Mean peak load forces (PLFs) for different conditions for different object sizes.

| $m_1$, $m_2$ sets | Mean PLFs ($N$) with standard deviations (in parentheses) for different object sizes | | |
|---|---|---|---|
| | Large | Medium | Small |
| $m_1 = 0.5\,\text{kg}$, $m_2 = 0.03\,\text{kg}$ | 2.9131 (0.1307) | 2.6020 (0.1151) | 2.4113 (0.1091) |
| $m_1 = 1.0\,\text{kg}$, $m_2 = 0.03\,\text{kg}$ | 2.9764 (0.1009) | 2.6554 (0.1052) | 2.4602 (0.1067) |

TABLE 4: Mean peak velocity with standard deviations (in parentheses) for different object sizes for different conditions.

| Object size | Mean peak velocity (m/s) | |
|---|---|---|
| | $m_1 = 0.5\,\text{kg}$, $m_2 = 0.03\,\text{kg}$ | $m_1 = 1.0\,\text{kg}$, $m_2 = 0.03\,\text{kg}$ |
| Large | 0.1497 (0.0149) | 0.1557 (0.0209) |
| Medium | 0.1345 (0.0157) | 0.1399 (0.0122) |
| Small | 0.1098 (0.0121) | 0.1176 (0.0119) |

magnitude of the peak load force (PLF) for each object size for conditions 1 ($m_1 = 0.5\,\text{kg}$, $m_2 = 0.03\,\text{kg}$) and 2 ($m_1 = 1\,\text{kg}$, $m_2 = 0.03\,\text{kg}$) separately and determined the mean PLFs, as shown in Table 3. We see that the mean PLFs for condition 2 are slightly larger than that for condition 1. We found previously that $m_1$ and $m_2$ are linearly proportional to the PLF, and $m_1$ affects the load force, but it does not affect the weight perception. On the other hand, $m_2$ affects both load force and weight perception [13, 23]. We assume that the larger $m_1$ in condition 2 has produced the larger PLF.

We have already found in Section 3.2.1 that the subjects feel the best maneuverability at $m_1 = 0.5\,\text{kg}$, $m_2 = 0.03\,\text{kg}$ and $m_1 = 1\,\text{kg}$, $m_2 = 0.03\,\text{kg}$. On the other hand, the actually required PLF to transfer the PAO should be slightly larger than the perceived weight [24], which is 0.052 N. We compared the perceived weights from Figure 4 to the PLFs (Table 3) for the large, medium, and small objects and found that the PLFs were very excessive. It means that the subjects apply the load forces that are extremely larger than the actual requirements. We assume that the excessive PLFs cause problems in the human-system interactions in terms of maneuverability, safety, and so forth that we discussed in the introduction. We also see that the magnitudes of the PLFs are proportional to the object sizes [13, 23, 24].

*3.2.4. Analysis of Motions.* Figure 5 shows the typical displacement, velocity and acceleration trajectories for a trial.

We derived the peak velocity and peak acceleration for each trial and determined their means for each object size in each condition separately as given in Tables 4 and 5 respectively. We see in the tables that the velocity and acceleration are large. We assume that the large peak load forces have resulted in the large accelerations that are harmful to the power assist system in terms of maneuverability, safety, and so forth.

## 4. Experiment 2: Improving the Human-System Interactions

Tables 3 and 5 show that the load forces and accelerations are excessive that cause problems in the human-system interactions as we discussed in Section 1. Experiment 2 aimed to design a novel control based on the results of experiment 1 to reduce the excessive load forces and accelerations, and thus to improve the human-system interactions.

*4.1. Novel Control Design and Implementation.* The novel control was such that the value of $m_1$ exponentially declined from a large value to 0.5 kg when the subject transferred the PAO with the power assist system and the command velocity of (4) exceeded a threshold. Equations (5) and (6) were used for $m_1$ and $m_2$, respectively, to augment the effectiveness of the control shown in Figure 3. The novel control is illustrated in Figure 6 as a flowchart. We determined the digit 6 in (5) by trial and error. In fact, the control shown in Figure 3 is

Improving Interactions between a Power-Assist Robot System and Its Human User in Horizontal Transfer of Objects Using a Novel Adaptive Control Method

145

TABLE 5: Mean peak accelerations with standard deviations (in parentheses) for different object sizes for different conditions.

| Object size | Mean peak acceleration (m/s$^2$) | |
|---|---|---|
| | $m_1 = 0.5$ kg, $m_2 = 0.03$ kg | $m_1 = 1.0$ kg, $m_2 = 0.03$ kg |
| Large | 0.2309 (0.0901) | 0.2701 (0.0498) |
| Medium | 0.2282 (0.0721) | 0.2542 (0.0153) |
| Small | 0.1887 (0.0298) | 0.2134 (0.0525) |

itself novel as it includes the ideas related to human's weight perception. However, the novelty in the control in Figure 3 is further enhanced as presented in Figure 6 through the exponential reduction of $m_1$.

We derived the relationship formula for $m_1$ in (5) empirically. The explanation on how to derive the empirical formula is as the following.

(i) Based on the time trajectory of the load force in Figure 5, we derived the magnitude of the peak load force (PLF) for each trial and determined the mean PLFs for each $m_1$ and $m_2$ set for each object size separately. We then plotted the graph taking the $m_1$ values of the twelve $m_1$ and $m_2$ sets as the abscissa and the mean PLFs for the twelve $m_1$ and $m_2$ sets for the three objects as the ordinate, and thus determined the relationships between $m_1$ and PLFs. The results showed approximately linear relationships between the inertial mass ($m_1$) and the PLFs.

(ii) We see in Figure 4 (our previously published articles also reported similar results) that humans do not feel the change in $m_1$ that is, $m_1$ does not affect the haptic perception of weight, but it affects the load force. On the other hand, $m_2$ affects both perceived weight and load force [13, 23, 27, 28].

(iii) Based on the information gathered in (i) and (ii), we see that the PLF linearly varies with $m_1$. Hence, if we exponentially reduce $m_1$ then the PLF will also reduce because it was our goal to reduce the excessive acceleration through the reduction in the excessive PLF. We want to reduce the excessive acceleration because it hampers the human-system interactions. On the other hand, this type of reduction in $m_1$ could affect the relationships in (2) that could change in the human's feelings especially the weight perception (in (2), the load force is represented by $f_h$), but we found empirically in Figure 4 that the reduction (change) in $m_1$ does not affect the human's haptic perception of the weight because weight perception is due to $m_2$, not due to $m_1$. It means that the effect of $m_1$ and $m_2$ on the human's haptic weight perception is different. Hence, the reduction in $m_1$ would also reduce the load force proportionally and the reduction in the load force would not adversely affect the relationships of (2) because the subjects would not feel the change of $m_1$. We used this valuable information to model

the exponential reduction of $m_1$ in (5). However, the magnitudes (digits) used in the formula for $m_1$ were determined based on the magnitudes of the PLFs by trial and error. The detailed procedures of deriving the formula are presented in [13, 23, 27, 28] for various conditions. It is also possible to justify the empirical formula using mathematical analysis based on (2).

(iv) The novel control scheme may be considered as an empirically-derived adaptive control method. When the system tends to lose its performances due to the excessive accelerations, the novel control changes itself based on the condition, reduces the accelerations through reducing the load forces, and thus helps the system adapt to the situations [29].

The procedures for experiment 2 were the same as that employed for experiment 1, but $m_1$ and $m_2$ were set as $m_1 = 6 * e^{-6t} + 0.5$, $m_2 = 0.03$ (condition 1.a) and $m_1 = 6 * e^{-6t} + 1.0$, $m_2 = 0.03$ (condition 2.a) for the simulation. Here, we ignore presenting the simulation details for $m_1 = 6 * e^{-6t} + 1.0$, $m_2 = 0.03$ because the concept and procedures for $m_1 = 6 * e^{-6t} + 0.5$, $m_2 = 0.03$ and $m_1 = 6 * e^{-6t} + 1.0$, $m_2 = 0.03$ are the same:

$$m_1 = 6 * e^{-6t} + 0.5, \tag{5}$$

$$m_2 = 0.03. \tag{6}$$

The performances of the human-robot system were broadly expressed through several criteria such as object motion, object mobility, naturalness, stability, safety, ease of use, and so forth, and in each trial the subject subjectively evaluated (scored) the system using a 7-point bipolar and equal-interval scale as follows.

(1) Best (score: +3);

(2) Better (score: +2);

(3) Good (score: +1);

(4) Alike (score: 0);

(5) Bad (score: −1);

(6) Worse (score: −2);

(7) Worst (score: −3).

### 4.2. Evaluation of the Novel Control

4.2.1. Reduction in PLFs and Peak Accelerations. We compared the mean PLFs for experiment 2 conducted at $m_1 = 6 * e^{-6t} + 0.5$, $m_2 = 0.03$ and $m_1 = 6 * e^{-6t} + 1.0$, $m_2 = 0.03$ to that for experiment 1 conducted at $m_1 = 0.5$, $m_2 = 0.03$ and $m_1 = 1.0$, $m_2 = 0.03$. The results are shown in Table 6. The results show that the PLFs reduced significantly due to the novel control.

The mean peak accelerations for different object sizes for experiment 2 are shown in Table 7. The results show, if we compare these to that of Table 5, that the peak accelerations reduced due to the application of the novel control. The

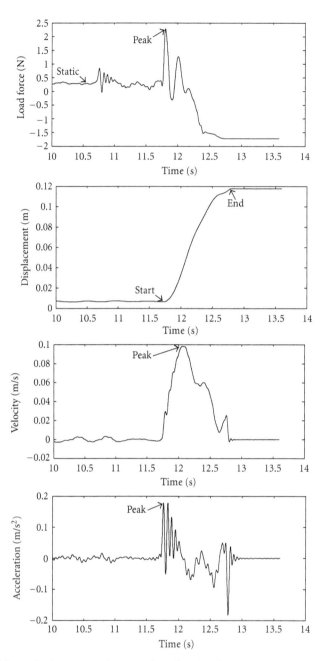

Figure 5: Time trajectories of load force, displacement, velocity, and acceleration for a typical trial when a subject transferred the small size PAO with the system at condition 1 ($m_1 = 0.5\,\text{kg}$, $m_2 = 0.03\,\text{kg}$).

Table 6: Mean peak load forces for different conditions for different object sizes after the application of the novel control.

| $m_1$, $m_2$ sets | Mean PLFs ($N$) with standard deviations (in parentheses) for different object sizes | | |
|---|---|---|---|
| | Large | Medium | Small |
| $m_1 = 6 * e^{-6t} + 0.5$, $m_2 = 0.03$ | 1.3569 (0.0154) | 1.1123 (0.0821) | 0.9901 (0.0910) |
| $m_1 = 6 * e^{-6t} + 1.0$, $m_2 = 0.03$ | 1.8646 (0.0707) | 1.5761 (0.1071) | 1.0990 (0.0885) |

Table 7: Mean peak accelerations with standard deviations (in parentheses) for different object sizes for different conditions after the application of the novel control.

| Object size | Mean peak acceleration (m/s$^2$) for two $m_1$, $m_2$ sets | |
|---|---|---|
| | $m_1 = 6 * e^{-6t} + 0.5$, $m_2 = 0.03$ | $m_1 = 6 * e^{-6t} + 1.0$, $m_2 = 0.03$ |
| Large | 0.1234 (0.0403) | 0.1404 (0.0302) |
| Medium | 0.1038 (0.0233) | 0.1220 (0.0107) |
| Small | 0.0884 (0.0111) | 0.1008 (0.0164) |

Improving Interactions between a Power-Assist Robot System and Its Human User in Horizontal Transfer of Objects Using a Novel Adaptive Control Method

147

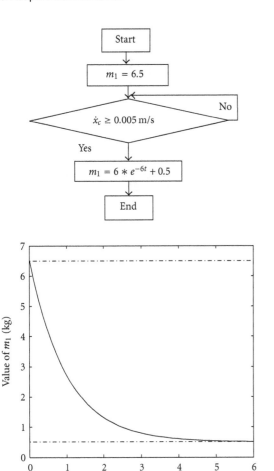

FIGURE 6: Flowchart and hypothetical trajectory of the inertial mass ($m_1$) for the novel control scheme.

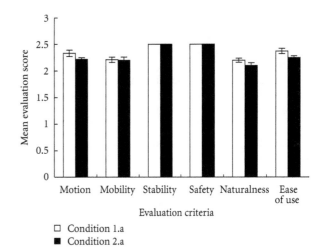

- □ Condition 1.a
- ■ Condition 2.a

FIGURE 7: Mean performance evaluation scores for the small size object for conditions 1.a ($m_1 = 6 * e^{-6t} + 0.5$, $m_2 = 0.03$) and 2.a ($m_1 = 6 * e^{-6t} + 1.0$, $m_2 = 0.03$) after the application of the novel control.

reason may be that the reduced peak load forces due to the novel control reduced the accelerations accordingly. We also found that the velocity reduced slightly due to the novel control.

*4.2.2. System Performances Improvement.* We determined the mean evaluation scores for the three objects separately. Figure 7 shows the mean evaluation scores for the small size object for two conditions (two $m_1$, $m_2$ sets). The scores for the large and medium size objects in each condition were almost the same as that shown in the figure for the small size object. The figure shows that the novel control produced satisfactory system performances.

It is seen in Figure 7 that there is no error bar (individual differences) for the stability and safety, which means that all the subjects evaluated and reported the same score. In fact, the stability and safety were evaluated on whether or not there were any oscillations when transferring the objects with the assist system. No oscillation indicates the stability and the system behaves safe for the user if there is no oscillation. The subjects almost did not report any oscillations during the experiment. This is why all the subjects scored the same value (2.5) for these two criteria. However, there are individual

differences for other criteria. The score 2.5 means that the subject's opinion was between 2 (better) and 3 (best). This special case of evaluation applies to only stability and safety.

We conducted the Analyses of Variances, ANOVAs (object size, subject) on the maneuverability scores, perceived weights, peak load force, peak velocity, peak acceleration, performance evaluation scores, and so forth for experiments 1 and 2 separately. We found that the variations between the object sizes were significant ($P < 0.01$ at each case) for the peak load force, peak velocity and peak acceleration. However, the variations between the object sizes were not significant for the maneuverability scores, perceived weights, and performance evaluation scores ($P > 0.05$ at each case) [24]. On the other hand, the variations between the subjects were not significant at each case ($P > 0.05$ at each case). Hence, the results may be used as the general findings. However, the generality may be increased if we increase the number of trials, object sizes, shapes, subjects, experiment protocols, involvement of the end-users such as the factory people, and so forth.

## 5. Discussion

*5.1. Weight Perception in Horizontal Transfer of Objects: A New Initiative.* The term weight perception used in this paper combines both the visual (optical) perception and the haptic perception, which involves the tactile perception by the touch through the skin, the proprioceptive perception by the relative position of the grasping parts of the body (fingers), and the kinesthetic perception by the relative movement or motions of the grasping parts of the body (fingers) [24, 30]. The ideal case or the first type of the weight perception occurs when the human grasps an object and lifts it against the gravity as we studied in [13]. The second type of the weight perception occurs if the human grasps the object and transfers it from one position to another position (on a surface), as it is presented in this article [17, 31]. We considered the second type of the weight perception though this type of weight perception is usually not investigated by other researchers. We, in this paper, investigated the horizontal weight perception because the practical applications of the power assist systems for transferring heavy objects horizontally need to consider this.

*5.2. Light-Weight Objects versus Heavy Objects.* The optimum/best value of $m_2$ (i.e., $m_2 = 0.03$ kg) derived in this paper does not mean the actual mass of the objects to be transferred in the industrial applications, rather $m_2$ means the value that should be put into the control program for getting the optimum maneuverability, safety, stability, and so forth when transferring heavy objects with the power assist systems.

Our ultimate goal is to develop a human-friendly power assist robot system based on the human characteristics for manipulating heavy objects in the industries that would provide satisfactory human-system interactions, as we mentioned in the introduction. However, we could not use a real robotic system, and heavy and large objects. Instead, we used a simulated system, low simulated and actual weights. We think that the following reasons motivated us to use the small and light-weight objects:

(i) we, at this stage, wanted to reduce the costs of developing the real system because a real robotic system convenient for manipulating large and heavy objects is costly;

(ii) we want to compare the findings of this paper to that of other state-of-the-art psychological experiment results, and for this purpose our object sizes and weights need to be small because the psychological tests usually use low weights and small size objects [24, 25, 32]. We think that such comparison with equal basis may produce important information that may help develop the real robotic system in the near future adjusting with the human perceptions such as naturalness, best feelings, and so forth;

(iii) we, in this paper, just wanted to understand human's characteristics and human's interactions with the power assist system in the horizontal object manipulation with the system and then to use the findings (e.g., motivation, problem statement, design ideas, assumptions, hypotheses, dynamic modeling, control programming, novel control strategies, system characteristics reflecting human-system interactions such as relationship between actual and perceived weights, force and motion characteristics, etc.) to develop a real robot capable of manipulating heavy and large objects in the near future. We believe that the findings we have derived will work (but magnitudes may change) for the heavy and large size objects. It may be true that the results are incomplete until we validate those using the heavy and large objects using a real robot. But, it is also true that the results are novel, unique, important, useful and

FIGURE 8: The 3-DOF power-assist system for manipulating objects. The arrows show the motion directions.

thus have potential applications for developing real robots for manipulating heavy and large objects in industries. We assume that the physics may behave in the same way when the reinforcement (force support) is a higher magnitude. If not, then the approaches and findings will clearly and definitely guide to develop the real robotic system for manipulating heavy objects. We will report the validation of the results using heavy and large objects and real robots in the forthcoming articles.

*5.3. 1-DOF System versus Multi-DOF System.* In this paper, we used an especially developed 1-DOF (horizontal motion) power assist system (Figures 1 and 2). The main target of this study was to understand human characteristics and human's interactions with the system for the object manipulation in the horizontal direction. We previously developed similar 1-DOF power assist systems to lift objects in the vertical direction and also conducted numerous studies to understand human characteristics and human's interactions with the system in the vertical lifting of the objects [13, 23, 27, 28]. However, we believe that the findings could be made more practical and accurate if an integrated 2-DOF (or 3-DOF) system consisting of both horizontal and vertical motions could be used for the experiments [31]. Such an integrated 3-DOF system having both horizontal (forward-backward and left-right) and vertical (up-down) motions is shown in Figure 8. This system may be used to validate the results of this paper. On the other hand, the constraint of the 1-DOF system may affect the subjective results, but the effects are at all not significant as we found in [33].

*5.4. Potential of the System to Fulfill the Requirements in Objects Manipulation.* The requirements for the successful manipulation of heavy objects with power-assist are as follows: (i) the perceived weight is optimum, (ii) the load force is slightly larger than the perceived weight, (iii) the motions, maneuverability, stability, safety, naturalness, comfort, situational awareness, efficiency, manipulating speed, and so forth, are satisfactory, (iv) the system is enough flexible to adjust with the objects of different sizes, weights, shapes, and so forth, (v) the objects can be manipulated in various

Improving Interactions between a Power-Assist Robot System and Its Human User in Horizontal Transfer of Objects Using a Novel Adaptive Control Method

149

degrees of freedoms for example, vertical, horizontal, and so forth, (vi) the system produces satisfactory performances even in the worst-cases, uncertain, rapid changing situations, disturbances, and so forth. The proposed system along with its previous works and future extensions may satisfy these requirements [12, 13, 23].

*5.5. Effectiveness and Accuracy of the Results.* The servomotor was kept in the velocity control mode. Another mode, the torque control mode, may be tested to verify the results. The results do not violate the size-weight illusion because the objects of different sizes were handled independently [32]. The evaluation methodologies of the human factors (e.g., weight perception) are subjective instead of objective. Nevertheless, the subjective evaluation is to be reliable because the subjective evaluations in the technical domains have already been proven effective and reliable in many cases [34]. However, accuracy of the findings may be enhanced by transforming the maneuverability evaluation scale from 5-point to 7-point and by improving the quality of the evaluation alternatives and evaluation criteria and by increasing the number of the subjects and the trials.

## 6. Conclusions and Future Works

In this paper, we successfully presented a 1-DOF power assist robot system for transferring objects by the human subjects in the horizontal direction. We included human features (e.g., weight perception) in the robot dynamics and control. We simulated the system and analysed the human-system interactions such as we determined the optimum manoeuvrability conditions for transferring objects with it. We also determined the psychophysical relationships between the actual and the perceived weights for the objects transferred with the system. We analyzed weight perception, load forces and motion characteristics, and so forth. We then used the findings to develop a novel biomimetic control method for the robot. The novel control was implemented and it was found improving the human-system interactions in terms of object mobility, safety, naturalness, maneuverability, and so forth. The novel control was designed following the bio-mimetic or the human-interactive approaches, and psychophysics was used that determined the relationships between the physical stimuli and the sensory responses [24, 35, 36].

The findings may help develop human-friendly power assist devices for handling heavy objects in industries such as manufacturing and assembly, mining, logistics and transport, construction, agriculture, and so forth. The findings are novel in the sense that the human cues are included in the robot dynamics and control, and a weight-perception-based model of the horizontal transfer of objects with power-assist is presented that was neither previously addressed by other researchers nor considered in our previous works. The findings may enhance the state-of-the-art knowledge and applications of psychology, robotics, biomimetics, control system, automation, human factors, HCI, HRI, interface design and evaluation, interactive system design, and so forth.

We will verify the results using heavy objects and real robotic systems in the near future. The system will be upgraded to a real multi-degree of freedom system and it will be evaluated properly for heavy objects. We will enhance the compliance of the actuation [37]. More human features will be investigated and be used to design the control to further improve the human-system interactions. The biomimetic and the psychophysical approaches to the control design will be considered for other assistive and interactive applications such as rehabilitation, healthcare, and so forth [22, 35, 37–39].

## Acknowledgment

The authors express their thanks and gratitude to the Japanese Ministry of Education, Culture, Sports, Science, and Technology.

## References

[1] H. Kazerooni, "Extender: a case study for human-robot interaction via transfer of power and information signals," in *Proceedings of the 2nd IEEE International Workshop on Robot and Human Communication*, pp. 10–20, November 1993.

[2] K. Kong, H. Moon, B. Hwang, D. Jeon, and M. Tomizuka, "Impedance compensation of SUBAR for back-drivable force-mode actuation," *IEEE Transactions on Robotics*, vol. 25, no. 3, pp. 512–521, 2009.

[3] H. Seki, K. Ishihara, and S. Tadakuma, "Novel regenerative braking control of electric power-assisted wheelchair for safety downhill road driving," *IEEE Transactions on Industrial Electronics*, vol. 56, no. 5, pp. 1393–1400, 2009.

[4] T. Kawashima, "Study on intelligent baby carriage with power assist system and comfortable basket," *Journal of Mechanical Science and Technology*, vol. 23, no. 4, pp. 974–979, 2009.

[5] T. Tanaka, Y. Satoli, S. Kaneko, Y. Suzuki, N. Sakamoto, and S. Seki, "Smart suit: Soft power suit with semi-active assist mechanism - Prototype for supporting waist and knee joint," in *Proceedings of the International Conference on Control, Automation and Systems (ICCAS '08)*, pp. 2002–2005, October 2008.

[6] G. Q. Liu, Y. C. Yan, J. Chen, and T. M. Na, "Simulation and experimental validation study on the drive performance of a new hydraulic power assist system," in *Proceedings of the IEEE Intelligent Vehicles Symposium*, pp. 966–970, June 2009.

[7] S. Lee, S. Hara, and Y. Yamada, "Safety-preservation oriented reaching monitoring for smooth control mode switching of skill-assist," in *Proceedings of the IEEE International Conference on Systems, Man and Cybernetics (SMC '08)*, pp. 780–785, October 2008.

[8] K. Osamura, S. Kobayashi, M. Hirata, and H. Okamoto, "Power assist control for slide doors using an ideal door model," in *Proceedings of the IEEE International Symposium on Industrial Electronics (ISIE '08)*, pp. 1293–1299, July 2008.

[9] K. Kosuge, H. Yabushita, and Y. Hirata, "Load-free control of power-assisted cycle," in *Proceedings of the 1st IEEE Technical Exhibition Based Conference on Robotics and Automation (TExCRA '04)*, pp. 111–112, November 2004.

[10] M. Ding, J. Ueda, and T. Ogasawara, "Pinpointed muscle force control using a power-assisting device: system configuration

and experiment," in *Proceedings of the 2nd Biennial IEEE/RAS-EMBS International Conference on Biomedical Robotics and Biomechatronics (BioRob '08)*, pp. 181–186, October 2008.

[11] T. Kusaka, T. Tanaka, S. Kaneko, Y. Suzuki, M. Saito, and H. Kajiwara, "Assist force control of smart suit for horse trainers considering motion synchronization," *International Journal of Automation Technology*, vol. 3, no. 6, pp. 723–730, 2009.

[12] S. M. M. Rahman, R. Ikeura, M. Nobe, and H. Sawai, "Design of a power assist system for lifting objects based on human's weight perception and changes in system's time constant," in *Proceedings of the 2nd Conference on Human System Interactions, (HSI '09)*, pp. 664–671, Catania, Italy, May 2009.

[13] S. M. M. Rahman, R. Ikeura, M. Nobe, and H. Sawai, "Design and control of a 1DOF power assist robot for lifting objects based on human operator's unimanual and bimanual weight discrimination," in *Proceedings of the IEEE International Conference on Mechatronics and Automation (ICMA '09)*, pp. 3637–3644, August 2009.

[14] M. M. Ayoub, "Problems and solutions in manual materials handling: the state of the art," *Ergonomics*, vol. 35, no. 7-8, pp. 713–728, 1992.

[15] A. M. Okamura, N. Smaby, and M. R. Cutkosky, "Overview of dexterous manipulation," in *Proceedings of the IEEE International Conference on Robotics and Automation (ICRA '00)*, pp. 255–262, April 2000.

[16] T. Doi, H. Yamada, T. Ikemoto, and H. Naratani, "Simulation of a pneumatic hand crane power-assist system," *Journal of Robotics and Mechatronics*, vol. 20, no. 6, pp. 896–902, 2008.

[17] S. Hara, "A smooth switching from power-assist control to automatic transfer control and its application to a transfer machine," *IEEE Transactions on Industrial Electronics*, vol. 54, no. 1, pp. 638–650, 2007.

[18] T. Takubo, H. Arai, K. Tanie, and T. Arai, "Human-robot cooperative handling using variable virtual nonholonomic constraint," *International Journal of Automation Technology*, vol. 3, no. 6, pp. 653–662, 2009.

[19] A. Niinuma, T. Miyoshi, K. Terashima, and Y. Miyashita, "Evaluation of effectiveness of a power-assisted wire suspension system compared to conventional machine," in *Proceedings of the IEEE International Conference on Mechatronics and Automation (ICMA '09)*, pp. 369–374, August 2009.

[20] T. Miyoshi and K. Terashima, "Study on horizontal power assisted system for overhead crane," *International Journal of Applied Electromagnetics and Mechanics*, vol. 24, no. 3-4, pp. 297–309, 2006.

[21] H. Seki, M. Iso, and Y. Hori, "How to design force sensorless power assist robot considering environmental characteristics—position control based or force control based," in *Proceedings of the 28th Annual Conference of the IEEE Industrial Electronics Society*, pp. 2255–2260, November 2002.

[22] L. Vanacken, R. Pinho, J. Sijbers, and K. Coninx, "Force feedback to assist active contour modelling for tracheal stenosis segmentation," *Advances in Human-Computer Interaction*, vol. 2012, Article ID 632498, 9 pages, 2012.

[23] S. M. M. Rahman, R. Ikeura, M. Nobe, and H. Sawai, "Controlling a power assist robot for lifting objects considering human's unimanual, bimanual and cooperative weight perception," in *Proceedings of the IEEE International Conference on Robotics and Automation (ICRA '10)*, pp. 2356–2362, May 2010.

[24] A. M. Gordon, H. Forssberg, R. S. Johansson, and G. Westling, "Visual size cues in the programming of manipulative forces during precision grip," *Experimental Brain Research*, vol. 83, no. 3, pp. 477–482, 1991.

[25] M. O. Ernst and M. S. Banks, "Humans integrate visual and haptic information in a statistically optimal fashion," *Nature*, vol. 415, no. 6870, pp. 429–433, 2002.

[26] L. Dominjon, A. Lécuyer, J. M. Burkhardt, P. Richard, and S. Richir, "Influence of control/display ratio on the perception of mass of manipulated objects in virtual environments," in *Proceedings of the IEEE Virtual Reality (VR '05)*, pp. 19–25, March 2005.

[27] S. M. M. Rahman, R. Ikeura, M. Nobe, and H. Sawai, "Control of a power assist robot for lifting objects based on human operator's perception of object weight," in *Proceedings of the 18th IEEE International Symposium on Robot and Human Interactive Communication (RO-MAN '09)*, pp. 84–90, Toyama, Japan, October 2009.

[28] S. M. M. Rahman, R. Ikeura, S. Hayakawa, and H. Sawai, "A critical look at human's bimanual lifting of objects with a power assist robot and its applications to improve the power-assist control," in *Proceedings of the IEEE International Conference on Robotics and Biomimetics (ROBIO '10)*, pp. 732–738, Tianjin, China, December 2010.

[29] K. Astrom, *Adaptive Control*, Dover, New York, NY, USA, 2008.

[30] D. Hecht and M. Reiner, "Stroop interference and facilitation effects in kinesthetic and haptic tasks," *Advances in Human-Computer Interaction*, vol. 2010, Article ID 852420, 2010.

[31] S. M. M. Rahman, R. Ikeura, M. Nobe, and H. Sawai, "Study on optimum maneuverability in horizontal manipulation of objects with power-assist based on weight perception," in *Mechatronics and Information Technology (ICMIT '09)*, vol. 7500 of *Proceedings of SPIE*, December 2009.

[32] J. R. Flanagan and M. A. Beltzner, "Independence of perceptual and sensorimotor predictions in the size-weight illusion," *Nature Neuroscience*, vol. 3, no. 7, pp. 737–741, 2000.

[33] S. M. Mizanoor Rahman, R. Ikeura, I. Shinsuke, S. Hayakawa, and H. Sawai, "Psychophysical relationships between actual and perceived weights for lifting objects with power-assist: consideration of constrained and unconstrained lifting," in *Proceedings of the 3rd International Symposium on System Integration (SII '10)*, pp. 152–157, Tohoku University, Sendai, Japan, December 2010.

[34] H. Kobayashi, R. Ikeura, and H. Inooka, "Evaluating the maneuverability of a control stick using electromyography," *Biological Cybernetics*, vol. 75, no. 1, pp. 11–18, 1996.

[35] H. L. Xie, Z. Z. Liang, F. Li, and L. X. Guo, "The knee joint design and control of above-knee intelligent bionic leg based on magneto-rheological damper," *International Journal of Automation and Computing*, vol. 7, no. 3, pp. 277–282, 2010.

[36] T. J. Li, G. Q. Chen, and G. F. Shao, "Action control of soccer robots based on simulated human intelligence," *International Journal of Automation and Computing*, vol. 7, no. 1, pp. 55–63, 2010.

[37] N. Costa, M. Bezdicek, M. Brown, J. Gray, and D. Caldwell, "Joint motion control of a powered lower limb orthosis for rehabilitation," *International Journal of Automation and Computing*, vol. 3, no. 3, pp. 271–281, 2006.

[38] J. Boeck, L. Vanacken, S. Notelaers, and K. Coninx, "Improved haptic linear lines for better movement accuracy in upper limb rehabilitation," *Advances in Human-Computer Interaction*, vol. 2012, Article ID 162868, 7 pages, 2012.

[39] H. Mi, A. Krzywinski, T. Fujita, and M. Sugimoto, "Robotable: an infrastructure for intuitive interaction with mobile robots in a mixed-reality environment," *Advances in Human-Computer Interaction*, vol. 2012, Article ID 301608, 10 pages, 2012.

# 14

# Virtual Sectioning and Haptic Exploration of Volumetric Shapes in the Absence of Visual Feedback

**Tatiana V. Evreinova, Grigori Evreinov, and Roope Raisamo**

*School of Information Sciences, University of Tampere, Kanslerinrinne 1, PINNI B, 33014 Tampere, Finland*

Correspondence should be addressed to Grigori Evreinov; grigori.evreinov@uta.fi

Academic Editor: Kerstin S. Eklundh

The reduced behavior for exploration of volumetric data based on the virtual sectioning concept was compared with the free scanning at the use of the StickGrip linkage-free haptic device. Profiles of the virtual surface were simulated through the penholder displacements in relation to the pen tip of the stylus. One or two geometric shapes (cylinder, trapezoidal prism, ball, and torus) or their halves and the ripple surface were explored in the absence of visual feedback. In the free scanning, the person physically moved the stylus. In the parallel scanning, cross-sectional profiles were generated automatically starting from the location indicated by the stylus. Analysis of the performance of 18 subjects demonstrated that the new haptic visualization and exploration technique allowed to create accurate mental images, to recognize and identify virtual shapes. The mean number of errors was about 2.5% in the free scanning mode and 1.9% and 1.5% in the parallel scanning mode at the playback velocity of 28 mm/s and 42 mm/s, respectively. All participants agreed that the haptic visualization of the 3D virtual surface presented as the cross-sectional slices of the workspace was robust and easy to use. The method was developed for visualization of spatially distributed data collected by sensors.

## 1. Introduction

Even in the absence of direct contact and visual feedback, people have to explore physical properties such as friction and roughness, compliance and stiffness of environment (in geophysics and monitoring), and materials (nondestructive testing). Complementing visual information, the existing haptic shape-rendering algorithms focus on rendering the interaction between the tip of a haptic probe and the virtual surface. Using haptic interface and analyzing the effects of different types of the force feedback, the operator of the hand-held detector can feel the change of roughness, rigidity, and other physical properties of a contact. However, human perception of spatially distributed data, for example, the surface topography with varying stiffness, relying on single-point-based exploration techniques often fails to provide a realistic feeling of the complex topological 3D surfaces and intersections [1–7]. Although manual palpation can be very effective, free scanning with a single-point inspection is unnatural and significantly increases the cognitive load to establish the right relations between successive samples of

sensory information separated in space and time [8]. Haptic recognition and identification of spatial objects, their unique shape, and location do not always lead to the correct decision [9, 10]. Therefore, there is a great challenge to develop the new techniques for tangible exploration and interaction with virtual objects [11] in order to facilitate interpretation of spatially distributed data obtained, for example, by the hand-held detector [12].

The main difference between interaction with physical objects using the fingers and using the rigid probe with virtual objects is that the natural manipulations occur with multiple areas of objects and fingertips and rely on multiple sources of haptic information. This being so, the important components of the surface exploration are the kinesthetic sense of distance to the surface of interaction [11] and self-perception of the finger joint-angle positions [13]. Competitive afferent flows allow the person to immediately sense the relative differences between adjacent locations by sharpening the curvature gradient due to the lateral inhibition phenomenon [14, 15].

The question of how to efficiently explore complex volumetric surfaces by relying on the haptic sense remains open.

The key issue to be solved is an accessible 3D frame of reference and means of displaying the specific exploratory patterns as a sequence of haptic probes [16]. What would happen when haptic visualization would be more complicated than just point-based local characteristics (physical parameter or perceptual quality) of the region under the cursor? Could the temporal structuring of sequentially presented spatial data facilitate their mental integration? Could exploratory movements across the volumetric surface, being kept in sync, help in haptic signals integration?

This paper begins with a discussion of related work. Then we present the method and design principles of the experimental setup and the results of comparative study of the two approaches for the presentation and exploration of the volumetric shapes in the absence of visual feedback. Finally, we summarize our results and draw conclusions. Some references are related to studies carried out with blind people. However, we had to note that the technique in the question was developed for engineers and technicians (sighted people) for alternative visualization of the surface topography and spatially distributed data collected by sensors [11, 17–20]. Thus, this is not the case for blind and visually impaired people.

## 2. Background

Depending upon tactile experience and topological imagination, even being explored with one or two hands, raised line drawings may be difficult for blindfolded-sighted observers to integrate nonvisual information to identify the overall pattern [8]. In some cases, an exploration of the swell paper images placed on the graphical tablet and augmented with audio feedback has facilitated the representation of the topology of a graphical environment [21], although the sonification of the graphs does not work flawlessly [22, 23].

In the experiments with elementary and composite planar geometric shapes [24], haptic and auditory modalities were combined to improve the mental representation of topological relations in the absence of visual feedback. However, the authors concluded that the constraints of single-point exploration techniques do not permit the presentation of certain basic concepts such as parallelism (of lines and planes) and intersection of 3D shapes in a simple and intuitive way.

Usually, when asked to identify the virtual object, subjects rely on sensory cues and previous experience gained through observation and manipulation involving a physical contact with an object embedded in specific contextual settings [25, 26]. To create the true mental image of a geometric shape, an observer has to collect any accessible information about the features of the object such as the local irregularities of the surface (edges, vertices, convex and concave features, and flatness), and then integrate tactile, proprioceptive and kinesthetic cues in a specific way [17, 27–32]. However, in the absence of visual feedback, identification of the objects having different levels of complexity (number and shape of elements and their symmetry and periodicity) is greatly affected by the conditions of the presentation and exploration techniques [33, 34]. In particular, objects having smooth

curved boundaries are more difficult to distinguish than polygons. This may lead to misinterpretation of rounded 3D shapes [21, 35].

A systematic exploration of successive locations creates a sequence of sensations from which the person hypothesizes and the imagination retrieves a virtual profile. This helps to identify the surface, that is, to recognize and classify the contact area as, for example, curved outward (convex), curved inward (concave), or flat [36]. Many attempts have been made to specify generic types of surface discontinuity [37–40]. However, to recognize the surface discontinuity, the person should not analyze the absolute parameters of the contacts in different locations but their relative position, that is, local irregularities such as shifts and displacements regarding the common reference point or the reference surface, or the relative finger displacements [11, 13, 36].

Some textural features of the virtual surface can be simulated using pseudographic tactile cells to display a small area of the surface around the pointer where visible irregularities can be transformed into the pattern of raised pins. With the appearance on the market of refreshable braille cells, for example, Metec AG [41], the module functionality was extensively tested by being physically connected to different input devices such as a stylus, mouse, and joystick [42]. An interaction with geometric shapes was also the subject of evaluating functionalities of such a reduced display area. It is interesting that the subjects preferred visualization techniques preventing the redundancy of information about the local details yielding a better presentation of the overall indicative features and trends [43–45]. Another approach to explore virtual images consisted of creating some kind of the haptic profilometer (or surface profiler), for instance, a two-axis H frame (absolute) positioning system with braille cells mounted on a carriage able to move along guiding rails [46]. With such a haptic display in the absence of visual and auditory feedbacks, blindfolded (sighted) persons were able to recognize the features and to identify polygonal tactile shapes from the list of the objects given.

It is important to note that the flat surface of interaction determines not only the sensory-motor coordination and strategy of exploration behavior adequate for the given task but also the way of mental processing (componential analysis, feature extraction, and classification) and reconstruction of the entire image or pieces of the image from the perceptual data collected. Moreover, an exploration strategy acts as a perceptual filter and mechanism of signal compression of sensory information. Depending on the velocity of scanning and the perceptual threshold, a variation of the probe positions is perceived sparsely but effectively allowing the user to differentiate the gradient of the surface, global and local irregularities. It is noteworthy that identifying small virtual objects, even augmented with static and dynamic friction, is a more difficult task than the recognition of physical models examined in a natural way by palpation.

To improve haptic simulation techniques, the researchers compared the accuracy of identifying virtual 3D objects and their physical models in the absence of visual feedback. In the absence of visual feedback, it is hard to imagine a proper frame of reference which would be accessible at any point in the interaction with different components of the virtual 3D object. Therefore, 3D shape recognition and identification demand much more cognitive resources than a perceptual analysis of flat graphs.

In earlier studies in the exploration of virtual objects, the experimenters used the PHANToM haptic device, and, later on, they used the PHANTOM Omni, Omega.3, Novint Falcon and other linkage-based force-feedback devices. However, by making an inspection with a rigid probe, the person could still make contact with a single point of the objects examined [9, 47]. Consequently, by analyzing the profile of the shapes through displacements of the tip of the rigid probe in order to be able to correlate all information collected, an observer has to choose the frame of reference and an optimal scanning strategy to discover the features of the curved surfaces [46]. When no common frame of reference is available, the person can explore a virtual 3D object piece-by-piece using occasional sources of reference such as easily detected landmarks (edges, vertices, and faces) or even the skin surface of the subdominant (opposite) hand.

The results reported by Stamm with coworkers [47] demonstrated the limits and problems of interpreting shapes and their components in haptic exploration of the corners and edges, the shape orientation and posture. Kyung with coworkers [48] showed that human performance during haptic inspection of geometric polygons using the grabbing force-feedback mouse was significantly better than with the point-based force-feedback interaction technique such as the PHANToM haptic device. Jansson and Larsson [49] investigated prominent features of synthetic human heads with the use of the PHANToM device. This research showed that increasing the amount of haptic information needed to recognize and identify virtual 3D objects soon overloads the ability of the perceptual system. The authors concluded that there are three possible solutions to display complex virtual objects and scenes in the absence of visual feedback: training the users, simplifying the information being communicated to the user, and developing more efficient haptic interaction techniques and devices.

However, haptic information for object recognition consists of not only perceptual components but also highly coordinated voluntary behaviors (navigation and exploration) and cognitive resources (mental representations of physical and conceptual attributes) [50, 51]. Therefore, the key question is how to efficiently display and coordinate these components making complex haptic information easy to perceive and understand.

In this paper, we report the results of the comparison of two approaches for the haptic visualization and exploration of volumetric shapes in the absence of visual feedback: the free scanning and the parallel scanning with reduced exploratory behavior. The research was aimed to evaluate the applicability and effectiveness of these two approaches.

## 3. Materials and Method

*3.1. The Participants.* Eighteen volunteers (ten males and eight females) from the local university participated in this study. The age of the participants ranged from 23 to 29 years with a mean of 24.5 years. None of them had participated in similar experiments before. None of them reported any hearing and sensory-motor problems. All participants were regular computer users and reported being right-hand dominant or using their right-hand most frequently. As it was stated in the introduction, only the sighted people were chosen to enable the evaluation of the benefits and shortcomings of the technique introduced.

*3.2. Method.* The human ability to integrate perceptual information over time and space provides the basis of mental imagery [32, 52]. Nevertheless, in our study, we relied on the fact that the sighted participants had the mental templates (visual-haptic models) of different volumetric objects. To detect specific points, object features, and spatial relations in the absence of visual feedback, an observer should be able to integrate the multiple-touch probes collected in the haptic space. An exploratory strategy is also an important factor and depends on the personal cognitive style of thinking (analytic, holistic, or detail-oriented) and individual haptic experience. Therefore, to facilitate mental processing, haptic information obtained from exploratory patterns should still be structured and firmly synchronized.

The "dimensions" of the haptic space (mapping) may nevertheless be different from the dimensions of the visual space adopted for linkage-based force-feedback devices [11]. To collect a sequence of haptic probes specifying the virtual surface, the person can explore the haptic space through self-directed behavior (or free exploration) using a suitable hardware and software providing corresponding haptic signals. Alternatively, a sequence of haptic signals can be generated and presented to the person during a specified time interval if it would be an actual scanning of the study area in some direction. We called this technique "reduced exploratory behavior" which can also be interpreted as motionless exploratory patterns.

For example, as can be seen from Figure 1, multiple-touch probes of the virtual object (the top view projection of the upper half of the ring torus) are displayed and perceived exclusively along the $z$-axis as a gradient of brightness and corresponding displacements of the points of grasp of the penholder in relation to the pen tip. These multiple-touch probes can be displayed on the time axis and belong to the imaginary section planes [32]. To collect information about the virtual surface, the person should mark only the initial position of the section plane on $y$-axis of the tablet within the slit of the stencil frame and start the scanning process by clicking the left button of the tablet. The displacements of the StickGrip along the $z$-axis could be proportional, for example, to the gray scale (brightness) level of the invisible image (ring torus). This could produce exploratory patterns perceived as the virtual cross-sectional slices without the need to physically scan the profile of each trajectory along the $x$-axis with the Wacom pen.

However, let us imagine a ripple surface. It is clear that the free scanning technique is independent of the orientation of the surface irregularities. This cannot be true for the parallel scanning technique. Nevertheless, by making the exploration of virtual shapes in the absence of visual feedback, we do not consider this interaction in the absence of the computer support. That is, the system/application could analyze spatially distributed (e.g., geophysical) data and manipulate the appearance of the image in an appropriate way so that specific features would become more prominent and distinguishable at the cross-sectional analysis.

In contrast to mimicking the visual space, the haptic exploration of the objects with the virtual sectioning concept and the parallel scanning technique with reduced exploratory behavior would have the following benefits:

(i) there is a fixed reference point within each section plane;

(ii) all reference points belong to the same axis ($y$), allowing a user to easily correlate exploratory patterns located in parallel sectional planes and to ascertain relationships, dependencies, and tendencies between corresponding segments located in parallel planes and presented at the particular moments of the timeline;

(iii) an exploratory pattern can be repeated within a certain timeframe (e.g., in less than 3 s, Figure 1) as many times as needed in order to form a correct mental image of each cross-section slice profile;

(iv) the virtual sectioning method can be applied to the entire haptic space, or to a part of the space, to explore one or several objects at a time.

Finally, the new scanning technique with the reduced exploratory behavior would contribute to the research on data visualization in haptic space.

*3.3. Apparatus.* In spite of advances in existing force-feedback techniques, the work reported here was performed using the StickGrip linkage-free haptic device, which presents a motorized pen grip for the Wacom pen input device as shown in Figure 2 [53].

The point at which the penholder is held is sliding up and down the shaft of the Wacom pen so that as the user explores the virtual surface with the pen, s/he feels that hand being displaced towards and away from the physical surface of the pen tablet (Wacom Graphire-4).

Using the Portescap linear stepper motor (20DAM4 0D2B-L) did not require any additional gears and led to low noise and equal torque with no differences in directionality of the shaft displacements that might confuse the user. The StickGrip has a range of 40 mm (±20 mm) of the grip displacements with an accuracy of ±0.8 mm for the Wacom pen having a length of 140 mm. The grip displacements with an average speed of about 25 mm/s of the point of grasp in this range give accurate feedback about the distance and direction (closer and further) regarding the surface of the pen tablet, and, consequently, such feedback is a part of the afferent information regarding the heterogeneity of the virtual surface. During preliminary tests of the setup, the two values of 42 and 28 mm/s were adopted for presenting virtual cross-sectional planes in the parallel scanning mode with an

accuracy of displacements better than 4%. However, the grip displacements (even at a velocity of 28 mm/s) still constrained the exploration and presentation of the virtual scan-lines when the gradient of deformation of the virtual surface was too high. The distance and direction of the grip displacements were coordinated with the structure of the virtual surface.

The workspace of exploration was bordered with a frame of $60 \times 85$ mm along the $y$-axis and the $x$-axis. The frame was used to limit unnecessary exploratory movements and redundant haptic information, in order to easily scan the virtual surface performing long strokes between opposite borders in any direction. The virtual surfaces were visualized as 8-bit grayscale images (Figures 4 and 5). Thus the experimenter could monitor the activity of the subjects as indicated in Figure 2 (at the bottom right).

To facilitate spatiotemporal coordination between the StickGrip displacements along the $z$-axis and the timeline corresponding to the $x$-axis of the virtual cross-sectional planes, the users had to rely on auxiliary sound signals. During the virtual scanning, auxiliary signals presented a sequence of short beeps (sine-wave tone pulses of 800 Hz at duration of 65 ms) with an interval of 360 and 240 ms as illustrated by white dots in Figure 3. The start/end points of the virtual trajectory were marked with the tone pulses of 2.8 kHz at duration of 46 ms. The end-point signal appears immediately at the end of the playback of each scanline.

However, the trajectory had a fixed length, and tone pulses were synchronized with the points of records (of the Stick-Grip displacements) along the timeline (Figure 1). Therefore the last interval was shorter as indicated in Figure 3.

The sequence of sound beeps was the same and it was independently of the type of shape. Therefore, participants could not use these sounds to identify the shapes or their features in the absence of haptic feedback. Sound signals were not used during free scanning mode because they could distract and confound the subjects being presented asynchronously with haptic information.

A microphone was used (Figure 2, on the left) to record the subjects' decisions as well as any comments given after the test. Short wav-files were used to deliver voice prompts to the subjects about the application status ("test on," "task was completed successfully").

*3.4. Procedure.* The same set of ten volumetric images was presented to the subjects in each experimental block. However, the subjects were not aware of the specific shapes, which were potentially going to be presented to them. One or two geometric shapes (cylinder, trapezoidal prism, ball, and torus) or their halves and the ripple surface (10 volumetric images) were explored with the StickGrip haptic device in the absence of visual feedback and identified in the three conditions (experimental blocks).

The three conditions were as follows:

(i) the baseline condition named free scanning was the (self-directed) free exploration of the virtual space;

(ii) the successive haptic exploration with the reduced exploratory behavior of cross-sectional profiles lying on parallel planes, named parallel scanning, was of

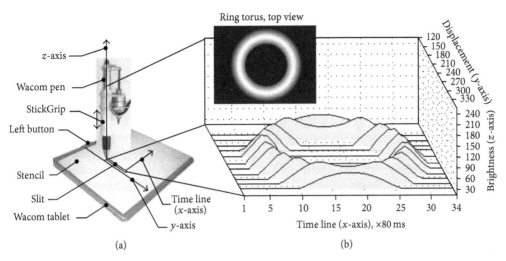

(a)

(b)

FIGURE 1: Dimensions of the haptic space (on the left) and visualization of exploratory patterns presented as the virtual cross-sectional slices of the upper half of the ring torus (on the right).

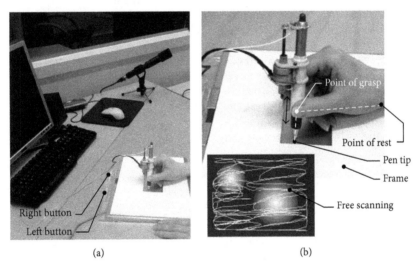

(a)

(b)

FIGURE 2: Experimental setup (on the left) and the schematic diagram specifying the reference points of the StickGrip grasp at exploration of the virtual surface (on the right). Virtual surface (on the bottom right), as viewed on the monitor of the experimenter.

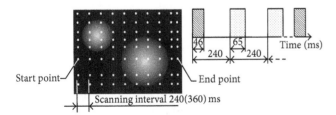

FIGURE 3: Auxiliary sound signals during the parallel scanning mode.

the virtual trajectories along the $x$-axis of the Wacom tablet at the scanning velocity of 28 mm/s;

(iii) the similar mode of the parallel scanning (with the reduced exploratory behavior) at the velocity of presenting virtual cross-sectional planes of 42 mm/s.

Audio markers accompanied the two conditions of parallel scanning.

To decrease perceptual learning and knowledge transfer, the participants performed the experimental session at once (three blocks). Both the blocks and volumetric images were presented in randomly assigned counterbalanced order.

Detailed verbal instructions were given to the participants regarding the testing procedure. The subjects started and finished the trials by clicking the right button on the tablet. When the subjects were ready to continue the test, they were instructed to press this button again. During the free scanning mode (baseline condition), the subjects were asked to explore the virtual profile of the surface within the workspace (the frame), to recognize and imagine the virtual shape(s), and to identify it (or them). When the participants finished scanning the surface, they were asked to click the right button on the Wacom tablet. Immediately after that, they had to make the decision by speaking it aloud (into the microphone), by giving a verbal description or title of the virtual image.

In another two blocks, the same virtual shape(s) were explored through successive playback of cross-sectional profiles of the virtual surface. To initiate the scanning process of each cross-section, the subjects had to click the left button of the tablet with the left hand (Figure 3) as many times as needed. The virtual trajectories played back at a given speed (42 or 28 mm/s) starting from the points indicated by the subject.

The subjects held the StickGrip like an ordinary pen. Since fast displacements of the StickGrip could slightly deviate the stylus from the intended direction (e.g., see upper tracks across the ball and ripples in Figure 4), subjects were asked to hold the StickGrip in a vertical position.

In general, the starting point could be any location pointed out within the workspace. However, to choose the starting point, the subjects were asked to move the StickGrip only along the left border of the frame. The right border of the frame was always the endpoint of the virtual trajectory. The subjects had to detect and memorize the features of the entire profile of each cross-section, to further integrate them and mentally retrieve the entire surface of the virtual shape(s). At any time when the subjects had a problem recalling the features of the virtual cross-section, they could examine such a region again.

Once the subjects had been instructed, they were briefly allowed to practice with the sequence of needed actions in two conditions by exploring the virtual pyramid with free and parallel scanning modes. The results of these trials were excluded from further analysis.

The experimental session (three blocks) took place in the usability laboratory as shown in Figure 2 (on the left) and lasted less than 60 minutes. The subjects were blindfolded and perceived the virtual space relying on kinesthetic and proprioceptive senses. To accomplish the test, the participants had to complete ten trials in each block of set tasks with no time limit. At the end of the test, they were given sound feedback ("task was completed successfully"). Between trials and blocks, the participants had a short (self-paced) break and could ask any questions. After the test the participants were interviewed about their experiences and problems.

The test was performed according to the ethical standards. Informed consent was obtained in accordance with the guidelines for the protection of human subjects. No private or confidential information was collected or stored.

*3.5. Design.* In order to reduce variance due to individual differences, the experiment was conducted as a within-subjects design in which each participant experienced all volumetric images identified in three conditions. There were four dependent variables: the task completion time of recognizing (by clicking the right button on the Wacom tablet) and identifying the virtual shape (by giving a verbal description or title of the virtual image), number of the virtual cross-sectional profiles (scan-lines) inspected in order to recognize and identify each shape, number of repeated inspections of the same scan-line, and number of volumetric images

correctly identified. The top view projection of virtual shapes (10 images) and three conditions of their exploration were considered as independent variables.

The reduced exploratory behavior was expected to improve human performance in recognizing and identifying volumetric images in the absence of visual feedback. Both conditions of exploration (reduced behavior versus free exploration and velocity of virtual scanning) and different levels of complexity of the virtual images (number of objects and elements/attributes, their symmetry and periodicity, and the gradient of the surface discontinuity) could have an impact on human performance.

The human performance was evaluated in terms of the task completion time, number of the virtual cross-sectional profiles (scan-lines) inspected, number of repeated inspections of the same scan-line, false recognition or/and identification (confusion matrices of the shapes presented), and exploratory strategies used. A variable number of components of the virtual image (1, 2 objects or many ripples) allowed us to differentiate the results of image interpretation. We could refer to recognition error when the number of objects was specified incorrectly and refer to identification error when the number of objects was correct but the description or title of the image was inappropriate.

## 4. Results and Discussion

In total, the results were collected from 540 trials during the haptic exploration of 10 virtual shapes (images) in three conditions (blocks) by 18 subjects. The statistical analysis was performed using SPSS 18 for Windows (Chicago, IL, USA) and Origin-Pro 8.6 for the 3D visualization of exploratory behavior.

*4.1. Analysis of Exploratory Strategies.* The typical tracks recorded during haptic exploration and identification of virtual shapes in the free scanning mode are presented in Figure 4. Here, we can only demonstrate that during inspection of virtual shapes in the free scanning mode, our blindfolded subjects did not use any specific strategy. By making continuous circular and linear movements (Figure 4), they merely repeatedly scanned the workspace to detect at least the more prominent and global features of the test objects (borders, vertices, convexity, concavity, and flat areas), which probably would better correspond to their own mental representations.

Nevertheless, exploration strategies were influenced by the method, techniques, and shape-related factors: relative position and size of the virtual shape(s) (two cylinders, two hemispheres, and two trapezoidal prisms), their inherent symmetry (ball and torus), and a specific relief having periodicity of the surface gradient (torus, two balls, and ripples) or not (the half ball). Most of the subjects reported that the free scanning mode demanded more cognitive effort to make mental matching of different pieces of trajectories which are separated in space and time. In particular, to determine spatial relationships among pattern components (adjacent edges, their slope, and the direction of slope), these

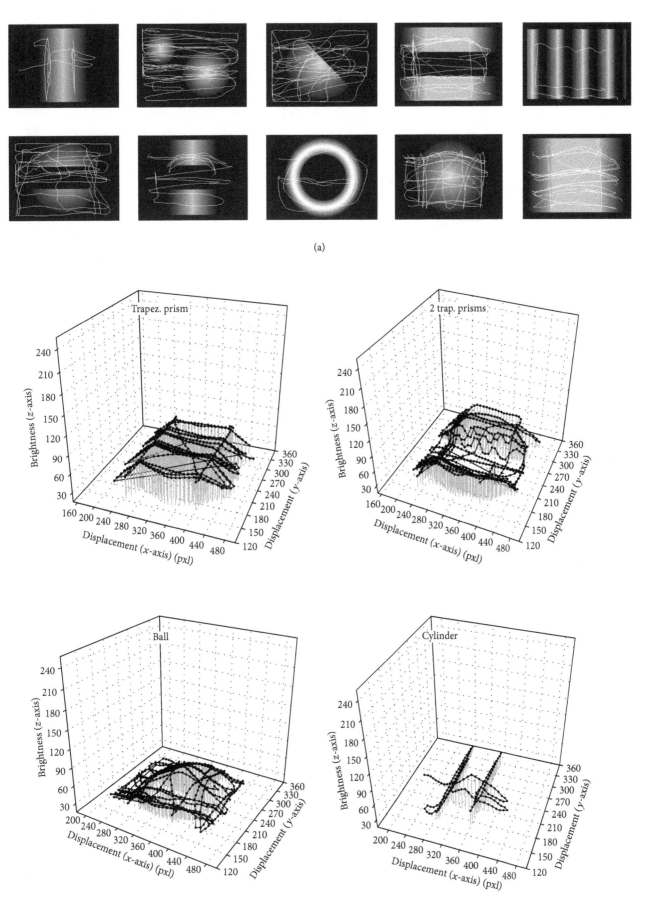

(a)

Figure 4: Continued.

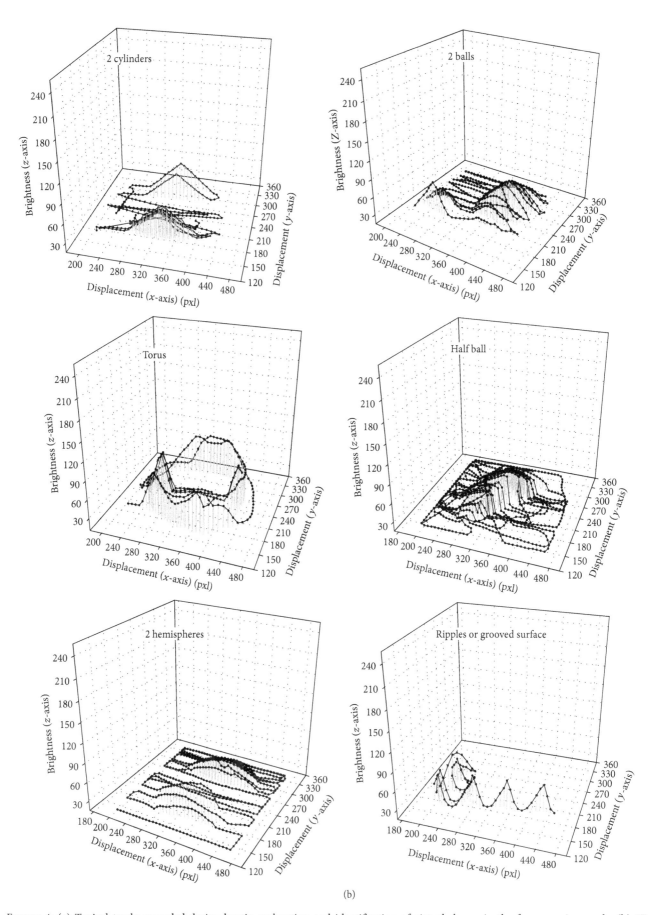

(b)

FIGURE 4: (a) Typical tracks recorded during haptic exploration and identification of virtual shapes in the free scanning mode. (b) 3D reconstruction of the virtual shapes explored in the free scanning mode.

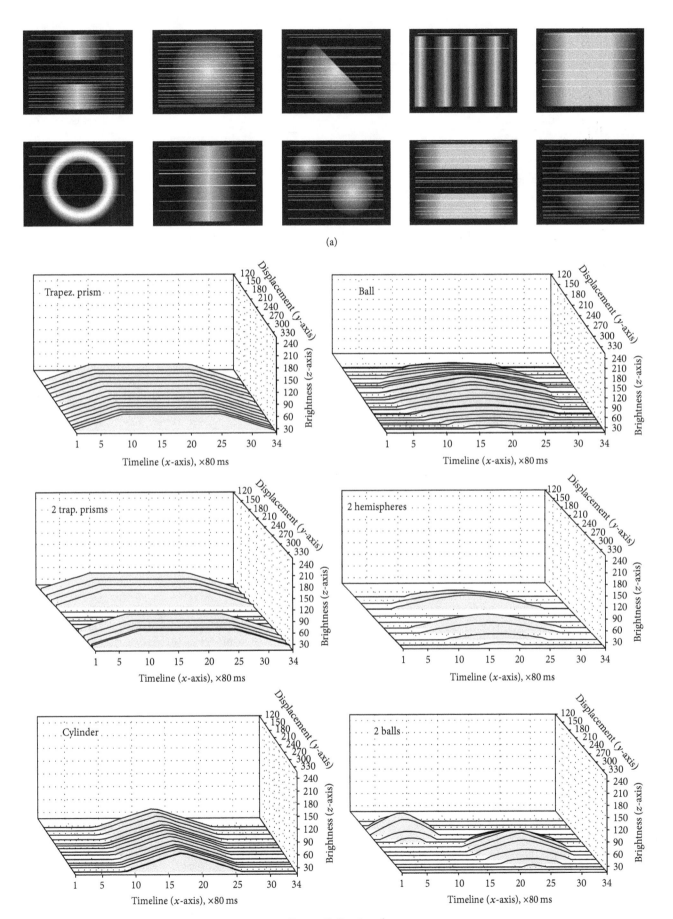

(a)

FIGURE 5: Continued.

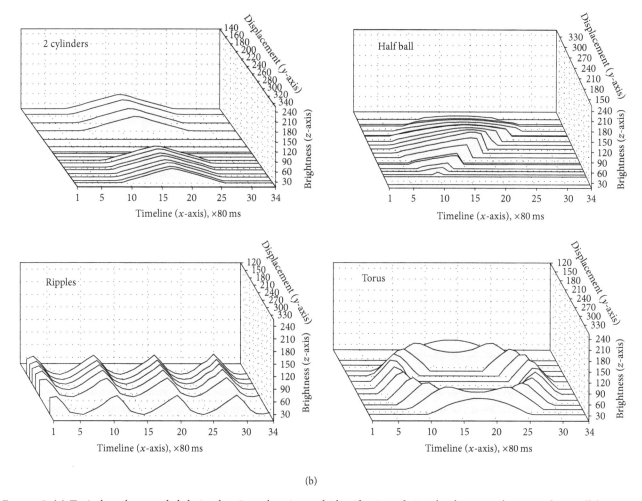

(b)

FIGURE 5: (a) Typical tracks recorded during haptic exploration and identification of virtual volumetric shapes in the parallel scanning mode. The repeated inspection and exploration in more detail were required with respect to shapes having smooth rounded surfaces. (b) 3D reconstruction of the virtual shapes explored in the parallel scanning mode.

components should be fully analyzed each in a separate location.

The typical tracks recorded during haptic exploration and identification of virtual shapes in the parallel scanning mode are presented in Figure 5. At the beginning of the exploration, the subjects tried to define the number of shapes within the frame relying on a sense of the roundedness, straightness, or flatness of exploratory trajectories and spatial intervals between them. They performed a rough inspection with a greater step between virtual cross-sections (ripples, trapezoidal prism, torus, and cylinder). Then, the subjects actually began their exploration of the workspace in more detail (ball, two balls, and two hemispheres) or just a detailed scanning of the key areas (two cylinders, two balls, and two trapezoidal prisms), which could help to identify the object in question.

Although identification of the ball and the half ball was often unsuccessful (Tables 1, 2, and 3), in the brief interview after the test, 14 subjects (78%) out of 18 reported that the ball, cylinder, half ball, and grooved surface (ripples) were the easiest haptic shapes to identify.

Ten out of 18 subjects (55.6%) reported that they actively used sound beeps to "measure" the length of edges and to build the mental model of the virtual shape (e.g., "3 beeps up, 4 beeps straight, and 3 beeps down"). Three out of these ten subjects preferred the low playback velocity of the virtual trajectory of 28 mm/s.

Three out of 18 subjects (16.7%) immediately after an explanation of the test procedure and a short practice asked for the volume of the sound beeps to be lowered, as they believed that these signals would distract them. For these subjects, the sound volume was lowered by about 20%. At the end of the test, they reported that the sound beeps did not distract them, but that only the start and stop sounds were useful from their point of view. It is likely that these subjects relied on a holistic encoding strategy by capturing each of the cross-sectional trajectories as a whole by making "in-air hand gestures." These three subjects outperformed the others approaching minimum completion time but with a rather high rate of false identification. However, we need more observations to validate our inferences.

TABLE 1: Confusion matrix of the virtual shapes recognition and identification (%) in the free scanning mode, averaged over all participants.

| Test objects | Cylinder | 2 Cylinders | Trapez. prism | 2 Trap. prisms | 2 Balls | A ball | 2 Hemisph. | Half ball | Torus | Ripples |
|---|---|---|---|---|---|---|---|---|---|---|
| Cylinder | *98.66* | | 0.67 | | | | | 0.67 | | |
| 2 Cylinders | | *97.99* | | | | | 2.01 | | | |
| Trapez. prism | 1.34 | | *97.32* | | | 1.34 | | | | |
| 2 Trap. prisms | **0.67** | 0.67 | | *97.99* | | | 0.67 | | | |
| 2 Balls | | | | | *98.66* | | | **0.67** | **0.67** | |
| A ball | 1.34 | | 0.67 | | | *95.31* | **0.67** | | 2.01 | |
| 2 Hemispheres | | 1.34 | | 1.34 | 0.67 | | *96.65* | | | |
| A half ball | | | | | **1.34** | 2.68 | 0.67 | *94.64* | 0.67 | |
| Torus | | **0.67** | | **0.67** | **0.67** | | | | *97.99* | |
| Ripples | | | | | | | | | | *100* |

TABLE 2: Confusion matrix of recognition and identification (%) of virtual shapes in the parallel scanning mode at the playback velocity of the virtual trajectory of 28 mm/s, averaged over all participants.

| Test objects | Cylinder | 2 Cylinders | Trapez. prism | 2 Trap. prisms | 2 Balls | A ball | 2 Hemisph. | Half ball | Torus | Ripples |
|---|---|---|---|---|---|---|---|---|---|---|
| Cylinder | *98.66* | | | | **0.67** | 0.67 | | | | |
| 2 Cylinders | | *97.99* | | 0.67 | 0.67 | | 0.67 | | | |
| Trapez. prism | 0.67 | | *98.66* | | | 0.67 | | | | |
| 2 Trap. prisms | | 0.67 | | *97.99* | | | | 1.34 | | |
| 2 Balls | | | | | *98.66* | | | 0.67 | **0.67** | |
| A ball | 0.67 | | 0.67 | | | *96.65* | **0.67** | 1.34 | | |
| 2 Hemispheres | | 0.67 | | 0.67 | 1.34 | | *97.32* | | | |
| A half ball | | | | | **0.67** | 3.35 | | *95.98* | | |
| Torus | | | | **0.67** | | | | | *99.33* | |
| Ripples | | | | | | | | | | *100* |

TABLE 3: Confusion matrix of recognition and identification (%) of virtual shapes in the parallel scanning mode at the playback velocity of the virtual trajectory of 42 mm/s, averaged over all participants.

| Test objects | Cylinder | 2 Cylinders | Trapez. prism | 2 Trap. prisms | 2 Balls | A ball | 2 Hemisph. | Half ball | Torus | Ripples |
|---|---|---|---|---|---|---|---|---|---|---|
| Cylinder | *99.33* | | 0.67 | | | | | | | |
| 2 Cylinders | | *97.99* | | 1.34 | | | | | **0.67** | |
| Trapez. prism | | **0.67** | *97.99* | | | 1.34 | | | | |
| 2 Trap. prisms | | | | *99.33* | 0.67 | | | | | |
| 2 Balls | | | | | *98.66* | | | | **1.34** | |
| A ball | | | 0.67 | | | *95.31* | | 4.02 | | |
| 2 Hemispheres | | 0.67 | | | | | *99.33* | | | |
| A half ball | 0.67 | | | | | 1.34 | | *97.99* | | |
| Torus | 0.67 | | | | **0.67** | | | | *98.66* | |
| Ripples | | | | | | | | | | *100* |

*4.2. Evaluation of Human Performance.* The goal was to analyze the differences between the two kinds of haptic visualization and exploration of virtual volumetric shapes supposing that mental representations of sighted people are quite similar.

*4.2.1. Task Completion Time.* By relying on the free scanning technique (a baseline condition), the mean task completion time of recognition and identification of the virtual shape was about 59 s with a standard deviation (SD) of about 19 s, varying from a minimum of 13 s (SD = 11 s) to a maximum

of 109 s (SD = 20 s) averaged over all participants. The box plots in Figure 6 show the typical pattern of differences in the individual performance under different conditions of exploration of the virtual geometric shapes.

Figure 7 illustrates the mean time of recognition and identification of the virtual shapes for each of the three exploration conditions averaged over all participants. During the parallel scanning mode at the playback velocity of the virtual trajectory of 28 mm/s, the mean task completion time was about 58 s (SD = 14 s) varying from a minimum of 16 s (SD = 12 s) to a maximum of 77 s (SD = 14 s) averaged over

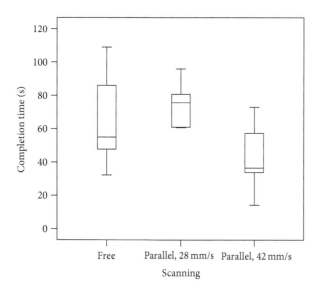

FIGURE 6: Typical results of one of the subjects: the task completion time in three conditions of exploration, recognition and identification of virtual shapes.

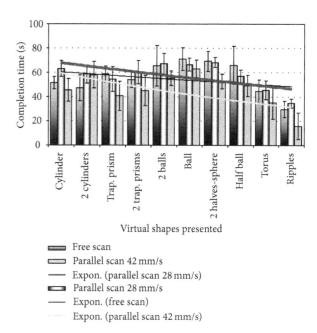

FIGURE 7: Mean completion time and trend lines of recognition and identification the virtual shapes for each of the three exploration conditions averaged over all participants.

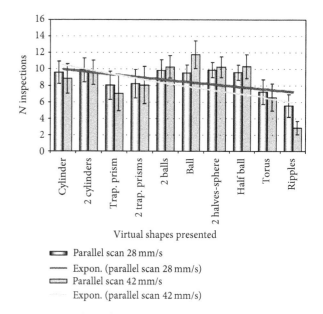

FIGURE 8: Number of inspections (scanlines) and trend lines of the same shape at the two scanning velocities averaged over all participants.

all participants. The number of virtual cross-sectional profiles (scan-lines) inspected varied from a minimum of 5 (SD = 1.9) to a maximum of 9.8 (SD = 1.2) with a mean of about 8.5 (SD = 2.6) averaged over all participants. The number of scan-lines of the same shape (Figure 8) varied from a minimum of 2.9 (SD = 1.7) to a maximum of 13 (SD = 1.2) with a mean of about 8.7 (SD = 2.7). The average number of repeated inspections of the same cross-section profile (scan-line) was about 1 (SD = 0.03) varying from a minimum of 1 to a maximum of 1.1 averaged over all participants.

During the parallel scanning mode at the playback velocity of the virtual trajectory of 42 mm/s, the mean of the task completion time (Figure 7) was about 46 s (SD = 19 s) varying from a minimum of 14 s (SD = 14 s) to a maximum of 89 s (SD = 8 s) averaged over all participants. The number of scan-lines of the same shape varied from a minimum of 2.6 (SD = 2) to a maximum of 12 (SD = 3) with a mean of about 8.5 (SD = 3) averaged over all participants. The average number of repeated inspections of the same scan-line was about 1 (SD = 0.04) varying from a minimum of 0.9 to a maximum of 1.1 averaged over all participants.

A grooved surface (ripples) was only the image that was successfully recognized by all participants with both scanning techniques and with minimum effort. To identify the virtual grooved surface (ripples), the subjects spent on average about 35 s (SD = 21 s) using the free scanning mode. During the parallel scanning mode at the playback velocity of the virtual trajectory of 42 mm/s, they needed significantly less time, only about 16 s (SD = 7 s) on average. The mean number of inspections was about 3 (SD = 1.6), which increased by approximately twofold (5.6, SD = 2.8) when lowering the playback velocity of the virtual trajectory.

The shapes having smooth rounded surfaces required more time to perform their inspection (Figure 7). In particular, using the free scanning technique ball, the two halves of the sphere and a half ball required 71 s (SD = 19 s), 69 s (SD

= 16 s), and 66 s (SD = 31 s) on average. Making inspection with parallel scanning mode at the playback velocity of the virtual trajectory of 28 mm/s, the times needed to recognize and identify these shapes were: 67 s (SD = 14 s), 68 s (SD = 12 s) and 57 s (SD = 17 s), respectively. At the playback velocity of the virtual trajectory of 42 mm/s, the task completion time diminished: 63 s (SD = 11 s) for the ball, 53 s (SD = 8 s) for the two hemispheres, and 49 s (SD = 11 s) for the half ball.

As regards task completion time, the results of the paired samples $t$-test revealed a statistically significant difference when the virtual surfaces were explored using the free scanning technique and the parallel scanning of frontal cross-sections at the playback velocity of the virtual trajectory of 42 mm/s: $t(9) = 3.713$ ($P < 0.005$); the correlation index was high and statistically significant 0.805 ($P < 0.005$). The difference in exploration of the virtual surfaces in the parallel scanning mode at two velocities (28 and 42 mm/s) was also statistically significant: $t(9) = 6.016$ ($P < 0.0001$), although the correlation index of this parameter was high and statistically significant 0.902 ($P < 0.0001$).

However, the paired samples $t$-test revealed no difference between the free scanning technique and the parallel scanning of frontal cross-sections at the playback velocity of the virtual trajectory of 28 mm/s: $t(9) = 0.796$ ($P > 0.1$), while the correlation index was high and statistically significant 0.853 ($P < 0.005$).

### 4.2.2. Number of Inspections (Scanlines).

Regarding the virtual cross-sectional profiles (scan-lines), the results of the paired samples $t$-test demonstrated that no difference was revealed either for the number of scan-lines $t(9) = 0.003$ ($P > 0.5$) or for the number of repeated inspections and the number of repeated inspections of the same cross-section: $t(9) = 0.204$ ($P > 0.5$) and $t(9) = 1.366$ ($P > 0.1$), respectively. Thus, the correlation between the numbers of scan-lines at two velocities (28 and 42 mm/s) was high as 0.947 and statistically significant ($P < 0.0001$).

The correlation between numbers of repeated inspections of the same scan-line was also high at 0.953 and statistically significant ($P < 0.0001$). The numbers of repeated inspections of the same cross-section revealed a weak correlation of 0.575 which did not reach statistical significance ($P > 0.05$).

### 4.2.3. Analysis of Errors.

The analysis of errors made (false recognition and identification) for each of the three exploration modes showed that the mean number of errors was less than 2.5% for 180 trials (10 virtual volumetric images being explored, recognized and identified by 18 subjects). In particular, the mean number of errors was 2.5% (SD = 1.6%) in free scanning mode and 1.9% (SD = 1.2%) and 1.5% (SD = 1.3%) in parallel scanning mode, at the playback velocity of the virtual trajectory of 28 mm/s and 42 mm/s, respectively (Figure 9).

The result of the paired samples $t$-test revealed no differences in human performance in terms of false recognition and identification of the virtual shapes at the playback velocity of the virtual scanlines of 28 mm/s and 42 mm/s $t(9) = 0.888$ ($P > 0.1$); the correlation index was low and not statistically significant: 0.585 ($P > 0.05$). The paired differences between errors made during the free scanning mode and parallel scanning at the playback velocity of 42 mm/s and 28 mm/s were statistically significant: $t(9) = 2.478$ ($P < 0.05$) and $t(9) = 2.827$ ($P < 0.05$). Indices of correlation were also significant: 0.691 ($P < 0.05$) and 0.926 ($P < 0.05$), respectively.

A further analysis of the confusion matrices of the virtual shapes recognition and identification (Tables 1–3) showed that shapes with different levels of complexity (number

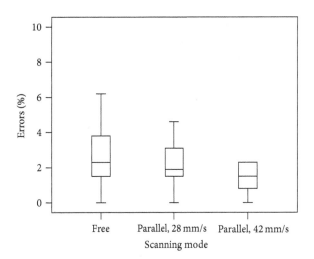

FIGURE 9: Percentage of false recognition and identifications in the three exploration modes.

of the shapes' elements, their symmetry and periodicity, and gradient of the surface discontinuity) required different perceptual and cognitive efforts to recognize and distinguish their specific features to integrate them into a coherent mental image.

As can be seen from the tables, false recognition and identification were much affected by the scanning mode and perceptual heterogeneity of the shape boundaries. In particular, careless inspection of the virtual profile of the surface within the workspace could be the reason of recognition errors when the number of objects was specified incorrectly. Another reason could be the growing redundancy of sensory information that can also soon overload the subjects to establish the right relations between successive samples. However, this kind of error was made more often in the free scanning mode (2.01%) than with the use of the parallel scanning technique (1.12%). In Tables 1–3, the thick lines border the error values of recognition.

The shapes having smooth rounded surfaces (the ball, the two hemispheres, and the half ball) were more difficult to distinguish than the cylinder, torus, or the ripple surface and could be a reason for their misinterpretation. These poorly identified objects in the confusion matrices are bordered. The contribution of poorly identified objects was about 4.5% of total errors made in the free scanning mode, 2.9% in the parallel scanning mode at the playback velocity of the virtual trajectory of 28 mm/s, and 2.5% in the parallel scanning mode at the playback velocity of the virtual trajectory of 42 mm/s.

## 5. Conclusion

The imaginary surfaces of virtual shapes can be perceived from the virtual trajectories simulated with displacements of the point of grasp of the penholder. During this study, virtual volumetric shapes with different levels of complexity were presented to blindfolded sighted participants using the StickGrip linkage-free haptic device, the virtual sectioning concept, and the parallel scanning technique with reduced exploratory behavior.

The virtual shapes with smooth rounded surfaces (a ball, the two hemispheres, and a half ball) were more difficult to distinguish, and completing their identification required about 70 seconds. These results corroborated the experimental observations which have also been noted in previous studies [21, 35]. The torus and grooved surface (ripples) were easily identified, and their exploration required much less cognitive effort and time (40–15 seconds). However, the case with a ripple surface demonstrated the need for adaptive adjusting of visualization parameters for presentation of the specific features with respect to the robustness and the sensitivity of the technique.

The number of scan-lines inspected in order to recognize and identify the shape and the average number of repeated inspections of the same scan-line revealed no statistically significant difference in the two exploration conditions. The average number of repeated inspections of the same scan-line was about one, while the scanning velocity of the virtual trajectories presenting cross-sectional profiles is a crucial parameter in the parallel scanning technique. At the speed of displacements of the penholder of 42 mm/s, the subjects achieved significantly better results than when scanning velocity was 28 mm/s. Nevertheless, these parameters could be customized or adjusted depending on information presented (e.g., density of the virtual surface irregularities). The speed of displacements of the penholder should be increased and adapted for visualization of volumetric data with a high gradient of spatial discontinuity.

All participants agreed that visualization of exploratory patterns presented as the virtual cross-sectional slices of the workspace was robust and extremely easy to use, which enabled them to create accurate mental images.

In further research, we plan to confirm the universality of the cross-sectional virtual scanning concept and the reduced exploratory behavior using the data sonification.

## Acknowledgments

The authors gratefully acknowledge the support of Finnish Academy Grant 127774. The authors would like to thank the reviewers for their valuable comments and suggestions to improve the quality of the paper.

## References

[1] P. Boytchev, T. Chehlarova, and E. Sendova, "Virtual reality vs real virtuality in mathematics teaching and learning," in *Proceedings of the WG 3. 1 & 3. 5 Joint Working Conference Mathematics and ICT: a 'golden triangle' (IMICT '07)*, D. Benzie and M. Iding, Eds., College of Comp. and Inf. Science Northeastern University, Boston, Mass, USA, 2007.

[2] K. Kahol and S. Panchanathan, "Distal object perception through haptic user interfaces for individuals who are blind," in *Newsletter ACM SIGACCESS Accessibility and Computing*, no. 84, pp. 30–33, ACM, New York, NY, USA, 2006.

[3] H. H. King, R. Donlin, and B. Hannaford, "Perceptual thresholds for single vs. multi-finger haptic interaction," in *Proceedings of the IEEE Haptics Symposium (HAPTICS '10)*, pp. 95–99, IEEE Haptics Symposium, Washington, DC, USA, March 2010.

[4] Y. Liu and S. D. Laycock, "A haptic system for drilling into volume data with polygonal tools," in *Proceedings of the Eurographics Association*, W. Tang and J. P. Collomosse, Eds., pp. 1–8, EG UK Theory and Practice of Computer Graphics, Cardiff University, 2009.

[5] N. Magnenat-Thalmann and U. Bonanni, "Haptics in virtual reality and multimedia," *IEEE Multimedia*, vol. 13, no. 3, pp. 6–11, 2006.

[6] S. Mayank, *Implementation and evaluation of a multiple-points haptic rendering algorithm [M.S. thesis]*, the Russ College of Engineering and Technology of Ohio University, 2007.

[7] W. Yu, R. Ramloll, and S. Brewster, "Haptic graphs for blind computer users," in *Haptic Human-Computer Interaction*, S. A. Brewster and R. Murray-Smith, Eds., pp. 41–51, Springer, Berlin, Germany, 2001.

[8] M. W. A. Wijntjes, T. van Lienen, I. M. Verstijnen, and A. M. L. Kappers, "Look what I have felt: Unidentified haptic line drawings are identified after sketching," *Acta Psychologica*, vol. 128, no. 2, pp. 255–263, 2008.

[9] G. Jansson and K. Billberger, "The PHANToM used without visual guidance," in *Proceedings of the 1st Phantom Users Research Symposium (PURS '99)*, pp. 27–30, Heidelberg, Germany, 1999.

[10] J. F. Santore and S. C. Shapiro, "Identifying an object that is perceptually indistinguishable from one previously perceived," in *Proceedingsof the 19th National Conference on Artificial Intelligence (AAAI '04)*, pp. 968–969, The MIT Press, July 2004.

[11] A. Withana, Y. Makino, M. Kondo, M. Sugimoto, G. Kakehi, and M. Inami, "Impact: Immersive haptic stylus to enable direct touch and manipulation for surface computing," *Computers in Entertainment*, vol. 8, no. 2, article 9, 2010.

[12] H. Yano, M. Nudejima, and H. Iwata, "Development of haptic rendering methods of rigidity distribution for tool-handling type haptic interface," in *Proceedings of the Eurohaptics Conference- 2005 and Symposium on Haptic Interfaces for Virtual Environment and Teleoperator Systems (WHC '05)*, pp. 569–570, 2005.

[13] H. Z. Tan, M. A. Srinivasan, C. M. Reed, and N. I. Durlach, "Discrimination and identification of finger joint-angle position using active motion," *ACM Transactions on Applied Perception*, vol. 4, no. 2, pp. 1–14, 2007.

[14] G. von Békésy, *Sensory Inhibition*, Princeton University Press, 1967.

[15] F. Vega-Bermudez and K. O. Johnson, "Surround suppression in the responses of primate SA1 and RA mechanoreceptive afferents mapped with a probe array," *Journal of Neurophysiology*, vol. 81, no. 6, pp. 2711–2719, 1999.

[16] R. L. Klatzky, S. J. Lederman, and J. M. Mankinen, "Visual and haptic exploratory procedures in children's judgments about tool function," *Infant Behavior and Development*, vol. 28, no. 3, pp. 240–249, 2005.

[17] T. V. Evreinova, G. Evreinov, and R. Raisamo, "Interpretation of Ambiguous Images Inspected by the StickGrip Device," in *Proceedings of the IADIS International Conference on Interfaces and Human Computer Interaction (IADIS IHCI '11)*, pp. 209–217, 2011.

[18] T. V. Evreinova, G. Evreinov, and R. Raisamo, "Estimating topographic heights with the StickGrip haptic device," in *Proceedings of the International Symposium on Multimedia Applications and Processing (MMAP '11)*, pp. 691–697, September 2011.

[19] T. V. Evreinova, G. Evreinov, and R. Raisamo, "Haptic visualization of bathymetric data, a case study," in *Proceedings of the Haptic Symposium (Haptics '12)*, pp. 359–364, 2012.

[20] T. V. Evreinova, G. Evreinov, and R. Raisamo, "Evaluation of effectiveness of the StickGrip device for detecting the topographic heights on digital maps," *International Journal of Computer Science and Application*, vol. 9, no. 3, pp. 61–76, 2012.

[21] P. Roth, L. Petnicci, and T. Pun, "From dots to shapes: an auditory haptic game platform for teaching geometry to blind pupils," in *Proceedings of the 7th International Conference on Computers Helping People with Special Needs (ICCHP '00)*, pp. 603–610, 2000.

[22] G. Evreinov and R. Raisamo, "An evaluation of three sound mappings through the localization behavior of the eyes," in *Proceedings of the 22nd International Conference on Virtual, Synthetic and Entertainment Audio (AES '02)*, pp. 239–248, New York, NY, USA, 2002.

[23] P. B. L. Meijer, "An experimental system for auditory image representations," *IEEE Transactions on Biomedical Engineering*, vol. 39, no. 2, pp. 112–121, 1992.

[24] S. Rouzier, B. Hennion, T. P. Segovia, and D. Chêne, "Touching geometry for visually impaired pupils," in *Proceedings of Euro-Haptics*, pp. 104–109, 2004.

[25] N. Gronau, M. Neta, and M. Bar, "Integrated contextual representation for objects' identities and their locations," *Journal of Cognitive Neuroscience*, vol. 20, no. 3, pp. 371–388, 2008.

[26] A. Theurel, S. Frileux, Y. Hatwell, and E. Gentaz, "The haptic recognition of geometrical shapes in congenitally blind and blindfolded adolescents: is there a haptic prototype effect," *PLoS ONE*, vol. 7, no. 6, Article ID e40251, 2012.

[27] I. Biederman, "Recognition-by-components: a theory of human image understanding," *Psychological Review*, vol. 94, no. 2, pp. 115–147, 1987.

[28] K. E. Overvliet, J. B. J. Smeets, and E. Brenner, "The use of proprioception and tactile information in haptic search," *Acta Psychologica*, vol. 129, no. 1, pp. 83–90, 2008.

[29] M. Singh, "Modal and amodal completion generate different shapes," *Psychological Science*, vol. 15, no. 7, pp. 454–459, 2004.

[30] S. Ullman, "The visual analysis of shape and form," in *The Cognitive Neurosciences*, M. S. Gazzaniga and E. Bizzi, Eds., pp. 339–350, MIT Press, Cambridge, Mass, USA, 1995.

[31] J. Voisin, G. Benoit, and E. C. Chapman, "Haptic discrimination of object shape in humans: two-dimensional angle discrimination," *Experimental Brain Research*, vol. 145, no. 2, pp. 239–250, 2002.

[32] B. Wu, R. L. Klatzky, and G. D. Stetten, "Mental visualization of objects from cross-sectional images," *Cognition*, vol. 123, no. 1, pp. 33–49, 2012.

[33] E. Foulke and J. S. Warm, "Effects of complexity and redundancy on the tactual recognition on metric figures," *Perceptual and Motor Skills*, vol. 25, no. 1, pp. 177–187, 1967.

[34] A. M. Kappers, J. J. Koenderink, and I. Lichtenegger, "Haptic identification of curved surfaces," *Perception and Psychophysics*, vol. 56, no. 1, pp. 53–61, 1994.

[35] K. van den Doel, D. Smilek, A. Bodnar et al., "Geometric shape detection with soundview," in *Proceedings of the 10th Meeting of the International Conference on Auditory Display (ICAD '04)*, vol. 47, no. 5, pp. 1–8, 2004.

[36] T. V. Evreinova, G. Evreinov, and R. Raisamo, "An evaluation of the virtual curvature with the StickGrip haptic device: a case study," *Universal Access in the Information Society*, vol. 12, no. 2, pp. 161–173, 2013.

[37] J. J. Koenderink and A. J. van Doorn, "Surface shape and curvature scales," *Image and Vision Computing*, vol. 10, no. 8, pp. 557–564, 1992.

[38] A. Pichler, R. B. Fisher, and M. Vincze, "Decomposition of range images using markov random fields," in *Proceedings of the 11th International Conference on Image Processing (ICIP '04)*, pp. 1205–1208, IEEE Computer Society Press, October 2004.

[39] G. Taylor and L. Kleeman, "Robust range data segmentation using geometric primitives for robotic applications," in *Proceedings of the 9th International Conference on Signal and Image Processing (IASTED '03)*, pp. 467–472, ACTA Press, August 2003.

[40] D. Weinshall, "Shortcuts in shape classification from two images," *CVGIP*, vol. 56, no. 1, pp. 57–68, 1992.

[41] A. G. Metec, http://www.metec-ag.de/, 2013.

[42] E. Lecolinet and G. Mouret, "TACTIBALL, TACTIPEN, TACTI-TAB Ou comment "toucher du doigt" les données de son ordinateur," in *Proceedings of the 17th international conference on Francophone sur l'Interaction Homme-Machine (IHM '05)*, pp. 227–230, ACM, New York, NY, USA, 2005.

[43] N. Noble and B. Martin, "Shape discovering using tactile guidance," in *Proceedings of EuroHaptics (EH '06)*, pp. 561–564, 2006.

[44] T. Pietrzak, A. Crossan, S. A. Brewster, B. Martin, and I. Pecci, "Exploring geometric shapes with touch," in *Proceedings of the 12th IFIP TC 13 International Conference on Human-Computer Interaction (INTERACT '09)*, pp. 145–148, Springer, Berlin, Germany, 2009.

[45] M. Ziat, O. Gapenne, J. Stewart, and C. Lenay, "Haptic recognition of shapes at different scales: a comparison of two methods of interaction," *Interacting with Computers*, vol. 19, no. 1, pp. 121–132, 2007.

[46] J. S. Chan, T. Maucher, J. Schemmel, D. Kilroy, F. N. Newell, and K. Meier, "The virtual haptic display: a device for exploring 2-D virtual shapes in the tactile modality," *Behavior Research Methods*, vol. 39, no. 4, pp. 802–810, 2007.

[47] M. Stamm, M. E. Altinsoy, and S. Merchel, "Identification accuracy and efficiency of haptic virtual objects using force-feedback," in *Proceedings of the 3rd International Workshop on Perceptual Quality of System (PQS '10)*, 2010.

[48] K. U. Kyung, H. Choi, D. S. Kwon, and S. W. Son, "Interactive mouse systems providing haptic feedback during the exploration in virtual environment," in *Proceedings of the 19th International Symposium (ISCIS '04)*, pp. 136–146, Springer, 2004.

[49] G. Jansson and K. Larsson, "Identification of haptic virtual objects with different degrees of complexity," in *Proceedings of Eurohaptics 2002 (EH '02)*, pp. 57–60, University of Edinburgh, Edinburgh, UK, 2002.

[50] S. Kelter, H. Grötzbach, R. Freiheit, B. Höhle, S. Wutzig, and E. Diesch, "Object identification: the mental representation of physical and conceptual attributes," *Memory and Cognition*, vol. 12, no. 2, pp. 123–133, 1984.

[51] M. A. Symmons, B. L. Richardson, and D. B. Wuillemin, "Components of haptic information: skin rivals kinaesthesis," *Perception*, vol. 37, no. 10, pp. 1596–1604, 2008.

[52] H. Bértolo, "Visual imagery without visual perception," *Psicológica*, vol. 26, no. 1, pp. 173–188, 2005.

[53] G. Evreinov, T. V. Evreinova, and R. Raisamo, "Method, computer program and device for interacting with a computer," Finland Patent Application, G06F ID, 20090434, 2009.

# 15

# *Zoo U*: A Stealth Approach to Social Skills Assessment in Schools

**Melissa E. DeRosier,**[1] **Ashley B. Craig,**[2] **and Rebecca P. Sanchez**[3]

[1] *3-C Institute for Social Development, 1901 North Harrison Avenue, Suite 200, Cary, NC 27513, USA*
[2] *Games Research Department, 3-C Institute for Social Development, 1901 North Harrison Avenue, Suite 200, Cary, NC 27513, USA*
[3] *Games Research Department, Center for Research in Emotional and Social Health, 1901 North Harrison Avenue, Suite 200, Cary, NC 27513, USA*

Correspondence should be addressed to Rebecca P. Sanchez, sanchez@cresh.org

Academic Editor: Leila Alem

This paper describes the design and evaluation of *Zoo U*, a novel computer game to assess children's social skills development. *Zoo U* is an innovative product that combines theory-driven content and customized game mechanics. The game-like play creates the opportunity for *stealth assessment*, in which dynamic evidence of social skills is collected in real time and players' choices during gameplay provide the needed data. To ensure the development of an engaging and valid game, we utilized an iterative data-driven validation process in which the game was created, tested, revised based on student performance and feedback, and retested until game play was statistically matched to independent ratings of social skills. We first investigated whether the data collected through extensive logging of student actions provided information that could be used to improve the assessment. We found that detailed game logs of socially relevant player behavior combined with external measures of player social skills provided an efficient vector to incrementally improve the accuracy of the embedded assessments. Next, we investigated whether the game performance correlated with teachers' assessments of students' social skills competencies. An evaluation of the final game showed (a) significant correlations between in-game social skills assessments and independently obtained standard psychological assessments of the same students and (b) high levels of engagement and likeability for students. These findings support the use of the interactive and engaging computer game format for the stealth assessment of children's social skills. The created innovative design methodologies should prove useful in the design and improvement of computer games in education.

## 1. Introduction

Social skills comprise a group of behaviors and knowledge that help children create and maintain friendships and navigate a multitude of situations involving other people. A child's social skills competence can strongly influence his or her sense of well being and adjustment [1, 2]. The importance of social skills and peer relationships increases through the elementary school years and into adolescence, with peers becoming key providers of support, advice, companionship, and affirmation [3]. Children with strong social skills and the relationships built on these skills tend to have more positive emotional, behavioral, and academic functioning. Positive peer relationships also function as a protective factor against negative outcomes in the face of stressful life events such as poverty [2, 4, 5]. In contrast, a lack of social skills competence can increase children's risk for poor adjustment across many areas of functioning. Children who experience problems in social interactions with their peers are more likely to exhibit depression [6], anxiety disorders [7], suicide [8], delinquency and antisocial behavior [9, 10], substance abuse [11, 12], educational underachievement [13, 14], and other mental health difficulties [2]. Children's risk for negative outcomes increases as peer problems become more chronic or severe [1].

A key to preventing the development of more serious maladjustment is intervening with problematic social behaviors before they become chronic and intractable [2, 15–17]. The first step in intervention is identifying children in need of social skills help with an effective assessment.

Recognition of these needs has led to inclusion of social goals in many Individualized Education Plans (IEPs), Student Support Team strategies, and overall school improvement plans. To meet these goals, schools must have access to assessment tools that are valid, easy to use, and able to identify students struggling with specific social skills as well as track students' response to intervention (RTI).

The gold standards of social skills assessments are naturalistic behavioral observation and behavior rating scales [18]. These methods, however, require extensive time and cost commitment and often have psychometric challenges such as unreliable or biased observers, lack of social comparison data, situational specificity, observer reactivity (i.e., students modify their behavior because they are being observed), and inappropriate recording techniques [19, 20].

A desire for alternative tools that provide rich accurate data and increase student engagement has led to a transdisciplinary interest in computer games for assessment and learning [21]. Computer games provide a promising avenue for the assessment of social skills and have several advantages over traditional methods. Once the assessment is developed, professional time and training to use the system is minimal. Subjective bias and reliability issues, as well as recording errors, are eliminated because behaviors are automatically scored rather than being coded by observers. Social comparison data can be collected efficiently from a large group of students. Situations that are important for assessment but unlikely to be observed in naturalistic observation because of low frequency can be engineered into the assessment. The issue of observer reactivity can be overcome with *stealth assessment* techniques, in which assessments are "woven directly and invisibly into the fabric" of the game [21] and players' choices during gameplay provide the data needed for assessment. This greatly reduces the likelihood that students will alter their behavior to please an observer.

Further, traditional measures of students' social skills generally lack sensitivity of measurement and have limited utility for informing identification of students for social intervention or for tracking a student's response to that intervention. Computer-based systems offer the potential for more effective, sensitive, and reliable social skills assessment compared to traditional methods. Technology also offers a more engaging platform for students, an affordable method for broad scale everyday use by schools, and a seamless means of integrating data-driven decision making into school-based social interventions. This type of comprehensive in-game modeling of an individual player's knowledge or skills is becoming more common as Intelligent Tutoring Systems research and technology are increasingly applied to computer games [18, 22–24].

In the present study, we used theory-driven content and customized game mechanics to design and evaluate a stealth assessment computer game to determine children's social skills levels. We used extensive game log data and user feedback to revise the game during an iterative testing procedure. When the game was finalized, we used aggregate log data to create performance indices in order to assess students' social skills aptitude and examined correlations

FIGURE 1: Dialogue selection menu.

between in-game performance and independent measures of social skills to establish the validity of our computer game for social skills assessment.

## 2. Method

*2.1. Development of Zoo U.* The primary design goal of *Zoo U* was to create virtual situations analogous to those commonly experienced by children in school settings in order to assess social problem solving strategies and aptitude. To accomplish this, we created *Zoo U* as a single-player point-and-click problem solving game situated in a school-like setting that, in addition to teacher and student NPCs (nonplayable characters), also contains zoo animals. The animals provide a bit of fun and fantasy to the school setting as well as opportunities for novel social problem solving tasks (e.g., working with other students to feed and care for the animals).

*Game Mechanics.* Each scene employs the same set of point-and-click mechanics and is rendered in 2.5 D, allowing for the appearance that the avatar can move in front of or behind objects in the scene via perceptual depth. For example, as depicted in Figure 1, the player is allowed to move to a location adjacent to one of the desks, which obscures the lower part of the avatar. The player clicks to move within a geometrically defined "walkable area" by using a modified A* algorithm to construct the walk path so that collisions between the avatar and objects in the scene are avoided.

*Zoo U* allows the player to initiate dialogue with NPCs by clicking on them. Players are informed of clickable objects and NPCs by the change in their standard cursor to one that glows blue. A subset of other objects in each scene also can be manipulated by clicking; some of these objects are integral for scene completion, and others are included as distractors similar to those in real world settings. The avatar initiates and/or responds to NPCs' dialogue by selecting from scripted dialogue choices (as shown in Figure 1) that are presented in random order. As the player moves the mouse over a choice, the corresponding actor-recorded audio is heard and the player selects a speech choice by clicking on it. In accordance with the principles of Intelligent Systems [25], in nearly all cases a player's choice in one dialogue bubble impacts the available dialogue choices in subsequent interactions with a particular NPC in each scene.

*Scene Content.* Subject matter experts (SMEs) used educational and developmental psychology theories and empirical research to develop six independent social scenes to assess distinct social competencies (emotion regulation, impulse control, communication, empathy, cooperation, and initiation).

In each scene, players are presented with a social problem that needs to be solved. Content was developed to elicit measurable player behaviors and dialogue choices known to be integral to the social skill competency being assessed in each scene. For example, in the impulse control scene the player needs to feed the elephant before the class can go to recess. Players have access to two NPCs (the teacher and a peer) with which the student can interact and seek assistance in solving the presented task, as well as a number of clickable objects (e.g., food crates). Dialogue choices were written to assess particular components of the measured social skill (e.g., asking the teacher a specific question about the animal's name rather than asking her a more impulsive question about recess). Some of the objects are problem relevant (e.g., a clipboard on the wall that provides instructions for feeding the elephant), and others are included as distractors (e.g., the food crates, none of which contain food the elephant can eat). For both distractor NPCs and objects, students are allowed some exploration (e.g., the student is allowed to talk with a less-than-useful peer once). Students' scores decline; however, if they diverge too far from on-task behavior.

In order to receive a high impulse control score, the player needs to control his or her impulses to click on the distractor objects and direct full attention to appropriately determine how they should feed the elephant. Of course, each social skill assessed in *Zoo U* has unique requirements, and each scene varies with regard to how much emphasis is placed on interaction with NPCs versus interaction with the environment to solve a problem. Whereas scenes like impulse control, cooperation, and initiation are largely scored on students' behaviors in the scene (e.g., clicking on objects and time spent between behaviors), and social skills like emotion regulation and communication place greater emphasis on the individual and sequence of dialogue choices made when talking to NPCs.

## 2.2. Iterative Testing

*Student Testing.* In order to optimize both the gameplay and assessment quality of *Zoo U*, two independent iterative evaluations were conducted with third- and fourth-grade students and their teachers in two schools in central North Carolina. Parental consent forms were sent to the homes of all third- and fourth-grade students ($n$ = 254) in regular classrooms. More than 90% of students received parental consent to participate. The first iterative test included students from one third- ($n$ = 16) and one fourth-grade

($n$ = 23) classroom and their teachers. Data collected from this initial sample were used to revise the content and gameplay options, as well as verify the difficulty of in-game challenges within each of the six social problem solving scenes. The revised scenes then were tested by a group of 187 students from 14 third- and fourth-grade classrooms and their teachers. Across both tests, students were approximately evenly divided across grades and genders and represented the full range of socioeconomic status with a racial distribution of 55% White, 32% African American, 7% Asian American, and 6% multiracial. Twenty-seven percent of students were of Hispanic/Latino ethnicity.

In both iterative test groups, testing took place during a regularly scheduled one-hour computer lab class at the school. Each child was assigned a computer on which to play *Zoo U* while research staff observed. Following the project introduction and computer orientation, students were given 30 minutes to complete the six *Zoo U* scenes. Teachers were asked to observe without providing assistance. Trained observers monitored and recorded students' level of attention, areas of difficulty, and reactions to *Zoo U* mechanics and content. Computer logs tracked the location and time of each mouse click so that students' interactivity could be mapped. The resulting data from the first iterative test group were used to refine any dialogue choices that did not relate in the expected directions with teacher ratings of students' social skills, as well as provide insights about particular game mechanics that gave students difficulty. The log data from the second iterative test were used to verify the refinements from the first iterative test as well as to calculate algorithms for students' performance in each *Zoo U* social problem solving task.

*Student Ratings of Zoo U.* After playing *Zoo U*, students completed a brief survey evaluating their experience with the software. We asked students to rate how fun/interesting the game was, how easy it was to use and understand, whether they liked the characters/graphics, whether they wanted to play more, and how much they liked it overall. Students rated these items on a four-point scale from 1 = "Not at all true for me" to 4 = "Very true for me." Research staff then led a group discussion to gather comments from students and suggestions for how to make the navigation or user experience better. In creating the second iteration of the game, we paid special attention to any ratings that were relatively low and refined the game accordingly.

## 2.3. Zoo U as a Valid Measure of Social Skills

*Game Log and Scoring.* At the time of the initial design of each scene, the SMEs created the content with the intention that children with varying levels of proficiency in the relevant social skill for that scene would perform differently. For instance, as shown in Figure 2, the impulse control scene contains three crates showing different possible foods for the elephant and a clipboard nearby labeled "Feeding Instructions," but the food crates are red herrings. Each time a player clicks a crate and attempts to feed the elephant that

FIGURE 2: Impulse control scene.

kind of food, the elephant sticks out its tongue and the avatar says, "I don't think he likes it."

We expected impulsivity to vary directly with the number of clicks on the food crates, but the optimal number of clicks that would indicate varying levels of impulsivity was not evident at the time of initial design (i.e., a priori). To establish these optimal thresholds, gameplay was captured to provide minute annotated logging of the times and locations of every player click event. We parsed these logs to provide aggregate data, such as how many times a player clicked on a particular in-scene object, average response time to a dialogue choice menu versus response time on a particular choice, and the sequence of problem solving choices made by a particular student.

We then calculated a composite performance index (i.e., an algorithm) for each of the six scenes based on the aggregate information generated by the parsed log files for each scene (e.g., the number of times a player clicked on an individual NPC). Performance indices consisted of three core game-based components. The first component was scored based on dialogue choices to determine the quality of the student's attempts to solve the problem by communicating with the NPCs. For example, when asking the peer NPC for information, credit was given when an on-task menu choice was selected, whereas credit was not given when an off-task dialogue choice was selected.

In contrast to this menu-driven scoring method, the other two components assessed the quality of the student's behaviors while he or she interacted with the scene. The second component measured the amount of time spent engaged in appropriate problem solving activities versus inappropriate ones. For impulse control, this component was reflected via percentage of total time spent engaged in appropriate problem solving behaviors and reading the provided instructions on the clipboard versus time spent off-task (e.g., choosing off-task dialogue options and clicking on distractor objects). The third component measured the ratio of on-task versus off-task behaviors while completing the scene. In the impulse control scene, this was accomplished by calculating the number of impulsive clicks, including clicks on unrelated objects, and objects that the student had already learned were not useful for solving the problem.

TABLE 1: Student usability ratings of Zoo U.

| Area rated | Mean (std) |
| --- | --- |
| Fun/interesting | 3.90 (.31) |
| Easy to use and understand | 3.95 (.22) |
| Liked characters and graphics | 3.80 (.45) |
| Want to play more | 3.95 (.22) |
| Overall liked | 3.90 (.31) |

*Teacher Ratings of Students' Social Skills.* An important aspect of this study was to examine the degree to which *Zoo U* performance was related to an independent external assessment of students' social skills (i.e., external validation). To this end, teachers completed an online survey rating the social skills of each of their students prior to students interacting with *Zoo U* (Table 1). This survey presented behavioral descriptors (e.g., "gets distracted easily," "good to have in a group"), and teachers rated the degree to which each descriptor was true of each student (from a low of "never true" to a high of "almost always true"). In order to target the teacher assessment more directly to the social skills and behaviors assessed through *Zoo U*, items for this survey were drawn from previously validated measures of social skills in this age group, including the Teacher Checklist [26], the Social Skills Rating Scale [27], and the Social Competence Scale-Teacher Version [28]. The resulting Social Skills Behavior Inventory (SSBI) [29] included 34 items across the six social skills scales (communication, cooperation, empathy, initiation, impulse control, and emotion regulation). Internal consistency for each subscale was acceptable (*mean Cronbach α* = .86) and was statistically similar for ratings of third- and fourth-grade students.

## 3. Results

*3.1. Student Ratings of Zoo U.* Overall, students rated *Zoo U* very positively with every area rated ≥3.8 on a four-point scale. In addition, researcher observations revealed high levels of student engagement with 96% on-task behavior and numerous positive comments about the game (e.g., "This is awesome!"; "When can I play more?"). Students easily understood how to navigate *Zoo U*, and analysis of usage data indicated a low rate of errors (e.g., misclicks). Researchers observed very few misunderstandings or requests for technical help. Desire for replay was also strong; after students had completed all six scenes of *Zoo U*, they were told that they could replay *Zoo U* a second time or go online to play other games for the remainder of the session. We were pleased that 89% of students elected to replay *Zoo U*.

*3.2. Zoo U as a Valid Measure of Social Skills.* To assess external validity, we conducted correlational analyses to examine the relations between *Zoo U* performance indices and the teacher ratings of students' social skills for each subscale. Table 2 displays these results. For all six scenes, the *Zoo U* composite performance index was significantly correlated with the teacher rating on the analogous SSBI

TABLE 2: Correlations between *Zoo U* composite performance and teacher ratings of student social skills.

| SSBI teacher rating scales | *Zoo U* composite performance index | | | | | |
| --- | --- | --- | --- | --- | --- | --- |
| | Imp con | Emo reg | Comm | Coop | Init | Emp |
| Impulse control | **.29**\*** | .31\*** | .15\* | .16\* | .17\* | .16\* |
| Emotion regulation | .15\* | **.30**\*** | .08 | .17\* | .25\** | .17\* |
| Communication | .26\*** | .28\*** | **.20**\** | .20\** | .27\*** | .19\* |
| Cooperation | .23\** | .31\*** | .12 | **.21**\** | .16\* | .17\* |
| Initiation | .17\* | .14\* | .08 | .18\** | **.27**\*** | .15\* |
| Empathy | .26\*** | .22\** | .10 | .17\* | .24\** | **.23**\** |

Note: \*\*\**P* < .0001, \*\**P* < .01, and \**P* < .05.

TABLE 3: Intercorrelations amongst *Zoo U* subscales.

| | Emo reg | Comm | Coop | Init | Emp |
| --- | --- | --- | --- | --- | --- |
| Impulse control | .23\** | .07 | .21\** | .15\* | .24\** |
| Emotion regulation | | .20\** | .09 | .26\** | .16\* |
| Communication | | | .07 | .19\* | .10 |
| Cooperation | | | | .21\** | .16\* |
| Initiation | | | | | .14 |

Note: \*\**P* < .01 and \**P* < .05.

subscale and correlated in expected ways with other SSBI subscales.

To ensure that *Zoo U* composite indices were discriminating amongst the targeted social skills, intercorrelations between *Zoo U* subscales were calculated to determine the degree to which *Zoo U* subscales were independent. Table 3 displays the results of those correlations. Although *Zoo U* subscales are related in a number of cases, the composition of those associations is expected given the overlap of social skills competencies in children's real world behaviors (e.g., it is not surprising that impulse control is correlated with emotion regulation).

## 4. Discussion

Computer games provide a promising avenue for the assessment of student skills. It is likely that computer-based assessments will be utilized heavily in the future, as the student assessment paradigm shifts from a single-source (e.g., teacher) time-intensive approach to a more multifaceted and interactive methodology that will require a new way of thinking about student identification. In the present study, experts in educational/developmental psychology and computer science collaborated to create and test an innovative stealth assessment of children's social skills. This study contributes to the improvement of computer games in education by describing a novel design methodology for developing these kinds of assessments.

This study underscores the potential cumulative value of assessing multiple dimensions of player behavior when formulating student performance indices. In-game data logs captured students' dialogue choices, behavioral choices, and time on task and off task. *Zoo U*'s performance indices were developed, tested, and refined based on both theory

and these data logs. These performance indices then were validated by measuring their association with a standard teacher report of students' social skills.

A key challenge in designing *Zoo U* was determining the appropriate level of difficulty in order to garner enough student variability in responses to develop useful performance indices. The starting point of our solution was to employ an iterative design process. The results of this process demonstrated that stealth assessment principals can be used in the context of identifying children's levels of social skills in ways that are commensurate with standard identification practices (i.e., teacher report). We currently are testing these performance-derived indices with a larger, more nationally representative sample of students to further calibrate the in-game assessment of students' social skills.

The results of this assessment study are linked to the promise of educational games' potential to offer opportunities for instruction and intervention to build children's social and emotional skills. Merrill [18] notes that "the present and future challenge in assessment is to find meaningful ways to make assessment results functional, in the sense of tying specific results to important social outcomes and to the development of effective instructional and therapeutic programs." We concur with the importance of this challenge and currently are developing a number of computer-based intelligent social tutoring systems that will utilize *Zoo U* assessment for the identification of students' social skills aptitude. The assessment capabilities of *Zoo U* offer flexibility for use as both a prepost assessment of intervention effects and as a way of modulating the difficulty so that students are continuously challenged but not frustrated (i.e., scaffolded learning). Utilizing this capability, we are developing tutorials for both universal and indicated populations with the intent of improving children's social skills strategies across a range of functioning.

In this study, we established the validity of *Zoo U* with one of the gold standards of social skills assessment, a behavior rating scale. Future research should further validate *Zoo U* by using the other gold standard, naturalistic observation. We believe that because *Zoo U* was developed specifically to provide game-based social problem solving scenarios analogous to authentic situations children encounter, ecological validity will be maintained and that many of the limitations (e.g., observer bias and reactivity, recording error) of naturalistic observation will be minimized.

*Zoo U* leverages innovative technologies to provide an engaging and powerful social skills assessment tool with real-time reporting functions for educators to easily track students' progress toward social goals. Online access makes *Zoo U* cost effective and enables easy access for students and schools across the nation, making it an appealing option for social skills assessment. Data derived through this new form of assessment can be used to inform decisions regarding implementation of social interventions by schools, to identify children in need of social skills interventions, and to track progress over the course of an intervention. Compared to standard measures, the engaging nature of computer games and the efficiency with which assessments can be conducted and scored make them less arduous for both students and teachers and more accessible, informative, and effective on a broad scale.

## Disclosure

The research reported in this article may lead to the development of a product for commercialization.

## Acknowledgment

This research was supported by U.S. Department of Education Grant ED-IES-10-P-0114.

## References

[1] J. Kupersmidt and M. DeRosier, "How peer problems lead to negative outcomes: an integrative mediational model," in *Children's Peer Relations: From Development to Intervention*, pp. 119–138, American Psychological Association, 2004.

[2] J. Parker, K. Rubin, S. Erath, J. Wojslawowicz, and A. Buskirk, "Peer relationships, child development, and adjustment: a developmental psychopathology perspective," *Developmental Psychopathology*, vol. 1, pp. 419–493, 2006.

[3] W. Furman and D. Buhrmester, "Age and sex differences in perceptions of networks of personal relationships," *Child Development*, vol. 63, no. 1, pp. 103–115, 1992.

[4] A. E. Kazdin, "Effectiveness of psychotherapy with children and adolescents," *Journal of Consulting and Clinical Psychology*, vol. 59, no. 6, pp. 785–798, 1991.

[5] S. Luthar, *Resilience and Vulnerability: Adaptation in the Context of Childhood Adversities*, Cambridge University Press, New York, NY, USA, 2003.

[6] M. Boivin and S. Hymel, "Peer experiences and social self-perceptions: a sequential model," *Developmental Psychology*, vol. 33, no. 1, pp. 135–145, 1997.

[7] S. A. Erath, K. S. Flanagan, and K. L. Bierman, "Social anxiety and peer relations in early adolescence: behavioral and cognitive factors," *Journal of Abnormal Child Psychology*, vol. 35, no. 3, pp. 405–416, 2007.

[8] J. V. Carney, "Bullied to death: perceptions of peer abuse and suicidal behaviour during adolescence," *School Psychology International*, vol. 21, no. 2, pp. 213–223, 2000.

[9] M. Brendgen, F. Vitaro, and W. M. Bukowski, "Affiliation with delinquent friends: contributions of parents, self-esteem, delinquent behavior, and rejection by peers," *Journal of Early Adolescence*, vol. 18, no. 3, pp. 244–265, 1998.

[10] M. E. Feinberg, T. A. Ridenour, and M. T. Greenberg, "Aggregating indices of risk and protection for adolescent behavior problems: the Communities That Care Youth Survey," *Journal of Adolescent Health*, vol. 40, no. 6, pp. 506–513, 2007.

[11] J. D. Hawkins, R. F. Catalano, and J. Y. Miller, "Risk and protective factors for alcohol and other drug problems in adolescence and early adulthood: implications for substance abuse prevention," *Psychological Bulletin*, vol. 112, no. 1, pp. 64–105, 1992.

[12] C. Spooner, "Causes and correlates of adolescent drug abuse and implications for treatment," *Drug and Alcohol Review*, vol. 18, no. 4, pp. 453–475, 1999.

[13] C. B. Fleming, K. P. Haggerty, R. F. Catalano, T. W. Harachi, J. J. Mazza, and D. H. Gruman, "Do social and behavioral characteristics targeted by preventive interventions predict standardized test scores and grades?" *Journal of School Health*, vol. 75, no. 9, pp. 342–349, 2005.

[14] L. J. Woodward and D. M. Fergusson, "Childhood peer relationship problems and later risks of educational under-achievement and unemployment," *Journal of Child Psychology and Psychiatry and Allied Disciplines*, vol. 41, no. 2, pp. 191–201, 2000.

[15] J. D. Coie, K. A. Dodge, R. Terry, and V. Wright, "The role of aggression in peer relations: an analysis of aggression episodes in boys' play groups," *Child development*, vol. 62, no. 4, pp. 812–826, 1991.

[16] M. E. DeRosier, J. B. Kupersmidt, and C. J. Patterson, "Children's academic and behavioral adjustment as a function of the chronicity and proximity of peer rejection," *Child Development*, vol. 65, no. 6, pp. 1799–1813, 1994.

[17] M. Greenberg, C. Domitrovich, and B. Bumbarger, "Prevention of mental disorders in school-aged children: current state of the field," *Prevention & Treatment*, vol. 4, no. 1, pp. 1–52, 2001.

[18] K. W. Merrell, "Assessment of children's social skills: recent developments, best practices, and new directions," *Exceptionality*, vol. 9, no. 1-2, pp. 3–18, 2001.

[19] K. W. Merrell, *Behavioral, Social, and Emotional Assessment of Children and Adolescents*, Laurence Erlbaum Associates, Mahwah, NJ, USA, 1999.

[20] K. W. Merrell and G. A. Gimpel, *Social Skills of Children and Adolescents: Conceptualization, Assessment, Treatment*, Laurence Erlbaum Associates, Mahwah, NJ, USA, 1998.

[21] V. J. Shute and F. Ke, "Games, learning, and assessment," in *Assessment in Game-Based Learning: Foundations, Innovations, and Perspectives*, D. Ifenthaler, D. Eseryel, and X. Ge, Eds., Springer, New York, NY, USA, 2012.

[22] Y. Cheong, A. Jhala, B. Bae, and R. M. Young, "Automatically generating summaries from game logs," in *Proceedings of the 4th Artificial Intelligence and Interactive Digital Entertainment International Conference (AIIDE '08)*, pp. 167–172, 2008.

[23] J. Rowe and J. Lester, "Modeling user knowledge with dynamic bayesian networks in interactive narrative environments," in *Proceedings of the 6th Annual AI and Interactive Digital Entertainment Conference*, pp. 57–62, Palo Alto, Calif, USA, 2010.

[24] A. Tveit and G. B. Tveit, "Game usage mining: information gathering for knowledge discovery in massive multiplayer games," in *Proceedings of the International Conference on Internet Computing (IC '02)*, Session on Web Mining, 2002.

[25] V. J. Shute and D. Zapata-Rivera, "Educational assessment using intelligent systems," Educational Testing Service Report RR-08-68, ETS, Princeton, NJ, USA, 2008.

[26] M. E. DeRosier and S. H. Mercer, "Improving student behavior: the effectiveness of a school-based character education program," *Journal of Research and Character Education*, vol. 5, pp. 131–148, 2007.

[27] F. Gresham and S. Elliott, *Social Skills Rating System*, American Guidance Service, Circle Pines, Minn, USA, 1990.

[28] Conduct Problems Prevention Research Group (CPPRG), Social Competence Scale (Teacher Version), 1990, http://www.fasttrackproject.org/.

[29] M. E. DeRosier, "Using computer-based social tasks to assess students' social skills: findings from the Zoo U pilot evaluation," Final Report for the U.S. Department of Education, Washington, DC, USA, 2011.

# 16

# Force Feedback to Assist Active Contour Modelling for Tracheal Stenosis Segmentation

**Lode Vanacken,**[1] **Rômulo Pinho,**[2] **Jan Sijbers,**[2] **and Karin Coninx**[1]

[1] *Hasselt University-tUL-IBBT Expertise Centre for Digital Media, Wetenschapspark 2, 3590 Diepenbeek, Belgium*
[2] *IBBT Vision Lab, Department of Physics, University of Antwerp, Universiteitsplein 1, N.1, 2610 Wilrijk, Belgium*

Correspondence should be addressed to Lode Vanacken, lode.vanacken@uhasselt.be

Academic Editor: Antonio Krüger

Manual segmentation of structures for diagnosis and treatment of various diseases is a very time-consuming procedure. Therefore, some level of automation during the segmentation is desired, as it often significantly reduces the segmentation time. A typical solution is to allow manual interaction to steer the segmentation process, which is known as semiautomatic segmentation. In 2D, such interaction is usually achieved with click-and-drag operations, but in 3D a more sophisticated interface is called for. In this paper, we propose a semi-automatic Active Contour Modelling for the delineation of medical structures in 3D, tomographic images. Interaction is implemented with the employment of a 3D haptic device, which is used to steer the contour deformation towards the correct boundaries. In this way, valuable haptic feedback is provided about the 3D surface and its deformation. Experiments on simulated and real tracheal CT data showed that the proposed technique is an intuitive and effective segmentation mechanism.

## 1. Introduction

Image segmentation in the medical field is an important step for the diagnosis and treatment of various diseases. In many cases, this task is performed manually [1, 2]. However, manual segmentation is widely acknowledged as being time consuming and intra- and interoperator dependent. Hence, some level of automation during the segmentation is desired, as it often significantly reduces the segmentation time. Medical image segmentation, in particular, is a very complex task, given the necessary precision required for object extraction and boundary delineation. A typical solution is to allow users to provide extra knowledge to or interfere with the segmentation process in order to refine the results yielded by the automatic steps, which is known as semiautomatic (or interactive) segmentation.

The Active Contour Model (ACM) [3] is a well-known shape deformation algorithm to delineate structures in images, and several semiautomatic versions of this algorithm have been proposed in the literature [4]. ACMs minimise an energy function that controls the bending and stretching of a given initial contour and the attraction by image features.

The expected result is that the contour matches the boundary of the structure of interest in the image. In 2D, the interface between user and algorithm is usually established with click/drag processes. However, if the data being segmented is three-dimensional, such as in 3D Computed Tomography (CT) images, a more refined interface is called for.

The present work sets forth a 3D segmentation interface for ACMs based on haptics. The chosen application is the segmentation of tracheal stenosis from chest CT scans. Tracheal stenosis is an unnatural narrowing of the trachea with traumatic, neoplastic, or idiopathic causes that, despite being relatively rare, can be life threatening [5]. In order to correctly diagnose and treat it, accurate assessment of the stricture is necessary, which determines the point where it starts, where it ends, and the degree of narrowing [6]. One way of performing this assessment is via segmentation [7], which needs to be especially accurate around the narrowed parts of the trachea, so that the parameters of the stenosis can be correctly calculated. Although the healthy trachea can in general be segmented very easily with, for example, region growing, the task may be challenging in cases of severe stenosis. As discussed in [7], this happens because the tracheal lumen at the narrowed region is often barely visible in the image. Triglia et al. [8] solved this problem by manually reconstructing the parts of the narrowed trachea that were not visible in the image, but this can be time consuming and prone to error. In [9], it was also shown that 3D ACMs are able to reconstruct missing parts of the trachea, but noise and the presence of neighbour organs in the image may hinder segmentation. The semiautomatic process proposed here is therefore meant to overcome such difficulties.

The proposed ACM can be steered by the user with 3D input from a haptic device. Conversely, the user is provided with valuable force feedback about the 3D surface and its deformation. This interaction creates a first-person 3D environment, which gives the user the feeling that a real shape is being manipulated. The net effect is an intuitive, interactive segmentation mechanism that improves over traditional 2D approaches. The method was evaluated with two sets of 3D CT images. The first is a real case of severe tracheal stenosis. The second set is a phantom of stenosis created from a real CT image, in which the oesophagus also appears in the image and may disturb the segmentation process. The results obtained with the proposed method were compared to a reference manual segmentation using traditional region growing.

This paper is organised as follows. Section 2 gives an overview of existing semiautomatic segmentation algorithms, including those employing 3D interfaces. Section 3.2 briefly reviews the ACM used in the segmentation of tracheal stenosis from CT images. In Section 4, the method to integrate haptics with ACM is fully described. The experiments and evaluation of the proposed method are given in Section 5. Section 6 presents a discussion of the results obtained, and the paper is concluded in Section 7.

## 2. Related Work

The work related to the research presented here can be categorised in primarily two different topics, namely, interactive segmentation and the addition of force feedback to segmentation. Both will be discussed in this section.

*2.1. Interactive Segmentation.* Given the difficulties in implementing fully automatic segmentation algorithms, interactive segmentation has long been a topic of interest in the literature. Qiu and Yuen [1] recently discussed current trends and the history of semiautomatic segmentations. Olabarriaga and Smeulders [2] presented an interesting survey focussed on interactive segmentation in medical images, discussing practical and subjective aspects of the problem. McGuinness and O'Connor [10] proposed a framework for the evaluation of interactive segmentation and evaluated four existing algorithms. McInerney and Terzopoulos [4] presented a survey of ACMs applied to medical images and described different ways of manipulating the deformable curves with user intervention.

In the field of segmentation of 3D images, Kang et al. [9] proposed a set of editing tools meant to interactively correct inaccuracies of automatic segmentation methods. They compared their tools with traditional slice-by-slice 2D segmentation approaches. Another similar and successful approach has been proposed by Heckel et al. [11], which applied variational interpolation in combination with a set of user-drawn, planar contours that can be arbitrarily oriented in 3D space. A natural evolution of such types of interaction tools is the use of more advanced, or even 3D, interfaces. Bornik et al. [12], for example, used immersive 3D spaces and tablets to manipulate deformable models in segmentation refinement, and Zudilova-Seinstra et al. [13] recently employed glove-based input for the delineation of medical data.

*2.2. Force Feedback during Segmentation.* As 3D interfaces evolved to haptics, so did the 3D user interaction in segmentation applications. Vidholm et al. [14, 15] used haptics such that seeds for the segmentation could be placed in good spots. Force feedback was applied based on data from MR images so that the user could recognise good seed locations. Similarly, Malmberg et al. [16] augmented a 3D wiring segmentation technique with force feedback. In this type of segmentation technique, the boundaries of the object to be segmented are contoured (wired). Force feedback using volume haptics was provided to better understand the object boundaries and thus enhance the wiring.

More related to the work presented here, Vidholm et al. [17] showed a technique which enables the user to push a deformable model to perform segmentation. Finally, when working with deformable models, the placement and shape of the initial surface to be deformed is also very important. Harders and Székely [18] proposed to extract the centre line of a tubular structure to create forces to guide a user on a path close to this centre line. While moving along the path, the user sets control points which define a spline-based centre line. This centre line, in turn, is used to calculate and generate a cylinder with dynamic width to represent the deformable model.

## 3. Segmentation of Tracheal Stenosis

In the following, we will briefly review the main concepts behind ACMs and how they are used to accomplish the tracheal stenosis segmentation.

*3.1. Active Contour Models.* ACMs, commonly known as snakes, are curves defined within an image domain that are able to move under the influence of internal forces derived from the curve itself and of external forces derived from the image data. The internal and external forces are defined in such a way that the curve will register to an object boundary or other desired features within an image. As defined by Kass et al. [3], a snake can be represented in 2D by a curve $\mathbf{v}(s) = (x(s), y(s))$, $s \in [0, 1]$, responding to an energy functional of the form

$$E = \int_0^1 [\kappa E_{\text{int}}(\mathbf{v}(s)) + (1 - \kappa) E_{\text{ext}}(\mathbf{v}(s))] ds, \tag{1}$$

where $\kappa \in [0, 1]$ is a weighting factor.

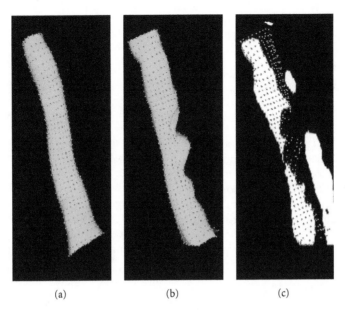

(a)            (b)            (c)

FIGURE 1: (a) The initial shape of the ACM (green) with the corresponding landmarks (red dots). (b) A step of the deformation algorithm. (c) The landmarks of the shape being deformed overlaid on an image of tracheal stenosis. Note the landmarks being attracted by the edges of the structures in the image.

The internal energy $E_{\text{int}}$ restricts the deformations by preventing the curve from breaking apart and avoiding the appearance of sharp corners. The external energy usually represents the gradient of an image $I$ convolved with a Gaussian function $G$ at scale $\sigma$, which causes the curve to be attracted by contours with high image gradients.

The objective is then to minimise (1), making the system a force balance equation of the form

$$\kappa \mathbf{F}_{\text{int}} + (1 - \kappa)\mathbf{F}_{\text{ext}} = \mathbf{0}, \tag{2}$$

where

$$\begin{aligned} \mathbf{F}_{\text{int}} &= -\nabla E_{\text{int}}, \\ \mathbf{F}_{\text{ext}} &= -\nabla E_{\text{ext}}. \end{aligned} \tag{3}$$

The minimisation is solved iteratively. The expected result is a curve that matches the high gradients of the image while being restricted by the internal constraints, according to the assigned weighting factors.

### 3.2. ACM for Tracheal Stenosis Segmentation.

The concepts above naturally extrapolate to 3D and can easily be adapted to a discrete domain. Within the context of the proposed application, a discrete surface is defined as $\mathcal{S} = (\mathcal{X}, \mathcal{T})$, where $\mathcal{X}$ is the set of points, or landmarks, with $\mathbf{x}_i, i = 1, \dots, n$, a point in this set, and $\mathcal{T}$ is the set of triangles connecting the points of $\mathcal{X}$.

The ACM is initialised with an estimation of the healthy shape of the trachea, obtained with the method proposed in Pinho et al. [7]. In this way, the initial shape tends to be near enough to the boundary of the narrowed trachea in the image. In addition, this shape conveys more intuitive information to the user. This improves on the approach proposed by Vidholm et al. [17], in which the initial surface does not necessarily resemble the target object.

The deformation algorithm iteratively loops through all the points in $\mathcal{X}$, applying the ACM forces locally, until no significant deformation has been made to the surface. Below, the internal and external forces are briefly presented and Figure 1 illustrates some steps of the algorithm. For a detailed description, we refer the reader to [7].

### 3.2.1. External Force.

The external force $\mathbf{F}_{\text{ext}}$ is derived from the image, which is first converted into a distance map $I_D$ indicating the distance from any point to the nearest edge (high image gradient). The gradient of $I_D$ defines how landmarks of the surface lying on a certain point of the image are influenced by $\mathbf{F}_{\text{ext}}$. Therefore, the external force applied to the landmark $\mathbf{x}_i$ of $\mathcal{X}$ is defined as

$$\mathbf{F}_{\text{ext}_i} = -\frac{|\nabla I_D(\mathbf{x}_i)|}{M} \nabla I_D(\mathbf{x}_i), \tag{4}$$

where $M$ is the maximum gradient magnitude in $I_D$.

### 3.2.2. Internal Forces.

The internal force $\mathbf{F}_{\text{int}}$ controls stretching and bending, in such a way that the surface is continuous (does not break apart) and remains smooth (has no sharp corners). The force tries to keep the landmarks equally spaced and tries to minimise the local Gaussian curvature of the surface. It is given by

$$\mathbf{F}_{\text{int}_i} = \gamma \mathbf{F}_{\text{elast}_i} + (1 - \gamma)\mathbf{F}_{\text{bend}_i}, \tag{5}$$

where $\gamma$ is a weighting factor.

$\mathbf{F}_{\text{elast}_i}$ is the elastic force applied to $\mathbf{x}_i$ of $\mathcal{X}$, defined as

$$\mathbf{F}_{\text{elast}_i} = D_i \frac{\mathbf{d}_{\text{elast}_i}}{|\mathbf{d}_{\text{elast}_i}|}, \tag{6}$$

where the directional component $\mathbf{d}_{\mathrm{elast}_i}$ moves the landmark towards a central point relative to its neighbours. The scalar component $D_i$, in turn, is a normalised measure of how much $\mathbf{x}_i$ deviates from this central point.

The bending force $\mathbf{F}_{\mathrm{bend}_i}$ is given by

$$\mathbf{F}_{\mathrm{bend}_i} = K_{G_i} \frac{\mathbf{d}_{\mathrm{bend}_i}}{|\mathbf{d}_{\mathrm{bend}_i}|}, \tag{7}$$

where $\mathbf{d}_{\mathrm{bend}_i}$ is either equal to $\mathbf{d}_{\mathrm{elast}_i}$ or it moves $\mathbf{x}_i$ along its normal if the landmark is not located at the open ends of the surface. In either case, the directional component moves $\mathbf{x}_i$ in such a way that the discrete Gaussian curvature computed at the landmark is minimised. The scalar component $K_{G_i}$ is a normalised measure of how much the curvature at $\mathbf{x}_i$ deviates from zero.

Finally, for each iteration $j$ of the deformation algorithm of the ACM,

$$\mathbf{x}_i^{(j)} = \mathbf{x}_i^{(j-1)} + \kappa \mathbf{F}_{\mathrm{int}_i} + (1-\kappa)\mathbf{F}_{\mathrm{ext}_i}. \tag{8}$$

# 4. Haptic Interaction in Active Contour Models

In this section, we will first give some theoretical background on the use of haptics and the benefits it can provide to 3D interaction. Afterwards, we will discuss how we integrated force feedback with ACMs when they are used to segment tracheal stenosis.

*4.1. Haptic Interaction.* Haptic interaction requires the existence of a device that serves as the interface between the user and an application. Not only does this device enable the user to provide input to the application, but also conveys to the user the reaction of the system to the provided input (force feedback), giving the user a sense of touch [19].

A first step towards adding force feedback to any application is deciding how to perform the haptic rendering. In our case, the trachea is represented using the surface description $\mathcal{S} = (\mathcal{X}, \mathcal{T})$ of Section 3.2. Using the haptic device, the user can interact with the triangular boundary of $\mathcal{S}$, pushing or pulling it. The haptic rendering takes care of interpreting the commands sent by the haptic device, transferring them to the surface, and returning to the user the force feedback given by the surface. This is performed using the algorithm described by Ruspini et al. [20], illustrated in Figure 2. The force feedback in this algorithm is calculated using Hooke's law:

$$\mathbf{F}_{\mathrm{user}} = -k\mathbf{y}. \tag{9}$$

When rendering force feedback, the force applied by the device to the user is calculated using $k\mathbf{y}$. The user actually slightly penetrates the surface and the distance of this penetration, $\mathbf{y}$, together with a constant $k$ is used to calculate this force. The constant $k$ represents the stiffness of the model and indicates how the surface being touched reacts as a function of $\mathbf{y}$. As a result, $\mathbf{F}_{\mathrm{user}}$ turns out to be as well the force applied by the user to the surface. The duality of $\mathbf{F}_{\mathrm{user}}$ is one of the advantages of haptics and is beneficial to both the system and to the user, increasing the sense of first-person interaction in the 3D environment.

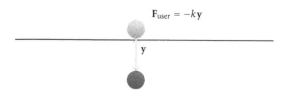

$$\mathbf{F}_{\mathrm{user}} = -k\mathbf{y}$$

FIGURE 2: Conceptual representation of haptic rendering. $k$ determines the stiffness of the surface and $\mathbf{y}$ the penetration distance between the haptic probe (red circle) and its projection on the surface border (green circle).

*4.2. Integration with ACMs.* As described in Section 3.1, the external force used in this work for the ACM derives from the gradient of a distance map $I_D$ that indicates the distance from any point in the original image to the nearest edge. In our haptic framework, $\mathbf{F}_{\mathrm{user}}$ acts as an additional external force to the ACM, creating the new force

$$\mathbf{F}_{\mathrm{hap}} = \mathbf{F}_{\mathrm{ext}} \pm \mathbf{F}_{\mathrm{user}}, \tag{10}$$

which changes (2) to

$$\kappa \mathbf{F}_{\mathrm{int}} + (1-\kappa)\mathbf{F}_{\mathrm{hap}} = \mathbf{0}. \tag{11}$$

Note that $\mathbf{F}_{\mathrm{user}}$ can represent two directions and, depending on its sign, can symbolise to the user either a pushing or pulling gesture.

Making $\mathbf{F}_{\mathrm{user}}$ an additional external force allows the user to interact with the segmentation in real time and provide additional input in order to enhance the segmentation results by correcting the ACM forces in cases in which it was not converging to the correct locations. Nonetheless, one pitfall of this added force is that users might strongly deform the tracheal surface, by either pushing or pulling it in the wrong direction. For instance, once the triangle being touched and its landmarks are identified, adding the force to only those landmarks would punch a hole in the surface and would make it very difficult to influence the ACM more globally. This effect is avoided by smoothly propagating the user force to the neighbour landmarks according to a Gaussian function of the distance from the landmark to the point of contact. Although other smoothing functions could be chosen, for example, a 3rd-order B-Spline, the Gaussian function represented a good compromise between physical correctness and computational cost. In addition, as already explained, the internal forces of the ACM tend to preserve the smoothness and continuity of the surface. As a result, with, for example, $\kappa = 0.8$ in (11), the surface will tend to automatically repair itself following any severe deformation.

In contrast, the weight $\kappa$ can take a lower value while the user is pushing or pulling the surface. With $\kappa = 0.5$, for instance, the user has more control over the deformation, since the internal forces of the ACM will be relaxed. This weight, however, is only applied to those landmarks being directly affected by the user force, which limits the deformations to a restricted area.

Another feature is the possibility to pause the ACM forces such that the user has complete control over the surface. This gives the user extra time to diagnose areas that are not converging to the desired locations. Pausing the ACM means that the forces are only applied to landmarks being pushed or pulled, that is, $\mathbf{F}_{hap_i} = \mathbf{F}_{user_i}$.

We further augmented the typical force equation with an extra transformation which depends on the gradient of the original image and alters the constant $k$ in (9) to

$$k' = k\frac{|\nabla I_D(\mathbf{x}_i)|}{M}, \qquad (12)$$

with $\nabla I_D(\mathbf{x}_i)$ and $M$ is the maximum gradient magnitude in $I_D$ (as defined in (4)).

If the magnitude of the gradient of the image at the point of contact with the surface is high, the surface will seem more stiff to the user. Conversely, if the magnitude is small the surface will seem more flexible. This change in stiffness provides the user with an interesting variation in the force feedback. Remember that the aim of the external force of the ACM is to guide the surface towards high gradients (edges) of the image. At these locations, the user will have more difficulty in pushing or pulling the surface, meaning that the surface may already be near or resting on the correct place. Yet, if the surface is in reality near a wrong edge, the user can still manipulate the segmentation by increasing the force exerted via the haptic device.

Finally, another aspect to be taken into account is the high update rate of 1 kHz necessary for stable realistic haptics [20]. This constraint does not match well with the ACM algorithm being used for segmentation, as one iterative loop of this algorithm is computationally intensive enough to take longer than one millisecond to run. Therefore, it is necessary to decouple the segmentation, graphics rendering, and haptic rendering in separate parts (threads) such that they can all run in parallel (see Figure 3). This guarantees that the user interaction is not hindered. The graphics thread constantly renders on the screen the new shape which is provided by the ACM thread. The ACM thread performs the ACM segmentation and after every iteration it also provides the haptic shape to the haptic thread. This thread on its turn provides the haptic rendering as well as the force from the user to the ACM thread such that it can be used during the segmentation.

At this point, we have covered all aspects involved in the proposed segmentation of tracheal stenosis using haptics. In the next section, the proposed method will be evaluated through a series of experiments.

## 5. Experiments

We carried out a number of experiments to evaluate whether the addition of haptics allows users to influence the ACM segmentation adequately. The idea was to collect the user impression of the system and to quantitatively evaluate the segmentation results. Since we would also like to judge the importance of the addition of force feedback, the experiments were divided into executions having force feedback switched on and off.

*5.1. Data.* We used two CT images in this series of experiments that clearly demonstrate the segmentation challenges

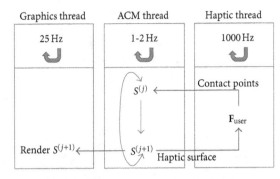

FIGURE 3: Diagram of the separate parts involved in the system. The ACM thread performs the ACM segmentation influenced by the forces provided by the user $\mathbf{F}_{user_i}$. After performing one iteration $j$ of the segmentation, the ACM thread provides the new shape $\mathcal{S}^{j+1}$ to the graphics rendering and haptic rendering threads.

mentioned in Section 1. The first image was a real case of severe stenosis extending along 2/3 of the trachea. The difficulty in this segmentation, when using traditional ACM, is that, due to the severity of the narrowing, the tracheal lumen at the narrowest location of the trachea is barely visible in the CT image of the patient. As a result, the edges of the tracheal wall are not well defined. With region growing, the segmentation is actually nearly split in two (see Figure 4(a)). Our aim here is to give fine control to the user such that he or she can steer the ACM to the correct locations using the defined forces.

In the second image, a phantom of stenosis was created from the CT scan of a healthy patient. In this scan, both the trachea and the oesophagus, located behind the trachea, are visible. They were first segmented with traditional, semi-automated region growing, generating a binary image. This binary image was further processed with a tool to manually create stenosis in an otherwise healthy trachea. In the tool, the user places an erosion mask on the trachea and iteratively erodes the regions below the mask until the stenosis achieves the desired shape (see Figure 4(b)). The difficulty in this case lies in the fact that the oesophagus is very near the trachea. Although the trachea alone could be segmented with, for example, region growing in this case, one could imagine a situation in which the two tubes would appear connected in the image (due to artefacts or anatomical anomalies), making region growing an inadequate choice. The consequence of such configuration to the ACM is that it directly affects its external force, to such an extent that the contour controlled by the traditional ACM cannot be attracted by the edges of the trachea. The idea is that the user steers the ACM into the capture range of the edges of the trachea, from where the ACM can continue, in principle, with no further interaction.

*5.2. Participants.* Four volunteers served as participants in this experiment, all of them had at least some experience with virtual environments. Although none of the participants had experience with medical images, one of them was familiar with segmentation algorithms. We judged that familiarity with virtual environments and haptics was more important

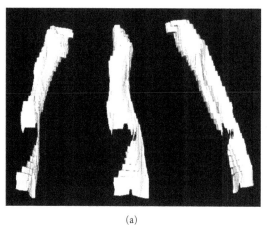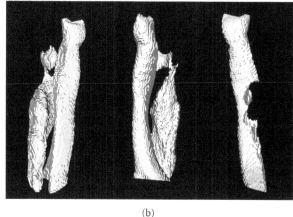

(a)                                                                                        (b)

FIGURE 4: (a) A real, very severe case of stenosis segmented with simple region growing. (b) The trachea and the oesophagus appearing together in the image, after segmentation, followed by the phantom stenosis created on the same trachea.

FIGURE 5: The set-up used to perform ACM segmentation for tracheal stenosis using a Phantom premium 1.5.

than with segmentation because our objective was to collect the impression the participants had about the human-computer interaction offered by the system.

*5.3. Hardware.* For input, two devices were used. As described earlier, we need first and foremost a device to provide force feedback to the users and to allow them to influence the segmentation. A PHANToM premium 1.5 was used for 6 DOF input and 3 DOF force feedback. This device is equipped with a stylus having a single button. The haptic set-up was similar to the one shown in Figure 5.

The second device was used for navigation capabilities and system control. It is required that the shape to be deformed can be viewed and touched from different angles and locations. A space mouse with 6 DOF was thus used for this task. Such devices are typically used by the nondominant hand and are therefore suited to be used in combination with

the PHANToM [21]. Regarding system control, the space mouse's buttons were used to start, pause, restart, finish the segmentation, and to disable or enable the display of visual features.

The computer set-up we used consisted of an Intel Xeon E5520 at 2.27 GHz, with 4 GB RAM and NVIDIA Quaddro FX 4800 graphics card. As display we used a 21-inch-wide screen with a resolution of 1680 by 1050.

*5.4. Software.* The application developed for the segmentations is responsible for establishing the interaction between the user and segmentation task. It displays to the user the ACM algorithm in action and provides to the algorithm the data received from the input devices. The application starts by displaying the shape to be deformed, already placed at the correct start location. Remember from Section 3.2 that the initial ACM shape is an estimation of the healthy trachea of the patient, obtained with the method proposed in [7]. In this way, the focus of the experiment was not on the placement of the initial shape, but only on the segmentation itself. The landmarks of the ACM shape are also visualised in the application, such that the user has a better view on how the deformations are occurring as the segmentation algorithm iterates.

In order to enhance the users' haptic feedback experience, three visual cues were included in the application. The first is to highlight the triangles being touched by the user. In this way, not only do the users perceive touch through the force feedback, but also they can be sure about the point of interaction. The second visual cue is a line emanating from the interaction point indicating the strength of the force exerted onto the shape. This is especially useful during a training phase, when the users can have a clearer idea about the relationship between the force applied through the haptics device and the actual deformation of the ACM shape. Finally, it is important that the user can see if the segmentation is succeeding in delineating the boundary of the trachea in the CT image. The application therefore integrates the visualisation of the 3D shape of the trachea

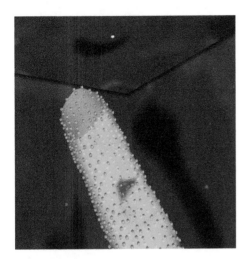

FIGURE 6: Visualisation of the interaction point (red) and its projections (yellow, pink and blue) onto the slices as well as the CT texture data on the slices representing the current interaction point position.

with 2D views of the CT image volume. These views are projections of the axial, sagittal, and coronal planes of the image volume. However, instead of the traditional visualisation of preselected slices of the image, the application projects on three fixed planes the slices corresponding to the closest integers derived from the coordinates of the interaction point (see Figure 6). Such feature provides the user with a clear indication of how the image data looks like at the current position of the haptic device.

*5.5. Procedure.* A repeated measures within-participant design was chosen to evaluate the proposed method. One completion of the segmentation task consisted of starting the ACM algorithm, interacting with the shape as the ACM iterates (possibly pausing the algorithm whenever necessary), and pushing the finish button of the space mouse when satisfied with the current ACM shape. Each participant performed the experiment in one session lasting about 40 minutes. The session was broken up into two force feedback conditions, that is, either force feedback was switched on or off. For each force feedback condition, the user conducted two segmentations on the two data sets earlier discussed, with conditions alternated between participants. Before starting the experiment, each user was introduced to the system using a practice data set. After the experiment, the users were asked to fill in a questionnaire in order to provide us with subjective feedback.

## 6. Results and Discussion

*6.1. Objective Results.* The objective results gathered from the experiments were the time it took to perform the segmentations as well as the quality of the resulting segmentation. Time was measured from the moment the users pushed the start button until the moment they pushed finish button. It is important to mention that the users were allowed to first

TABLE 1: Statistics of segmentation quality.

| | Real data | | | Phantom data | | |
|---|---|---|---|---|---|---|
| | Sensitivity | DSC | Jaccard | Sensitivity | DSC | Jaccard |
| ACM | 0.896 | 0.737 | 0.583 | 0.902 | 0.855 | 0.747 |
| Hap | 0.871 | 0.685 | 0.523 | 0.886 | 0.850 | 0.743 |
| Hap (ff on) | 0.873 | 0.684 | 0.521 | 0.922 | 0.874 | 0.777 |
| Hap (ff off) | 0.870 | 0.687 | 0.525 | 0.849 | 0.826 | 0.709 |

navigate towards the ACM shape and inspect it for a while before starting the segmentation.

*6.1.1. Segmentation Times.* On average, participants took 206 seconds (3 minutes and 26 seconds) to complete one segmentation task. For the condition in which force feedback was present, the users performed the segmentations in 213 seconds and for the other condition participants were slightly faster, with 200 seconds. Although this difference can be considered negligible, a possible explanation for this is the fact that users could exert stronger forces when force feedback was switched off.

*6.1.2. Segmentation Quality.* To compare the quality between the traditional ACM and the version using haptics, we measured the overlap, $O \in [0, 1]$, between the segmentations obtained with the two methods and a reference manual segmentation obtained with semiautomatic region growing. In terms of true and false positives and negatives, the overlap was quantified in 3 different ways:

Sensitivity (true positive rate): $O = \text{TP}/(\text{TP} + \text{FN})$,

Dice similarity [22]: $O = 2\text{TP}/(2\text{TP} + \text{FP} + \text{FN})$,

Jaccard similarity [23]: $O = \text{TP}/(\text{TP} + \text{FP} + \text{FN})$.

Table 1 shows results obtained with the traditional ACM and the version using haptics, the latter further subdivided into force feedback switched on and off, as explained earlier. The results for the version using haptics are an average of the several runs of the application with the four participants of the experiments. In all cases, the traditional ACM performed slightly better, but the difference was in reality rather marginal. What is worth noticing is that, with the phantom stenosis, haptics with forced feedback switched on was noticeably better than its switched-off counterpart. We believe that this can be explained by the fact that the user can really feel the external force exerted by the edges of the oesophagus on the segmentation, therefore being able to counteract it with the aid of the haptics device.

*6.2. Subjective Results.* From the subjective feedback given by the participants, we were able to deduce several opinions which are interesting to take into account when creating segmentation systems like the one presented here.

We asked the participants to grade several statements using a Likert scale with 1 indicating strongly disagree and 5 strongly agree. An overview of the answers given about segmentation can be seen in Figure 7 and with regard to the

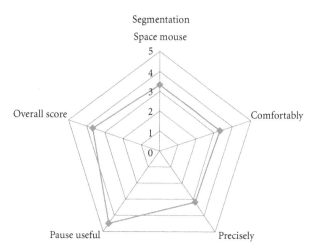

FIGURE 7: Segmentation questionnaire scores from the subjective feedback.

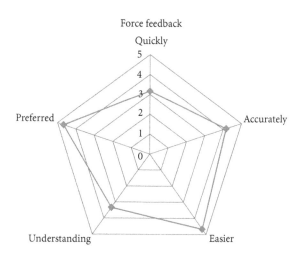

FIGURE 8: Force feedback questionnaire scores from the subjective feedback.

force feedback in Figure 8. The values are the averages of the users' scores.

The scores for the segmentation indicate that the space mouse was perceived as an adequate device to perform navigation and system control with a slightly positive score ($M = 3.33$ SD $= 0.81$). Similarly, the mechanism was found to be comfortable and precise. A very interesting result is that the pause feature is found to be very useful ($M = 4.5$ SD $= 0.55$). Typically, users first let the ACM algorithm run for a while until they could see areas which were not deforming correctly. When those areas were found, they paused the simulation and edited the ACM shape until either satisfied with the end result or until they were reassured that the ACM algorithm could converge to the desired solution on its own. When asked to give the system an overall score, it was perceived as above average ($M = 3.67$ SD $= 0.52$).

The force feedback scores were in general very positive. A slightly worse score can be seen when the participants were asked if force feedback aids in performing the segmentation quickly. They were indeed indecisive about this (SD $= 1.33$ with $M = 3.17$). Some found it to be slower due to the fact that when force feedback was switched off they could push harder than their own comfort would allow when compared to when force feedback was switched on. Other users found force feedback reassuring and that it gave them a perceived increase in speed. Still, force feedback was overall found to be easier, preferred, and more accurate.

In postexperiment discussions, users reported it took some time to get acquainted with the system and the segmentation task. They also reported that without force feedback they felt less in control over the segmentation. One user even reported that it was impossible to carry out the segmentation without force feedback, since it was very hard to indicate if he or she was touching the shape or not. Although they also indicated that without force feedback it was possible to deform the shape more quickly, they preferred the higher sense of control offered when the force feedback was switched on rather than being faster when it was switched off.

Finally, the participants commented that the pause feature of the application's interface indeed gave them a mechanism to further control the segmentation process. It removed the need to compete with the deformations caused by the ACM algorithm, thus enabling easy manipulation of the shape. In the end, they found the system helpful in catching occasional mistakes made by the automatic part of the application.

*6.3. Discussion.* From the experimental results, we can deduce that our system shows potential to be used for segmentation of tracheal stenosis. It took less than 5 minutes to perform a segmentation in which the ACM was executed together with a user interacting with the ACM shape. The addition of force feedback was evaluated as beneficial to the quality of the interaction with the system. Furthermore, the ability to pause the ACM was found to be a very important feature which allows the user to take the time to apply his own changes to the current shape as well as to give full control over the final shape.

One of the observed downsides, however, is that it is very hard for a user to evaluate whether the current shape is good or bad. Sometimes it is very easy to diagnose wrong deformations, but with stenosis unexpected deformations are common. The visualisation used for the slices provides a good overview during interaction with the shape, but in order to diagnose the quality of the current shape the borders would have to be followed closely, which is not easy nor efficient. It is even potentially dangerous as accidental deformations can occur when unintentionally touching the shape borders while tracing them.

## 7. Conclusion

In this paper, we presented a 3D segmentation interface for tracheal stenosis from chest CT scans. We proposed a semiautomatic method that overcomes typical segmentation difficulties such as noise and the presence of neighbour organs in the image. Our method is based on Active Contour

Models augmented with 3D input from a haptic device. An evaluation was performed using two CT data sets and four users. The results indicated that the addition of haptics provided the users with valuable force feedback about the 3D surface and its deformation. Furthermore, the addition of a pause function during the interaction with the ACM proved to be an important part of the proposed method.

In future work, we would like to evaluate our system with more data sets and with users which are familiar with diagnosing tracheal stenosis, such that we could verify that our method is able to improve the diagnosing tasks.

# References

[1] G. Qiu and P. C. Yuen, "Interactive imaging and vision—ideas, algorithms and applications," *Pattern Recognition*, vol. 43, no. 2, pp. 431–433, 2010.

[2] S. D. Olabarriaga and A. W. M. Smeulders, "Interaction in the segmentation of medical images: a survey," *Medical Image Analysis*, vol. 5, no. 2, pp. 127–142, 2001.

[3] M. Kass, A. Witkin, and D. Terzopoulos, "Snakes: active contour models," *International Journal of Computer Vision*, vol. 1, no. 4, pp. 321–331, 1988.

[4] T. McInerney and D. Terzopoulos, "Deformable models in medical image analysis: a survey," *Medical Image Analysis*, vol. 1, no. 2, pp. 91–108, 1996.

[5] N. Spittle and A. McCluskey, "Lesson of the week: tracheal stenosis after intubation," *British Medical Journal*, vol. 321, no. 7267, pp. 1000–1002, 2000.

[6] P. M. Boiselle, J. Catena, A. Ernst, and D. A. Lynch, "Tracheobronchial stenoses," in *CT of the Airways*, pp. 121–149, Humana Press-Springer, 2008.

[7] R. Pinho, K. G. Tournoy, and J. Sijbers, "Assessment and stenting of tracheal stenosis using deformable shape models," *Medical Image Analysis*, vol. 15, no. 2, pp. 250–266, 2011.

[8] J. M. Triglia, B. Nazarian, I. Sudre-Levillain, S. Marciano, G. Moulin, and A. Giovanni, "Virtual laryngotracheal endoscopy based on geometric surface modeling using spiral computed tomography data," *Annals of Otology, Rhinology and Laryngology*, vol. 111, no. 1, pp. 36–43, 2002.

[9] Y. Kang, K. Engelke, and W. A. Kalender, "Interactive 3D editing tools for image segmentation," *Medical Image Analysis*, vol. 8, no. 1, pp. 35–46, 2004.

[10] K. McGuinness and N. E. O'Connor, "A comparative evaluation of interactive segmentation algorithms," *Pattern Recognition*, vol. 43, no. 2, pp. 434–444, 2010.

[11] F. Heckel, O. Konrad, H. Karl Hahn, and H.-O. Peitgen, "Interactive 3D medical image segmentation with energy-minimizing implicit functions," *Computers and Graphics*, vol. 35, no. 2, pp. 275–287, 2011.

[12] A. Bornik, R. Beichel, and D. Schmalstieg, "Interactive editing of segmented volumetric datasets in a hybrid 2D/3D virtual environment," in *Proceedings of the 13th ACM Symposium Virtual Reality Software and Technology (VRST '06)*, pp. 197–206, November 2006.

[13] E. V. Zudilova-Seinstra, P. J. H. de Koning, A. Suinesiaputra et al., "Evaluation of 2D and 3D glove input applied to medical image analysis," *International Journal of Human Computer Studies*, vol. 68, no. 6, pp. 355–369, 2010.

[14] E. Vidholm, X. Tizon, I. Nyström, and E. Bengtsson, "Haptic guided seeding of mra images for semi-automatic segmentation," in *Proceedings of the 2nd IEEE International Symposium on Biomedical Imaging*, pp. 288–291, April 2004.

[15] E. Vidholm, S. Nilsson, and I. Nyström, "Fast and robust semi-automatic liver segmentation with haptic interaction," in *Proceedings of the MICCAI*, vol. 2, pp. 774–781, 2006.

[16] F. Malmberg, E. Vidholm, and I. Nyström, "A 3D live-wire segmentation method for volume images using haptic interaction," in *Discrete Geometry for Computer Imagery*, vol. 4245 of *Lecture Notes in Computer Science*, pp. 663–673, 2006.

[17] E. Vidholm, M. Golubovic, S. Nilsson, and I. Nyström, "Accurate and reproducible semi-automatic liver segmentation using haptic interaction," in *Medical Imaging: Visualization, Image-Guided Procedures, and Modeling*, vol. 6918 of *Proceedings of SPIE*, p. 69182Q, 2008.

[18] M. Harders and G. Székely, "Improving medical segmentation with haptic interaction," in *Proceedings of the Virtual Reality*, pp. 243–250, March 2002.

[19] G. C. Burdea, *Force and Touch Feedback for Virtual Reality*, Wiley Interscience, 1996.

[20] D. C. Ruspini, K. Kolarov, and O. Khatib, "The haptic display of complex graphical environments," in *Proceedings of the 24th Annual Conference on Computer Graphics and Interactive Techniques*, pp. 345–352, 1997.

[21] A. Kulik, J. Hochstrate, A. Kunert, and B Froehlich., "The influence of input device characteristics on spatial perception in desktop-based 3D applications," in *Proceedings of the Symposium on 3D User Interfaces*, pp. 59–66, 2009.

[22] L. R. Dice, "Measures of the amount of ecologic association between species," *Ecology*, vol. 26, no. 3, pp. 297–302, 1945.

[23] P. N. Tan, M. Steinbach, and V. Kumar, *Introduction to Data Mining*, Addison-Wesley, 2006.

# 17

# Evaluating User Response to In-Car Haptic Feedback Touchscreens Using the Lane Change Test

**Matthew J. Pitts,[1] Lee Skrypchuk,[2] Tom Wellings,[1] Alex Attridge,[1] and Mark A. Williams[1]**

[1] *WMG, University of Warwick, Coventry CV4 7AL, UK*
[2] *Jaguar & Land Rover Research, Jaguar Land Rover, Coventry CV3 4LF, UK*

Correspondence should be addressed to Matthew J. Pitts, m.pitts@warwick.ac.uk

Academic Editor: Mark Dunlop

Touchscreen interfaces are widely used in modern technology, from mobile devices to in-car infotainment systems. However, touchscreens impose significant visual workload demands on the user which have safety implications for use in cars. Previous studies indicate that the application of haptic feedback can improve both performance of and affective response to user interfaces. This paper reports on and extends the findings of a 2009 study conducted to evaluate the effects of different combinations of touchscreen visual, audible, and haptic feedback on driving and task performance, affective response, and subjective workload; the initial findings of which were originally published in (M. J. Pitts et al., 2009). A total of 48 non-expert users completed the study. A dual-task approach was applied, using the Lane Change Test as the driving task and realistic automotive use case touchscreen tasks. Results indicated that, while feedback type had no effect on driving or task performance, preference was expressed for multimodal feedback over visual alone. Issues relating to workload and cross-modal interaction were also identified.

## 1. Introduction

The touchscreen interface is synonymous with ubiquitous computing, being found in an ever-widening array of devices. This is due in part to the ease-of-use of the interface, with co-location of the input and display; and an interaction mode familiar to even novice users [1]. Having become established as the de facto standard interface for today's multi-function smartphones [2], the emergence of the tablet computer has led to further entrenchment of the technology in the consumer market [3]. Touchscreens are also widely used in cars, where the flexibility of the interface also allows designers to create cleaner cockpit layouts free from the clutter of multiple pushbutton controls.

It is the direct nature of touchscreen interaction however that poses the largest challenge to automotive Human Machine Interface (HMI) designers. As visual attention must be directed to the touchscreen during use, the interface imposes significant levels of visual workload upon the user; over 70% of the time taken to complete an in-vehicle touchscreen task can be spent looking away from the road [4]. This has implications for safety: accident risk is correlated to both the duration and frequency of glances away from the forward roadway [5], and large-scale studies have found that up to 60% of crashes, near-crashes, and incidents can be attributed to visual distraction from the primary driving task [6]. This problem is exacerbated the lack of tactile and kinaesthetic feedback [7] that would normally be provided by a traditional mechanical control such as a pushbutton or dial.

This paper reports on the findings of a study into the effects of multimodal touchscreen feedback in an automotive context, conducted in 2009 and originally reported in [8]. The initial findings from the earlier publication are extended with a revised analysis of the subjective data and the addition of objective measures of task performance and driving behaviour, along with discussion of contemporary studies.

## 2. Touchscreens and Multimodal Interaction

The multiple resource theory model of workload [9] states that each sensory channel has a discrete and finite level of processing capacity, beyond which performance is degraded. By diverting some of the workload demands of HMI interaction from the visual to other senses, the overall level of distraction may be reduced. Given that touchscreen interaction employs vision and touch, the opportunity exists to improve performance through exploitation of the haptic channel.

Multimodal feedback has been the subject of numerous research studies. A review of 43 such studies [10] indicated that combining visual feedback with auditory or tactile feedback led to reduced reaction times and improved performance measures, although error rates were not improved. Studies on the effects of haptic feedback in handheld touchscreen devices indicated improvements in subjective workload [11] and reduced task completion times [12]; in both of these cases, improvements were also observed in error rates.

There have also been a number of relevant studies relating to automotive touchscreen use. Lee and Spence [13] used an automotive-themed attention task to assess dual-task performance using a touchscreen telephone secondary task. Their findings indicated that reaction times and task completion times were both improved when combined visual, audible, and haptic feedback was applied; this was complemented by a reduction in reported subjective workload. Serafin et al. [14] conducted on-bench and static vehicle evaluations of an automotive user interface on a touchscreen equipped with haptic feedback. Results showed that users showed strong preferences for trimodal feedback over visual alone; however, no evaluations were conducted under dynamic driving conditions.

Richter et al. [15] discussed the evaluation of a haptic touchscreen interface in an automotive scenario, using the Lane Change Test to create the driving environment. Their findings indicate improved error rates and task completion times with haptic feedback enabled. The authors' own follow-up study [4] evaluated the effects of haptic feedback on the performance of an abstracted touchscreen task in an immersive simulated driving environment. Results showed reduced task completion time along with subjective preference for combined visual and haptic feedback.

In general, the studies described above provide evidence of the potential benefits, both objective and subjective, of haptic feedback to improve interaction with in-vehicle technology.

## 3. The Lane Change Test

The context in which a product is evaluated can have a significant influence on the user's perception of usability [16]. It is therefore important to replicate the context of use when collecting user-derived data [17]. When evaluating automotive HMI technologies, this requires the use of an environment which represents the cognitive, visual, and physical workloads of the primary driving task. The use of driving simulators has become more popular in recent years as the cost of hardware has been reduced and capability increased [18], offering advantages over instrumented vehicle studies in terms of safety, cost, repeatability, and ease

of data collection [19–21]. The term "driving simulator" however covers a wide range of systems with varying technical complexity. Hardware configurations can range from desktop-PC-based solutions with a single screen and a gaming controller through to fully immersive solutions utilising panoramic projections, real vehicle cabins, and full motion platforms. Clearly, the implications of cost and complexity vary accordingly, with an outlay of a few thousand pounds in the former case and several million in the latter.

The Lane Change Test (LCT) is a software-based approach to providing a standardised, low-cost method for the evaluation of in-vehicle technology. LCT was originally developed as part of the Advanced Driver Attention Metrics (ADAM) project investigating next-generation in-car user interfaces [22]. LCT provides a simple simulated driving task which represents the manual, visual, and cognitive demands of real-world driving. The driving task is performed in parallel with secondary user interface tasks, and variations in driver response are recorded and used to calculate quantitative measures of performance.

LCT is designed to facilitate the evaluation of any type of in-vehicle technology, both OEM and aftermarket, and to allow for all types of sensory interaction. It is, however, limited to domestic vehicle applications due to the vehicle dynamics model and assumptions of driver position. Driving inputs are made through a standard PC gaming wheel and pedals; while the LCT method can be used using a simple bench-top setup or in driving simulators with varying degrees of fidelity, lane change trajectories are improved with a driving simulator setup compared to a desktop computer [23]. LCT is the subject of ISO standard 26022 : 2010 [24], which outlines the experimental conditions and methodology required to conduct an LCT-based evaluation study, thus removing much of the variability often apparent in approaches to driving simulator studies [18].

Validation studies of LCT have indicated strong correlations in the measured effects of secondary task performance to both high-fidelity driving simulators [25] and real-world driving scenarios [22]. Recent research has concentrated on the development and validation of new metrics for use with LCT, adding extra measures of the effect of secondary tasks on aspects of driver performance [26].

LCT has been shown to be effective in identifying degradation in driving performance in the presence of secondary tasks [27, 28]. However, earlier studies using LCT highlighted differences in results, possibly attributable to variations in the application of the method between studies [28]. It is worthy of note that these earlier studies were conducted prior to the official publication of ISO 26022 : 2010 which specifies the experimental approach to the use of LCT.

## 4. Study Outline

It is clear that the potential exists for the performance of automotive touchscreen interfaces to be improved through the addition of haptic feedback. A study was therefore designed to investigate the effects of visual, audible, and haptic feedback on objective task performance and user response to touchscreen interaction in an automotive use scenario. The aim of the study was to evaluate the objective and subjective benefits of haptic feedback relative to the visual and auditory modalities commonly employed on touchscreen interfaces, when delivered in different combinations of feedback stimuli. The study sought to obtain data relevant to the real-world benefits of multimodal feedback through the use of participants who are all vehicle owners and have experience of touchscreen technology, along with realistic automotive touchscreen use cases.

*4.1. Research Questions and Hypotheses.* The research questions for the study were as follows.

(i) Does the addition of haptic feedback affect driving performance when operating in-car HMI?

(ii) Does the addition of haptic feedback affect task performance when operating in-car HMI?

(iii) Does the addition of haptic feedback improve the user experience?

(iv) Does the addition of haptic feedback make in-car technology easier to use?

Based on the benefits of haptic feedback described in Section 2, hypotheses were formed that (a) the addition of haptic feedback would improve driving and task performance, (b) the addition of haptic feedback would improve users' affective response to the touchscreen interface, and (c) the addition of haptic feedback would reduce subjective workload.

## 5. Methodology

The following chapter describes the methodology used to test the hypotheses described above, outlining the experimental approach and evaluation setup.

*5.1. Experiment Design.* The study used a dual-task approach with users completing realistic automotive use case tasks (described in Section 5.5) while engaged in a driving task based on LCT. A $1 \times 4$ within-subjects experiment design was employed, with feedback type as the independent variable. Four levels of feedback were employed: visual only (V), audible + visual (AV), haptic + visual (HV), and audible + haptic + visual (AHV). All participants experienced all four levels of feedback, and the study was counterbalanced for feedback presentation order, with the design perfectly balanced for multiples of 24 participants.

*5.2. Participants.* A total of 54 people were recruited with 48 completing the evaluation; three respondents were withdrawn from the study after exhibiting an adverse reaction to the simulated driving environment, two exhibiting poor driving performance, and a further one experiencing issues with the touchscreen tasks. All participants had at least one year experience of driving in the UK and also had experience of in-car touchscreen use. The demographic breakdown is given in Table 1.

TABLE 1: Participant demographic breakdown.

| Age range | 18–25 | 26–35 | 36–45 | 46–55 | 56+ | Total |
|---|---|---|---|---|---|---|
| Female | 2 | 4 | 12 | 2 | 1 | 21 |
| Male | 3 | 4 | 5 | 6 | 9 | 27 |
| Total | 5 | 8 | 17 | 8 | 10 | 48 |

FIGURE 1: Experiment setup.

*5.3. Experiment Setup.* The evaluation utilised the Lane Change Test software to create a simulated driving environment, as described above. To enhance the physical validity (fidelity) of the evaluation environment, a simple dash buck was employed, consisting of an aluminium frame supporting a vehicle instrument panel and centre console supplied by Jaguar Land Rover. A Logitech G25 gaming wheel was attached to the frame in the correct position, with the touchscreen mounted in the centre console in an approximation of its in-vehicle position. The participant was seated in front of the buck in a vehicle seat, thus replicating the ergonomic conditions of a real vehicle. The buck was situated in front of a rear-projected screen which displayed the driving simulation, as shown in Figure 1.

*5.4. Evaluation Interface.* The touchscreen hardware used for the study was an 8.4" TouchSense haptic touchscreen demonstrator unit from Immersion Corporation (Immersion Corporation: http://www.immersion.com/), which served as both the input surface and visual and haptic display. This consists of a resistive touchscreen fitted with Immersion's proprietary electromechanical haptic feedback actuators and controller. The unit imparts haptic sensations to the user's finger through a lateral displacement of the screen surface and is capable of reproducing a range of haptic effects; to maintain consistency a single effect was used throughout the study, selected on the basis of a preliminary study described in Section 5.6.

Given that context has a significant effect on the perception of usability of technology [16], the touchscreen task was also designed to provide an authentic user experience. This was achieved by using a direct replication of the graphical user interface from the Jaguar XF premium saloon car, as shown in Figure 2. The interface was programmed to perform logging of the task completion data, recording the start and end times of each touchscreen task. These

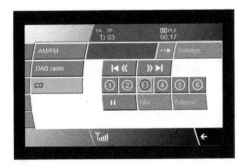

FIGURE 2: Touchscreen evaluation interface screenshot.

values were then used to compute the task completion times reported in Section 6.2.

Graphics were supplied by Jaguar Land Rover in Adobe Flash format; the interface logic was then recoded in Actionscript 3.0 to incorporate the experimental controls and enable capture of task completion data. Visual feedback was provided by a change in colour of the button when pressed. Haptic feedback was produced on press and release of the button. The audible stimulus was the acknowledgement tone used on the Jaguar XF touchscreen interface, with a fundamental frequency of approximately 1 kHz and a duration of around 70 ms. This was delivered over headphones, providing a degree of acoustic isolation from the sound of the haptic touchscreen actuators.

*5.5. Touchscreen Tasks.* Touchscreen tasks were based on real life use case scenarios experienced in production vehicles and implemented on the interface described above. The selected use cases represented a range of functionality across the system, requiring different amounts of menu level navigation and button presses to complete the task. These are summarised in Table 2.

A mixed-task approach was adopted whereby participants completed all eight tasks during each drive, thus proving an aggregate measure of driving performance for each feedback condition. This approach overcomes difficulties of determining relative task workload for tasks of mixed duration [27], as used here. Tasks were modified between trials where possible to avoid repetition; for example, by requesting a different radio frequency or climate setting, without altering the required number of button presses. The order of presentation of use cases was varied for each feedback state, again to reduce potential learning effects.

*5.6. Preliminary Study.* It was important to ensure that the haptic effect used for the evaluation did not provoke a negative reaction from the participants, as this may bias opinions of the haptic touchscreen technology. A simple preliminary study was therefore conducted in order to ascertain which of the available preprogrammed haptic effects was most preferred by users. 34 participants were recruited, all within the automotive industry, with 50% experts in the design of touchscreen interfaces.

The study used a custom interface programmed in Adobe Flash to test preference for haptic feedback effects.

TABLE 2: Touchscreen use cases.

| Task | Button presses required | Menu navigation levels |
|---|---|---|
| Dial UK phone number and initiate call | 13 | 1 |
| Play track number 4 from specified CD | 7 | 2 |
| Select specified contact from phone book | 4 | 3 |
| Adjust HVAC fan speed | 4 | 1 |
| Select specified DAB preset | 3 | 2 |
| Tune FM radio to specified frequency | 3 | 1 |
| Set seat heating/cooling to specified level | 3 | 0 |
| Set climate control to auto/off | 2 | 1 |

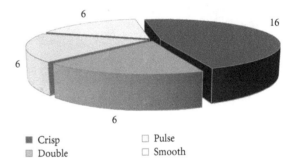

■ Crisp     □ Pulse
▨ Double   □ Smooth

FIGURE 3: Most preferred haptic feedback effect type.

Participants were presented with 20 different haptic effects in sets of 5, where each set was from one of the preprogrammed "click" effect groups: all of these stimuli were impulsive and designed to provide a haptic sensation reminiscent of a mechanical push switch but are differentiated by their duration and frequency characteristics.

Stimulus presentation order was randomised to avoid bias. Participants selected their most preferred effect from each group and were then asked to select an overall preference from the four preferred effects previously selected. Participants were asked to operate the touchscreen with their left hand as would be the case in a right-hand-drive car and wore ear defenders to avoid cross-modal interaction from the sound produced by the haptic touchscreen actuators.

While no overall preference for a specific haptic effect was found, one group of effects, "Crisp Click", was more strongly preferred, with 16 of 34 users selecting effects from this group (Figure 3). A binomial test of this result showed statistical significance ($P < 0.05$, one-tailed). The effect used in the main study was therefore chosen from this group and consisted of an impulsive stimulus with overall duration of approximately 80 ms and fundamental frequency of 130 Hz, illustrated in Figure 4.

*5.7. Driving Task.* The LCT driving scenario involves driving down a straight, three-lane roadway at a limited constant

FIGURE 4: Selected haptic feedback effect waveform.

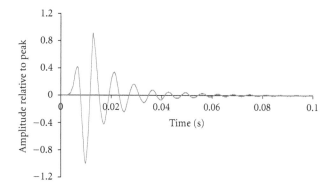

FIGURE 5: Lane Change Test screenshot [29].

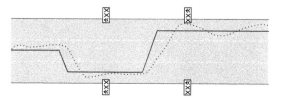

FIGURE 6: Lane Change Test deviation analysis [24].

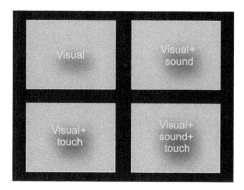

FIGURE 7: Touchscreen feedback introduction screen.

speed of 60 km/h. Signs are positioned at regular intervals along the roadway which indicate the correct lane that the driver should occupy. At the appearance of each set of signs the driver is required to make a lane change manoeuvre such as to occupy the indicated lane. A screenshot of the LCT scenario is shown in Figure 5 [29].

The simulated track length is 3000 m, corresponding to 3 minutes of driving at a constant 60 km/h. Within this duration, 18 pairs of signs are displayed, corresponding to a lane change manoeuvre every 9 seconds.

The driver's trajectory through the lane changes is compared to a normative model, the idealised path though along the track, which is identical for each participant. Deviations from the normative path are calculated using the LCT analysis tool software to provide a measure of mean deviation (MDev) for each drive. MDev values for the dual-task conditions are compared to those from a baseline measure, where the participant is engaged in the primary driving task only. Figure 6 shows an example of deviation from the normative path, an output from the LCT analysis tool [24].

### 5.8. Training Procedure.

A five-stage training procedure was employed. Firstly, participants completed a demographic questionnaire about their experience of driving and touchscreen device use, along with a consent form. Participants were informed of the details of the study and also made aware of the potential symptoms of simulator sickness. It was made clear to participants that they were free to withdraw at any time and should stop immediately if they began to feel unwell.

The second phase of the training involved introducing the participants to the touchscreen and the different types of feedback that they would be experiencing. This was achieved using the simple interface shown in Figure 7, which consisted of four buttons, each of which produced one of the four combinations of feedback defined in Section 5.1. Audible feedback was delivered over headphones in order to provide acoustic isolation from the sound of the touchscreen's haptic feedback actuators. As participants were non-expert users, the term "touch feedback" was used to refer to haptic feedback throughout the study.

The third element of the training involved familiarisation with the touchscreen evaluation interface. Each of the tasks involved in the study was demonstrated by the experimenter and repeated by the user until they were confident in using the interface. Once this stage had been reached participants were introduced to the driving task. Practice drives without secondary tasks were conducted until the participant was confident in performing the driving task; due to its simple nature, this stage was generally reached within a short period of time. This phase also served to provide baseline driving data for the single task condition, which was recorded once the participant was comfortable with the driving task. The final stage of the training was to include the secondary task in the practice drive; this was conducted using visual feedback only, with tasks selected at random by the experimenter.

### 5.9. Data Sources.

Variation in driving performance was monitored using the mean deviation (MDev) parameter from LCT, as described in Section 5.7. This is calculated as an overall value for each drive (hence each feedback condition). Touchscreen task performance was measured by task completion time, from initiation of the task to its successful completion.

Subjective measures of users' experience of the touchscreen interface were collected via questionnaire after each drive. A range of parameters were measured, including hedonic rating, confidence in button press, difficulty of the touchscreen task, interference with the driving task, and, when haptic feedback was enabled, the strength and realism of the haptic stimulus. Most measures employed a 9-point rating scale with semantic anchors at the end- and mid-points; hedonic rating was measured using the 9-point hedonic rating scale which features semantic anchors at every point [30].

An additional follow-up questionnaire was administered at the end of the study, which featured a most/least preferred feedback condition choice and two further questions to determine opinions on the effects of haptic feedback on pleasure and ease of use, using 5-point Likert scales.

*5.10. Analysis.* Driving and touchscreen task performance data was analysed using within-subjects ANOVA, with post hoc pairwise comparisons made using Tukey's HSD test. Subjective data was analysed using the nonparametric Friedman's test and post hoc paired Wilcoxon signed rank tests using the normal approximation. Statistical significance is determined at $\alpha = 0.05$ (two-tailed) in all cases.

# 6. Results

Results from the objective and subjective measures employed are detailed below. For all figures error bars indicate the 95% confidence interval.

*6.1. Driving Performance.* Driving performance was measured by the mean deviation from the normative path: the average amount that the driver moved from the modelled path through the LCT scenario. One participant displayed difficulties with the driving task, resulting in consistently high mean and standard deviation values for lateral deviation which were well outside the expected range; data from this participant was therefore rejected. Mean values for each feedback state were then filtered for outliers then subjected to a one-way, within-subjects ANOVA, the output of which is shown in Figure 8. Outliers were identified based on the interquartile range method described by Tukey [29] and defined as occurring outside the range

$$Q_2 \pm 1.5(Q_3 - Q_1), \qquad (1)$$

where $Q_2$ is the median of the data set and $Q_1$ and $Q_3$ the 25th and 75th percentiles. 3 data points were removed, corresponding to 1.3% of the remaining data. Baseline driving performance was included in the analysis as a fifth level of the independent variable.

The difference due to the independent variable was shown to be statistically significant ($F(4, 184) = 12.492, P < 0.001$). A Post hoc Tukey HSD test, corrected for familywise type I error as per Cicchetti [31] indicates that differences exist only between the baseline condition and other means ($q(5, 184) = 3.90, W = 0.16$). This indicates that, while there was no significant difference in driving performance due

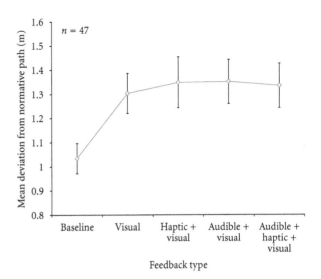

FIGURE 8: Effect of feedback type on mean Deviation (MDev).

to feedback state, mean deviation increased from 1.03 m to 1.33 m when touchscreen tasks were introduced, an increase of 29%.

*6.2. Task Performance.* Mean task completion time (TCT) for each task under each experimental condition was calculated and data filtered for outliers as described above. A two-way, within-subjects ANOVA analysis was then performed, with feedback type and task as factors. The results are shown in Figure 9, with tasks ranked by task completion time and plotted against the required button presses for each task.

Mean TCT ranged from 5.00 seconds (climate control, AHV) to 21.64 seconds (CD task, HV). Task time roughly follows the number of button presses required to complete the task. No significant differences were observed between the feedback states ($F(3, 138) = 1.039$, NS); however differences due to task were significant ($F(7, 322) = 59.56, P < 0.001$). A Post hoc Tukey HSD test applied to mean TCT for each task across all feedback states indicates that the phone dialling and CD tasks were significantly different to all other tasks at the $\alpha = 0.05$ level, with overall mean TCT of 19.35 and 19.62 seconds, respectively ($q(8, 322) = 4.35, W = 4.48$). The climate control task required the lowest task completion time of 7.27 seconds; this was significantly different to the phone, CD, FM, and fan speed tasks.

*6.3. Subjective Data.* The subjective response scores from the questionnaires were collated, filtered for outliers, and subjected to statistical analysis using the nonparametric Friedman's test at the $\alpha = 0.05$ level. Post hoc tests of pairwise significance were conducted using the paired Wilcoxon signed rank test with a Šidák correction [32] maintaining familywise significance at $\alpha = 0.05$. The outcomes from the analyses are detailed below.

*6.3.1. Hedonic Rating.* Figure 10 shows the mean hedonic rating for each feedback state. While there is a statistically

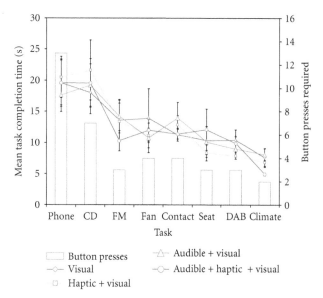

FIGURE 9: Touchscreen task completion time.

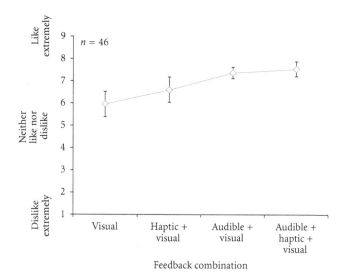

FIGURE 10: Hedonic rating.

significant increase in rating score with multimodal feedback ($\chi^2(3)$ = 44.82, $P$ < 0.001), post hoc tests indicate that introducing haptic feedback alone does not improve performance over visual feedback. However, audible + visual ($z$ = 4.47, $P$ < 0.001) and audible + haptic + visual ($z$ = 4.29, $P$ < 0.001) do offer a significant improvement over visual alone. Combined audible, haptic, and visual feedback also attracted a significantly higher rating than haptic + visual feedback ($z$ = 3.71, $P$ < 0.001).

*6.3.2. Confidence Rating.* A similar pattern is observed for confidence rating, as shown in Figure 11. Differences across feedback states were again shown to be significant ($\chi^2(3)$ = 32.97, $P$ < 0.001), with post hoc tests indicating significant improvements from visual feedback alone with the addition of audible ($z$ = 4.32, $P$ < 0.001) and combined audible and haptic feedback ($z$ = 4.55, $P$ < 0.005).

*6.3.3. Touchscreen Task Difficulty.* Figure 12 shows the rating scores for touchscreen task difficulty. The difference in rating score across feedback types is significant ($\chi^2(3)$ = 11.46, $P$ < 0.01), albeit smaller in magnitude than observed previously, with an increase of less than one scale point. Post hoc tests indicate significant differences between the "visual" and "audible + visual" conditions ($z$ = 3.10, $P$ < 0.001) and between the "visual" and "audible + haptic + visual" conditions ($z$ = 2.76, $P$ < 0.001). Note that the touchscreen task was rated as "more than moderately difficult" for all feedback conditions.

*6.3.4. Driving Interference.* The scores for driving task interference again follow a similar pattern (Figure 13). Difference across feedback conditions was found to be significant ($\chi^2(3)$ = 13.80, $P$ < 0.01), with improvements seen over visual feedback with the addition of auditory ($z$ = 3.19, $P$ < 0.001) and auditory + haptic feedback ($z$ = 3.54, $P$ < 0.001).

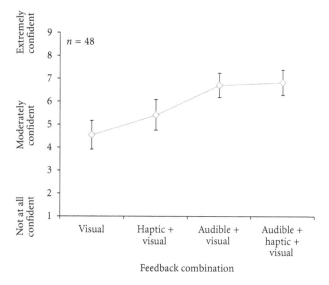

FIGURE 11: Confidence rating.

Again, mean ratings for all conditions indicate a "more than moderate" level of interference with the driving task.

*6.3.5. Haptic Feedback Perception.* The subsequent two questions deal with user perception of the haptic effect itself. A Wilcoxon signed-rank test performed on mean ratings of the perceived strength of the haptic feedback stimulus showed significant differences with and without audible feedback ($z$ = 3.64, $P$ < 0.001), indicating that the magnitude of the haptic effect was perceived to be higher in the presence of audible feedback (see Figure 14(a)), thus suggesting a multimodal interaction between the two stimuli. Without audible feedback, the mean haptic feedback strength rating of 3.51 indicates that participants perceived the effect to be weaker than optimal.

Users were also asked to rate the similarity of the feel of the touchscreen haptic feedback to that of a real switch.

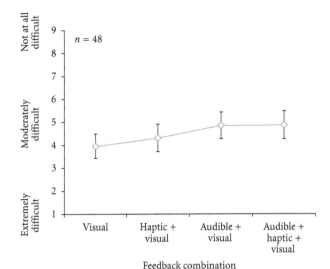

FIGURE 12: Touchscreen task difficulty rating.

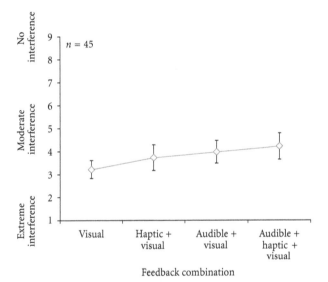

FIGURE 13: Interference with the driving task.

Again, a significantly higher rating was achieved when both audible and haptic feedback were present ($z = 4.32$, $P < 0.001$; Figure 14(b)).

*6.3.6. User Experience.* Participants were asked if each of the feedback types presented enhanced the user experience. As with previous measures, a trend was seen indicating preference for enhanced feedback, with combined audible, haptic, and visual feedback attracted the highest rating, a mean of 4.04 corresponding to "agree" on the Likert scale. Differences across feedback types were significant ($\chi^2(3) = 38.13$, $P < 0.001$), with significant pairwise differences seen between the visual/audible + visual ($z = 4.19$, $P < 0.001$), visual/audible + haptic + visual ($z = 4.58$, $P < 0.001$), and haptic + visual/audible + haptic + visual ($z = 3.52$, $P < 0.001$) pairs. These results are shown in Figure 15.

Additional questions included in the follow-up questionnaire aimed to understand preference for feedback combination and the effect of haptic feedback specifically on the user experience. Figure 16 shows the most/least preferred choices for each feedback type, with "most preferred" choices shown as positive and "least preferred" as negative. Clearly, visual only feedback was strongly least favoured, with combined audible, haptic, and visual feedback most preferred, with 27 out of 48 choices. Participants were also asked to rate their agreement with the statements "Touch feedback makes the touchscreen easier to use" and "Touch feedback makes the touchscreen more pleasurable to use," using 5-point Likert scales. The mean scores of 4.27 and 4.07 ($SD = 0.65$ and 0.74, resp.) indicate that, on average, participants agreed with these statements.

*6.3.7. Order Effects.* Subjective rating data from the hedonic, confidence, and interference ratings were reanalysed to examine potential effects of presentation order. Results indicate that, while presentation order had no significant effect on hedonic rating ($\chi^2(3) = 6.17$, $P = 0.10$) or touchscreen task difficulty ($\chi^2(3) = 2.07$, $P = 0.56$), there was a significant effect on interference with the driving task over the duration of the study ($\chi^2(3) = 22.46$, $P < 0.001$), with the level of interference becoming lower as the study progressed.

## 7. Discussion

Results clearly show that lateral control performance is not significantly affected by the type of feedback presented. However, mean deviation increased significantly relative to a baseline when touchscreen tasks were introduced, highlighting the increase in workload experienced due to the inclusion of the secondary task. The application of multimodal feedback was not able to mitigate this increase. This concurs with the findings of Rydström et al. [33], who measured lateral deviation while engaged in haptic and visual secondary tasks, again using the LCT method.

Task performance also showed no significant differences due to feedback type, but there were large differences in task completion time across the different tasks. This is to be expected given the varying levels of task complexity; indeed, the pattern of task completion time roughly followed the minimum number of button presses required to complete the task. The debate into what tasks should be allowed while a vehicle is in motion is beyond the scope of this paper; however, the duration of most intensive task used, telephone dialling, sits approximately on the limit of the "15-Second Rule" for acceptable static task completion times defined under SAE J2364 [34].

The apparent lack of objective effect of multimodal feedback is contrary to findings in the literature which indicate that the addition of haptic stimuli to existing feedback sources will have benefits in terms of task performance and error rates. Given the specific nature of the sensory and workload demands imposed by the driving task, it is logical to consider these results in reference to studies that feature

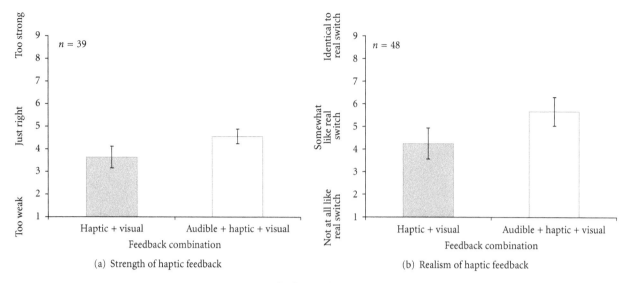

(a) Strength of haptic feedback

(b) Realism of haptic feedback

FIGURE 14: Haptic feedback effect strength and realism.

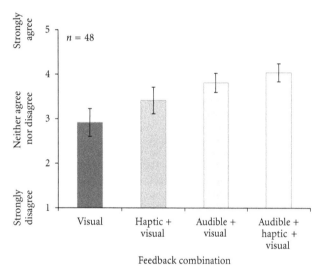

FIGURE 15: Does the feedback enhance the user experience?.

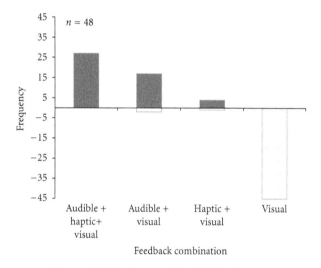

FIGURE 16: Most/Least preferred feedback type.

similar experimental conditions, that is, the evaluation of multisensory feedback using a touchscreen-based secondary task in a simulated automotive driving scenario.

In one such study, Lee and Spence [13] evaluated reaction time to driving and touchscreen tasks with the same combinations of feedback used in this study. Results indicated that a significant difference in reaction time existed between the visual only and trimodal (audible, tactile, and visual) combinations; as with this study, there was no significant difference between the visual only and bimodal visual + tactile condition. The touchscreen task required interaction with a telephone keypad, as opposed to the menu-based tasks employed in this study. A significant effect of bimodal (audible + tactile) feedback intensity on reaction times was also noted, indicating a workload-related perceptual threshold effect.

Richter et al. [15] conducted a study to evaluate a haptic touchscreen implementation, using the LCT to provide the driving context. Their secondary touchscreen task was also based on a telephone keypad. Improvements were shown in number entry error rates for small (but not large) buttons with the addition of haptic feedback, while the effect on task completion time was inconclusive. It should be noted that this study featured a small sample size (5 respondents) and no measures of significance were reported.

While not in total agreement, the differences to the findings of the above are not sufficient to invalidate this study. The influence of task complexity and perceived feedback magnitude on users' subjective responses is discussed below.

*7.1. Effects of Workload and Cross-Modal Interaction on Perception of Haptic Feedback Magnitude.* The results from the rating of haptic feedback strength indicate that haptic feedback alone was not sufficiently strong to provide positive confirmation to the user. The effect employed in the study was chosen on the basis of the findings of the preliminary study described in Section 5.6, with the intention that this process would reject inappropriate effects, including those which were of insufficient magnitude. While all of the participants indicated that they could feel the haptic feedback in the training phase, a number reported difficulty in sensing the stimulus during the tasks. This suggests that the workload demands of the concurrent driving and touchscreen tasks reduced participants' ability to detect the haptic stimulus; this agrees with the findings of Leung et al. [35] who observed a reduction in haptic sensitivity when participants were under cognitive workload.

The effects of cross-model interaction between tactile and auditory stimuli are well established [36–38], with significant links between the neural mechanisms for processing tactile and auditory information. It is therefore to be expected that the perception of the haptic stimulus will be effected by the presence of its auditory counterpart. Indeed, in this study, haptic feedback was perceived to be stronger when audible feedback was also present. Interestingly, the haptic feedback stimulus was also perceived to be more realistic (more like a real switch) in the presence of the audible stimulus; even though the latter was not representative of the sound made by a switch (a "beep" rather than a "click"), its presence supported the mental model of switch use during users' interaction with the touchscreen.

*7.2. The LCT and Workload.* Measures of perceived touchscreen task difficulty and interference with the driving task also showed improvements with enhanced feedback, albeit with smaller differences. For both measures, scores indicated a "more than moderate" level of overall difficulty/interference. This suggests that the combined performance of the driving and touchscreen tasks placed significant workload demands on the participants. While the perceived level of interference was reduced in the presence of multimodal feedback, objective driving performance as measured by mean deviation was not improved.

Analysis of order effects indicated that, while presentation order had no effect on touchscreen task difficulty, there was a significant effect on interference with the driving task, with the level of interference becoming lower as the study progressed. As the perceived difficulty of the touchscreen task was constant throughout (no significant order effect), it is assumed that the perceived demands of concurrent performance of the driving and touchscreen tasks diminished as the study progressed.

The immediate implication is that participants did not receive sufficient training prior to commencing the evaluation. Petzoldt et al. [39] found that training, especially in the dual-task condition had a significant effect on mean deviation in an LCT-based study. As described in Section 5.8, training/practice was provided on the driving and touchscreen tasks both individually and concurrently. Clearly there is a limit to the extent to which participants can be trained within the practical constraints of the study, and Petzoldt et al. again identify that there are no guidelines

within the ISO standard for training requirements for LCT. Furthermore, as the experiment design was counterbalanced, any order bias present should not introduce bias to the independent variable in this study.

It may be suggested that the use of tasks based on a real vehicle interface imposed a high level of cognitive and visual workload on the user, by compounding the demands of interacting with the interface and recalling the correct sequence from memory. Given that the purpose of the study was to evaluate the effectiveness of the feedback mechanism rather than the graphical user interface, an alternative, less demanding task may provide clearer results at the expense of physical validity. A subsequent study conducted by the authors [4] used an abstracted "search and select" touchscreen task requiring participants to locate and press a target button within a 3 × 3 array. This task featured a lower training threshold, and it was found that subjective workload, when measured using the same scales applied in this study, was lower and order effects nonsignificant.

The nature of the workload experienced should also be considered. The LCT driving task is, in essence, very straightforward: there is no other traffic on the roadway and no requirement to moderate speed. Cognitive and physical demands must therefore be assumed to be low; by implication the operation of LCT requires significant visual attention. The use of an objective visual workload measure, such as eyes-off-the-road time, or a diagnostic subjective workload measure such as NASA-TLX [40] would provide evidence to support this hypothesis.

*7.3. Haptic Feedback and User Experience.* Hedonic rating scores indicate a preference for trimodal feedback, showing a trend across feedback states which is repeated for ratings of confidence. While combined audible, haptic, and visual feedback attracts the highest mean scores, no significant differences are shown for the addition of haptic feedback to other feedback states. This concurs with the findings of Serafin et al. [14], which indicated preference for "enhanced" (multimodal) feedback over visual alone, with trimodal feedback attracting the highest rating scores.

The trend in improved performance with multimodal feedback seen in the hedonic rating scores was repeated in the user experience questions. Participants "agreed" that trimodal audible, haptic, and visual feedback enhanced the user experience. Combined visual, audible, and haptic feedback was chosen as "most preferred" by 27 of 48 respondents. This, along with results indicating that users "agree" that haptic feedback makes the touchscreen both easier and more pleasurable to use indicate strong user acceptance of the technology.

The provision of feedback is an essential part of the user experience, informing the user of the state of the system under use and confirming that their expected outcomes have occurred. A failure to provide relevant and clear feedback can frustrate the user and negatively affect their perception of the usability of the system [41]. The results discussed above suggest that the benefits of the application of haptic feedback were, within the context of this study, subjective and affective. There is therefore potential to explore the technology solely in terms of its contribution to the user experience. Studies into the feel quality of mechanical switchgear [42, 43] have shown that vehicle users can differentiate between and express a preference for specific haptic characteristics. A system such as that tested which offers the potential for haptic feedback to be tailored to a user's specific requirements would provide an opportunity to optimise affective response to interaction with the HMI; this would also allow users to select the stimulus magnitude required for their personal preference and tactile acuity. In the increasingly competitive automotive industry, features that delight users improve the emotional response to the product and help to provide differentiation in a crowded marketplace [44].

## 8. Conclusions

The findings of the study showed subjective benefits for multimodal feedback in automotive touchscreens but were unable to provide evidence of objective benefits in terms of driving or task performance. Feedback type was found to have no effect on lateral deviation or touchscreen task-completion time. In the latter case the time required to complete the task was, understandably, dominated by task complexity in terms of button presses and menu level navigations required. Driving performance was, however, degraded from a baseline measure when touchscreen tasks were introduced, highlighting the distraction caused by operation of in-car technology.

Measures of subjective user response indicate a preference for multimodal feedback over visual alone, with hedonic rating, confidence, difficulty, and driving interference all showing an improvement and combined visual, audible, and haptic feedback being most strongly preferred. While no specific benefit was demonstrated for haptic feedback over audible, users indicated that haptic feedback improved the usability and user experience of the touchscreen interface. Prior research indicates that haptic interaction can be used to improve users' affective response to interfaces, suggesting that haptic touchscreen technology offers vehicle manufactures an opportunity to exploit this potential in the context of in-car technology.

The study also highlighted issues with dual-task workload and training when conducting HMI evaluation studies using the Lane Change Test. While LCT is designed to provide a measure of task workload through decrements in driving performance, it is difficult to diagnose the exact nature of the workload experienced by the user with the measures employed. The application of an objective measure of visual workload and/or a diagnostic subjective workload measure may help to clarify the findings from future studies in this respect.

This work could be extended by evaluating the performance of expert users in the dual-task scenario to understand the effect of training and learning effects throughout the study. Further evaluations could be conducted using measures of visual workload, as described above. Finally, correlation of the LCT-based results with repeat evaluations using an instrumented vehicle or high-fidelity simulation environment would help to determine the external validity of the approach.

## Acknowledgments

The authors would like to thank Dr. Carl Pickering and colleagues at Jaguar Land Rover Research for their technical support and input into this study. This research was conducted as part of the Warwick Innovative Manufacturing Research Centre (WIMRC) Project: "Designing the Next-Generation of HMI for Future Intelligent Vehicles" under the Premium Vehicles Customer Interface Technologies (PVCIT) Centre of Excellence. The PVCIT is a collaborative research project between leading automotive companies and research partners, including Jaguar Land Rover and Tata Motors European Technical Centre. The £4.7 million project is funded by the Advantage West Midlands (AWM) and the European Regional Development Fund (ERDF).

## References

[1] A. Sears, C. Plaisant, and B. Shneiderman, "A new era for high precision touchscreens," in *Advances in Human-Computer Interaction*, H. R. Hartson and D. Hix, Eds., pp. 2–3, Ablex Publishing, New Jersey, NJ, USA, 1992.

[2] Gartner Incorporation, Gartner Says Touchscreen Mobile Device Sales Will Grow 97 Percent in 2010, March 2010, http://www.gartner.com/it/page.jsp?id=1313415. (Accessed 18th August 2011.)

[3] DisplaySearch, Touch Screens in Tablet PCs Forecast to Reach 60M in 2011, March 2011, http://www.displaysearch.com/cps/rde/xchg/displaysearch/hs.xsl/110314_touch_screens_in_tablet_pcs_forecast_to_reach_60m_in_2011.asp. (Accessed 18th August 2011.)

[4] M. J. Pitts, G. E. Burnett, L. Skrypchuk, T. Wellings, A. Attridge, and M. A. Williams, "Visual-haptic feedback interaction in automotive touchscreens," *Displays*, vol. 33, no. 1, pp. 7–16, 2012.

[5] W. W. Wierwille, "Development of an initial model relating deiver in-vehicle visual demands to accident rate," in *Proceedings of the 3rd Annual Mid-Atlantic Human Factors Conference*, pp. 1–7, Blacksburg, Va, USA, March 1995.

[6] S. G. Klauer, T. A. Dingus, V. L. Neale, J. D. Sudweeks, and D. J. Ramsey, "The impact of driver inattention on near-crash/crash risk: an analysis using the 100-car naturalistic driving study data," Tech. Rep. DOT HS 810 594, National Highway Traffic Safety Administration, Washington, DC, USA, 2006.

[7] G. E. Burnett and J. M. Porter, "Ubiquitous computing within cars: designing controls for non-visual use," *International Journal of Human Computer Studies*, vol. 55, no. 4, pp. 521–531, 2001.

[8] M. J. Pitts, M. A. Williams, T. Wellings, and A. Attridge, "Assessing subjective response to haptic feedback in automotive touchscreens," in *Proceedings of the 1st International Conference on Automotive User Interfaces and Interactive Vehicular Applications (AutomotiveUI '09)*, pp. 11–18, ACM, Essen, Germany, September 2009.

[9] C. D. Wickens and J. G. Hollands, *Engineering Psychology and Human Performance*, Prentice Hall, Upper Saddle River, NJ, USA, 3rd edition, 2000.

[10] J. L. Burke, M. S. Prewett, A. A. Gray et al., "Comparing the effects of visual-auditory and visual-tactile feedback on user performance: a meta-analysis," in *Proceedings of the 8th International Conference on Multimodal Interfaces (ICMI '06)*, pp. 108–117, Alberta, Canada, November 2006.

[11] I. Poupyrev, S. Maruyama, and J. Rekimoto, "Ambient touch: designing tactile interfaces for handheld devices," in *Proceedings of the 15th Annual Symposium on User Interface Software and Technology*, pp. 51–60, Paris, France, October 2002.

[12] E. Hoggan, S. A. Brewster, and J. Johnston, "Investigating the effectiveness of tactile feedback for mobile touchscreens," in *Proceedings of the 26th Annual CHI Conference on Human Factors in Computing Systems (CHI '08)*, pp. 1573–1582, Florence, Italy, April 2008.

[13] J.-H. Lee and C. Spence, "Assessing the benefits of multimodal feedback on dual-task performance under demanding conditions," in *Proceedings of the 22nd British HCI Group Annual Conference on People and Computers: Culture, Creativity, Interaction*, vol. 1, pp. 185–192, British Computer Society, Liverpool, Uk, September 2008.

[14] C. Serafin, R. Heers, M. Tschirhart, C. Ullrich, and C. Ramstien, "User experience in the US and Germany of in-vehicle touch-screens with integrated haptic and auditory feedback," in *Proceedings of the SAE World Congress*, Detroit, Mich, USA, April 2007.

[15] H. Richter, R. Ecker, C. Deisler, and A. Butz, "HapTouch and the 2+1 state model: potentials of haptic feedback on touch based in-vehicle information systems," in *Proceedings of the 2nd International Conference on Automotive User Interfaces and Interactive Vehicular Applications (AutomotiveUI '10)*, pp. 72–79, Pittsburgh, Pa, USA, November 2010.

[16] N. Bevan, "Usability is quality of use," in *Proceedings of the 6th International Conference on Human Computer Interaction*, A. Ogawa, Ed., Elsevier, Tokyo, Japan, July 1995.

[17] A. P. O. S. Vermeeren, E. L. C. Law, V. Roto, M. Obrist, J. Hoonhout, and K. Väänänen-Vainio-Mattila, "User experience evaluation methods: current state and development needs," in *Proceedings of the 6th Nordic Conference on Human-Computer Interaction: Extending Boundaries (NordiCHI '10)*, pp. 521–530, Reykjavik, Iceland, October 2010.

[18] G. Burnett, "Designing and evaluating in-car user-interfaces," in *Handbook of Research on User-Interface Design and Evaluation for Mobile Technology*, J. Lumsden, Ed., pp. 218–236, IGI Global, Hershey, Penn, USA, 2008.

[19] S. T. Godley, T. J. Triggs, and B. N. Fildes, "Driving simulator validation for speed research," *Accident Analysis and Prevention*, vol. 34, no. 5, pp. 589–600, 2002.

[20] M. P. Reed and P. A. Green, "Comparison of driving performance on-road and in a low-cost simulator using a concurrent telephone dialling task," *Ergonomics*, vol. 42, no. 8, pp. 1015–1037, 1999.

[21] T. W. Hoyes, N. A. Stanton, and R. G. Taylor, "Risk taking in simulated environments: evidence relevant to risk homeostasis theory," in *Traffic and Transport Psychology: Theory and Application*, J. Rothengatter and E. Carbonell-Vaya, Eds., pp. 203–208, Elsevier, Amsterdam, The Netherlands, 1997.

[22] S. Mattes, "The lane-change-task as a tool for driver distraction evaluation," in *Quality of Work and Products in Enterprises of the Future*, H. Strasser et al., Ed., p. 57, Ergonomia, Stuttgart, Germany, 2003.

[23] M. P. Bruyas, C. Brusque, H. Tattegrain, A. Auriault, I. Aillerie, and M. Duraz, "Consistency and sensitivity of lane change test

[24] according to driving simulator characteristics," *IET Intelligent Transport Systems*, vol. 2, no. 4, pp. 306–314, 2008.

[24] ISO 26022:2010—Road vehicles—Ergonomic aspects of transport information and control systems—Simulated lane change test to assess in-vehicle secondary task demand.

[25] J. Breuer, K. Bengler, C. Heinrich, and W. Reichelt, "Development of driver attention metrics (ADAM)," in *Quality of Work and Products in Enterprises of the Future*, H. Strasser et al., Ed., pp. 37–40, Ergonomia, Stuttgart, Germany, 2003.

[26] K. Young, M. G. Lennéa, and A. R. Williamsona, "Sensitivity of the lane change test as a measure of in-vehicle system demand," *Applied Ergonomics*, vol. 42, no. 4, pp. 611–618, 2010.

[27] J. L. Harbluk, J. S. Mitroi, and P. C. Burns, "Three navigation systems with three tasks: using the lane-change test (LCT) to assess distraction demand," in *Proceedings of the 5th International Driving Symposium on Human Factors in Driver Assessment, Training and Vehicle Design*, pp. 24–30, Montana, Mont, USA, June 2009.

[28] E. Mitsopoulos-Rubens, K. L. Young, and M. G. Lenné, *Utility of the Lane Change Test in Exploring the Effects on Driving Performance of Engaging in Additional in Vehicle Tasks While Driving*, Monash University Accident Research Centre, Victoria, Australia, 2010.

[29] Institute of Ergonomics, Lane Change Test Screen Shot, Technische Universität München, 2012, http://www.lfe.mw.tum.de/_media/de/research/labs/lct.jpg.

[30] H. Stone and J. L. Sidel, *Sensory Evaluation Practices*, Elsevier Academic Press, San Diego, Calif, USA, 2004.

[31] D. V. Cicchetti, "Extension of multiple-range tests to interaction tables in the analysis of variance: a rapid approximate solution," *Psychological Bulletin*, vol. 77, no. 6, pp. 405–408, 1972.

[32] H. Abdi, "The bonferonni and Šidák corrections for multiple comparisons," in *Encyclopedia of Measurement and Statistics*, N. Salkind, Ed., Sage, Thousand Oaks, Cailf, USA, 2007.

[33] A. Rydström, C. Grane, and P. Bengtsson, "Driver behaviour during haptic and visual secondary tasks," in *Proceedings of the 1st International Conference on Automotive User Interfaces and Interactive Vehicular Applications (AutomotiveUI '09)*, pp. 121–127, Essen, Germany, September 2009.

[34] SAE J2364—Navigation and Route Guidance Function Accessibility While Driving.

[35] R. Leung, K. MacLean, M. B. Bertelsen, and M. Saubhasik, "Evaluation of haptically augmented touchscreen GUI elements under cognitive load," in *Proceedings of the 9th International Conference on Multimodal Interfaces (ICMI '07)*, pp. 374–381, Nagoya, Japan, November 2007.

[36] V. Occelli, C. Spence, and M. Zampini, "Audiotactile interactions in temporal perception," *Psychonomic Bulletin and Review*, vol. 18, no. 3, pp. 429–454, 2011.

[37] S. Soto-Faraco and G. Deco, "Multisensory contributions to the perception of vibrotactile events," *Behavioural Brain Research*, vol. 196, no. 2, pp. 145–154, 2009.

[38] C. Spence and M. Zampini, "Auditory contributions to multisensory product perception," *Acta Acustica united with Acustica*, vol. 92, no. 6, pp. 1009–1025, 2006.

[39] T. Petzoldt, N. Bär, C. Ihle, and J. F. Krems, "Learning effects in the lane change task (LCT)—evidence from two experimental studies," *Transportation Research F*, vol. 14, no. 1, pp. 1–12, 2011.

[40] S. G. Hart and L. E. Staveland, "Development of NASA-TLX (Task Load Index): results of empirical and theoretical research," in *Human Mental Workload*, P. A. Hancock and N. Meshkati, Eds., pp. 239–250, Elsevier Science Publishing, Amsterdam, The Netherlands, 1988.

[41] D. A. Norman, *Emotional Design : Why We Love (or Hate) Everyday Things*, Basic Books, New York, NY, USA, 2004.

[42] T. Wellings, M. Williams, and C. Tennant, "Understanding customers' holistic perception of switches in automotive human-machine interfaces," *Applied Ergonomics*, vol. 41, no. 1, pp. 8–17, 2010.

[43] T. Wellings, M. A. Williams, and M. Pitts, "Customer perception of switch-feel in luxury sports utility vehicles," *Food Quality and Preference*, vol. 19, no. 8, pp. 737–746, 2008.

[44] T. Wellings, M. A. Williams, and C. Tennant, "Tactility, craftsmanship and the NPI process," Tech. Rep., SAE Transactions Journal of Passenger Cars: Mechanical Systems, 2005.

# 18

# Objective and Subjective Evaluation of Online Error Correction during P300-Based Spelling

**Perrin Margaux,**[1,2] **Maby Emmanuel,**[1,2] **Daligault Sébastien,**[3]
**Bertrand Olivier,**[1,2] **and Mattout Jérémie**[1,2]

[1] *Lyon Neuroscience Research Center (CRNL), INSERM, CNRS, Dycog team, 95 Boulevard Pinel, 69500 Bron, France*
[2] *Université Claude Bernard Lyon 1, 69000 Lyon, France*
[3] *CERMEP, 95 Boulevard Pinel, 69500 Bron, France*

Correspondence should be addressed to Mattout Jérémie, jeremie.mattout@inserm.fr

Academic Editor: Surjo R. Soekadar

Error potentials (ErrP) are alterations of EEG traces following the subject's perception of erroneous feedbacks. They provide a way to recognize misinterpreted commands in brain-computer interfaces (BCI). However, this has been evaluated online in only a couple of studies and mostly with very few subjects. In this study, we implemented a P300-based BCI, including not only online error detection but also, for the first time, automatic correction. We evaluated it in 16 healthy volunteers. Whenever an error was detected, a new decision was made based on the second best guess of a probabilistic classifier. At the group level, correction did neither improve nor deteriorate spelling accuracy. However, automatic correction yielded a higher bit rate than a respelling strategy. Furthermore, the fine examination of interindividual differences in the efficiency of error correction and spelling clearly distinguished between two groups who differed according to individual specificity in ErrP detection. The high specificity group had larger evoked responses and made fewer errors which were corrected more efficiently, yielding a 4% improvement in spelling accuracy and a higher bit rate. Altogether, our results suggest that the more the subject is engaged into the task, the more useful and well accepted the automatic error correction.

## 1. Introduction

A brain-computer interface (BCI) is a system that connects the brain to a computer directly and avoids the need for peripheral nerve and muscle activities to execute user's actions. A major aim of BCI research is to allow patients with severe motor disabilities to regain autonomy and communication abilities [1]. This raises the crucial challenge of achieving a reliable control by measuring and interpreting brain activity on the fly. Due to the highly complex, noisy, and variable nature of brain signals, especially those obtained with noninvasive recordings using scalp EEG, the computer sometimes misinterprets the signals and makes a decision that does not match the user's intention. In this context, it is highly relevant to look for a way to detect and correct errors. One way to tackle this issue is to appeal to the hybrid BCI approach [2], where it has been shown that BCI

performance could be improved by supplementing the first-order brain signal with second-level information to aid the primary classifier and to improve the final decision or BCI output [3]. This complementary signal can be either of a cerebral origin or of a very different nature [2].

Along that line, a couple of recent studies have proposed to use error-related brain signals in BCI applications. It has been established for years that the brain produces specific evoked responses in case of errors. The error-related negativity (ERN or Ne, [4, 5]) and error positivity [6, 7] are phase locked to the motor response in alternative forced-choice tasks, whereas the feedback-related negativity (FRN or feedback ERN) is produced in response to negative feedbacks [8] (see [9] for a review on ERN and FRN). In a human-computer interface, the ERN has already been used to detect errors online [10]. In BCI, an FRN like signal has been observed in response to erroneous feedback [11]. Ferrez and del R. Millan used the term "interaction error potential," as the decision results from the interaction between the user and the machine. Indeed, either one or both may be responsible for the error [12].

In particular, the well-known P300-speller has been used to compare classifiers in their performance to discriminate between correct and incorrect trials [13–15], in order to achieve real-time automatic error detection. In [15], the authors compared several classifiers offline, using a three-fold cross-validation procedure. The best classification was obtained with an LDA applied on polynomial coefficients. It was then used to evaluate the putative improvement due to ErrP detection, by estimating the ensuing reduction in the number of trials needed to properly spell a letter. They found that four out of five subjects could benefit from error detection, provided that the accuracy of the P300-Speller would remains below 75%. The same group was the first to test online automatic error detection in a P300-Speller BCI. The ErrP was detected with a 68% specificity (the probability of detecting a correct trial) and a 62% sensitivity (the probability of detecting an error trial), in two out of three subjects. However, this was not sufficient to improve the information transfer rate [13]. Finally, in a recent P300-Speller study, healthy and motor-impaired participants increased their bitrate by 0.52 (in bits/trial) using online error detection during copy spelling [14]. However, these studies implemented and evaluated automatic error detection but not automatic error correction. In other words, they could eventually suppress a wrong letter by detecting the ensuing ErrP but did not attempt to immediately replace this letter by another highly probable one [13, 14]. In the current study, we evaluated both error detection and correction, where correction was based on the second best guess of a probabilistic classifier.

In a previous experiment, we tested automatic error detection offline [16]. We achieved a very high specificity (above 0.9) and a fairly good sensitivity (up to 0.6), which yielded a significant improvement in offline spelling accuracy in about half of the participants considering an automatic correction based on the second best guess of the classifier. Importantly, it turned out that, for about 50% of the error trials, the second best guess of the classifier corresponded to the true target. Interestingly, this good correction rate (GCR) correlated with the spelling accuracy over subjects, suggesting that more attentive subjects would produce more distinguishable feedback response signals and should be more prone to benefit from automatic correction.

In the current study, we implemented and tested automatic error correction online, in a fairly large group of subjects. To ensure a high error rate in most participants, we used settings that render the spelling fast and challenging. We also evaluated subjective perception of error correction in each participant by means of a questionnaire. Importantly, the group would clearly split in-between participants with low and high ErrP detection specificity. We thus also report and discuss the difference between those two groups, both at the psychological and neurophysiological levels.

The paper is organized as follows. First, Section 2 describes the experimental design in details, including the online OpenViBE scenario that we implemented for spelling

and error detection and correction. It also describes the evaluation procedure we used to analyze data offline. Results are exposed in the next section and discussed in the final section of the paper.

## 2. Methods

*2.1. General Principle of the P300-Speller.* The P300-Speller is a BCI paradigm developed to restore communication in locked-in patients [17]. The P300 signal is an EEG positive deflection that occurs approximately 300 ms after stimulus onset and is typically recorded over centro-parietal electrodes. This response is evoked by attention to rare stimuli in a random series of stimulus events (the oddball paradigm) [18] and is even stronger when the subject is instructed to count the rare stimuli [19]. It can be used to select items displayed on a computer screen [17, 20]. In practice, all possible items are displayed while the user focuses his attention (and gaze) onto the target item. Groups of items are successively and repeatedly flashed, but only the group that contains the target will elicit a P300 response. Correct spelling thus relies on both the user's attentional state and the ability for the BCI to detect the P300 response online.

*2.2. Participants.* Sixteen healthy subjects took part in this study (7 men, mean age = 28.2 ± 5.1 (SD), range 20–37). They all signed an informed consent approved by the local Ethical Committee and received monetary compensation for their participation. All participants reported normal or corrected-to-normal vision. All subjects had no previous experience with the P300-Speller paradigm or any other BCI application.

*2.3. Experimental Design*

*2.3.1. Setup.* Participant's brain activity was simultaneously recorded with 56 passive Ag/AgCl EEG sensors (VSM-CTF compatible system) and 275 MEG axial gradiometers (VSM-CTF Omega 275). However, only 32 EEG electrodes were used for the online and offline analysis reported in this paper. The EEG electrode placement followed the extended 10–20 system (see Figure 1). Their signals were all referenced to the nose. The ground electrode was placed on the shoulder and impedances were kept below 10 kΩ. Signals were sampled at 600 Hz.

*2.3.2. Stimuli.* We used a standard 6 × 6 matrix of items for stimulation [17], which we combined with our own implementation of the P300-speller in OpenViBE [21, 22]. We moved away from the traditional row and column way of flashing items, by adapting the pseudorandom stimulation procedure proposed by Townsend et al. [23]. Townsend and collaborators showed that this improves the spelling accuracy significantly since it minimizes the risk for the subject or patient to be distracted by the letters adjacent to the target. Therefore, we constructed six pairs of groups of six letters, each pair being associated with a particular item of the matrix. This item then belongs to two groups

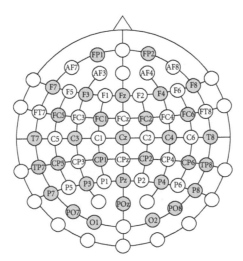

FIGURE 1: EEG channel montage. Only yellow channels were used for the online and offline analysis reported in this paper.

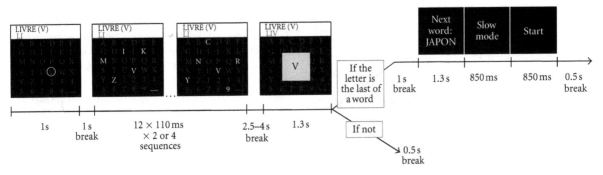

FIGURE 2: The course of one trial. The target letter is indicated by a green circle, for 1 second. Letters are flashed by group of 6 letters. After a delay, the letter chosen by the P300 classifier is displayed for 1.3 seconds. If the letter is the last of the word, a 4.5 second break occurs during which a display indicates the next word and the difficulty level (slow or fast spelling mode). If not, there is a short 0.5 s break before the next green circle appears.

only and those two groups have only this single item in common (see Figure 2). In other words, a unique pair of groups of nonadjacent letters is defined in order to replace the original pair of row and column that was associated with a unique possible target [24]. This way of flashing letters also minimizes the probability that a letter will be flashed twice in a row, which minimizes the risk for the user to miss one target presentation. The flash duration was equal to 60 ms and we set the stimulus onset asynchrony (SOA) to 110 ms. We chose these small parameter values in order to make the trials as short as possible. This has a twofold advantage. It enables us to acquire more trials per subject and it makes the spelling more difficult [22]. Both aspects are essential to generate enough error trials and study error detection and correction.

*2.3.3. One Trial.* We call a trial the succession of stimulations and observations that are needed to select one item (see Figure 2). Each trial is thus made of several sequences depending on the spelling condition. A sequence of stimulations corresponds to the successive flashing of all the groups, once and in a pseudorandom order. The longer the trial (i.e.,

the more sequences per trial), the more observations to rely on for the BCI to find the target.

We used two spelling conditions: a fast, more error-prone condition, made of short (2-sequence long) trials and a slower, less risky one, made of four-sequence long trials. These two modes are fairly fast and challenging, which ensures the recording of many trials per subject, among which enough error trials for subsequent analysis.

Since we used copy spelling, each trial started with the presentation of the current target, both at the top of the screen and within the matrix, using a green circle for 1 second. There was no break in-between sequence. At the end of each trial, 2.5 to 4 seconds after the last flash, the feedback was displayed in a blue square at the middle of the screen for 1.3 seconds. It was simultaneously written on the top of the screen (see Figure 2). This large presentation at the center of the visual field was made to favor clear single-trial responses to feedbacks. Participants were explicitly instructed to wait for the feedback at the middle of the screen and not to blink during feedback presentation.

In the session including automatic correction (see below), the second best guess of the classifier was used to replace the current feedback, in an orange square, whenever an ErrP would have been detected. In this case, the new feedback was presented for 1 second and the item was also simultaneously corrected at the top of the screen (see Figure 2). After a 0.5 second break, the new target for the next trial was presented.

*2.3.4. Full Procedure.* The experiment was divided into five parts.

(1) *Installation and Instructions.* After having read about the experiment and signed an informed consent form, each subject was prepared for EEG/MEG data acquisition. During preparation, the subject was asked to read the task instructions. Finally, a couple of typical trials were presented so that the subject would be familiar with stimulus presentation before starting the actual experiment.

(2) *Speller Training.* The aim of the first session was to gather training data in order to set the supervised algorithms subsequently used in the test phase, for individual feature selection and classification. Precisely, those data were used to both compute the individual spatial filters and class parameters. In this training session, subjects were all required to successively copy spell the same 36 items (the whole matrix). Each item or trial was spelled using 3 flash-sequences. The session lasted about 10 minutes and was interleaved with short breaks after the 12th and 24th items. No feedback was provided.

(3) *Speller Testing and Error Detection Training.* After training, the subjects had to go through four true spelling sessions, lasting approximately 12 minutes each. Each session was made of twelve 5-letter words. Subjects received feedback after each letter and words were separated by a 4.5 second break. Within a word, letters were spelled using the same number of sequences (either 2 or 4) and short- and long-lasting words were counterbalanced within sessions. The responses to feedbacks over those four sessions were used to train the feature extraction and classification algorithms for subsequent error detection.

(4) *Speller and Error Correction Testing.* In the fifth spelling session, participants had to spell twenty 5-letter words that they had chosen themselves before the beginning of the whole experiment. Still, it consisted in copy spelling since those words were entered in the computer by the experimenter before the actual session. All letters were spelled using two sequences only (fast mode). This last session lasted 17 minutes approximately. Importantly, whenever an error was detected, automatic correction applied.

(5) *Debrief.* After recording, participants had to fill in a questionnaire. Using marks between 1 and 10, they had to respond to questions about their perception of the performance of the machine, the difficulty of the task, the quality, and usefulness of the correction.

*2.4. Feature Extraction.* We used similar preprocessing steps and feature extraction algorithms to process the responses evoked by flashes (for spelling) and feedbacks (for error detection), respectively. Raw data were first downsampled to 100 Hz and bandpass filtered between 1 and 20 Hz, online. 100 Hz here corresponds to a good compromise between the need to sample above 60 Hz (the so-called engineer Nyquist frequency to avoid aliasing) and the advantage of reducing the dimension of the data for online processing. Feature extraction then consisted in linear spatial filtering, whose effect is to reduce the dimension of the data as well as to maximize the discriminability between the two classes (i.e., between targets and nontargets, during spelling, and between error and correct feedbacks, during error detection) [25]. The xDAWN algorithm provides orthogonal linear spatial filters that can be learned from training samples [25]. Based on our previous studies [16, 22], we used a five-dimensional filter for both spelling and error detection. As mentioned above, those filters were learned based on the first session, for subsequent spelling, and based on the first four spelling sessions which included feedbacks, for error detection in the last session. For online spelling, the features consisted in the spatially filtered epochs from 0 to 600 ms after flash onset. The evoked response thus included both the P300 and the early visual response [22, 26, 27]. For online error detection, the features consisted in the spatially filtered epochs from 200 to 600 ms after feedback onset [28].

*2.5. Feature Classification.* We used a mixture of multi-dimensional Gaussian model as a classifier. The model parameters (i.e., the mean and variance of each of the two Gaussians) were learned from the same training samples as the parameters of the xDAWN algorithms, for the spelling and error detection task, respectively. Importantly, we assumed conditional independence in time and space between features (naïve Bayes hypothesis) [16, 22]. This makes the real-time computation of the posterior probability of each new feature very efficient. This is particularly relevant for the spelling part, since it enables the BCI to update its posterior probability or belief about the target location, after each new observation or flash.

Indeed, for spelling, all items are initially assumed to be equiprobable targets. At each new observation, this belief is updated following Bayes rule, by optimally combining the data likelihood and priors. The obtained posteriors then furnish the prior for the next observation, in a Markovian fashion.

For error detection, a decision was made after each single feedback observation. Hence Bayes rule was applied once per trial only. We used individual priors based on each subject's averaged error rate, as given by the first four spelling and ErrP training sessions.

*2.6. Evaluation of Online Error Detection.* To evaluate ErrP classification, we use the common confusion matrix for a two-class problem (see Figure 3). It involves the estimation of the following complementary measures (reported in percent in the results section):

| | | Outcome | |
|---|---|---|---|
| | | Error | Correct |
| Predicted | Error | TP | FP |
| | Correct | FN | TN |

| | | Feedback (speller outcome) | |
|---|---|---|---|
| | | Incorrect | Correct |
| ErrP detection | Error | ErrP classifier recognises an error. The second best-guess from the classifier replaces the incorrect letter (good case). | ErrP classifier recognises an error. The second best-guess from the classifier replaces the actually correct letter (worst case). |
| | Correct | ErrP classifier does not recognises an error, event though the letter displayed is actually incorrect (bad case). | ErrP classifier does not recognises an error. The letter is indeed correct (best case). |

(a)           (b)

FIGURE 3: Confusion matrix for a general binary problem (a) and in the context of error correction (b), adapted from [14]. TP: true positive; FP: false positive; FN: false negative; TN: true negative.

(i) sensitivity = TP/(TP + FN), that is, the capacity to correctly detect errors;

(ii) specificity = TN/(TN + FP), that is, the capacity to correctly detect correct trials;

(iii) accuracy = (TP + TN)/(TP + TN + FP + FN), that is, the global efficacy of the classifier.

*2.7. Evaluation of Online Error Correction.* We computed three quantitative measures to evaluate error correction, both at the single subject and group levels.

We denote the first one by $\theta$. It is the percentage of error trials for which the classifier's second best guess corresponded to the actual target. Note that $\theta$ is independent of error detection and only measures how well the classifier might help correcting errors automatically. We estimated $\theta$ based on the whole five spelling sessions.

The second measure evaluates automatic error correction on the very last session. It is the good correction rate (GCR) and corresponds to the percentage of detected true error trials that were appropriately corrected. While $\theta$ is an offline (predictive) measure, GCR is an online (true BCI behavioral) measure of performance.

Finally, we estimated the individual gain in spelling accuracy due to automatic error correction in the last session. It is simply the difference between the observed accuracy and the one that would have been observed with no online correction.

A commonly used although imperfect measure of BCI performance is the bit rate [29], originally derived from [30]. It can be computed from the following formula:

$$br = \log_2(M) + (1 - p) \cdot \log_2 \frac{1 - p}{M - 1}, \tag{1}$$

where $M$ is the number of classes and $p$ is the accuracy of the P300 classifier. We report br in bits per minute and use it to compare the spelling accuracy with and without online correction as well as the accuracy that would have been observed if error detection would have been simply followed by the opportunity to spell the letter again. To estimate the latter, we consider that the letter would be spelled again once, with an accuracy corresponding to the one observed online for each subject. Importantly, the respelling of a letter includes a short instruction indicating that the user should focus onto the same target again [14].

For each of the above parameters, we also report the obtained values at the population level. Importantly, since the subjects did not show the same amount of errors, computing the average values for TP, FN, and other parameters would yield a bias estimate of what could be predicted at the population level. Therefore, we rather report the values obtained by concatenating all the trials over subjects, that is, by considering the so-called metasubject. We refer to such quantities at the population level as metavalues. As an example, the metasensitivity corresponds to the sensitivity of the metasubject with mTP true positive and mFN false negative (mTP and mFN being the sum of TP and FN over all the 16 participants).

Finally, the spelling accuracy using automatic correction was related to the specificity, the sensitivity, and the GCR using the following simple formula:

$$Pc = P \cdot \text{Spec} + (1 - P) \cdot \text{Sens} \cdot \text{GCR}, \tag{2}$$

where $P$ indicates the spelling accuracy in the absence of correction and $Pc$ the spelling accuracy after automatic correction. The correction becomes useful as soon as $Pc > P$, which for a given initial spelling accuracy and GCR yields the following limit condition on error detection sensitivity and specificity:

$$\text{Spec} > 1 - \frac{(1 - p) \cdot \text{Sens} \cdot \text{GCR}}{p}. \tag{3}$$

*2.8. Additional Offline Analysis.* Subjects clearly separated between a low (below 0.75) and a high (above 0.85) ErrP detection specificity group. We compared those two groups in terms of performance, responses to questionnaire, and electrophysiological measures. Because of the small sample size in each group, we used the nonparametric Mann-Whitney test for statistical inference.

The electrophysiological responses we considered for quantitative comparisons are the differences between averaged responses to target and non-target stimuli, or to correct and incorrect feedbacks, respectively. These were computed from the downsampled and bandpass filtered data (see Section 4). We compared the amplitudes and latencies of the negative and positive peaks of these differential responses.

For the responses to feedback, only the (last) session with correction was considered. We computed the difference between responses to correct and incorrect feedbacks on

| | | Outcome | |
|---|---|---|---|
| | | Error | Correct |
| Predicted | Error | 23.7% | 7.6% |
| | Correct | 14% | 54.7% |

FIGURE 4: Confusion matrix for ErrP detection (group results).

central electrode Cz, as in [14]. We typically observe a first negative component (between 250 and 450 ms) followed by a positive component (between 350 and 550 ms), which we denote by neg-ErrP and pos-ErrP, respectively.

For the responses to flashes, we used the data from all sessions. We computed the difference between the averaged responses to target and non-target stimuli and selected the channels exhibiting the maximum absolute differences at the group level. We thus focused our comparison on channel P7 for a negative peak difference in time window 150–270 ms and on channel P8 for positive peak difference in time window 250–500 ms. These two components correspond to the N1 and P300 responses, respectively. N1 is known to be associated with automated stimulus processing that is affected by early attentional processes [31] and to be preponderating at parieto-occipital sites [27].

For each participant, both the amplitudes and latencies of the peaks of the above-defined components were used for subsequent analysis and statistical comparisons. Note that for technical reasons, the electrophysiological data of one participant (S08) could not be saved during the experiment. Therefore, all the results relying on offline evoked potential analysis were obtained from the other 15 subjects.

## 3. Results

*3.1. Performance in Spelling.* In fast mode (including the last session), the online spelling accuracy was 64% ± 21 (SD). In slow mode, it was 80% ± 18 (SD). Accounting for the delay between two trials (5.8 s), this corresponds to rates of 4.52 ± 1.2 (SD) and 4.31 ± 1 correct letters per minute, respectively. The information transfer rate is higher in fast mode, meaning that the loss in accuracy is compensated by the speed increase.

*3.2. Performance in Error Detection.* The metavalues for the percent of true positive, false positive, false negative, and true negative are shown in Figure 4. The individual sensitivity and specificity values are given in Table 1. At the group level, the (meta) sensitivity, specificity, and accuracy obtained 63%, 88%, and 78%, respectively.

Interestingly, the spelling accuracy correlates with ErrP detection specificity over subjects ($P < 0.01$, $r = 0.68$, Figure 5(a)).

What is very much striking is the split into two groups according to the individual specificities in error detection. Six

subjects have quite low specificities, below 75%, while specificities for the other 10 subjects rise above 85% (Figure 5(a)).

*3.3. Performance in Automatic Error Correction.* Individual $\theta$ and gains are given in Table 1. At the group level, the GCR obtains 34%, meaning that for one hundred well-detected errors, thirty-four have been well corrected. The metavalue for $\theta$ is 36%, which is very close to the GCR. Over subjects, $\theta$ correlates with global spelling accuracy ($P < 0.0001$, $r = 0.87$). Precisely, the less the errors during initial spelling, the higher the probability to effectively correct for those errors (Figure 5(b)).

$\theta$ also correlates with specificity ($P < 0.01$, $r = 0.72$) and accuracy of ErrP detection ($P < 0.01$, $r = 0.63$, Figure 5(c)), as well as with responses to questions Q1 ("How well did you control the machine?", $P < 0.001$, $r = 0.75$) and Q2 ("Did the machine perform well?", $P < 0.05$, $r = 0.60$).

Over the whole group, the spelling accuracy raised by 0.5% due to automatic error correction, relative to a 62% initial accuracy (i.e., without correction). However, interindividual variability proved quite large. Automatic error correction yielded an improvement in 50% of the subjects (with a maximum gain of 12%), while it caused a degradation of spelling accuracy in 37.5% of the subjects (with a maximum drop of 19%).

Table 2 shows the bit rates corresponding to the three compared spelling modes: no correction, predicted correction based on automatic error detection, and hypothetical respelling and online automatic correction. Over subjects, the information transfer rate decreases when we move from automatic correction to automatic detection and respelling. Moreover, the highest bit rate is obtained for the no correction case. However, when restricting the comparison to the high specificity group, the highest bit rate is obtained during automatic correction.

Figure 6 provides a graphical representation of individual performance in terms of sensitivity and specificity in error detection. It also summarizes the behavior of the different groups, by displaying the metaspelling accuracy corresponding to the whole group, the low specificity group and the high specificity group, respectively. For those three groups, it further emphasizes the boundaries given by (3), that is, the minimum required trade-off between specificity and sensitivity. Precisely, given the observed GCR and spelling accuracy (in the absence of any correction) for each group, each boundary represents the limit above which the automatic correction becomes fruitful. The more a subject lays above the boundary, the higher the expected increase in spelling accuracy (e.g., S10 had a 12% gain of accuracy). Conversely, the more a subject lays below the boundary, the larger the expected drop of spelling accuracy (e.g., S01 had a 19% drop of accuracy).

*3.4. Self-Evaluation Questionnaires.* Questions and averaged ratings are reported in Table 3. Individual responses for Q1, Q2, and Q8 are detailed in Table 1. Interestingly, the group average answer to Q2 equals 6.6, which is very close to the observed global spelling accuracy of 68.5%. Moreover, the

TABLE 1: Individual and group performance in spelling, error detection, and correction. The first three columns indicate the subject number and demographic information such as gender and age. The next two columns indicate the spelling accuracy (percent of correct letters) for the whole five sessions (mixing words spelled with 2 and 4 sequences) and for the fifth session alone (the one dedicated to online evaluation of error correction, without considering the online correction), respectively. The next four columns indicate the individual sensitivity, specificity, $\theta$, and gain in spelling accuracy obtained in the last session, reported in percent. The last four columns show the individual responses to the most relevant questions (see Table 2 for a full description). The last three lines provide results at the group level (first line) and after having distinguished between low specificity (second line) and high specificity (third line) performers.

| Subjects | Dem. info. | | Spelling accuracy | | ErrP detection | | Correction | | Questionnaire | | | |
| | Sex | Age (year) | Sessions 1 to 5 | Session 5 only | Sens. | Spec. | $\theta$ | Gain | Q1 | Q2 | Q8 | Did you prefer with or without correction? |
|---|---|---|---|---|---|---|---|---|---|---|---|---|
| 1 | m | 34 | 82% | 80% | 35% | 69% | 47% | −19% | 5 | 5 | 2 | without |
| 3 | m | 25 | 32% | 25% | 72% | 68% | 25% | 1% | 1 | 1 | 2 | without |
| 4 | f | 31 | 44% | 36% | 75% | 69% | 24% | −2% | 6 | 5 | 1 | without |
| 6 | f | 20 | 42% | 31% | 81% | 61% | 23% | 0% | 4 | 8 | 8 | with |
| 12 | m | 23 | 66% | 56% | 48% | 70% | 39% | −9% | 7 | 6 | 4 | without |
| 14 | f | 23 | 52% | 50% | 70% | 72% | 35% | −1% | 4 | 6 | 5 | without |
| 2 | f | 32 | 65% | 56% | 68% | 93% | 39% | 7% | 5 | 7 | 6 | with |
| 5 | m | 28 | 70% | 72% | 46% | 96% | 46% | 3% | 7 | 7 | 5 | with |
| 7 | f | 37 | 93% | 89% | 27% | 97% | 44% | −3% | 8 | 8 | 1 | without |
| 8 | f | 29 | 90% | 87% | 62% | 97% | 59% | 0% | 5 | 7 | 2 | without |
| 9 | f | 26 | 72% | 65% | 69% | 88% | 41% | 1% | 6 | 7 | 7 | with |
| 10 | f | 22 | 84% | 79% | 90% | 99% | 58% | 12% | 7 | 8 | 7 | without |
| 11 | m | 26 | 91% | 88% | 25% | 95% | 61% | −2% | 8 | 8 | 4 | without |
| 13 | m | 23 | 55% | 41% | 59% | 90% | 40% | 11% | 5 | 6 | 9 | with |
| 15 | m | 27 | 63% | 50% | 34% | 94% | 45% | 6% | 7 | 8 | 8 | with |
| 16 | f | 25 | 94% | 91% | 67% | 99% | 50% | 3% | 8 | 8 | 9 | with |
| | Summary | | | | | | Metasubject | | | | | Summary |
| All | 7 m; 9 f | 26.9 | 69% | 62% | 63% | 88% | 36% | 1% | 5.8 | 6.6 | 5.0 | 44% with |
| Spec < 0.75 | 3 m; 3 f | 26 | 53% | 46% | 69% | 69% | 29% | −5% | 4.5 | 5.2 | 3.7 | 17% with |
| Spec > 0.85 | 4 m; 6 f | 27.5 | 78% | 72% | 56% | 95% | 45% | 4% | 6.6 | 7.4 | 5.8 | 60% with |

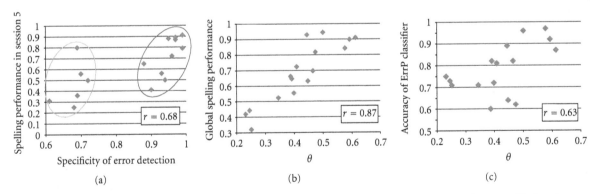

FIGURE 5: (a) Correlation between the spelling accuracy (rate of correctly spelled letters) in session 5 (without considering the correction) and specificity of error detection. The green circle includes participants with low specificity while the red one includes participants with high specificity. (b) Global spelling accuracy as a function of $\theta$. (c) Accuracy of error detection as a function of $\theta$. Each diamond represents a participant, and $R$ values represent correlation coefficients.

response to Q2 correlates with global spelling accuracy over individuals ($P < 0.05$, $r = 0.61$). And it also correlates with responses to Q1 ($P < 0.01$, $r = 0.74$). Answers to Q1 and Q2 further correlates significantly with error detection specificity (resp. $P < 0.05$, $r = 0.59$, and $P < 0.01$, $r = 0.62$), as well as with the observed gain in spelling accuracy due to automatic correction ($P < 0.05$, $r = 0.54$). The gain in spelling accuracy also correlates positively with the subject's answer about the usefulness of automatic correction (Q8, $P < 0.05$, $r = 0.61$).

TABLE 2: Bits per minute for the three compared spelling modes: no correction at all, automatic detection and predicted correction due to respelling, and automatic correction (online results).

| Subjects | Spelling mode (bits/min) | | |
| --- | --- | --- | --- |
| | No correction | Error detection and respelling | Error detection and automatic correction (online) |
| S01 | 21.75 | 16.27 | 13.55 |
| S03 | 3.25 | 3.01 | 3.27 |
| S04 | 6.00 | 5.45 | 5.14 |
| S06 | 4.69 | 5.45 | 4.37 |
| S12 | 12.23 | 9.68 | 8.88 |
| S14 | 10.20 | 8.97 | 9.39 |
| S02 | 12.23 | 13.01 | 14.24 |
| S05 | 18.29 | 18.68 | 19.23 |
| S07 | 26.10 | 25.63 | 24.43 |
| S08 | 25.08 | 25.48 | 24.79 |
| S09 | 15.51 | 15.34 | 15.38 |
| S10 | 21.30 | 23.51 | 26.59 |
| S11 | 25.58 | 24.78 | 24.40 |
| S13 | 7.42 | 7.82 | 10.43 |
| S15 | 10.20 | 10.30 | 11.97 |
| S16 | 27.15 | 28.07 | 28.61 |
| Metasubjects | | | |
| All | 13.06 | 12.70 | 12.81 |
| Spec < 0.75 | 9.03 | 7.71 | 7.37 |
| Spec > 0.85 | 18.21 | 18.77 | 19.56 |

TABLE 3: Questionnaire and averaged ratings over the whole group ($N = 16$). Ratings ranged between 1 (most negative response) and 10 (most positive response).

| Questions | Averaged ratings ± SD |
| --- | --- |
| Q1. How well did you control the machine? | 5.8 ± 1.9 |
| Q2. Did the machine perform well? | 6.6 ± 1.8 |
| Q3. Was the task difficult? | 4.6 ± 2.5 |
| Q4. Was the task tiring? | 5.9 ± 2.3 |
| Q5. Was the task motivating? | 7.9 ± 1.4 |
| Q6. Could you predict errors? | 4.9 ± 3.1 |
| Q7. How much did errors upset you? | 7.3 ± 2.2 |
| Q8. Was the automatic error correction useful? | 5.0 ± 2.8 |

Finally, to the last (binary) question: "Did you prefer the spelling with or without correction?" a short majority reported a preference for no correction (56%). However, when distinguishing between the low and high specificity groups, we find that 83% of the former preferred without correction whereas 60% of the latter preferred with correction.

3.5. *Electrophysiology*. The grand average feedback-related responses in correct and incorrect trials as well as their difference are depicted in Figure 7. Scalp topographies are also represented for each condition and for the two latencies corresponding to the negative and positive peaks of the difference. The negative peak average latency is 350 ms ± 49 (SD) after feedback onset, while the positive peak average latency is 480 ms ± 51 (SD).

The pos-ErrP amplitude correlates with the accuracy of error detection ($P < 0.01$, $r = 0.64$, Figure 8(a)), while the neg-ErrP amplitude correlates with the sensitivity of error detection ($P < 0.01$, $r = -0.70$, Figure 8(b)). Hence the larger the difference between responses to correct and incorrect trials, the more efficient the automatic error detection. Besides, we found a significant relationship between the initial spelling accuracy (without correction) and both the amplitude and the latency of the pos-ErrP. Indeed, the higher

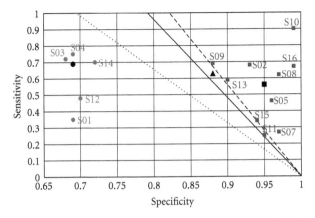

FIGURE 6: Error detection sensitivity as a function of error detection specificity. All subjects are represented as well as the global meta-subject (triangle) and the two metasubjects for the low specificity (circle) and high specificity (square) groups, respectively. The lines are the boundaries above which the automatic correction becomes fruitful, for the three groups (plain, dotted, and dashed, resp.).

the spelling accuracy, the larger ($P < 0.05$, $r = 0.58$) and the earlier ($P < 0.05$, $r = -0.55$) the positivity.

Similarly, the group average responses to target and non-target stimuli as well as the difference between the two are depicted on Figure 9. Figure 9 also shows the topographies obtained for those three responses, at the peak latency of the N1 (229 ms ± 19 (SD)) and P300 components (380 ms ± 72 (SD)).

The amplitude of the N1 component correlates with both the global spelling accuracy ($P < 0.05$, $r = -0.55$, Figure 8(c)) and $\theta$ ($P < 0.01$, $r = -0.72$). The larger the negative difference between the responses to target and non-target stimuli, the higher the spelling accuracy and the $\theta$. This corroborates what has been already observed in healthy subjects using the P300-speller, namely, that spelling accuracy depends on the ability to focus on the desired character, which yields a larger N1 response and provides a complementary feature to the P300 in order to achieve good classification [26].

Note that for correlations involving neg-ErrP or N1 amplitudes, values are negative since the amplitudes are negatives.

*3.6. Between-Group Differences.* The low specificity group performed spelling significantly poorer than the high specificity group (53% compared to 78%, $P < 0.05$). They also benefit significantly less from automatic correction ($P < 0.05$): correction improved the spelling accuracy by 4% in the high specificity group, while it degraded it by 5% in the low specificity group (Table 1). Accordingly, participants showing a low specificity tend to perceive the machine as less efficient ($P < 0.05$) and felt like they had fewer control on the BCI ($P < 0.05$). In agreement with their lower spelling accuracy, the subjects in the low specificity group also present a significantly lower value for $\theta$ (0.29 compared to 0.45, $P < 0.05$).

Finally, the latency of neg-ErrP peak proved shorter ($P < 0.05$, Figure 10(b)) and the amplitude of the N1 peak proved larger ($P < 0.01$, Figure 10(c)) for the high specificity group.

We found no significant differences between the two groups on other physiological parameters or on answers to questions Q3 to Q8.

## 4. Discussion

*4.1. Performance in Spelling and Error Detection.* We used our own implementation of the P300-speller BCI for the evaluation of online automatic error correction in 16 healthy volunteers. We considered two spelling conditions, namely, a slow and a fast mode, whose trial length was guided by our own previous experiments [16, 22].

In the current study, the online spelling accuracy proved fairly high. On average, participants could spell about 4.5 correct letters per minute, to be compared with 1.57 correct letters per minute in [14]. This high performance level might be partly attributable to the use of the xDAWN algorithm for spatial filtering [32] and to the departure from the row-column paradigm adapted from [23]. This initial high spelling accuracy has to be kept in mind when interpreting the outcome of error correction. Indeed, it might be that the effectiveness of error detection and correction depends upon the ongoing bit rate, which directly relies on the speed-accuracy trade-off that was targeted when choosing specific stimulation settings (i.e., short- or long-flash durations, short or long sequences).

Regarding the responses to feedback, we observed fronto-central evoked signals whose time courses resemble the ones that have been described recently in a BCI context [12, 14, 16]. As we already noted in [23], those components that are usually referred to as interaction ErrP in BCI [2], exhibit spatial and temporal patterns that strongly resemble the ones of feedback responses classically reported in cognitive neuroscience studies [8]. This suggests that although contextual modulations can be observed [33, 34], responses to feedback may present spatial and temporal components that are independent of the context but specific to the core process of learning from external outcomes. It stresses out the question of what part of the signal and underlying process is specific to a BCI type of interaction and what part is not.

As in a couple of earlier studies [13, 14], we showed that those responses to feedbacks can be detected online, from single trials. At the group level, we obtained 88% specificity and 63% sensitivity. For comparison, Dal Seno and collaborators tested two subjects and obtained an averaged specificity and sensitivity of 68% and 62%, respectively [13]. In nine healthy subjects, Spuler and collaborators report a 96% specificity and 40% sensitivity [14]. Note that in the latter study, the authors used a biased classifier to favor specificity. Indeed, a high specificity guarantees that correctly spelled letters will not be detected as errors mistakenly.

In our experiment, we did not use a biased classifier. However, specificity was higher than sensitivity for most of the subjects. This is because spelling accuracy is fairly high,

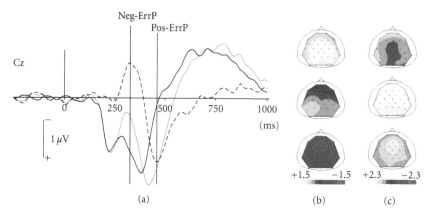

FIGURE 7: Grand average event-related dynamics ($-250$ ms to 1000 ms, channel Cz) associated with responses to correct feedbacks (black solid line), responses to incorrect feedbacks (grey solid line), and the difference between the two (black dashed line) (a). Zero time corresponds to feedback onset. Topographies for correct (top), incorrect trials (middle), and their difference (bottom) correspond to the latencies of the peaks of the neg-ErrP (b) and pos-ErrP (c), respectively.

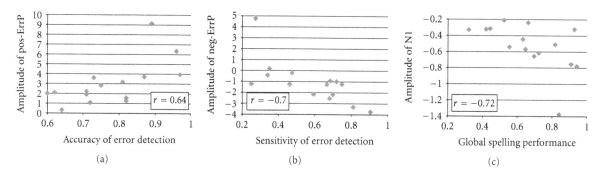

FIGURE 8: (a) Amplitude of pos-ErrP as a function of the accuracy of error detection (microvolts). (b) Amplitude of neg-ErrP as a function of the sensitivity of error detection (microvolts). (c) Amplitude of N1 as a function of the global spelling accuracy (microvolts). Each diamond represents a participant, and $R$ values represent correlation coefficients.

which yields much more training samples for the correct than for the incorrect feedback responses. Indeed, sensitivity higlhy depends upon the quality of the learning of the error class. As an example, subject S07 made 13 errors only. In [14], the authors recommend the use of at least 50 samples to train the ErrP classifier. Hence, part of the interindividual variability in sensitivity is simply due to the variability in the initial spelling accuracy between subjects, which directly affected the quality of the training. However, this is not the case for specificity since as a corollary, high spelling accuracies yield a lot of training samples for the correct class. We obtained 84 training samples in the poorer performer (S03).

Nevertheless, the current results for error detection are slightly worse than the ones we obtained offline in a previous experiment [16]. This might be due to several factors. One factor might be the offline use of ICA, to clean up the signals in our previous study. Second, the use of fairly fast modes here induced smaller interval between two consecutive feedbacks, which might have diminished the expectancy for each new outcome. A known possible cause for smaller feedback responses [35, 36]. The latter effect might not be seen in patients where more sequences

would typically be implemented. However, there is certainly room for improvement. At least two lines of research are worse mentioning in that respect. One is to make use of preexisting databases to tune the algorithms and suppress individual training [14]. However, this does not seem to be a good option in patients [14]. The second option, which could be used in combination with the first one, would be to use adaptive algorithms and keep updating the individual parameters while using the BCI. Reinforcement learning methods might prove very useful in this context [35].

### 4.2. Global Performance in Automatic Error Correction.

The novelty of our approach comes from the implementation and online evaluation of automatic error correction. Whenever an error is detected, we simply proposed to replace the supposedly erroneous choice by our classifier's second best guess. We evaluated the efficiency of this automatic correction through the computation of the good correction rate (GCR). At the group level, the GCR was equal to 34%. On the one hand, this is much higher than chance level ($1/35 = 2.86\%$), which speaks in favor of applying this strategy for automatic error correction. On the other hand, this is too low to yield a significant gain in spelling accuracy (0.5% only).

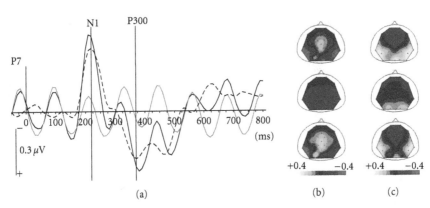

FIGURE 9: Grand average event-related dynamics ($-50$ ms to $800$ ms, channel P7) associated with responses to target flashes (black solid line), response to non-target flashes (grey solid line), and the difference between the two (black dashed line) (a). Zero time corresponds to feedback onset. Topographies for correct (top), incorrect trials (middle), and their difference (bottom) correspond to the latencies of the peaks of the N1 (b) and P300 (c), respectively.

However, the meta-bit-rate is slightly better with correction than with detection only. This highlights the efficiency of even poor automatic error correction compared to sole error detection which requires cumbersome additional spelling. In order to improve the GCR, one promising option is to use priors from a dictionary in order to bias the classifier [36]. It might improve both the initial spelling accuracy and the ensuing GCR.

### 4.3. The Importance of Interindividual Differences.
Beyond results at the group level, we observe a large interindividual variability. Specificity of error detection enabled us to clearly distinguish between two groups of participants: the low ($<75\%$, $N = 6$) and the high ($>85\%$, $N = 10$) specificity group. Our analysis revealed that those two groups differ not only in terms of specificity but also in terms of electrophysiological responses, initial spelling accuracy, $\theta$ values, and spelling accuracy gain as well as in their subjective perception of the BCI experience.

One obvious possible explanation is that the high specificity group corresponds to subjects who were more engaged into the task, which yields electrophysiological responses with large signal-to-noise ratio. Indeed, the N1 and P300 responses are known to reflect the participant's involvement in the task ([27, 37], see also [38] for a review on the P300 and [31] for a review on the N1). The P300 has been shown to increase with motivation in a BCI context [39] as well as the ensuing feedback-related negativity (the neg-ErrP) [16, 33]. As an expected consequence of a higher signal-to-noise ratio, the spelling accuracy increases as well as the $\theta$. We indeed observe that physiological amplitudes in response to flashes, spelling accuracy, and $\theta$ are strongly and positively correlated. Similarly, the larger the ErrP, the more efficient the error detection, especially in terms of specificity. This is in agreement with the correlations we observed between the spelling accuracy, $\theta$, and specificity and the perception of the BCI by the user (Q1 and Q2). Indeed, a high $\theta$ associated with an efficient ErrP classification yields a significant improvement due to automatic correction.

All the correlations and group differences we observed are coherent with the hypothesis of a role of task engagement. However, we should remain cautious in our interpretations. This assumption requires further in-depth investigations. Indeed, we could not show any significant correlation between objective measures and the subjective responses to motivation-related question (viz. Q5 and Q7).

Nevertheless, our conclusion can be refined by looking closely at the results in the high specificity group ($N = 10$). In this group, only 2 subjects experienced a drop of spelling accuracy due to automatic error correction. Accordingly, 6 subjects reported a preference in favor of a spelling including automatic correction. Six subjects showed a higher bit rate when using the automatic correction compared to no correction. And 7 out of the 10 participants obtained a higher bit rate with automatic correction compared to automatic detection with predicted respelling. Three out of the 4 participants, who reported preference for spelling with no correction, did not improve their spelling accuracy with correction. Interestingly, the last one (S10) who obtained the largest improvement ($+12\%$), surprisingly, reported verbally that efficient correction required too much attentional effort. All those results demonstrate the putative usefulness of automatic error correction but highlight the fact that it should certainly be used in a different way depending on the user's profile.

### 4.4. Requirements for Automatic Correction to Be Relevant.
In theory, any initial spelling accuracy could benefit from automatic correction, provided that the sensitivity, the specificity, and the GCR are high enough. All studies concur in stating that specificity is a primary requirement, in order to avoid the highly frustrating situation of automatically discarding a correctly spelled item. But contrary to Visconti and colleagues [15], our results show that the better the spelling accuracy, the more relevant the correction. At first, this might sound counter-intuitive, since the higher the spelling accuracy, the more difficult the rare error detection. However, we do observe that good performers achieve

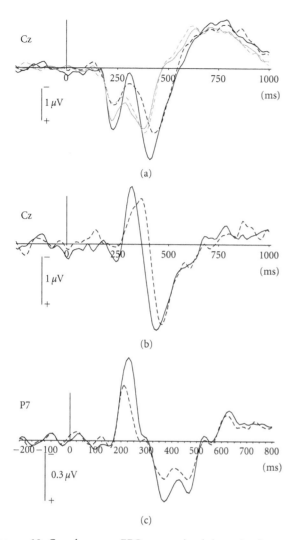

FIGURE 10: Grand average EEG event-related dynamics for group with a high specificity in solid line ($N = 10$) and group with a low specificity in dashed line ($N = 6$). (a) Responses to bad (grey) and good feedbacks (black) in channel Cz. (b) Difference of bad and good feedback responses in channel Cz. (c) Difference of target and non-target responses in channel P7.

better correction. Indeed, we show that both ErrP detection accuracy and $\theta$ (the subsequent ability to automatically correct for errors) are closely related to the spelling accuracy. In other words, the higher the spelling accuracy, the higher the performance in error detection and correction. As also supported by larger averaged ErrP and P300 responses, these results suggest that the more the subject engages into the task, the higher the performance in terms of both spelling accuracy and error correction. This is a strong indication in favor of a possible use of the P300-speller to train subjects in their abilities to focus attention [40].

## 5. Conclusion

The BCI presented here is the first online P300-Speller employing automatic correction by another item when an ErrP is detected. Our results are competitive in terms of ErrP detection, although they could probably be improved using adaptive training and a biased classifier. The automatic correction could also be improved, possibly by using the information from a probabilistic dictionary. However, it proved already relevant in terms of bit rate, compared to classical automatic ErrP detection alone. It also proved significant in most of the participants who had the best initial spelling accuracy. Importantly, the correction needs to be adjusted to each participant, depending on their initial spelling accuracy and preference.

## Acknowledgment

This work is supported by the French ANR project ANR-DEFIS 09-EMER-002 CoAdapt. We thank Dominique Morlet for technical help.

## References

[1] B. H. Dobkin, "Brain-computer interface technology as a tool to augment plasticity and outcomes for neurological rehabilitation," *Journal of Physiology*, vol. 579, part 3, pp. 637–642, 2007.

[2] J. D. Millan, R. Rupp, G. R. Muller-Putz et al. et al., "Combining brain-computer interfaces and assistive technologies: state-of-the-art and challenges," *Frontiers in Neuroscience*, vol. 4, article 161, 2010.

[3] T. O. Zander, C. Kothe, S. Welke, and M. Roetting, "Utilizing secondary input from passive brain-computer interfaces for enhancing human-machine interaction," in *Foundations of Augmented Cognition Neuroergonomics and Operational Neuroscience*, pp. 759–771, San Diego, Calif, USA, 2009.

[4] J. W. Gehring, B. Goss, M. G. Coles, D. E. Meyer, and E. Donchin, "A neural system for error detection and compensation," *Psychological Science*, vol. 4, pp. 385–390, 1993.

[5] M. Falkenstein, J. Hohnsbein, and J. Hoormann, "Event-related potential correlates of errors in reaction tasks," *Electroencephalography and Clinical Neurophysiology*, vol. 44, pp. 287–296, 1995.

[6] J. Hohnsbein, M. Falkenstein, and J. Hoormann :, "Error processing in visual and auditory choice reaction tasks," *Journal of Psychophysiology*, vol. 3,, p. 32, 1989.

[7] M. Falkenstein, J. Hohnsbein, J. Hoormann, and L. Blanke, "Effects of errors in choice reaction tasks on the ERP under focused and divided attention," in *Psychophysiological Brain Research*, C. H. M. Brunia, A. W. K. Gaillard, and A. Kok, Eds., pp. 192–195, Tilburg, The Netherlands, 1990.

[8] W. H. R. Miltner, C. H. Braun, and M. G. H. Coles, "Event-related brain potentials following incorrect feedback in a time-estimation task: evidence for a "generic" neural system for error detection," *Journal of Cognitive Neuroscience*, vol. 9, no. 6, pp. 788–798, 1997.

[9] S. Nieuwenhuis, C. B. Holroyd, N. Mol, and M. G. H. Coles, "Reinforcement-related brain potentials from medial frontal cortex: origins and functional significance," *Neuroscience and Biobehavioral Reviews*, vol. 28, no. 4, pp. 441–448, 2004.

[10] L. C. Parra, C. D. Spence, A. D. Gerson, and P. Sajda, "Response error correction—a demonstration of improved human-machine performance using real-time EEG monitoring," *IEEE Transactions on Neural Systems and Rehabilitation Engineering*, vol. 11, no. 2, pp. 173–177, 2003.

[11] G. Schalk, J. R. Wolpaw, D. J. McFarland, and G. Pfurtscheller, "EEG-based communication: presence of an error potential," *Clinical Neurophysiology*, vol. 111, no. 12, pp. 2138–2144, 2000.

[12] P. W. Ferrez and J. J. Del, "Error-related EEG potentials generated during simulated brain-computer interaction," *IEEE Transactions on Biomedical Engineering*, vol. 55, no. 3, pp. 923–929, 2008.

[13] B. Dal Seno, M. Matteucci, and L. Mainardi, "Online detection of P300 and error potentials in a BCI speller," *Computational Intelligence and Neuroscience*, vol. 2010, Article ID 307254, 5 pages, 2010.

[14] M. Spuler, M. Bensch, S. Kleih, W. Rosenstiel, M. Bogdan, and A. Kubler, "Online use of error-related potentials in healthy users and people with severe motor impairment increases performance of a P300-BCI," *Clinical Neurophysiology*, vol. 123, no. 7, pp. 1328–1337, 2012.

[15] G. Visconti, B. Dal Seno, M. Matteucci, and L. Mainardi :, "Automatic recognition of error potentials in a P300-based brain-computer interface," in *Proceedings of the 4th International Bran-Computer Interface Conference*, 2008.

[16] M. Perrin, E. Maby, R. Bouet, O. Bertrand, and J. Mattout, "Detecting and interpreting responses to feedback in BCI," in *Proceedings of the 5th International Brain-Computer Interface Workshop & Training Course*, pp. 116–119, Graz, Austria, 2011.

[17] L. A. Farwell and E. Donchin, "Talking off the top of your head: toward a mental prosthesis utilizing event-related brain potentials," *Electroencephalography and Clinical Neurophysiology*, vol. 70, no. 6, pp. 510–523, 1988.

[18] M. Fabiani, D. Karis, and E. Donchin, "P300 and recall in an incidental memory paradigm," *Psychophysiology*, vol. 23, no. 3, pp. 298–308, 1986.

[19] N. K. Squires, K. C. Squires, and S. A. Hillyard, "Two varieties of long latency positive waves evoked by unpredictable auditory stimuli in man," *Electroencephalography and Clinical Neurophysiology*, vol. 38, no. 4, pp. 387–401, 1975.

[20] E. Donchin, K. M. Spencer, and R. Wijesinghe, "The mental prosthesis: assessing the speed of a P300-based brain-computer interface," *IEEE Transactions on Rehabilitation Engineering*, vol. 8, no. 2, pp. 174–179, 2000.

[21] Y. Renard, F. Lotte, G. Gibert et al., "OpenViBE: an open-source software platform to design, test, and use brain-computer interfaces in real and virtual environments," *Presence*, vol. 19, no. 1, pp. 35–53, 2010.

[22] E. Maby, G. Gibert, P. E. Aguera, M. Perrin, O. Bertrand, and J. Mattout :, "The OpenViBE P300-speller scenario: a thorough online evaluation," in *Proceedings of the Human Brain Mapping Conference*, 2010.

[23] G. Townsend, B. K. LaPallo, C. B. Boulay et al., "A novel P300-based brain-computer interface stimulus presentation paradigm: moving beyond rows and columns," *Clinical Neurophysiology*, vol. 121, no. 7, pp. 1109–1120, 2010.

[24] H. Cecotti and B. Rivet :, "One step beyond rows and columns flashes in the P300 speller: a theoretical description," *International Journal of Bioelectromagnetism*, vol. 13, no. 1, pp. 39–41, 2011.

[25] H. Cecotti, B. Rivet, M. Congedo et al., "A robust sensor-selection method for P300 brain-computer interfaces," *Journal of Neural Engineering*, vol. 8, no. 1, Article ID 016001, 2011.

[26] P. Brunner, S. Joshi, S. Briskin, J. R. Wolpaw, H. Bischof, and G. Schalk, "Does the 'P300' speller depend on eye gaze?" *Journal of Neural Engineering*, vol. 7, no. 5, Article ID 56013, 2010.

[27] M. S. Treder and B. Blankertz, "(C)overt attention and visual speller design in an ERP-based brain-computer interface," *Behavioral and Brain Functions*, vol. 6, article 28, 2010.

[28] E. Lopez-Larraz, I. Iturrate, L. Montesano, and J. Minguez, "Real-time recognition of feedback error-related potentials during a time-estimation task," in *Proceedings of the 32nd Annual International Conference of the IEEE Engineering in Medicine and Biology Society (EMBC '10)*, pp. 2670–2673, 2010.

[29] J. R. Wolpaw, N. Birbaumer, W. J. Heetderks et al., "Brain-computer interface technology: a review of the first international meeting," *IEEE Transactions on Rehabilitation Engineering*, vol. 8, no. 2, pp. 164–173, 2000.

[30] C. E. Shannon and W. Weaver, *The Mathematical Theory of Communication: Presence of an Error Potential*, University of Illinois Press, Chicago, Ill, USA, 1949.

[31] R. Naatanen and T. Picton, "The N1 wave of the human electric and magnetic response to sound: a review and an analysis of the component structure," *Psychophysiology*, vol. 24, no. 4, pp. 375–425, 1987.

[32] B. Rivet, A. Souloumiac, V. Attina, and G. Gibert, "xDAWN algorithm to enhance evoked potentials: application to brain-computer interface," *IEEE Transactions on Bio-Medical Engineering*, vol. 56, no. 8, pp. 2035–2043, 2009.

[33] N. Yeung, C. B. Holroyd, and J. D. Cohen, "ERP correlates of feedback and reward processing in the presence and absence of response choice," *Cerebral Cortex*, vol. 15, no. 5, pp. 535–544, 2005.

[34] R. B. Mars, E. R. A. De Bruijn, W. Hulstijn, W. Miltner, and M. Coles, "What if I told you: "You were wrong"? brain potentials and behavioral adjustments elicited by performance feedback in a time-estimation task," in *Errors, Conflicts, and the Brain Current Opinions on Performance Monitoring*, MPI of Cognitive Neuroscience, pp. 129–134, Leipzig, Germany, 2004.

[35] A. Rachez, T. Proix, E. Maby, J. Mattout, and E. Daucé, "Direct policygradient for online learning in BCI," *International Journal of Bioelectromagnetism*, vol. 13, no. 1, pp. 52–53, 2011.

[36] T. M. Vaughan, D. J. McFarland, G. Schalk et al., "The wadsworth BCI research and development program: at home with BCI," *IEEE Transactions on Neural Systems and Rehabilitation Engineering*, vol. 14, no. 2, pp. 229–233, 2006.

[37] A. Datta, R. Cusack, K. Hawkins et al., "The P300 as a marker of waning attention and error propensity," *Computational Intelligence and Neuroscience*, vol. 2007, Article ID 93968, 9 pages, 2007.

[38] T. W. Picton, "The P300 wave of the human event-related potential," *Journal of Clinical Neurophysiology*, vol. 9, no. 4, pp. 456–479, 1992.

[39] S. C. Kleih, F. Nijboer, S. Halder, and A. Kübler, "Motivation modulates the P300 amplitude during brain-computer interface use," *Clinical Neurophysiology*, vol. 121, no. 7, pp. 1023–1031, 2010.

[40] E. Maby, M. Perrin, O. Bertrand, G. Sanchez, and J. Mattout, "BCI could make old two-player games even more fun: a proof of concept with, 'Connect Four'," *Advances in Human-Computer Interaction*. In press.

# Permissions

The contributors of this book come from diverse backgrounds, making this book a truly international effort. This book will bring forth new frontiers with its revolutionizing research information and detailed analysis of the nascent developments around the world.

We would like to thank all the contributing authors for lending their expertise to make the book truly unique. They have played a crucial role in the development of this book. Without their invaluable contributions this book wouldn't have been possible. They have made vital efforts to compile up to date information on the varied aspects of this subject to make this book a valuable addition to the collection of many professionals and students.

This book was conceptualized with the vision of imparting up-to-date information and advanced data in this field. To ensure the same, a matchless editorial board was set up. Every individual on the board went through rigorous rounds of assessment to prove their worth. After which they invested a large part of their time researching and compiling the most relevant data for our readers. Conferences and sessions were held from time to time between the editorial board and the contributing authors to present the data in the most comprehensible form. The editorial team has worked tirelessly to provide valuable and valid information to help people across the globe.

Every chapter published in this book has been scrutinized by our experts. Their significance has been extensively debated. The topics covered herein carry significant findings which will fuel the growth of the discipline. They may even be implemented as practical applications or may be referred to as a beginning point for another development. Chapters in this book were first published by Hindawi Publishing Corporation; hereby published with permission under the Creative Commons Attribution License or equivalent.

The editorial board has been involved in producing this book since its inception. They have spent rigorous hours researching and exploring the diverse topics which have resulted in the successful publishing of this book. They have passed on their knowledge of decades through this book. To expedite this challenging task, the publisher supported the team at every step. A small team of assistant editors was also appointed to further simplify the editing procedure and attain best results for the readers.

Our editorial team has been hand-picked from every corner of the world. Their multi-ethnicity adds dynamic inputs to the discussions which result in innovative outcomes. These outcomes are then further discussed with the researchers and contributors who give their valuable feedback and opinion regarding the same. The feedback is then collaborated with the researches and they are edited in a comprehensive manner to aid the understanding of the subject.

Apart from the editorial board, the designing team has also invested a significant amount of their time in understanding the subject and creating the most relevant covers. They scrutinized every image to scout for the most suitable representation of the subject and create an appropriate cover for the book.

The publishing team has been involved in this book since its early stages. They were actively engaged in every process, be it collecting the data, connecting with the contributors or procuring relevant information. The team has been an ardent support to the editorial, designing and production team. Their endless efforts to recruit the best for this project, has resulted in the accomplishment of this book. They are a veteran in the field of academics and their pool of knowledge is as vast as their experience in printing. Their expertise and guidance has proved useful at every step. Their uncompromising quality standards have made this book an exceptional effort. Their encouragement from time to time has been an inspiration for everyone.

The publisher and the editorial board hope that this book will prove to be a valuable piece of knowledge for researchers, students, practitioners and scholars across the globe.

# List of Contributors

**Xu Sun**
Science and Engineering, University of Nottingham Ningbo, 199 Taikang East Road, Ningbo 315100, China

**Andrew May**
Loughborough Design School, Loughborough University, Ashby Road, Loughborough, Leicestershire LE11 3TU, UK

**Lotfi Derbali and Claude Frasson**
Departement d'Informatique et de Recherche Operationnelle, Universite de Montreal, C.P. 6128, Succursale Centre-Ville, Montreal, QC, Canada H3C 3J7

**Alexander Astaras and Nikolaos Moustakas**
Lab of Medical Informatics, Medical School, Aristotle University of Thessaloniki, Thessaloniki, Greece
Department of Automation, Alexander Technological Educational Institute of Thessaloniki, Thessaloniki, Greece

**Alkinoos Athanasiou**
Lab of Medical Informatics, Medical School, Aristotle University of Thessaloniki, Thessaloniki, Greece
Department of Neurosurgery, Papageorgiou General Hospital, Thessaloniki, Greece

**Aristides Gogoussis**
Department of Automation, Alexander Technological Educational Institute of Thessaloniki, Thessaloniki, Greece

**Satoshi Suzuki**
School of Science and Technology for Future Life, Department of Robotics and Mechatronics, Tokyo Denki University, 2-2 Kanda-Nishiki-cho, Chiyoda-ku, Tokyo 101-8457, Japan

**Fumio Harashima**
Tokyo Metropolitan University, 1-1 Minami-Osawa, Hachioji-Shi, Tokyo 192-0397, Japan

**Katri Salminen, Veikko Surakka, Jani Lylykangas, Jussi Rantala and Roope Raisamo**
Tampere Unit for Computer Human Interaction, School of Information Sciences, University of Tampere, Kanslerinrinne 1, 33014 Helsinki, Finland

**Teemu Ahmaniemi, Dari Trendafilov and Johan Kildal**
Nokia Research Center, Itamerenkatu 11-13, 00180 Helsinki, Finland

**Junji Watanabe**
NTT Communication Science Laboratories, Nippon Telegraph and Telephone Corporation, 3-1, Morinosato-Wakamiya, Atsugi, Kanagawa 243-0198, Japan

**Yusuke Godai**
Graduate School of Electro-Communications, University of Electro-Communications, 1-5-1, Chofugaoka, Chofu, Tokyo 182-8585, Japan
Machinetool Division, Mayekawa Electric. Co., Ltd., 2000, Tatsuzawa, Moriya, Ibaraki 302-0118, Japan

**Hideyuki Ando**
Graduate School of Information Science and Technology, Osaka University, 2-1, Yamadaoka, Suita, Osaka 565-0871, Japan

**Camilla Grane and Peter Bengtsson**
Division of Human Work Science, Department of Business Administration, Technology and Social Sciences, Lulea University of Technology, 97187 Lulea, Sweden

**Chad C. Tossell and Philip Kortum**
Department of Psychology, Rice University, 6100 Main Street, MS-25, Houston, TX 77005, USA

**Clayton W. Shepard, Ahmad Rahmati and Lin Zhong**
Department of Electrical and Computer Engineering, Rice University, 6100 Main Street, MS-25, Houston, TX 77005, USA

**Mathieu Simonnet**
CNRS UMR 6285 LabSTICC-IHSEV/HAAL, Telecom Bretagne, Technopole Brest-Iroise, CS 83818-29238 Brest Cedex 3, France

**Stephane Vieilledent**
LaTIM-Inserm U 1101, Universite de Brest (UEB), Brest, France

**Thomas D. Parsons**
Clinical Neuropsychology and Simulation (CNS) Lab, Department of Psychology, University of North Texas, Denton, TX 76203, USA

**Albert A. Rizzo**
Institute for Creative Technologies, University of Southern California, Playa Vista, Los Angeles, CA 90094, USA

**Christopher G. Courtney**
Institute for Creative Technologies, University of Southern California, Playa Vista, Los Angeles, CA 90094, USA
Department of Psychology, University of Southern California, Los Angeles, CA 90089, USA

**Michael E. Dawson**
Department of Psychology, University of Southern California, Los Angeles, CA 90089, USA

**Mary Fendley and S. Narayanan**
College of Engineering and Computer Science, Wright State University, Dayton, OH 45435, USA

**David Pitman and Mary L. Cummings**
Humans and Automation Lab, Massachusetts Institute of Technology, 77 Massachusetts Avenue, Cambridge, MA 02139, USA

**S. M. Mizanoor Rahman**
Institute for Media Innovation, Nanyang Technological University, 50 Nanyang Drive, Singapore 637553

**Ryojun Ikeura**
Division of Mechanical Engineering, Graduate School of Engineering, Mie University, Tsu, Mie 514-8507, Japan

**Tatiana V. Evreinova, Grigori Evreinov and Roope Raisamo**
School of Information Sciences, University of Tampere, Kanslerinrinne 1, PINNI B, 33014 Tampere, Finland

**Melissa E. DeRosier**
3-C Institute for Social Development, 1901 North Harrison Avenue, Suite 200, Cary, NC 27513, USA

**Ashley B. Craig**
Games Research Department, 3-C Institute for Social Development, 1901 North Harrison Avenue, Suite 200, Cary, NC 27513, USA

**Rebecca P. Sanchez**
Games Research Department, Center for Research in Emotional and Social Health, 1901 North Harrison Avenue, Suite 200, Cary, NC 27513, USA

**Lode Vanacken and Karin Coninx**
Hasselt University-tUL-IBBT Expertise Centre for Digital Media, Wetenschapspark 2, 3590 Diepenbeek, Belgium

**Romulo Pinho and Jan Sijbers**
IBBT Vision Lab, Department of Physics, University of Antwerp, Universiteitsplein 1, N.1, 2610 Wilrijk, Belgium

**Matthew J. Pitts, Tom Wellings, Alex Attridge and Mark A. Williams**
WMG, University of Warwick, Coventry CV4 7AL, UK

**Lee Skrypchuk**
Jaguar & Land Rover Research, Jaguar Land Rover, Coventry CV3 4LF, UK

**Perrin Margaux, Maby Emmanuel, Bertrand Olivier and Mattout Jeremie**
Lyon Neuroscience Research Center (CRNL), INSERM, CNRS, Dycog team, 95 Boulevard Pinel, 69500 Bron, France
Universite Claude Bernard Lyon 1, 69000 Lyon, France

**Daligault Sebastien**
CERMEP, 95 Boulevard Pinel, 69500 Bron, France

Printed in the USA
CPSIA information can be obtained
at www.ICGtesting.com
JSHW051437221024
72173JS00006B/1497

9 781632 400253